BELIEVER'S BOOK II

Henry Mugabo

Published by New Generation Publishing in 2019

First Edition

ISBN: 978-1-78955-741-1

www.newgeneration-publishing.com

New Generation Publishing

BELIEVER`S BOOK

The , **BELIEVER`S BOOK** ,have taken years of, writing , reading teachings, editing, and experience but I would like to thank the Almighty God, who has empowered me to accomplish my, **Dream and Vision** ,I couldn't have done this book without his Mighty Powerful hand , and his goodness , this book is not the work of only one person, many people have been of great support and help , I want to Express my sincere gratitude to my **Spiritual ,Mother and Father** of the new generation, **Pastor, Elizabeth ,Nabulime, Pastor, William, of, Jesus is more than able Ministries** , their support Spiritual, , enthusiastic cooperation , their suggestions ,guidance have always been valuable, am grateful for them for their contribution towards the Believers- book , I wish to express my grateful thanks to my brother Joseph ,**Minister- BLessing, Traxton** ,for wise Advice ,Counsel and Encouragement , all the way ,**My Sisters and Brothers of Jesus is More than able Ministry**, for their belief in the book and sustaining me all the way,, I thank them sincerely ,**My Editor , Sharon and Esther** ,who have used their editorial ,skills ,wise Judgement ,and faith to bring this book **Believers book**, to fruition, **Amen**,

I Could have kept this knowledge private, but everything in me shouted, Don't you dare to share with the Public about the word of God on **Believing (faith)** I feel that am keeping a promise to God to do his will ,the most important information I have ever been given by God ,It has been demonstrated ,through me to change millions of people daily experience, by believing in the ,**BELIEVERS- BOOK** ,the believers book continues to play its part in the urgent task of transforming the generation of Today, **Amen**

BELIVER'S BOOK

CONTENTS

INTRODUCTION

THE, BELIEVERS, BOOK, - Is written to meet Ever changing generation of Today ,that God is still the same, Yesterday, Today and Forever **(Hebrews,13;8),**With Divine Supernatural Power to, Heal , Bless, Anoint ,Save , Redeem, Restore, Resurrect , Promote , give Wisdom, fill us with the Holy Spirit, Move mountains in our daily life , "nothing is too hard for him" **(Jeremiah, 32;27; Jesus 32;17; Luke 18;17)** The secret to Success is Believing ,and this keep you on truck ,to achieve your purpose and reach your destiny in life -God earnest desire for you and me is to have life in all its fullness**, (John10;10)**Saved, Redeemed, Restored ,Victorious, Health, Happy, Anointed and fully imbued in the Holy Spirit **, But how can we enjoy such Communion with all Its blessing, and Benefits ,If we don't Believe? ,**

With fleshing blend of sound Spiritual Explosion, and Practical insight **Henry - Mugabo ,** A College, graduate in this insight of Spiritual growth , wants to Share with you the Principal of Believing **(Faith)**as the key to everything-**,Faith-(Believe)Pleases God more than anything (Hebrews,11;6)** God is not pleased ,on how much you read your Bible , how much you Speak in tongues , give in Church , Sing or Praise him without your faith ,it's nothing ,**Henry, Mugabo-** In his ,**FIRST VOLUME- BELIEVER`S-BOOK ,**He gives a clear understanding of **,God's name, Worship , Praise , Future , Purpose, Favour , Blessing , Love, Gifts ,** and more , When you believe you see the power of God and his manifestation in life , when you put your believe to work the more it becomes, if your believe or faith is weak it shows you are not exercising your believe ,which indicates there is doubt in your heart resulting into ,**Weak- Faith ,** and the cure for Weak- Faith is acting on the word of God ,if you want your believing to be strong, start believing in the word and acting on its promises , **Amen**

In, **BELIEVER`S BOOK 11- Henry-,Mugabo** ,Gives you an insight on guiding principles on ,**Focus , Vision , Prayers , Holy Spirit, Salvation ,Success, Marriage ,Self-Discovery**.and more that will improve both your relationship you and God , to release your blessing ,**How can he do that?** the Answer is **Believe,(Hebrews,11;6)** that God still on the throne to fulfil his promises, signs and wonders still happen**(Miracles)Your ,Spiritual growth, Marriage, Issue ,Economic, Issues ,Addiction ,Curses, Issues ,Healing , Deliverance, Moves mountains** ,Believe in God word and his promises ,do the word of God ,his promise still stand, and he never fail us, keep this book of Law **(Bible)** On your lips, meditate on it day and night, so that you may be careful to do everything written in it, then you will be prosperous and successful,**(Joshua,1;8)** Heavens and earth will pass away, but my words will never pass away **(Mathew,24;35)** So is my word that goes out from my mouth, It will not return to me empty ,but will accomplish what I desired and achieve the purpose for which I sent it **(Isaiah,55;11),We are the Chosen, Redeemed ,Anointed, to overcome, Poverty, Sickness, Captivity of all kind, Believe**, the Lord is lifted high , the Lords right hand has done mighty things, I will not die ,but live and proclaim what he has done **(Psalm,118;5)**His stretched hand, break bondages, fight battles, break chains **,Live by Faith in God , Jesus Christ ,Holy -Spirit ,and his Word,(Bible)and Act** ,In order to achieve your goal and fulfil your purpose ,and reach your destiny and have a Jolly life, the **BELIEVER`S- BOOK,** Is in your hand ,the choice is yours , you will have the edge in your life, Do not be conformed to this world, but let God transform you inwardly ,by a complete change of your mind ,then you will be able to know the will of God -what is good ,and is pleasing to him and is perfect **(Romans,12;2)Believe, Amen**

FOCUS

FOCUS-is paying particular attention on something/or centre of interest Focus is the key to accomplish what is necessary-Easy Word to spell, It contains only ,***Five letters-*** but Powerful word, In order to achieve success and move forward, you have to be focused ,Jesus was focused to set human beings free from Sin ,some people focus on positive things (***Which are Godly)***Some people negative things (***which are ungodly***)There many things in the world we can be focused on like, Properties, Politics ,Fame Posh life, children,work As a Christian our main aim is to focus on God and Jesus Christ, and positive things ,that brings us closer to our God **(Righteousness, and Holiness)** Focus on Christ does not mean that we should not live how other people live, but means we should not copy what they do, which is out of Christianity ,focus on Jesus means we get rid away with the things of the world that pulls us from being connected to God- It is a disciplined style of life, and when you get rid of the world life you see the , Blessing of God ,Victory, Favour , Open doors ,Opportunities, Overcome obstacles and Forces of Darkness ,through Jesus Christ doing everything for you ,If you stay focused, thing are possible. When you experience difficulties, you can positively change, your outlook, reduce your stress and concentrate on achieving the best elements that may have not been achieved , if focus is not available. **Without, goals** – you will end up going into somebody else's ,dreams or direction. but develop your map today, and set your goals as well as focus. **Amen**

To focus means bringing your attention to the centre of something intently to gain clarity.

A negative focus- this can result in our missing of possibilities along our paths.

Focus is key- To accomplish what is necessary and being that focus is a word of five letters for instance, many take it for a mock ,yet it is one of the powerful tool to create order, and forwardness in our lives,

Focus on a good thing – focus positively with a target and forget the loses or challenges along the path of doing something. Let your eyes look straight ahead ,fix your gaze directly before you give careful thoughts to the path for your feet , and be steadfast in all your ways , do not turn to the right or left keep your foot from the Evil **(Proverb,4;25-27) Amen**

Successful people focus – they don't easily get distractions by simply ignoring the most unwanted. don't waste your time to win people to understand you, Don't waste time on unnecessary friends ,don't allow people with **(22;hours)**conversation without nothing building you, Allow people of**(15 minutes)**with positive ideas ,you can't live a positive day when you focusing on negative ,focus don't pay attention to negative talking People always have to say ,people normally don't talk about ordinary people but successful people, always talk about winners, not losers ,don't worry about the past look forward, the more favour you have the more opposition, stop allowing yourself upset Sanballat ,Geshem sent this massage ,Come let us meet together in one of the village on the plain of Ono, but they were scheming to harm me, so I sent a massage them with this reply ,I am carrying on a great project and I cannot go down , why should the work stop , while I leave it and go down to you ,Four times they sent the massage and each time I gave them the same answer , , when it come to the building of the walls of Jerusalem Nehemiah, discovered that everyone around him wanted him to succeed but he on the other side he had also opposition who wanted him to stop the work (enemies) they threatened him with rumours and threats ,nevertheless he completed the work because he stayed focused on what mattered most and he refused to be distracted ,**(Nehemiah,6;2;3)**when you decide your life priorities are they will help you to reach your God assigned assignment , when the odds are against you ,Ask yourself , what are the biggest priorities in life settle those in mind, **Amen**

<u>Review your goals</u> – More than twice a day is important for you understand whether you are meeting targets or not. Focus is the end result of achieving goals .**Amen**

QUESTION?

HOW CAN WE STAY FOCUS IN THE WORLD OF TRIALS ,PROBLEMS, BUSY DAYS, AND EVIL TODAY?

The answer is ,**STAY FOCUSED** (Let us strip off every weight that slows us down, and let us run with endurance the race God has set before us *(Hebrews,12; 1)* God has given us two things needed to run and win in life, *Time and Energy* ,and you can't afford to waste them, why do we have such hard times saying no? Two of the most common reason are fear of rejection ultimately you must ask yourself this question *whose approval am I seeking? God or man approval?* Fear of missing out good opportunities ,We assume that whatever opportunity knocks we must answer the door and say yes to whatever is standing there ,that's a mistake, Opportunity does not equal Obligation, there will always be more opportunity than there is time to pursue them ,so you must choose your opportunity, prayerfully and wisely ,greater people know how to keep their mind focused, know how to inspire and motivate their followers ,to keep pushing the main chance ,they don't let side issues overwhelm them ,so stay focused ,when you focus on being a blessing God makes sure you are always blessed in abundance, I find hope in the darkest of the days and focus in the brightest, I do not judge the universe (Dalai-lama) Our main purpose we Christians to **Focus on the things of heaven not of the world,** for you are have died and your life is hidden in Christ, your life is in Christ ,and then when he appears then too will appear with him, and share his glory **(Colossians 3;2)** Don't look at, houses, fame ,cars ,family ,Jesus is for you as you praying here interceding for you ,we pray in times of trials and think we would not have a change , not only God motivate other believers to pray for you, but Jesus is doing the same in heaven and prays for you ,We are meant not to dwell on what went wrong, instead focus on what to do next, spend energy on what to do next moving forward, and finding answers and solutions to problems and trials, the truth is most people spent much of their time and energy scattered than they should have been focused,   and when you are scattered you are filled with uncertainty, not being sure of what is important, where to start and, how to get done, what they are focused on that increase personal stress, leaving you lost and cause mental disorder in life, Live life to the fullest and focus on the positive ,being focused first on your God will help you to be more productive and committed in everything you do ,the oppressed look to him and are glad, that they will never be disappointed **(Psalm34;5)** Being focused will help you to achieve quicker the results that you really want, When you are focused it is quicker to take action and achieve a break-through in life- It's good to be focused on the most important things in life ,Being focused will improve your personal and professional life , being focused help you to listen to people , ideas better also come with solutions to any problems quicker , being focused provide your life with personal power because **(a)**Provide you with strength to complete **(b)**Organise your action **(c)**Expand your sense of clarity **(d)** Re-change your inner spirit work within you from inside out We need to have focus on the people we live with you can't have 40 best friends choose 3 or 5 among them those who are always encouraging you always on your side in all situations evaluate them Jesus had 12 disciples but he choose **(3three)** among them who had faith when he went to heal a child in the house The scripture says "then he did not let anyone else go on with him except ***Peter James and his brother John*** they arrived at Jarius house where Jesus saw the confusion and had all the loud crying and wailing he went and said to them why all this confusion? Why are you crying? the child is not dead -she only sleeping, they laughed at him so he put them out took the child father and mother and his three disciples and went into the room where the child was lying ,he took her by hand and said to her "***Talitha -Koum which means little girl*** ,I tell you get up she got up once and started walking around, she was **(12,years)** when this happened they were all completely amazed, But Jesus gave them order strict orders not to tell anyone and said give her something to eat**(Mark,5;37;42)** you have to focus on who is in your circle ,people you eat lunch with ,you spend your time with, you speak to ,you call on your telephone ,are they God fearing, if they are not

5

positive show them the door out, **_kiss good bye to them_** ,if you stay with them you will miss your destiny, It's better to be lonely for a long time ,than being with someone who will poison your life, and make you to miss your creation purpose ,know people you give your time, many battles come our way into life but you need to know which battle to fight, if the battle is distractive leave it you don't need to pay people to win them ,not everybody is going to understand you, focus on people who are making a different in your life, don't give up of doing good, because of friends the more God promote you need to become ignoring people, don't go the radio station and modern technology, and get carried out about what they say and write about you ,God and Christ is enough for you, the one who is in you is greater than the universe, The things we need to focus on- Jesus and so is able now and always to save those who come to God through him, because he lives forever to plead with God for them (**Hebrews7;25**)Do your best to present yourself to God as approved worker, who has no need to be ashamed rightly handling the word of truth(**2Timothy2;15**)For it is better to suffer doing good, if that is Gods will than for evil things (**1Peter3;17**) Focus on Good things than evil things (**1Thessolonians5;21**)Let love be genuine abhor what is evil hold fast to what is good(**Romans12;9**)When I was a child I spoke like a child I thought like a child I reason like a child when I become a man I gave up childish ways (**1Corinthians,13;11**) Whatever your hand finds to do it with your mighty, for there is no work or thought knowledge or wisdom in sheol to which you are doing (**Ecclesiastes;9;10**)My dear Christian brothers and sisters ,who also have been called by God think of Jesus who God sent to be the highest priest of the faith we profess (**Hebrews;3;1**) Focus on Jesus instead of storms ,It is better to trust in the lord than depending on human beings, and human leaders with their promises (**Psalm;118;8-9**)**Focus on the decree** have decided to obey your law until the day I die(**Psalm;119;112**)Your word is a lamp to guide me ,and a light for my path, I will keep my solemn promises to obey your just instructions(**Psalm;119;105**)The scriptures can direct our attentions towards the spiritual gaps, many times our busyness hardness our heart to the reality of the shortcomings and sinful ways however by allowing Gods word (**Gods sword the bible,**) Our visions are softened and we can see clearly the way of the lord ,study the word -bible with greater diligence than any other activity of your day, **Focus on eternal life** -but we wait for what God has promised new heavens and new earth where righteous will be at home(**2Peter3;13**)<u>**Focus on the Grace;**</u> For whoever finds me finds life ,and obtains favour from the lord (**Proverb;8;35**) Blessed are those who keep his testimonies, who seek him with their whole heart(**Psalm;119;2**)I will instruct you and teach you in the way you shall go I will counsel you with my eyes upon you (**Psalm;32;8**)But teach me your way O God that I may walk in your truth unite my heart to fear your name (**Psalm 86;11**) Your word is a lamp to my feet and light to my path (**Psalm 119;105**) for whatever boast I made to him about you I was not put to shame but just as everything we said to you was true so also our boasting before Titus has proved true (**2Corinthians 7;14**)For God gave us the spirit not of fear but of power and love and self- control (**2Timonty1;7**)but he who endures to the end will be saved (**Mathew;24;13**)So put on your God armour now than when the evil days comes, you will be able to resist the enemy attack, and after fighting to the end you will still hold your ground ,remain in faith (**Ephesians;6;13**)<u>Focus on the grace</u>- set your hope on the grace to be brought to you when Christ is revealed to you at his coming some time we are very proud because we are serving in Church .fasting long hours spending too much time in prayers and bible study we can be tempted to forget about grace we may start to feel a bit proud of ourselves for being so faithful to God without focusing on how he gives the grace to us to do it is Gods unmerited favour on our lives that gives us the ability to do the work of the righteousness Christians take a moment to reflect on his rich grace on your life and thank God for that, **Amen Focus on Jesus** -You have been raised to life with Christ so set your heart on the things in heaven where Christ seats /sit on his throne at the right hand side of God keep your mind fixed on things above so when you die your life is hidden with Christ in God(**Colossians 3;2**)**Let us focus on Jesus** on whom our faith depends, from the beginning to end he did not give up because of the cross on the contrary because of the joy that was waiting for him he thought nothing of the disgrace of dying on the cross and he is now seated on the right hand of Gods throne, it is easy to be caught up by things of the world and neglect the hope we have next-there is nothing bad being involved in politics ,work, family demands but problem arise when we let them take over our lives ,that we forget his place in our life pray that God will renew an expectancy of eternal life that will release the pressure of worldly concern ,When the days drew near for him to be taken up he set his face to go to Jerusalem (**Luke 9;51**)Jesus said any one who starts to plough and then keeps looking back is of no use to the kingdom of God/ Lord(**Luke 9;62**-focus on the future not the past)(**Colossians 2;6;8; Peter2;1;25; 1John;2;1;29;Titus 2;11;12 Philippians;39;24 Romans 11;5;23;Daniel,11;32**),the bible says my people perish because of lack of wisdom (**Hosea 4;6**)God has a plan /purpose for you we need to find out what it is if any one lack wisdom ask God that gives all men in abundance look at the principle in(**Proverb,4;20;27**)We need to learn Gods talk ,Jesus said that he who speaks what the father speaks(**John 8;28**)Dear fellow Christians don't look as the world see things but as the word of God declares it (**1Corinthians;4;18**)Put on the armour of God(**Ephesians 6;11;18**)<u>Focus on to Jesus</u> the pioneer and perfect or of our faith ,from the beginning to the end, he did not give up because of the cross on contrary because of the joy that was waiting for him he thought of nothing of the disgrace of dying on the cross and now is seated at the right side of God throne(**Hebrews12;2;3Philippians 1;6 Hebrews;12;2;11**) Jesus is at the finishing line with a great group of witness on the side line cheering us forward those who do marathon focuses on crossing the finishing line those who are distracted by the crowds weather tend to lose their speed - costing them the race let us keep focus on Jesus to win the kingdom Jesus is the saviour of the world , Joy , victory , he overcome and his name break chains and bondages in our life, **Focus on God;** the oppressed look to him and are glad they will never be disappointed the helpless call to him and answers he saves them from all their troubles His angels guards those who honour the lord and rescue them from danger take time at work pray at home pray everywhere Focus on his presence God will magnifies his glory on your life Seek the kingdom of God and his righteous and all things will be added to you (**Mathew;6;33**)Commit your work to the Lord, and your plans will be established(**Proverb16;3**)For those who live according to the fresh set/focus their minds on the things of the fresh but those who live according to the spirit set their minds on the things of the spirit(**Romans;8;5**)Be totally committed to God (**Romans;12;1;2**)Renew your mind in, In conclusion my brothers and sisters fill your mind with those things that are good that deserve praise things that are true , noble right pure , lovely ,and honourable , put in practice what you learnt and received from both from my words and from my actions and the God who gives us peace will be with you, (**Philippians;4;6;9**) **Riches in heaven (Mathew 6;19;33)** Run to win the race ,Set your goals mind for your -self (**1Corinthians;9;24;27; Hebrews;2;1**)Do not allow fear let you turn focus to God don't let the negative cause you to lose sight of the positive in future weigh both sides carefully don't let the storms blind you from Gods power to help you and his promises to guide you(**Numbers;14;4 &13;13**)Don't streak back and don't be double minded (**James,1;6;8**) Identify avoid destructions, keeping Christ first can be difficult in our daily life, when we have so many things have surrounded us threatening side and can take away our faith , we should take away our eyes off what we can do in the flesh and we focus on what we can do with Christ, I have all the strength to face all conditions by the power that Christ gives me(**Philippians;4;13**)Don't believe someone because he sounds like authority or says words you hear each the bible and check his teachings with God's word (**1Thessolonians;5;19;22**)The bible should be your main guidance in all situation ,don't listen to any authoritative preacher ,who contradicts Gods word, make the bible your final authority in life, Jesus said many will come in my name and deceive even the most elect (**Mathew;24;4;5 and Ephesians 4;14;15**)**Focus thought on Jesus-whom we acknowledge as our apostle and high priest**)My brothers and sister ,who also have been called by God -think of Jesus whom God sent to be the high priest of the faith we profess -he was faithful to God who chose him to do this work Just as Moses was faithful in his work **(Hebrews;3;1)**A man who builds a house, receives more honour than house itself, in the same way Jesus receives more honour than Moses, Every house in fact is build by somebody ,and God is the one who builds all houses, **(Psalm,127;1)**but Christ is faithful as the son in charge of Gods houses ,pay attention to your thoughts ,and ask God to help you discipline you, **Amen**, **Focus on your, faith-**that God is in control, take time and see how God really loves you unconditionally ,how he can do things without asking no body ,Focus on the lord instead of worries problems fear ,He God knows what we need and will provide and you shall have it **Focus on the Right Path-** listen my son be wise and give serious thought to the way you live ,don't associate with people who drink too much wine or stuff themselves with food ,Every day there different paths in life for us to take, we chose every day the path of righteousness ,Some time the right path is filled with uncertainty -problems, and trials ,you ask yourself Does really God hear my Prayers? How is this all going to work ,if we really trust in the lord he will surely lead us to the right path, It is our responsibility to choose the right path,even if it brings pain, set your heart on the right path**(Proverb 23;19)It is important to be focused** ,because we all know that **Mistakes bring us down when-** we tend to lose our enthusiasm for doing what it takes to move forward ,the way to deal with common hindrance to motivation is to switch to being focused from the mistakes ,and develop a way not to allow it again in our life ,**Disappointments discourage-**   the bigger the vision/ dream ,the more disappointment you will face, and it can be very discouraging when you put a lot of time and energy into a project ,and you don't get a reward ,when you tend to come short you tend to feel you have wasted your time ,the solution to overcome disappointment to think for a long term result Instead of a short term result ,Focus on developing good work habits ,and you will increase your motivation level once you start you will gain from your effort- **Obstacles ,frustrate-**obstacles appears to seem unmovable ,they are not permanent, put your focus on what you want, then you are more willing to do whatever it takes to get it ,you need to make your ,dreams /vision big ,that you will be more than willing to pay a big price in order to have it , you can manage your life better being focused ,Managing life better means a change in your life path ,and you have to change life today -because tomorrow may be too late, Successful people manage their lives by change, unsuccessful people are passive and they don't make changes in their lives, you have to move from the position the of looser to winning - winning the difficulties and adapting to new changes overcoming the suspension of life meeting your desires and living your life fully, experience knowledge examine your relationship with your God and others ,take decisions to change/focused ,understand the difference between I have and I want to self –confidence, positive thinking ,managing your stress improve , your mood by improving your health, clear mind good mood, follow some health tips and be courageous and you will manage life ,**<u>What makes us to lose focus</u>?** Doubt ,Circumstances, Friends ,Bad Company, not consulting good counsellors, focus on things you don't have, -keeps you to be -pre-occupied to enjoy the things you don't have, focus on what you have instead of things you don't have, It is good to focus on the good things and what we have than focusing on what we have lost ,and were losing -Always have a good altitude remembering always to focus on the positive- if you stay focused on the positive ,when you experience difficulties you can positively change your, outlook, reduce stress ,and concentrate on achieving things that otherwise may not have been possible for you, focus on potentials instead of your limits ,successful people have focus they don't easily get distracted ,they ignore things which are completely unnecessary in their lives, review your goals more than twice a day, in order to be focused on achieving them ,You must stay focused on the end results to achieve your goals-Focus your energy on greatness **Nelson Mandela** focused on how to liberate ,**South Africa** and **Jesus** focused on how to set you free from sin, and have hope again ,negative focus can result in our entirely missing the possibilities in our path ,One more reason why we lose focus is the fact we not awake of our priorities, if you focus on saving money you will save money ,Without goals you will end up following someone else map (**Direction**) There more scripture for more reading ,and understand why we should be focused ,to keep your right kind of focus , you have to focus on your, vision ,Develop your map today, set your goals and focus ,to focus means to bring your attention to the centre, to concentration on something intently in order to gain clarity, when you are focused you can be victorious , Save money , Get married-if you are single ,Start a business of no losses ,Discover many things in life; **Amen**

DISTRACTION

DISTRACTION-It is something that makes it difficult to think / to pay attention to something /act of distracting, obstacles to attention ,there is always distraction when we are planning to move forward ,or move on ,or when we are focused -Distraction tap in and capture our attention, many Christians are distracted today from serving God, because of various reasons ,distraction is always there even if you don't ask for one, but as Christians we have to say no to distraction, so we can find our destiny with the word of God, clothe yourself with the full Armour of God, so that you may be able to stand against the schemes of the devil **(Ephesians 6;11)** We believe that God is the captain of our ship ,when you start losing the sight of your captain, you start to steer your own ship, but not only does this it leads to going a wrong side but can lead to trials, Sin, missed opportunity, and missed blessing, when you lose sight of your Captain, you start to worry ,and fear crops up ,you start thinking that Am in by myself, -God said he will guide you but instead of focusing on him ,you start focusing on the huge waves, distraction from God could be because of sin, but that's not always the reason ,don't let the noise of the world keep you away from hearing from God, It is not only sin that distract us from God there many reasons which distract us from God **(1)Ourselves(2)Doubt(3)Money(4)Hobbies(5)Relationship/Friends(6)Phone-call(7)Watching-Television**-Sometimes we are distracted by technology all day and we acknowledge God only right before we go sleep with a 30 seconds prayer and this shouldn't be quick prayers are selfish one we don't even take time to say thank you Lord ,we meant to do Gods will by praising him and worshiping him ,but we allow other things to consume our time like ,**Overtime** ,work on Sunday ,and Bank-holidays, Instead of going to church, We are meant to fix our eyes on our captain God, and we know where to find him ,Satan always tries his best to distract you, and more when you try to build a relationship with God he will distract you more, God says draw near me ,and I will draw near you, keep praying, many times people pray but they are distracted and think it's not going to work, because of lack of faith doubt distract them ,Spent time with God his is with you on the journey, he is guiding you to the right path, if you persevere in prayers at the right time he will answer you, have faith the more you focus on yourself the more distracted you will be from the proper path, -the more you know him the more the spirit will make you like him, the more you will understand his love utter sufficiency for all of life difficulties and that's the only way to know real satisfaction ,God did not create you to be distracted in life ,God created you to be/ live a Jesus infused life -life is full of distraction but you have to stay focused, **Dangers of being distracted taking your eyes off God and Jesus**

Christ (1) Peter got distracted by the storms around him ,Peter spoke up Lord if it is real you order me to come out on the water to you Jesus said Come so peter got out of the boat and started walking on water ,but when he noticed the strong wind he was afraid and started to think down in the water, Save me Lord he cried at once Jesus reached out and grabbed hold of him and said how little faith you have, why did you doubt? they both got into the boat and the wind died down ,then the 10 disciples worshiped him Jesus ,Truly you are a son of God they exclaimed, **Mary and Martha**- Martha was distracted by the dinner ,As Jesus and the disciples continued on their way to Jerusalem they came to a certain village, where a woman named Martha welcomed him into her home, her sister Mary sat at the lords feet, listening to what he taught, but Martha was distracted by the big dinner, she was preparing she came to Jesus and said Lord doesn't seem unfair to you that my sister Just sits here while I do all the work, tell her to come and help me, but the Lord said Dear Martha you are worried and upset over all these details ,there is only one thing worth being concerned about Mary has discovered it, will not be taken away from her (Jesus)**Satan seeks to distract** us in any way possible ,Be alert be on your watch- your enemy the enemy the devil rooms around like a soaring lion ,looking for someone to devour ,be firm in your faith and resist him, because you know all other believers in the world are going through the same kind of suffering ,but after you have suffered for little while the God of grace who call you to share the Eternal life and Glory in union with Christ will himself perfect you ,and give you firmness strength and a sure foundation to him ,be the power for ever (**1Peter5;8**) **Other friends /relationship may distract you from the Lord**-Does this sound as if am trying to win human approval ?no indeed what I want is Gods approval, Am I trying to win the approval of human beings or of God am trying to please people (am trying to be popular with people)if I were still trying to do so I wouldn't be a servant of God (**Galatians1;10**) **Other activity can distract you from God** -you may give much attention to other activity other than God,not having time with God in prayers- you may have time to spend with the poor and needy ,but forgetting time for God in prayers, but this is what I have against you -you don't love me as you did at first, if you don't turn from you sins I will come to you and take your lamp stand from its place -but this is what is in your favour you hate what Nicolaitans do as much as I do if you have ears then listen to what the spirit says to the churches, to those who win the victory ,I will give the right to eat the fruit of the tree of life that grows in the garden of God (**Revelations 2;3;4**)**Worries of life can distract us from God** What to Eat, Clothes, Money ,bills ,Employment, but the word of God encourages us and say "So don't ever worry by saying what are we going to Eat ,what to Drink or what are we going to Wear because it's the unbelievers who are eager for all those things surely you heavenly father know that you need all of them

,but first be concerned by Gods kingdom and his righteous and all of these things will be provided as well (**Mathew 6;31;33**)God is the source when your clothes are torn he knows to clothe you ,when your fridge he will fill it, Stop storing up your treasure for yourselves on earth ,where months and rust destroy ,and where thieves breaks in and steal but keep storing up treasure for yourselves in heavens ,where months and rust do not destroy, and where thieves do not break in and steal ,because where your treasure is there your heart will be also (**Mathew 6;19;21**)**Distracted by the world and what's in the world ,**Fame, Politics, Economy Magazines ,Football ,Television -shops Phones and calls from-friends Face book and What's up, is the biggest distraction of human life ever in modern technology and world ,we tend to love those things in the world more than God and ,if any one loves the world the love of the father is not in him because you can't love two masters at ago (**John 2;15**)In life you have the power to say this is not how my story will be your life is controlled by what you focus on **Solution to all the distraction we face in today** life (**1**) Do not be conformed to this world but be transformed by the renewal of your mind, that by testing you may discern what is the will of god what is good and acceptable and perfect (**Romans 12;2**) (**2**)Fix your Eyes on Jesus the pioneer and perfecto of the faith ,who in view of joy set before him endure the cross disregarding, its shame and he has sat down on the right hand of the throne of god (**Hebrews 12;2**)If ye the be risen with Christ, seek those things which are above where Christ sit on the right hand of God your affections on things above not on the things on the earth (**Colossians 3;1;2**)look straight ahead and fix your eyes on what lies before you (**Proverb 4;25**)Let all the world look at me for salvation for Am God there is no other God (**Isaiah 45;22;23**)Always we must stop everything and go to a quite place to hear from God ,then Jesus said lets go off ourselves to a quite place and rest a while he said this because there were so many people coming and going that Jesus and his disciples didn't have time to eat (**Mark 6;31**) **Focus on the lord by meditating on scriptures** -this book of the law shall not depart from your mouth but you shall meditate on it day and night so that you may be careful to do accordingly to all what is written in it for then you will make your way prosperous and then you will have success (**Joshua,1;8**) **We must prioritise our time** utilise our time and on daily basis have Prayer time Very early the next morning before day light Jesus got up and left then he went out of the town to a lonely place where he prayed But Simon and companion went out searching for him and when they found him they said to everyone is looking for you ,but Jesus said we must go on the other side (village around here)I have to preach in them because that's why I came for ,so they travelled over Galilee preaching in the synagogues ,The bible states it clearly -Then be careful how you live do not be unwise ,but be wise making the best use of your time the times are Evil,(**Ephesians,5;15;16**)**Amen**

13

BEST QUOTES ABOUT DISTRACTION;

I would put a picture here but it will distract you from your bible study, You cannot do big things if you are distracted by small things, Distraction destroys action, if it's not moving you towards your purpose leave it, Negativity distract me from goals so I simply do not entertain it ,I do laugh at it, In United kingdom, America Europe ,Africa, Asian, there is a lot of activity to distract you from God, like Football ,Cricket ,Tennis Boxing, East enders ,Ex-factor, and many other things but you have to be focused on what you want, either your God or activities ,It is not bad to enjoy them but don't allow them to overtake your life and serving God, You have to close some doors because they are not helping-Your results are the product of either personal focus or personal distraction, the choice is yours, Mind your own business always work hard avoid distraction, Every day set simple goals of being more awake and less distracted ,I can write all the things I will do in the morning ,afternoon evening ,when the mind is clear and there is no distraction ,Work is hard -distraction is plentiful and time is short, Am here to build something for a long term, anything for a short time is distraction ,there will be always doubters, obstacles, mistakes but with hard work no limitation, Girls /Boys were always my distraction in school Boys sometimes can be distractive ,but girls keep focused to their education and finish and graduate, At the end of the day Men/women are distraction weather you like it or not ,Always stay true to yourself and never let somebody else distract you from your goals and ambitions, Starve your distraction feed your vision focus and purpose in life, the best way to switch off from distraction is to switch them off turn/them off or practice saying no it's the only way to reduce distraction ,Successful people never worry about what others are doing ,Children are not distraction from the most important work ,but there are the most important work in life, and you have to care about them ,No matter how busy a person is ,If they really care they will find time for you, Love when you are ready not only when you are lonely ,Be happy ,smile, Ignore the noise, focus on your work; **Amen**

DOUBT AND FAITH

Doubt is unbelief in (Gods existence) Many people doubt in their God, Word, Faith, Salvation ,their existence in the world ,Churches, Environment, Marriages ,Family ,Finances, Jobs ,and many are struggling to find the truth, which is in the word of God **(Bible)** Faith is a gift- For its is by Gods grace that you have been saved through faith ,It's not the results of your own effort, but God's gift that no one can boast about **(Ephesians 2;8)** Faith is complete confidence in a Person **(God-Holy Spirit)**, Plan, strong belief in, Divine supernatural Power, that controls Human destiny and plans ,*(Human-kind)*- Faith is important as the Air we Breathe , while the Oxygen in the Air nourishes the body ,Faith nourishes the Heart and Soul *,It takes faith to believe in God and Jesus Christ, It takes faith to believe what God say is always true and right ,It takes faith to walk in that Every day*; It is by faith that we understand that the universe was created by Gods word, so that what can be seen was made out of what cannot be seen **(Hebrews,11,3)**, Jesus said you don't need a lot of faith even little one can move mountains ,It was because you haven't enough faith answered Jesus ,I assure you that ,if you have faith as big as a mustard seed you can say to this hill go from here to there ,and it will go you could do anything **(Mathew,17;20)**,In life we can ask for more faith ,The Apostle said" to the Lord make our faith greater the Lord said," if you had faith as big as a mustard ,you could say to this mulberry tree -pull yourself in the sea and it would obey you **(Luke 17;5)**- Having faith means -recognizing that you have no control that what will be -will be , and that there is a great power on the throne ,and universe that control everything **(God)** A lot of things we do not understand only God has the answer ,and get up and believe in him, not your own understanding -What gives life is Gods Spirit ,human power has no use at all , the words I have spoken to you bring Gods life -giving spirit, yet some of you do not believe, What attracts good things it's because we believe and expect good things to come ,when we believe in bad things to come we also attract that mind of bad things, Jesus knew from the very beginning who were the one that would not believe and which one would betray him **(John;6;63)** As Christian our main goal is to grow mature in **Faith(Believe in the above God)**that he will do what you want, It is a belief that God will do what is right, Faith know that there is power in name of Our Almighty God, Faith is more precious than Gold that perishes ," the bible says their purpose is to prove that your faith is genuine even gold which can be destroyed is tested by fire and so your faith which is more precious than Gold must be tested ,so that it may endure , then you will receive praise and glory and honour on the day when Jesus is revealed **(1 Peter 1;7)** **Faith is the foundation to Salvation**- yet we know that a person is put right with God only through faith in Jesus Christ, never by doing what the Law requires ,we too have believed in Christ Jesus, in order to be put right with God, through our faith in Christ ,and by not doing what the law requires ,for no one is put right by doing what the law requires **(Galatians 2;16)** It is by Gods grace, that you have been saved through faith ,it is not by the result of your own effort, but God's gift so that no one can boast about it **(Ephesians 2;8-9)** Whoever believe in him has eternal life **, (John 3;16)** and shall not come to judgement but has passed from death to life **,** the Just shall live by faith**(Romans,1;17)Faith brings all the benefits of Salvation- into our lives** this includes healing prosperity ,love Joy, **(1Peter1;8)** Deliverance from demons and the curses sanctification, of the mind motion ,the salvation of the soul and any other benefit which the word of God promises **,** The name of God is more powerful than the giants with a sword , Goliath said to David, come on and I will give your body to the birds and animals to eat, David answered you are coming against me with a sword ,spear and Javelin but I come to you in the name of the Almighty God of Israelite armies ,which you have defied this very day the Lord will put you in my power, I will defeat you and cut off your head and, I will give the bodies of Philistines soldiers to animals to eat then the whole world will know that Israel has a God **(1Samuel,17;44;46)**What is say is this " Gods massage is near you on your lips and in your heart "that is the massage of Faith that we preach , if you confess that Jesus is Lord and believe that God raised him from death you will be saved , for it is by faith that we are put right with God it is by our confession that we are saved the scripture says that whoever believe in him will not be disappointed , this includes every one because there is no different between Jews and gentiles God is the same Lord of all and richly blesses all who call to him, But how can they call to him for help -if they have not believed ? and how can they believe, if they have not heard the massage ? and how can they hear it , if is not proclaimed and how can the massage be proclaimed if the massagers are not sent out as the scripture says how wonderful is the coming of the massagers- who bring good news but not all have accepted the good news, **Isaiah** himself said "Lord who believed our massage ,So the faith comes by hearing the massage, and the massage comes through preaching Christ -*but I ask is it true that they did not hear the massage?* of course they did- for as the scriptures says" the sound of their voice went out to all the world ,their words reached the ends the earth *,again I ask did the people of Israel not understand ?* **Moses** himself is the first one to answer "I will use the called nations to make my people Jealous and by means of a nation of fools ,I will make my people angry, "and Isaiah is even bolder when he says " found by those who were not looking for me , I appeared to those who were not asking for me " But concerning Israel he says" all day long I held out my hands to welcome a disobedient and rebellious people " **(Romans,10;8;21)** *There is a* *thousand /million ways you can please God but you cannot please God without faith-*For he who comes to God must believe that he is a rewarder of those who diligently seek him *(Hebrews 11;6)*,**Faith has a price to pay and a price to receive faith reward,** Look at him they said to each other listen to his challenge King Saul has promised to give a big reward to the man who kills him the king will also give him a daughter to marry and will not require his father's family to pay taxes **(1Samuel;17;25;26)Faith says I can't save the impossible** -A man of faith dares the impossible and God bails him with extra ordinary exploits - yes said "Jesus if you yourself can everything is possible for the person who believes **(Mark;9;23)**I have all the strength to face all conditions by the power that Christ gives me**(Phillipians;4;13)**Faith brings answer to prayers "and whatever thing you ask in prayers believing you will receive it **(Mathew,21;22)** Since God tells us to pray for our daily bread **(Mathew;6;11)**faith is therefore the key to material provision ,**Faith, Speaks-** It is never afraid of mockery ,don't keep quite on what you believe let your faith speak it will soon mock your mockers with a miracle-the scripture says" I spoke because I believed in the same spirit of faith we also speak because we believe **(2Corinthians;4;13),Faith shifts to avenge any mockers of God** -no matter how big the size of the mocker ,David couldn't tolerate the mockery of God of Israel ,David said to Saul "your majesty no one should be afraid of this philistine I will go and fight him "no "answered Saul "how could you fight him? you are just a little boy and he has been a soldier for all his life your majesty ,David said I take care of my father's sheep ,whenever a lion or bears carries off a lamb I go after it attack it and rescue the lamb ,and if the bear or lion turns on me ,I grab it by the throat and beat it to death ,I have killed lions and bears ,I will do the same to this heathen philistine who has defied the army of the living God the Lord has saved me from the bears and lions he will save me from this philistine**(1Samuel 17;32;37)**It's your turn to face anything mocking you in life knowing God is in control*(poverty ,sickness ,stagnation ,addiction, fear ,doubt)* **Faith is a Spiritual force through which our Ministry for Christ becomes effective -** I assure you that whoever tells this hill to get up and throw itself in the sea and does not doubt in his heart , but believes that what he says will happen it will be done for him **(Mark 11;23)** faith then is a major key to Ministry success , it brings you what you want to your Ministry and by Imparting it to others through your life and Ministry of God's Word you enable them to receive the blessings of God s grace ,**Faith is the Major key for effective healing ministry and deliverance-** Ministry Jesus Christ is the same *"Yesterday ,Today, and Forever, (Hebrews 13;8),* **Men of faith are men of Victory -** People with faith have moved mountains in life ,they can pick the head of their oppressors at any time - and so without a sword David defeated and killed Goliath with a sling and a stone ,he ran to him, stood over him ,took

Goliath sword out of its sheath and cut off his head and killed him when the philistines saw that their hero was dead they ran away then the men of Israel and Judah shouted and ran after them pursuing them all the way to Gath and to the gates of Ekron ,the philistines fell wounded all along the roads that leads to Shaaraim as far as Gath and Ekron ,When the Israelites came back from pursuing the philistines they looted their camp David picked up Goliath head and took it to Jerusalem but kept Goliaths weapon in his own tent **(ISamuel;17;50-54)It's better to have Faith that pleases God than the one that moves mountains** -because God can always carry over by faith Enock was translated that he should not see death and was not found because God had translated him before his translation he had his testimony that pleased God**(Hebrews;11;5)Faith kills giants without a sword - giants falls and flee** ,-A man of faith is never scared, because he know he can kill them without a sword only his sword is the word of God, and believing what it says , today take courage face and kill your giants by faith today (poverty , sickness , losses , addiction ,delay , stagnation and so without a sword David defeated and killed Goliath with a sling and a stone**(1Samuel;17;50)It's better to have a building faith** -,What matters build your faith and your faith will build the rest ,but you my friends keep on building yourselves up your most sacred faith ,pray in the power of the holy spirit and keep yourselves in the love of God as you wait for our lord Jesus Christ in his mercy to give you eternal life **(Jude;1;20;21)Faith has happy endings** -ends with Joy ,good reports and celebrations the faith of David brought good things triggered joy and celebrations in all cities of Israel ,to have faith is to be sure of the things we hope for ,to be certain of the things we cannot see it was by faith that people of ancient times won God approval **(Hebrews;11;1-2)**as David was returning after killing Goliath and as the soldiers were coming back home women from every town in Israel come out to meet King Saul they were, singing Joyful songs, dancing , and playing tambourines and lyres in their celebrations the women sang "Saul has killed thousands but David tens of thousands **(1Samuel;18;6;7)Faith does not wait for encouragement** -David asked the men who were near him "what will the man get who kills this philistine and frees Israel from this disgrace? After all whose is this heathen philistine to defy the army of the living God they told him what would be done for the man who killed Goliath? Eliab, David's eldest brother heard David talking to the men, he was angry with David, what are you doing here? Who is taking care of those sheep of yours out there in the wilderness? you cheeky brat ,you just come to watch the fighting!**(1Samuel;17;26;28) Faith moves God to act** - faith does not need fear or doubt moves God when Jesus saw his friends he said to the Paralytic ,son your sins are forgiven , the lame man got up grabbed his mat and went home ,when Jesus saw the faith of the lame friends ,he moved on their behalf and healed their friends, unless we ask in faith without

18

doubting we won't receive what we are asking **(James,1;5;7)Faith acts-** like a magnet drawing the fulfilment of Gods promises into your life, so what are you wishing for its Gods will you can have it with your faith, work hard believe and get up early it's the best part of the day **Faith without work is dead** -a man of faith will fill his empty water pots to the brim and watch for a miracle ,he will do his best and wait God to do the rest **(Jn;2;7-10)Faith is when you act as God is telling you** -,Faith is active reliance on God it is believing in action , so as the body without a spirit is dead so also faith without action is dead **(James;2;26) Faith is not all about good intentions** -faith is action ,good intentions have never delivered any trophy to anybody, the whole army of Israel had good intentions to finish Goliath but David took action and delivered victory - Goliath started walking towards David again and David ran quickly towards the philistine battle line to fight him he put his hand into his bag and took out a stone which he slung at Goliath ,it hit him on the forehead and broke his skull and Goliath fell face downwards on the ground **(1Samuel;17;48;49)** -Like our saviour Jesus Christ through the power of the Holy spirit, It takes faith to grow spiritually in Jesus Christ and what hinders to grow spiritually in faith (The Apostle said to the Lord make our faith greater -The lord answered if you had Faith as big as a mustard seed, you could say to this mustard berry tree pull yourself up by the roots ,and plant yourself in the sea and it would obey, and for this reason I tell you when you pray and ask for something believe it that you have received it and you will be given whatever you ask, pray forgive anything you have against anyone*(Luke;17;5;Mark11;23-24;Mathew ;21;21)*Faith strengthen us during trials because we live in a sinful fallen world we will face difficulties ,but our faith is what keeps us strong during hard times we have the enemy and it's our faith that act as a shield to protect us from Satan plots , above all taking faith with which you will be able to quench all the fiery darts of the wicked *(Ephesians 6;16) Faith makes you to became a big nation,(church ,family, organisation)* it was by faith that made Abraham to became a father even though he was too old and Sarah herself could not have a child ,he trusted God to keep his promise though Abraham was practically dead from this one man came as many descendants as they are stars in the sky as many as numberless grains of sand on the shore sea*(Hebrews 11;11;13) Our faith quickness our desire-* Jesus Answered her you are a woman of great faith ! what you want will be done for you ,and at that very moment her daughter was healed *(Mathew, 15;28 ;A woman of faith with her daughter who had demons)Faith help us to encourage others* - Unshakeable faith is noticeable and it encourages others to be firm in their faith too- We always give thanks to God the father of our Lord Jesus Christ when we pray for you , For we have heard of your faith in Christ and of your love for all Gods people *(Colossians 1;3-4)* It is easy to stay committed to faith in God when you see others doing the same, choose to stand strong in faith and inspire others to do the same - I remember the sincere faith you have the kind of faith that your grandmother Lois and mother Eunice also had ,I am sure that you have it also (**2 Timothy 1;5**)*Faith fuels what we do* - We demonstrate our faith in God by what we do and how we live -For as the body without the spirit is dead so faith work is dead faith and work- work together to move forward genuine faith is validated by actions that follows action done without faith is useless , we must act in faith thus also faith by itself it does not have work is dead ,but someone will say "you have faith and I have works show me and I have works show me your faith without work and I will show you faith with work "*(James 2;17;18) Faith is important to get rid of our, self doubt , fears, in order to build self esteem and self confidence,* To keep your faith alive, you have to obey ,Gods word and doing the best, Choose faith by saying I can do all things through Christ, remember that I have commanded you to be ,determined and confident don't be afraid or discouraged for I the Lord your God am with you, whenever you go (**Joshua;1;9**)If you believe that you are destined to be a great success ,and you hold to this belief no matter what happens then there is nothing in the world that can stop you from becoming that great success .if you believe that you are a good person with God given abilities and that you are going to do remarkable and greater things with your life that belief will express itself through all your actions and will eventually became a reality the, biggest responsibility you have is to change your belief on the inside so that you are consistent with the realities you wish to enjoy on the outside- Its good always your expectation to be higher in Jesus name -To him who by means of his power working in us is able to do much more than we can ask for , even think of(**Ephesians;3;20**) Some of you have become proud because you have thought that I would not be coming back to visit you,if the Lord is willing however I will come to you soon and then I will find out for myself the power which these proud people havc and not just what they say ,for the kingdom of God is not a matter of words but of Power which do you Prefer? shall I come to you with a whip or in a spirit of Love and gentleness ?(**1Corinthians 4;18;21**)**Where you are is not your destination, God is taking you to a better place have faith**- It was by faith that made Abraham obey when God called him to go out to a country which God had promised, to give him ,he left his country without knowing where he was going ,by faith he lived as a foreigner in the country God had promised him he lived in tents as did Isaac and Jacob who received the same promise from God,(**Hebrews;11;8;10**)With faith you raise higher ,you overcome obstacles and you move forward into your, blessings and victory, Take time to go to church that faith activates Gods Power, and that faith opens door for God to move on your behalf ,Put a smile on your face when you feel discouraged ,put action behind your faith ,chose faith overcome doubt and fear ,and live in the freedom God has for you -Don't dig up in doubt what you planted in Faith-your faith can move mountains and your Doubt can create more mountain, for you in life, you can tell what your beliefs really are by looking what you do ,you always express your true values in your actions ,you act on the outside consistent with who really are and what you really believe on the inside, the best way to determine your faith is to think about how you behave ,when you are angry, upset or under-pressure of any kind, this is when they come out ,Circumstances do not make a man -they only reveal him to himself . whatever you expect with your confidence becomes your own self fulfilling prophecy (You are the first prophet to yourself) you are telling your success when you talk about how you think things are going to turn out in your life-your expectation determines your attitude ,and your attitude causes people to behave towards you, in a way that reflects what you are thinking inside if you expect to be successful, you will be happy – if you expect to be surrounded by prosperous and healthy people around you that is what will happen ,you can tell your true expectations by listening to the words you use to describe upcoming events -talk positive about the future believe in success and wonderful things, expect the best, be open to possibility that happens ,successful people maintain an attitude of positive expectancy, and have a wealth mind ,belief ,be kind ,patience, gentleness , loving people ; I Believe you you are God of miracle who heals the sick resurrect the dead the one who does the impossible ,The God who was to come ,The power of the risen one ,God,**Amen**

QUESTION?

HOW TO OVERCOME DOUBT AND INCREASE IN FAITH?

Put your trust in the lord and stand firm ,have faith and you will succeed in life, I Have been crucified with Christ and I no longer live but Christ lives in me, the life I now live in the body I live by faith in the Son of God who loved me and gave himself for me **(Galataians;2;20)**In life you will never succeed if you don't believe that you deserve what you want - Visualise your goals make an effort to go for it, and always stay positive that its yours Faith comes by hearing and hearing by the word of God **(*Roman;10;17*)**So then faith comes from hearing the massage and the massage comes through preaching the massage of Jesus Christ the reason the bible has out sold other books is because is God word and faith comes by hearing the word the word of God- Your faith will grow strong when you read his word ,and it works when you do what it says, it is the solution to all the problem you face today- -the word they heard did not profit them being mixed with faith in those who heard it **(Hebrews;4;2)**Constant hearing and attention to the word of God produces faith , especially if you attend it with an open mind and heart, pay attention to what I say my son, Listen to my words never let them get away from you remember them and keep them in your heart they will give life and health to anyone who understands them **(Proverb 4;20;22)** what we listen to affects what we believe if you listen to doubt people you will doubt ,if you listen to people who lie you will lie ,and this produce deception eventually ,the mind will accept something that thing is heard often enough and persuasively enough that's why we should keep listening to the word of God through ,Preachers ,Christian, Tapes confessions of the word , daily fellowship with godly Christians , this will cause us to believe the truth from our hearts ,By choosing faith you become a contender for the Human Spirit, giving hope to those in need- keep your thoughts Positive, because your thoughts,-become your words -Keep your words positive because your words becomes -your behaviour ,keep your behaviour positive because your behaviours becomes- your habit ,keep your habits positive because your habits- becomes your behaviours **(Mahatma Gandhi)**It's not good enough to read Gods word you must internalise it, and then vocalise it, We say all kinds of things but the truth that we don't really believe them, because they don't show up the way we live ,we want to see things with our naked eyes or see miracles happening in the present not in the future-in life ,be Positive with every ideas surrounding your dreams ,think about the possibility of what you plan to do and approach it with an optimistic action stay positively- If you tell yourself you are fine you will,-When you go through negative situations don't think about it make it positive**(Yoko-Ono)**Staying positive doesn't mean that things will turn out Ok, rather it is knowing that you will be Ok, no matter how things turn out-Positivity believing**(Faith)**will block the negative thoughts that overwhelm you ,during hard times , stay positive and you will achieve more than what you set yourself for, Have fun ,be yourself ,enjoy life and stay positive-No matter what you face don't forget if you are positive positivity will find you and embrace you A fantastic positive attitude makes a great day! Smile **(Mary-Bradford)**Never doubt you were born to do great things ,An attitude of positive expectation is the mark of superior personality- if you have a positive attitude and constantly strive to give your best effort eventually you will overcome your immediate problems ,and find you are ready for greater challenges -Positive thoughts leads to positive results before you leave the house ,you need to make up your mind that you are going to stay in faith and enjoy the day, no matter what comes your way - you have to decide a head of the time**(Joel-Osteen)** I have the ability to build myself up or break myself down **(Hayley-Williams)**Optimism is happiness magnet if you stay positive good things and good people will be drawn to you It makes a big difference in your life when you stay positive and believing you will see opportunities instead of Obstacles Positive anything is better than negative nothing **(Elbert-Hubbard)** Positive thinking will let you do everything better than negative thinking will Positive believers sees the Invisible feels, the intangible and achieves the impossible-Dwell on the beauty of life watch the stars and see yourself running with them **(Marcus -Aurellus)**When it rains ,it Pours ?but soon ,the sun shines again ,stay positive better days are on their ways ,keep your face to the sunshine and you cannot see a shadow**(Helen-Keller)**Whenever you go no matter what the weather always bring your own sunshine, believe you can do and you are halfway there -Gods time is the best, but we should change and believe that God is who he is ,we should trust him ,for opportunities trust him regardless of the situation some say my faith is low ,I wish I had faith like **,Mary ;Henry ,Erica ,Rose ,David,** or so and so ,there is no mystery about to close the gap between yours and others what you have to do to spend your time reading the word (***bible***)Scriptures take control of your time re-arrange your priorities, if you are serious about growing in faith it's a price you must be willing to pay ,it takes approximately *56 hours* to read the bible through, if you read *40 chapters a day* and you would complete within a month if you read *9 chapters* of the new testament each day you would complete it within *30 days* but you must read it systematically regularly and expectantly when Satan attached Jesus in the wildness Jesus quoted scriptures to him that's why the **(*Psalmist;119;11*)**Say keep your law in my heart so that I will not sin against you ,the book of Proverb has **31**chapters here is an idea since they are **31 days** in a month why not read one chapter in this wisdom book every day to be wise you must study the word be strong in faith believe it to be successful in life you must practice it-Love yourself it is important to stay positive because beauty comes from the inside out **(Jenn-Proske)**I stay positive strength comes within ,Choosing to be positive ,and having a grateful attitude is going to determine how you are going to live your life **(Joel-Osteen)**Faith is being sure of what you hope for **(*Hebrews11;1*)*By faith Abraham was called*,** Noah was warned about the floods and built an Ark ,Abraham left everything all was the word of God if you don't sense a strong leading by God himself then stepping out in faith is not yours, faith is willing to delay Gratification, when you step out on faith you must be willing to accept the fact that what you desire may or may not happen soon, Abraham took him**(25years)**Joseph took him**(13years)**if you are someone who is believing in immediate blessing stepping out on faith is not yours -***Faith is moving forward without all the facts-*** Even though he didn't know where he was going ,Abraham had to leave, God only gives you enough information to see right /light ,in front of you, and he often times conceals the details about the journey along the way ,If you are someone who is looking for all the facts before you move on faith is not yours-Positive believing is empowering ,Positive action is achieving - surround yourself with positive people and situation and avoid negativity- Accept that not all your questions and requests will be answered some take longer than expected some take a short time "*There something that the Lord our God has kept secret but he has revealed hid law and we and our descendants are to obey it forever;* **(Deuteronomy;29;29)Faith is about willing to leave what is comfortable-** like a stranger in a foreign country its difficult for many because we value comfort predictability and certainty the problem is if we value it too much we will never see Gods power when God calls you must be able to leave your family, job, romantic relationship ,church ,you have to take strong decisions and be sure that God is leading you make decisions with prayers and seeking wise counsels if you dwell on comfort you will never move on **Faith believes in supernatural power of God-** faith commands you to do something that you have never done before- if you believe in the natural realms stepping out on faith is not yours - You need to have Gods faith that there is nothing to Hard with God, everything is possible so long as you believe -Successful people do not spend much time thinking about what must be done ,Instead they spend twice much as much time reflecting on what they have already done ,and on how they have accomplished what they set out to do the power of expectation and believe is within you ,things turn out best for people who make best of the way things turn out pursuing a God given dream is a bumpy ride as every reader in the bible found out and only those who think right succeed ,the greatest gap between successful people and unsuccessful people is a *thinking* **gap**, this is especially so when it comes to failure ,Successful people see failures as a regular part of success and they get over it -Successful people their altitude is not a pitfalls their altitude is a challenge and what is nature telling them ?such tenacity only comes from right thinking and it's a hallmark of all successful people they keep trying ,learning and keep moving forward they win the battle in their minds and then they overflows into what they do if you absolutely can't stay positive, don't go negative just cruise neutral for a while until you can get back up -We should learn to be led by the spirit ,since we live by the Spirit let us keep in step with the spirit (**Galatians;5;25)**If a Christian life is about having a personal relationship with God ,then God must still speak to us today ,but a relationship can't be built on one day speech ,First it requires commitments and communication ,between two personals in which each speaks and listens to the other ,you are controlled by the spirit ,if the spirit of God lives in you(**Romans;8;9)**That means having a spirit controlled responses and making spirit led decision, When you follow Gods life you no longer consists of that which you can see ,felt or figured out it includes walking by faith, trusting him, learning to know his voice and leading of the spirit , Some of us we are reluctant to do that because we have seen people who claim to be doing it, and their approaches scare us, so when we sense the spirit leading we doubt it analyse it ,conclude it ,isn't logical and don't pay attention to it   some of us we want to pay attention to it but we are not sure we know that is really speaking to us we wonder is this *Gods voice or our own desire* ? all Christians have experienced and they question them who am I the spirit to speak to me among others this is why Paul wrote since we live by the spirit let us keep in step with the spirit - Spiritual guidance is learned one step at a time even the most mature believers will stumble and get it wrong at a time no problem ,the lord delights in a man way he will not fall for the lord upholds him in his hands(**Psalms;*37;23-24)***Use your measure of faith-God has dealt to each one a measure of faith (**Romans;12;3**) and we just have to use the faith God has given us and develop our faith , And because of Gods gracious gift to me ,I say to every one of you do not think of yourself more highly than you should, Instead be modest in your thinking ,and judge your self-according to the amount of faith God has given you, is equal to the assignment he has given you ,so What are you facing today? tell yourself you can handle this is nothing, what is more important is your faith ,Jesus told Peter Satan has asked for you that he may shift you as wheat ,but I have prayed for you that your faith should not fail, and when you turn back to me you must strengthen your brothers (***Luke; 22; 31-32***) Faith is more important than career and success. Money or reputation, everything can be taken away from you, but if you have faith is having a direct line to God, as a prayer of faith goes up his power flows down; **Amen** as a result you are more than an adequate for the challenge -Failure is never final , as long as your faith does not fail , that's why Satan will do everything he can to keep you from spending time each day reading your ,bible, what it say is this, Gods massage is near you on your lips and in your heart that is the massage of faith we preach (**Romans,10;8**)Paul called this massage he preached the word of faith ,because the word the word will cause faith to love into your heart, God will build assurance ,confidence faith in your heart then you are to exercise faith ,Jesus said if you have Faith like a mustard seed you will say to this mountain to move here to there and it will (***Mathew;17;20)***If there is any obstacle in your life this can only be moved by your faith ,and you do not need a full truck lorry of it ,just a mustard seed think of a tiny seed has a power to grow overcome obstacles and become a mighty tree, what matter is not the size of your faith ,but the quality of it determines your success so today use the measure of your faith to overcome Barriers in your life ,Rocks around you Braving storms, Withstanding animals ,Marriage problems, Addictions, Diseases ,Careers and other threats in your life, your faith will deliver you your doubt does not qualify you anywhere ,do not doubt but believe (**John;20;24;29;Lk24;37-45**)He was greatly surprised because the people did not have faith(**Mark;6;6 Jesus rejected at Nazareth**)Thomas one of the **12 disciples** was not with them when Jesus came the other disciples then said to him we have seen the lord ,so he said to them unless I see in his hands and put my finger into print of the nails into his sides ,I will believe after eight days he appeared to them where inside then ,Jesus came and Thomas was with them the door being shut and stood in the midst and said peace to you then he said to Thomas reach your finger here and look at my hands and reach your hands here and put inside do not doubt but believe Thomas said my God and my lord Jesus said to him do you believe because you see ?Happy are those who believe without seeing-Thomas expressed his doubt to others /disciples but the lord knows the thought of man **(Psalm94;11)**Some of us we would have looked at Thomas and said he is not qualified to be a disciple but Jesus he recognised an honest heart and seeking soul and he showed up to answer the question of doubt dear fellow sisters and brothers your doubt don't take you anywhere in life, if you doubt take your doubts in prayers to the lord and he will answer you even before you leave his presence or after , and you will be saying my lord my God has done it for me, if you want to change your habits /morals from bad to good receive good things you should believe in God for good things, when you are in storms and problems in life and don't know where to go speak to yourself and say faith does not fail me ,you can have an expression of faith yet you do not enjoy the fruits and benefits of it, you can get excited about sermons in church yet nothing changes in life, you have to mix with a what you think say and do faith is not an emotion, it is a decision to stand on God word ,a catalyst facilitates a changes it makes things to happen ,**Seeds-** without sunshine means no **flowers Flour-** without yeast produces no **bread -Blue** without yellow you cannot have **green -An egg** without sperm you cannot have a **baby A spark**-without air you cannot have a **flame-** Faith makes Gods word to work in your life without it nothing can happen - Without specific catalyst certain results cannot be achieved to make spiritual progress is not enough to read a bible from page to page or to listen to sermons in church the active ingredients to understanding is faith after we hear Gods word we must act on it and trust Gods word his promise will bloom into our life once we activate our life with faith release your faith today in every part of your life water your life and seeds with faith and you will harvest the best in life **,How happy you are to believe that Lords massage will come true ?(Luke1;45;Marys visit to Elizabeth)**,Believe that you will see Gods favour today, because faith is today believe that this is the day God has choose for you to rejoice and is your best day **(Psalm,118;24)** Believe that today is the day God has choose for you to prosper, this is the day God is raining or sending rain in your business ,Today is your day of greatness, believe it today is your day of promotion, toady is your day of healing, today is my day to be delivered from my addiction, I believe that my blessing is today ,is my day to be forgiven my Sins, and Debts ,believe that today is my day to plan for my Wedding, I believe today that today is the day you have choose for me to meet New friends , to uplift me, move me from a higher level day ,to increase me, today is the day to Promote me at my work place, today is the day to Restore my loses, today is the day to receive, Direction from you, today is the to receive Wisdom understanding and knowledge from you, God today I believe that ,I will Lend and not borrow ,God, I believe and I have faith that today is the day to turn my story around , Jesus healing the man he found on the pool healing the woman who was bleeding and healing the son of the army official ,To receive from God you have to seek his kingdom first, Faith causes God to act God meets you at your level of expectation, if you are expecting in a hundred year you will receive after a 100 years but if your expectation and faith is today now good things are coming and expect them God is still making wonders and miracles ,God is still on the throne ,Dear Christian stop believing in money ,friends ,fame, jobs, politicians, environment , believe in the lord, Jesus Christ in the word of God, and the Holy Ghost for a change in your life ,for Healing ,Victory ,Divine opportunities ,Success, Protection ,Deliverance and fighting your battles ,those who rush to other gods bring many trouble on themselves ,I will not take part in their sacrifices ,I will not worship their God -You lord you all I have and you give me all my needs my future is in your hands how wonderful your gifts to me how good they are!**(Psalm;16;4;6)The Lord said to Moses choose one of the Leaders from each of each Twelve tribes send them as spies to explore the Land of Canaan which am giving to the Israelites Moses obeyed and from the wilderness of Paran he sent out leaders as follow Reuben - Shammua son of Zaccur Simeon-Shaphat son of Hori Judah-Caleb son of Jephunneh Issachar- Igal son of Joseph Ephraim -Hoshea son of Nun Benjamin- Palti son of Raphu Zebulum- Gaddiel son of Sodi Manasseh-Gaddi son of Susi Dan-Ammiel son of Gemalli Asher-Sethur son of Micheal Naphtali -Nahbi son of Vophsi Gad-Geuel son of Machi these are the spies Moses sent to explore the land he changed the name of Nun to Joshua** when Moses sent them out he said to them go North from here into the southern part of Canaan and then on into the hill country find out what kind of country it is how many people live there and how strong they are find out whether the land is good or bad and whether the people live in open towns or fortified cities find out whether the soil is fertile and whether the land is wooded and be sure to bring back some of the fruits that grows there (it was the season when grapes were beginning to ripen; **Numbers 13;20 read more) 10** out of the 12 came back and said the land is fortified people who live there are like Giants in the land there is no way we can get that land **(Numbers;13;28)** but **2** out of them said the land is ours Caleb silenced the people who were complaining against Moses and said we should attack now and take the land we are strong enough to conquer it but those who had gone with Caleb said no we are not strong enough to attack them the people are more strong than we are so they spread false report among the Israelites about the land they had explored they said even that land doesn't produce enough to feed who live there every one we saw was very tall and we saw giants there the descendants of Anak we felt as small as grasshoppers and that's is how we must have looked to them if you want to increase in faith you should **(1)Gods Power**-the 10 negative spies said we can't attack those people they are stronger than we the **(2Positive-Spies)** said if the lord is pleased with us he will lead us into that land and he will give to us, Many people today undermine Gods power and what he can do, they are like the 10 spies don't disregard Gods power but give all the credit to him if you fail to recognise Gods power you will always struggle in your life and faith sometime resources our education abilities influence connections looks limited we forget that God is involved and invests in our life and his power exceeds our expectations ,the bible says this generation of Israelites did not receive the blessing of the promised land that God intended for them to receive, because they did not have Faith ,there must be some, blessings, opportunities, favour ,open doors that God wants to release to you ,the only key to unlock them is to have faith ,To increase in Gods faith and overcome doubt in life, you have to **(2)Remember Gods past faithfulness**---his amazing miracles, and things he has done in your life , God performed great miracles in the past **Parting the red sea** -Moses held his out his land over the sea and the lord drove the sea back, with a strong east winds it blew all night and turned the sea a dry land, the water was divided and the Israelites went through the sea on dry ground, with walls of water on both sides **(Exodus;14;21;22)**Water from the rock -The lord said to Moses take some the leaders of Israel with you and go on a head of the people take along with the stick with which you struck the Nile I will stand before you on a rock at mountain Sinai strike the rock and water will come out of it for the people to drink Moses did so in the presence of the leaders this place was named Massah and Meribah because the Israelites complained and put the lord to the test when they asked **"is the lord with us or not?(Exodus17;6)The lord fought battles for the Israelites** -The lord said to Moses write an account of this victory so that it will be remembered tell Joshua that, I will completely destroy the Amalekites Moses built an altar and named it the lord is my Banner he said hold high the banner of the lord the lord will continue to fight against the Amalekites for ever**(Exodus;17;14)**He provided clothes for 40 years the lord led the Israelites through the desert your clothes and sandals never wore out you didn't have bread to eat and wine or beer to drink but the lord provided for your needs in order to teach you that he is your God **(Deuteronomy;29;5)**God even said to them how long will they refuse to believe in me, In spite of all the signs I have performed among them**(Numbers;14;11)**if you look at your life experience remember what he has done for you, It gives confidence to trust in him the next time your faith is tested look back and recount your past victories, healings, favour

,and mercies, Think in a thousand years whose going to care**(Sheaf-Cooper)**Focus on good things in life reflect on your past achievement and look on to your God Tell yourself if I don't try I will never know -don't doubt yourself you are a perfect example of talent and beauty**(Annie Pryatel)**This year my abilities will always outweigh my doubts think positive you can do it -**Act on your faith not your doubt** Noah and Abraham did (Noah build an Ark Abraham offered his son Isaac Moses David Faced Goliath Joshua marched Jericho David Joshua when thrown in the lions)doubt your doubt not your faith don't let your faith go away from you because you are in the valley of problems of darkness when you find yourself there don't be attempted to give in to your doubts fear and worries just keep walking- nothing is gained by giving up every step gained is away to doubt your doubt soon enough the light will shine on you keep going to what you know is true Romans **(8:-)**for am persuaded and he declares nothing in all the universe can separate us from the love of God in Christ our lord, I know who I have believed something in you think hope you know in times of trouble keep going to what you know is right/true**(2Timothy1;12)**People today live in life of negativity and doubt in their area of health, sickness, employment ,marriage, their happiness and joy, has been affected, such will be the spread of evil that many people love will grow cold, but whoever that holds up will be saved and this good news will be preached through all world for a witness to all nation and then the end will come **(Mathew;24;12)** If we take our eyes off Jesus and focus on the evil of this world and our circumstances ,then we are fallen by the negativity of the world, forgetting the love of God and Jesus that God is able to do anything ,To him by means of his power working in us is able to do so much more than we can ever ask for or even think**(Ephesians;3;20)**For the lord loved the world that ,he gave his only son that whoever believe in him should not die**(John;3;16)** Do not be worried and upset Jesus told them believe in God and believe in also in me **(John;14;1 Jesus the way to the father)** call on to me when trouble comes I will save you and you will praise me show mercy to those who have doubt save others by snatching them out of fire and others show mercy mixed with fear but hate their very clothes stained by their sinful lusts**(Jude;1;22)If you stop doubting and focus on Christ God and his word,** in the midst of trials and circumstances you can walk over the waters, and all the trials, and circumstances and be a winner and prosper/victorious, When Peter took his eyes off Jesus and his word Peter looked at the stormy sea ,he began to sink instead of focusing on Jesus and his promises, Peter focused on the circumstances and that why he began to think ,Satan is using the evil and negative things of the world to attract your attention and capture you can get discouraged by listening to **(3)Third factor to overcome Doubt and increase in faith is stop-**negative thinking ,-believing in negative ,newspaper or reading news paper of negativity, believing in negative politics ,and the negative reports of environment ,and negative perspective of wars, and get rid of negative friends ,who are full of and doubt in God's ,Love, Mercy ,Favour, Blessings ,Protection, Miracles, Healing, and your love for him grows cold when your boss tells you are laid off ,or doctor say you have been diagnosed with cancer, your wife /spouse they are leaving you, stay positive -keep speaking Gods word over your circumstances, and problems, my words shall not return to me void ,but shall accomplish what I please and prosper, in things which I sent it(**Isaiah 55;11**)Look at the (**10 Negative Spies**) they spread bad reports among the Israelites about the land they had explored as a result the whole nation of 2 million were filled with fear instead of faith because they allowed themselves to be influenced by (**10Spies**) and their negative reports they had no faith like the (**2Spies**)if you surround yourself with negative reports ,negative people, who fear who have negative thinking, have few or no testimonies, they will influence you and your faith-***Faith is contagious and Doubt* is contagious,** then be careful of the ,Environment you live in ,and reports you read, and listen to- you will miss what God have for you, if you allow those negativity in your life, Spend much time as you can with people of faith , the Spirit of faith will touch your life also - keep company with the wise and you will became wise, if you make friends with stupid people , you will be ruined (**Proverb,13;20**) **God talks in faith - God gives life to the dead and calls those things** -things which do not exist as though they did as the scriptures, I have made you a father of many nations so the promise is good in the sight of God in whom Abraham believed -the God who brings the dead to life, and whose command brings into being what did not exist Abraham believed and hoped, even when there was no reason for hoping and so became the father of many nations just as the scripture says" your descendants will be as many as stars (**Romans,17;18**) It's through words that covenant and promises are made its through words that our faith our fears are expressed ,bad words open the doors for bad things ,habits, to work Gods word open the door for God to work words of faith produces faith , words of fear attracts the spirit of fear, A man belly shall be satisfied with the fruits of his mouth and with the increase of his lips shall be satisfied,(**Proverb,18;20**)Your reward depends on what you say and what you do ,you will get what you deserve , Faith works by love - (**Proverb 12;14**)We feed on the words we speak, what we speak comes back to affect our own heart and our own spiritual conditions, for when we are in union with Christ Jesus neither, circumcision nor the lack of it as Sons and daughters of God we are called to be imitators of God filled with Gods spirit (Ephesians 5;1;8) when we are in Christ and we have the promises of God , we have the right to speak something God has promised as if it existed even before our natural sense are conscious of it, it's our faith that gives substance to this confession of things not seen , if we have believed God for a Child , Yacht, Plane ,House, Finances, deliverance , provision,   before we see it, we should realise that God has already sent his angels and given all things that pertain to life and godliness **(2 Peter 1;3)** and all spiritual blessings - Let us give thanks to the God and father of our Lord Jesus Christ , for in union with Christ he has blessed us by giving us every Spiritual- blessing in the heavenly world **(Ephesians 1;3)** the effective receiving depends on our faith   makes any difference what matters is faith that works through love **(Galatians 5;6 ;the Centurion Mathew,8;5;13 Woman of Canaan Mathew,15;21;28)** were motivated by their love for another in coming to Jesus and were both described as having great faith ,let us believe God for others to be blessed in a Spirit of love , and as we give ourselves God will give blessings to us also- do not judge others and God will not judge you ,do not condemn others and God will not condemn you forgive others and God will forgive you ,give to others and God will give you ,indeed you will receive a full measure a generous helping poured into your hands- all that you can hold the measure you use for others is the one that God will use for you **(Luke 6;36-37)**this is related to the idea of **Seed of faith** by planting a seed in term of some form of giving God will release a multiplied harvest in return ,if we endure and do not faint -you need to be patient ,in order to do the will of God and receive what he promised **(Hebrews 10;36)** ,**When you pray you must believe and do not doubt at all-** Whoever doubt is like a wave in the sea, that is driven and blown about by the wind, people like that are unable to make up their minds, and undecided in all ,they must not think that they will receive anything from the lord(**James;1;6;7**) **Pray in tongues to increase in faith- and be full of the Spirit** ,when you pray in tongues you edify , yourself (**1Corithians,14;4**)and build yourself up in your most Holy faith, praying in tongues is the key to being full of the Spirit , since faith is the fruit of the Spirit all things are related together ,**Seek holiness- purity of heart pursue peace with all men and holiness without which no one will see the Lord (Hebrews,12;14)**It is with the heart that man believes **(Romans10,10)**to the extent the heart has , uncleanness un-forgiveness, and other bad morals within the man will lose his spiritual perception of the Lord ,which enables his heart to believe , purity feed each other , We have Three kinds of faith, *Weak, moderate, and Greater ,faith* (1)**Weak faith** staggers/ stagers- these hear the words but do nothing my brothers and sisters what good is it for people to say that they have faith if their actions do not prove it can that faith save them suppose there is a brother or sister who needs clothing and do not have enough to eat what good is there in your saying God bless you keep warm and eat well if you don't give them the necessities of life? So it is with faith if it is alone without faith is dead **(James, 2;14;17)** you fools do you want to be shown that faith without action is useless? (**James; 2; 20**) (2)**Moderate faith**- they have faith and believe but do not act then the

Jewish authorities replied with question what miracle can you perform to show us that you have a right to do this? Jesus answered tear down this temple and in three days, I will build it again, are you going to build it again in three days ,they asked him, it has taken forty- six years to build this temple, but the temple Jesus was talking about was his body ,so when he was raised from death his disciples remembered that he had said this and they believed the scripture ,and what Jesus said **(John; 2; 18; 20)Do you believe there is only one God?** The demons also believe in God **(Mark;1;24)**demons also believe ,Jesus is the lord **(Mark3;11;12)** demons also know about the Bible **(Mathew;4;6)** demons also believe in eternal punishment **(Luke;8;30) (3) Greater/<u>Strong faith</u>**- is firm show me how can anyone can have faith without action I will show you my faith by action **(James;2;19)**this faith is a combination of faith and action where belief affects behaviours how was ancestor Abraham put right to God ? It's through his action when he offered his son Isaac on the Altar can't you see? his faith and action worked together his faith was made perfect through his actions and the scripture came true that said "Abraham was then almost 100 years old but his faith did not weaken when he thought of his body which was already practically dead or of the fact that Sarah could not give children his faith did not leave him and he did not doubt Gods promise his faith filled him with power and gave praise to God he was absolutely sure that God would be able to what he promised believed God and because of his faith God accepted him as righteous the words he was accepted a s righteous were not written for him alone there were written for us who believe in him who raised Jesus our Lord from death **(Romans;4;19;23)**and so Abraham was called a friend of God**(James;2;21;23)**you see then that that it is by peoples action that they are put right with God not only with God and not by their faith alone**(James;2;24)**It was the same with the prostitute Rahab she was put right with God through her actions by welcoming the Israelite spies and helping them to escape by a different road**(James;2;25)**So then as the body without the spirit (breath) is dead, So also faith without action is dead**(James;2;26)**There will always be people to help but you have to distinguish between those who need and those who want decide who you can help them to know how to fish for themselves your helping could some time help you to minister to them the goodness of God and what he can do and learn how to say **"No "**Ask in faith without double mind someone with a double mind is unstable in his ways he stagers between two side (which way)Pauls letter about faith says have done my best in the race I have run a full distance and I have kept the faith and now there is awaiting for me the victory prize of being put to right to God which the lord the righteous will give me on that day and not only to me but all those who wait with love for him to appear(**2Timothy;4;7**)The natives saw the snake hanging on Paul and said to one another this man must be a murderer but the fate will not let him live even though he escaped from the sea but Paul shook off the snake into the fire without being harmed at all they were waiting for him to swell up or suddenly fall down dead but after waiting a long time not seeing anything unusual happening to him they changed their minds and said is God (**Acts;28;4;Paul in Malta**) Each of us have different issues and problems but have the same principle of faith, **Be wise in your words you say**- your words can heal ,peoples life and can cage them as well, Gods word is anointed ,and has power when its spoken to change the spiritual atmosphere , be sure that the book of law is always read in your worship study it day and night and make sure you obey everything written in it then you will be prosperous and successful (**Joshua,1;8**) Confession of God's word saying the same thing ,as Gods word brings you to a place the Lord will move you to fulfil it - For it is by faith that we are put right with God it is by our confession that we are saved (**Romans,10;10**)My Christian brothers and sisters who also have been called by God think of Jesus whom God sent to be the high priest of the faith we profess (**Hebrews 3;1**) Praise the Lord you strong and mighty angles ,who obey his commands ,who listen to what he says (**Psalm,103;20**) We should live our own faith ;Success is personal ,stop the error and trial life, believe in victory ,success, never expect the world to create opportunities for you we are made in the image of God likeable valuable to God like Jesus Christ ,everything of Jesus belongs to us, whoever shall say to the mountain will move ,don't say something and ran away ,David was facing terrible circumstances, Saul was trying to kill him David running for 13 years his possession taken his wives and children taken his servant wanted to stone him, things looked bleak, David was in the situation where everyone in the natural said be discouraged and dismayed, but David encouraged himself in the lord prayed, and encouraged himself only a matter of hours until what God had promised him came to pass and he become a king if he had doubted and given up he would have lost all (**1Samuel;30;6**) keep feeding your faith and starve your doubt, He who knows nothing doubts nothing We doubt about our knowledge whether we truly know enough to move forward sometime about the choice we make but if anyone of lack wisdom should pray to God who will give it to us and stop doubting(**James;3;5;7**)Associate with people who don't doubt, for advice seek from God and good counsellors, God flows through people, but if they have doubt about what they eat ,God condemn them ,when they eat because their action is not based on faith and anything that is not based on faith is a sin (Do not make one another fall(**Romans14;23**)If you become discouraged you stop the flow of Gods power,Acknowledge (doubt)but don't be caught up in doubt(**Ray Benoit**)Faith no one can please God without faith ,whoever comes to God must have Faith that God exists and rewards those who seek him (**Hebrews;11;6**)*We should always be full of faith*-the scriptures" says the whole group was pleased with the apostles proposal so they chose Stephen a man full of faith Prochorus, Nicanor, Timon, Parmenas and Nicolaus a gentile from Antioch who had earlier been converted to Judaism the group presented them to the apostles who prayed and placed their hands on them **(Acts 6;5;6)***We should be rich in faith-the bible says* "listen my dear brothers and Sisters, God chose the poor people of this world to be rich in faith and to posses the kingdom ,which he promised to those who love him **(James;2;5)***We need perfect faith*-how was our ancestor Abraham put right with God? It was through his action when he offered his son Isaac on the Altar can't you see? his faith and action worked together his faith was made perfect through his action **(James,2;22)***We need overcoming faith* - because every Child of God is able to defeat the world and we win victory over the world by means of our faith, who can defeat the world? only the person ,who believe that Jesus is the son of God **(1 John; 5; 4; 5; our victory over the world)***When you read the bible you see how Jesus responded to people who had faith* ,Why are you so frightened Jesus answered how little faith you have then he got up and ordered the wind and the waves to stop and there was a great calm everyone was amazed what kind of man is this? even the winds and the waves obey him **(Mat;8;26;Mk4;40;)** Come answered Jesus so Peter got out of the boat and started walking on the water to Jesus but when he noticed the strong wind he was afraid and started to think down save me lord he cried at once Jesus reached out and grabbed him and said how little faith you have why did you doubt? they both got into and the wind died **(Mathew14;29;32;Jesus walk on water)**We   receive from God according to our faith ;The two blind men had it knowing that it will be done, and Jesus touched their eyes saying according to your faith be done to you,**(Mathew;9;29)***To the Roman centurion Jesus*-says to the officer Go home and what you believe will be done for you**(Mathew;8;13)**and the officers servant was healed that moment To the woman with the haemorrhage Jesus says take heart your faith has made you well **(Mathew;9;22)***Jesus said to the Woman of faith*- the bible says the woman came and fell to his feet and said help me sir she said Jesus answered it isn't right to take the children's food and throw it to the Dogs that true sir she answered but even the dogs eat the left over's that fall from their masters table so Jesus answered her you are a woman of Great faith what you want will be done for you and at that very moment her daughter was healed **(Mathew;15;25;28)***The blind Bartimaeus*, They came to Jericho and as Jesus was leaving with his disciples and a large crowd a blind beggar named Bartimaues son of Timaues was sitting by the road when he heard that it was Jesus Son Nazareth he began to shout Jesus son of David take pity of me many of the people scolded him and told him to be quite but he shouted even more loudly Son of David take pity of me Jesus stopped and said call him so they called the blind man cheer up they said get up he is calling you he throw off his cloak jumped up and came to Jesus what do you want me to do for you Jesus asked him? Teacher the blind man answered I want to see again Go Jesus told him your faith has made you well at once he was able to see and followed Jesus on the road **(Mark; 10; 46; 52)***To the lepers* who returned to give Jesus thanks to Jesus said there were Ten who were healed where are the other nine? Why is this foreigner the only one who came back to give thanks to the God? and Jesus said to him Get up and go your faith has made you well **(Luke; 17; 17; 19)** Those were the days of expectant faith and whenever among Gods people today that the same expectant faith re-merges the healing power of God is seen at work again, what were are witnessing of the renewing power of God at work within his church at present is only beginning compared with what needs to be seen with what God our father wants for us Jesus is asking you today ,do you believe? as he asked the two blind men ,do you believe am able to do this ?answer him honestly where you know there is doubt be open with God, about it ask the holy spirit to witness the prayer and healing promises of the lord to your heart, when you know he wants to heal you pray the prayer of faith ,and hold on to your father promises until the answer comes to pass ,Jesus approached every situation from a spiritual angle ,we often limit the working power of God because we consider the problem with our minds, instead of hearing with faith ,if your Christian life depends upon your rational thinking then you will limit God to the level of your mind, you make him smaller than yourself in truth, he is infinitely greater and his power is beyond your understanding beyond anything that your mind can conceive ,approach every situation with no limitation of your mind, seeing the potential of the spirit ,the spirit encourages faith ,believing God can turn the problem into an opportunity to witness his work is at hand to see ,his glory revealed ,the spirit will declare Gods word to you ,What is to be relationship between the mind and the spirit then? The mind to be submitted to the spirit for the spirit will enlarge your mind and expand your thinking to include the impossible things of God, **Paul** warns "you are the slave of the one who you obey either Sin- which leads to death ,or Obedience -which leads to righteousness ,don't obey your, fears ,doubt, and feelings of inadequacy ,obey the spirit for ,he speaks faith to you, God doesn't want you to be a mindless with a non intellectual approach to your faith in him ,he wants to fill your mind with his thoughts and rejoice that your intellect understanding more fully his ways **Beliefs of Christians(1)***All Christians believe in the resurrection of Jesus Christ* -and if Christ has not been raised from death then we have nothing to preach and you have nothing to believe **(1Corinthians;15;14)** all ,the Testimony, Missionary ,work ,would have been a wastage of time his resurrection gives us faith and hope that one day we will resurrect **(2)***Jesus is the only way to Heaven* (Salvation)there is no salvation in no one else God has given no other name on earth by which we must be saved the bible state it clear that Salvation is to be found through him alone in the world there is no one else whom God has given who can save us **(Acts;4;12)**We have to reject the idea that all roads leads to God Jesus didn't lie when he said Am the way the truth and the life no one goes to the father except by me **(John;14;6)does the bible has errors?** Because it says all scriptures is inspired by God and is useful for teaching the truth rebuking ,errors correcting faults and giving instructions for right living **(2Timothy;3;16)has the Church been wrong for 2000 years?** For it is God's grace that you have been saved through faith it is not the result of your own effort but God's gift so that no one can boast about it God has made us what we are and in our union with Jesus Christ he has created us for a life of good deeds which he has already prepared for us to do **(Ephesians 2;8;10)** *Christians we believe in the Humanity of Jesus Christ* -Jesus must be both fully God and full man why it significant it was necessary for him to be made in every respect like us so that he could be a merciful high priest **(Hebrews;2;14)**him to be a mediator between God he had to experience what we experience He had to be fully God because it's impossible for another man to save another Man from his sins when they are the same then Jesus could offer a sacrifice that would take away the sins of people **(Hebrews;2;18)** had to come to live a Godly life **(4)***Christians we believe in the Bible and what it says*- the bible is a final Authority on all matters decision .Vision, Blessings, Victory ,Protection salvation Judgement Marriage , Faith , Death , Sin and its wages and more the writings of the bible contains no errors or contradictions if we start arguing about it means that God did not inspire its writings man wrote it for his benefits and can lead to many that God cannot be trusted in his word **(5)***All Christians believe in one true God* eternally in three person the Father ,Son ,and holy spirit with each person being fully God ,sharing the same essence and attributes -To you alone O lord to you alone and not to us must glory be given because of your constant love and faithfulness**(Psalm;115;1)Who can heal us deliver ,Protect us, Make Miracles ,Bless us,** Ask yourself where does doubt come from is it your intuitive or your fearful self-Ask that question and listen to the very first thought that comes into your head believe that one**(Wendy Chadwick)**Ask yourself what will happen if I doubt this doubt?**(Gareth-Stubbs)**Ask yourself what will happen in years- years if I keep doubting tell yourself if I don't try then I will never know don't doubt yourself you are perfect example your talents and beauty know without doubting that you were created for amazing things Your goals minus-doubt equal =reality believe while others are doubting Realise that doubt is fear and fear is forgetting everything**(Sherri Levy)**Put one foot in front of the other and keep going**(Rose)**Notice that doubt is just a thought and don't believe it**(Rami-liesaho)**The doubtful vibe that you send out into the universe will only create more doubt refocus and believe(**Tiffany Helton**)See doubt as a means of improve yourself break through the barriers of doubt to Better yourself(**Deepak-**)Start with love be still with love and work through with love(**Pamela-Paraison**),Nobody becomes great without self- doubt but you can't let it consume you(**John McKay**)The only doubt you have the less likely it is that the creation will come to life (**Yanni**)Never doubt your intelligence and common sense (**Anita-Foley**)Know without a doubt that you were made for amazing things(**Josh Hinds**)Persevere and don't let any self- doubt distract you(**Catherine Pulpier**)The only limit to our realisation of tomorrow will be our doubt of today(**Franklin-Delano Roosevelt**)A mind troubled by doubt cannot focus on the course of victory(**Arthur-Golden**)Positivity in our life is a function of our thinking so think positive stay positive(**Simi- Ngr**)Our doubts are traitors and make us loose the good we often might win by fearing to attempt(**Jane-Addams**)Success takes time, persistence determination ,and most important believing in God, we receive from him ,whatever we ask because we obey his commands and do whatever please him, what he commands is what we believe in his son Jesus Christ ,and love one another as Christ commands us (**1John;3;22**)you like to receive praise from one another, but you do not try to win praise from the one who alone is God, How then can you believe ,do not think however that am the one who will accuse you to my father ,Moses in whom you have put your hope is the one who will accuse you, if you have already believed in Moses you would have already believed in me because ,he wrote about me, but since you don't believe what he wrote how can you believe what I say, Christian stop doubting believe in your bible, Christ, and God, Holy spirit, he will make a way for you where there is no way ,Delete the negative ,Accentuate the positive(**Donna-Karan**)**Faith opens-** your eyes to see that Gods promises are for your personality; *Faith helps you to discover your purpose in life , helps to know Gods Promises, power of God , Christ, and Holy Spirit ,It's a path way for finding solution ,helps to tap in your/my, anointing , blessing , Favour, Hope, Patience , grace , helps to overcome doubt , Fear, Stress , provide inner Strength , teaches to give back to God Tithing and offering , Faith helps us to have a need to help the needy , Love , Being kind, Self -control , look at the future as Great, Salvation , helps us to tap in our Dreams and Gifts , Calling , how we can Fight our Battles (Giant killers /Giants, helps to know the fruits of the Holy Spirit/and Characteristics , and exercise them , Faith means things are ok, faith is a strong conviction or belief in something for which there may be no tangible proof, -complete trust ,confidence or devotion , trust in the Lord to make things right at the beginning and end ,*But you man of God avoid all these things strive for righteousness godliness ,faith ,love ,endurance and gentleness ,run your best race in faith and win eternal life for it was to this life that God called you ,when you firmly professed your faith before many witness before God who gives life to all things and before Jesus Christ ,who firmly professed his faith before Pontius Pilate ,I command you to obey your orders and keep them faithfully until the day when our Lord Jesus Christ appear **(I Timothy,6;11;14)** be prepared to fight for faith in storms <**Amen**

QUESTION?

WHAT TO DO WHEN YOU DOUBT IN YOUR FAITH?

Obey God and the Conviction of the Holy -Spirit-It is your walk with God that will give you strength ,God will not reveal to you great things to you until when you are faithful in the things he is showing you now ,obedience to the spirit ,and what is showing you, and directing you to do through the word or through conscience, is important in the growth of your faith , **Living faith-** will help you to take steps of obedience and act on what God is saying to you ,**Amen**

Stop kicking yourself you are not the first -David did how much longer will you forget me Lord? how much longer will you hide away from me,**(Psalm;13;1)John did** -who was knew much about Jesus when John the Baptist heard in prison about things that Christ was doing he sent some of his disciple to him "tell us they asked "Jesus are you the one John said was going to come or should we expect someone else ,Jesus answered Go back and tell John what you are hearing and seeing ,the blind can see, the lame can walk ,those who suffer from dreaded skin diseases, are made clean, the deaf hear ,the dead are brought back to life and the good news, is preached to the poor ,how happy are those who have no doubt about me **(Mathew11;2;6)** For Herod had arrested and imprisoned, John as a favour to his wife Herodias (the former wife of the rods brother Philip John had been telling Herod is against the law to marry her -Adultery issue In **Mathew;14;3;4) in Mathew 14;10** we see John was beheaded in prison -I assure you that John the Baptist is greater than ,anyone who has ever lived but the one who is least in the kingdom of heaven is greater than John **(Mathew;11;11)**Jesus also doubted at about three O'clock, Jesus cried out with a loud shout "Eli, Eli, Lema Sabachthani? "Which means "My God why did you abandon me?" **(Mathew; 27; 46)**So don't condemn yourself for doubting ,you are not the first **(2)Turn yourself towards God-** rather than turning away from him,**(Mathew 11;2;3)**John sent his disciple to Jesus to see but many Christians when they doubt they turn away from God but turn to God like John he turned right where he was Jesus or God is not condemning you he is going to meet you if you turn to him **(3)Don't base your faith on your circumstances-** John doubted because he was in prison, yet before Prison he was believing in Jesus (don't let circumstance ripe you off your faith in God) **(4)Pay attention to the Evidence and**

believe in the unseen to John saw all the miracles Jesus performed healing the blind lame, raising the death to life Jesus was saying look back and see all what I did or look at the word of god what was written in the bible there is no errors it's the evidence of God's word so don't doubt in it, God is of supernatural power don't limit him in all your circumstance, get rid of your unbelief and believe **(5)In life don't be Overwhelmed that Everything you want will come to pass,** -they some things God has for you and some which are not for you, is he who knows what you deserve at the right time and season **Give thanks to the results before you see it-** don't complain ,that shows doubt, God love and answers to your situations give thanks to all situations **(1Thessalonians,5;18)Develop a life style of Worship and Praise -** this drive the forces of darkness in life away and brings the throne of God into our circumstances - Praising is an act of faith ,and helps our faith to grow - worshiping is admiring God through the Spirit if you can perceive who God is ,his power , faithfulness Love , your trust and faith in him will grow , let us then always offer praise to God as our sacrifice through Jesus which is the offering presented by lips that confess him as Lord **(Hebrews 13;15) Amen**

QUESTION?

WHY DO CHRISTIANS TODAY EXPERIENCE MUCH DOUBT?

*(1)***Because doubt satisfies our need for self- protection** we don't want to be wrong to get hurt or fail so our subconscious reasoning says it's easier not to trust to lower our expectations so I won't be disappointed but *,you are disappointed aren't you? ,*Why because of your doubt **(2)Because doubt comes easily-** We don't wake up in the morning and say to ourselves today we going to believe in God but doubt moves in the Vacuum it takes over when we don't do the right thing *(3)*Faith comes by hearing and by the word of God **(Romans;10;17)**If you don't keep your mind filled with the word of God you will be taken away by doubt in your life we forget that the word of God is full of promises of God and God can do whatever he promises *(4)Because doubt is easier to* **catch than the common cold and its carriers are words** the bible says you are trampled by your own words *(**Proverb;6;2**)*The word you speak listen too will either build you or destroy, Increase your faith or decrease ,words are powerful things, they determine your outlook and approach to life, so in order to move from doubt to faith you must start eliminating unscriptural words in your life**(5)Because doubters are easily to be found-** Sometimes people around us dwell on all the obstacles and difficulties opening doors to doubts and once that stream starts flowing in you get carried with it *(Joshua;1;2-3)*He said the lord my servant Moses is dead get ready now you and all the people of Israel and cross the river Jordan

into the land that am giving them as I told Moses I have given you all my people the entire land that you will be marching over Joshua had already tested the joy of the promised land but he had to go back and wait until the death of Moses and every doubters in Israel was buried ,observe some of our old ways must die, Moses represented the old system it was good for then but now when you align yourself with *what was instead of what is* you are not ready there so many folks you need to impress you are so bound with so many philosophies, that when God say to you it's time to move you have to consult somebody else, when God told Joshua, Moses my servant is died arise and go over this Jordan you and all this people to the land which am giving them ,there was only one answer Yes Lord ,you must honour the past ,but don't get stuck in it ,you must stand on the truth, but seek God first ,for fresh instructions ,decisions and directions your doubts must be buried, only two out of the twelve spies who went into the promised land believed God that would do it for them ,the others doubted and died into the wildness and every doubt ,Dear friends what is holding you back has got to die and buried too , your critics and voice of anxieties gather them all together put them in the box, and bury them ,stand on the top of the box and say ashes to ashes, dust to dust, before you can move a head you must understand and live by those principles , the evidence of your faith is in your works, for it is what you believe in that you will, be active in ,no man will believe in you more than yourself, **Amen**

VISION

VISION -means seeing beyond your current reality-Creating and Inventing what does not exist now/,art of seeing what is invisible to others -Everyone should have a Vision in life for your purpose, and destiny - *A vision that your future Life , and relationship with God , Finances ,Marriage ,Children ,Career, destiny is brighter ,* If you don't have a vision your reality will always be determined by others, every moment A vision is important in your area of life is a golden one for those who have visions to reorganise it, and do something about it, If you can't find joy in life may be you have a vision problem ,Our visions starts with our desires always write your desires on paper think everything you will desire to do, don't Panic your vision is your dream, that keeps coming back is the desire for you ,the thoughts of a righteous man are always good ,if you don't have a vision of who you want to be in life/ how you want to succeed you begin to lack a drive and your life becomes just an order of events, we are not limited by our abilities but by our vision, anything is possible within a big vision, when you build your vision big you have to plan for action ,Vision is a picture or idea you have in your mind or yourself -yourself your business or anything is going to happen, Ask God to enlarge your vision to show you how much more he has for you beyond, what you have ever seen or felt or heard or known ,It is there but is waiting for you, When your vision comes from God he will give you the strength ,wisdom connection relationship and resources to make it happen ,because he is the author and finisher of our faith ,Let us keep our eyes fixed on Jesus on whom our faith depends from the beginning to end, he did not give up because of the cross on contrary because of the joy, that was awaiting on him he thought nothing of the disgrace of dying on the cross and now is seated on the right hand side of Gods throne, think of what he went through how he was put with so much hatred from sinners-Acknowledge him (God)and he shall direct your path *(Proverb3;6)*<u>*Men shall dream dreams and see visions*</u> *(Joel2;28)*So do not let yourself become discouraged and give up, let your vision motivate you to perform to the best of your ability in your present position,, lord I pray I know that where am I right now isn't where you are taking me give me a glimpse of your vision for my future so that my understanding may grow in your timing, give me patience along the way and faith to trust and believe that you are always working for good; open my eyes so that I can see beyond touch my hears so that I can hear your word ,touch my heart, so that I can love you more ,and the visions you have given me and make a change in the world, build. churches ,schools ,hospitals, help the needy, and my family ,heal the sick ,Preach your Gospel everywhere in the world, Invent something new, liberate the oppressed, live for others and give , Vision is from God you don't tell him what to do ,*The difference between Dreams and Vision - Dreams are received While a person is sleeping and Vision while a person is awake, and they are often in Spirit* your vision may be smaller ,but remember that the future belongs to those who sees possibilities ,before they become obvious, **Late Nelson Mandela Madiba** -had a vision to liberate **south Africa** but came as a small vision **President Barrack Obama to rule America** ,The key to fill your Vision is discipline, **Vision**-is the source of Discipline is the route of leadership ,because your discipline attracts people ,discipline comes from Vision, Everything you do must be motivated by your Vision -Vision helps you to identify yourself, if in life you want to became a successful in life do not seek to became a person of value make yourself Valuable and people will pay for your Value, (your conferences, Books)Don't became a common man Everywhere doing everything ,A man without Vision is sampling life, Vision controls your choices- tells you what to do and what not to do, and gives you destiny -you are not here to do Everything only a few things are necessary ,What is necessary someone will say that "that am allowed to do anything "yes but not everything is good for you, I could say that am allowed to do anything but am not going to let anything make me a slave **(1Corithians 6;12)**Make yourself a person of value, Jesus himself he said am the bread of life sometime vision will take you to, **Prison- Nelson Mandela)** but all these is to test you, but get used to challenges-Vision comes in phases and is fulfilled in phases life is simple understanding your Potential ,Your Vision is not outside of you, Your future is not a head of you, A forest is not a head of a seed ,your brain is pregnant of Brain delivering any time ,Vision should be clear and simple Visions ,having a vision is not only enough there has to be commitment to act out on it, if you build castles in the air you have to put a foundation under them and any Vision requires setting up specific steps to achieve it, Steps are called goals, aims, they establish a plan for accomplishing your mission ,you will generally have one vision but many goals, and each gives you a reach, brings you closer to fulfilling your vision, building a vision is not difficult as long as you know what is in you ,see for yourself in the future the best vision is insight if you can dream it you can do it where there is no vision the people perish **(Proverb;29;18)**Create your future from the future not the past, people only see what they are prepared to see but not far, ,Surround yourself with positive successful people -There two days you can't do anything yesterday and tomorrow, there time for games and vision ,dream it ,wish it ,and do it, If a man lacks the use of his eyes it does not mean he does not have a vision ;**Amen**

IMPORTANCE OF VISIONS

A strong vision connects you with a passion and a great potential **regardless of what is going on in the world or challenge it makes you wake up in the morning and do something** (2)*Having a vision is most important in the* path of your success in life you feel much valuable as a person when you set and achieve visions and goals (3)*Vision- helps you to know when, what, why-*you are doing the things you are doing Discovering yourself helping you to see what others have not seen or considered worthy bringing the best out of you many people of people used in the bible looked like losers before but after were seen as winners after night with Jesus when they had caught nothing Jesus told them from now you will catch men(**Luke5;10**)they ended up building churches writing books having their names named after races (**1Corinthians;6;19;20**) (4)*Visions- inspires you to reach something you want-*,change in future and interest you have we have great talents and abilities, but without a vision you won't be motivated to do it (5) **Visions - helps you** *to open your mind to a brighter future and production as it's an idea of the future and a strong wish*(6)**Vision helps to overcome obstacles**-it helps you to wait when seasons are not conducive/tough (7)**Vision- helps you to focus** and create a purpose that becomes a measurement for your success your life matters without you what could be ?so vision gives you a purposes ,Successful leaders can see the future and still stay focused on the present, a vision is a target in which a leader focuses on resources and energy, vision still helps the leaders to see today as it is and calculate the future that grows and improve (8)**Vision**-can help the organisations to work together for a main goal and achievements it(*a)Your life style and plans (b) Use of time (c)Use of Energy (d) How to spend your Money and Investments (e)Priorities in life (f)How to spend your leisure time games to play movies to watch (g)How to choose your diet (h) The Importance of Vision to leadership (a)helps readers to clarify purpose visions gives them direction*, When people without a vision are distracted people with visions have a direction to follow ;After this Abram had a vision and heard the lord said do not be afraid Abram I will shield you from danger and give you Greater reward God promised Abraham in you all the families of the world shall be blessed the word of God comes in vision(**Genesis;15;1**)I will bless those who bless you but I will curse those who curse you and through you I will bless all nations(*Genesis;12;3*)That's a big vision but God knew that Abraham had the faith to embrace it Jacob packed up all he had and went to Beersheba where he offered sacrifices to the God of his father Isaac God spoke to him in vision at night and called "Jacob Jacob! yes he answered "I am God the God of your father he said "do not be afraid to go to Egypt I will make your descendants a great nation there I will go with you to Egypt and I will bring your descendants back to this land Joseph will be with you when you die (Jacob and his family go to Egypt to meet Joseph Jacob took everything and the number of the descendants who went to Egypt was;66 not including his sons and wives two sons were born to Joseph in Egypt bringing to &;70 the total number of Jacob family who went there **(Genesis;42;1;26)**The lord gave this answer write it down clearly on clay table what I reveal to you so that it can be ready at glance putting in writing because it is not yet to come but the time is coming quickly and what I show will come to pass it may seem slow in coming but wait for it will certainly take place and it will not be delayed and this is the massage those who are evil will not survive but those who are righteous will live because they are faithful to God (***Habakkuk2;2;4***) That night Paul had a vision in which he saw Macedonia standing and begging him come over and help us as soon as Paul heard this vision we got ready to Macedonia because we decided God had called us to preach the Good news to the people there *(Pauls vision Acts 16;9)*Moses had married a cushite women and Miriam and Aaron criticized him for it they said has the lord spoken only through Moses hasn't spoken through us? The lord heard what they said Moses was humble man more than anyone on earth suddenly the lord said to Moses Aaron and Miriam I want the three of you to come down in a pillar of cloud stood at the entrance of the tent and called out Aaron Miriam the two of them stepped forward and the lord said "now hear what I have to say !when there are prophets among you*I reveal myself to them in vision and speak to them in dreams its is different when I speak with my servant Moses I have put him in charge of all my people Israel so I speak to him face to face he has even seen my form clearly and not in riddles how dare you speak against my servant*(Numbers 12;6)* One night Joseph had a dream and when he told his brothers about it they hated him even more ,he said listen to my dream I had we were all in the field trying sheaves of wheat when my sheaf got up and stood up straight yours formed a circle round mine and bowed down to me do you think you are going to be a king and a ruler over us his brother asked so they hated him even more because of his dreams and because of what he said to them Joseph had another dream and said it to his brother I had another dream in which I saw the sun the moon and eleven stars bowing down to me he also told his dream to his father and his father scolded to him "what kind of dream is that? Do you think you're Mother, Bothers and I am going to come and bow down to you?"Joseph brothers were jealous of him but his father kept thinking about the matter**(Genesis;37;5;10)**This is happening even in our today's life, when we dream big not all people are happy of our vision and dreams, A vision should be personal but all the power belongs to God, and he will do whatever it requires for your vision and dream to be fulfilled (***Read-Jeremiah;11;20 to encourage you about your dreams and visions***)At this point I had another vision and I saw an open door in heaven and the voice sounded like a trumpet which I heard speaking to me before "said come up here and I will show you what must happen after this at once the spirit took control of me *(Revelation;4;2-)*What you were born to do is bigger than you doing now -If you hate what you have to do in order to pursue your vision something is wrong ,examine your motives see if there is inconsistence between who you are and what you are trying to accomplish *,Have you taken the ownership of the vision ?Do you have a heart for it?* If pursuing your vision is causing /causes you to violate your values then you need to get another vision may be the problem is your altitude *(1)* **Are you to idealistic***?* You must accept the way your vision is unfolding and change your expectations concerning how long it *takes 90/100of* all disappointment stem from un realistic expectation*(2)***Have you stopped dreaming daily** you must let yourself-dream a little bit every day explore possibilities and embrace options be creative continuing to dream actually helps you to move forward*(3)***Do you appreciate each small step of progress** one way to feel fulfilled is to celebrate success ,recognise when you pass milestones thanking God for your progress will encourage you to move forward *(4)Have you made a personal growth to your Goal* ? The only way to fulfil your big vision is to grow with it the bigger the vision the bigger to do to achieve it What God is revealing to you today in your current situation is how long can you grow the greatest reward of pursuing vision is who you become as a result thank you Lord for greater vision In me in my life be single minded **(James;1;8)**a double minded man is unstable in all his ways people like that are unable to make up their minds and undecided in all they do they will not receive anything from our God gave us clear vision that we may know where to stand and what to stand for any dream that is not clear won't help you get you nowhere *What* do you want to accomplish in life ? What do you want to complete? Who do you want to become **what does success mean to you?** *if you* cannot define it you won't be able to achieve it ,most people don't get what they want because they have not defined their dreams *in clear and compelling* details ,one writer wrote and said the indispensable first step to getting the things you want out of life is this **(1)**Decide what you want instead of saying I want to get out of debt say I will pay all of my debts by 31 January, Instead of saying ,I won't lose 12 stone say by 1 July, I will lose some stones instead of saying , I won't improve my leadership say, I will read one leadership book every month, being specific does not mean necessary mean having every little details thought out before you move forward but your main goal should be clear ,the rest will unfold as you move forward making adjustment as you go the question you need to ask yourself ,am I single minded**(Proverb 4;25;27)**fix your gaze directly before you**(2)**Look straight ahead with honest confidence don't hang your head in shame, plan careful what you do and whatever you do will turn outright, avoid evil and walk straight don't go one step off the right way it does not take much your mind to drift and dream but it takes greater effort to set your mind to the task of developing a clear goal of having a clear and compelling dream one leader said for me /him the whole process start with a question I must ask myself the dream is always rooted in the dreamer in his or her experience ,circumstances talents and opportunities I ask what am I feeling what am I sensing what is my intuition telling me? What am I seeing what am I thinking what do my intellect and common sense say? a clear picture may come to you at once in lighting but in built fashion but in most people it does not work that way most people needs to be working at it redrawing it if the process is difficult that's no reason give up in fact if it is too easy may be you are not dreaming big enough just keep working on it because a clear dream is worth fighting for it if you can get a clear sense of where you are well on your way to understanding and embracing the things God put you on earth to do Vision can be difficult even seemingly impossible to achieve out of reach but not out of sight , Moses spent the First two thirds 2/3of his life working out what God wanted him to do trying to do things his way only to fail but he had a heart for God and a vision from God and eventually he succeeded and you will do it in Jesus name When creating a vision you have to focus on the things that(1) gives you life and meaning(2)Do not limit yourself brainstorm imagine and dream(3)Know exactly who you are know what you want to become this includes your habits if you are unclear about yourself you are unclear about the future(4)Do not rely much on friends ideas and ideologies you can learn from them but never become like them be yourself though friends are more important than brothers anyone who is willing to get you to your destiny stay with them stay away from failures if in your group you are the smartest and friends are asking you questions leave the group and get a group you will be asking questions (5)Stop cheering for others who are living their vision commit yourself to your success and follow the steps required to achieve ;**Amen**

QUOTATIONS ON VISION

(*a*)Your vision will only come clear only when you look into your heart, who looks outside dreams who looks inside awakens (***Carl Jung***)(*b*)The best way to predict the future is to create it(***Alan Kay***)(*c*)***The*** Empire of the future are Empire of the mind(d) Where there is no vision people perish (***Proverb;29;18***)(*f*)If you can dream about it, you can do it(**Walt Disney**)(*g*)To accomplish great thing ,we must dream as well act (***Anatole-France***)(*h*)Create your future from your future not from the past(***Werner-Erhard***)(*I*)Leadership is the capability to translate vision into reality(***Warren -Benin's***)(*J*)You have got to think about big things while you are doing small things so that all the small things go in the right directions*(K)*Pain pushes until vision pulls (***Michael Beckwith***)A possibility is a hint from God one must follow it(-***Soren Kierkegaard***)(*L*)It is not what the vision is it's what the vision does(***Peter Senge***)The best vision is insight(***Malcolm Forbes***)*(M)*Vision is not just a picture of what could be it is an appeal to our better selves it is a call to become something more(**Rosabeth,Moss-Kanter**)People only see what you are prepared to see(***Ralph Waldo Emerson***) Father lord thank you for your word and let your word touch nations about visions let them dream and have vision and let their dreams come to pass though some take longer we believe in you and trust in you because your word remain forever and forever You said" And so I tell you what you prohibit on earth will be prohibited in heaven and what you permit on earth will be permitted in heaven and I tell you more whenever two of you on earth agree about anything you pray for it will be done for you by my father in heaven for where two or three come together in my name am there with them *(Mathew18;18-19);Amen*

SUCCESS

SUCCESS----In life is achieving what God created you to be, not Fame Houses,, Cars, Women ,Children you have- You matter because you are you and you matter to the end of your life ,**Make God your source** ,am the lord God who teach you for your own good and direct you in the way you should go,*(Isaiah 48;17) Success without God ends in failure and everything you are doing you have to be serious ,because anything you are not serious about , you cannot make the most out of it ,a road to success in life is to have Morals, without Morals success is useless to anyone who achieve it ,Morals play a very important role in humankind* ;Make God your life coach good success is putting God your first priority allowing him to put everything together for you ,give your boss a hard work he/she deserves ,but trust in the only one, who Promised to use his wonderful riches to give you everything you need (**Philippians 4;19**)the world owes you nothing, but Success- Success is doing the best you can with what you have ,where you are,-It is not based on Circumstances ,Wealth ,Power, Experience , Platform or Future Potentials -<u>**God gave us a gift of Success**</u> - The psalmist prayed for victory, said "this was done by the Lord what a wonderful sight ,it is !this is the day of the Lords Victory Let us be happy ,let us celebrate !save us Lord ,save us !give us success, O Lord (**Psalm;118;23;25**)**There are two types of success (a) Success that fulfils Gods will for your life (b) Success that is temporal which can leave you feeling empty and dies when you die** ,It doesn't how many times you have failed you will Succeed, God is not concerned about where you are now, but to the next level of Success ,the road to the righteous travel is like the sunrise, getting brighter and brighter until day light has come (**Proverb 4;18**)All of us then , reflect the glory of the Lord with uncovered faces, and that the same glory coming from the Lord who is the Spirit transform us into his likeness in an ever greater degree of glory (**2,Corinthians;3;18**) **God always abundance and great blessings ,he wants to give to every individual great life ,** *God has made provisions for our success, but we need to position our , ourselves to enjoy Success, the provision is greater ,and why everyone is not enjoying success, it's because they have not taken their positions, -Position must meet with Position* ,the scriptures says "Arise and shine for thy light has come and the glory of the lord (**Isaiah;60;1-2**)**Success is when God arise on you** ,We are redeemed in three major way *(1)Locality (2)Identity (3)Destiny* ,(a)Locality where you stay -which he used when he raised Christ from death and seated him at the right side in the heavenly word (heaven above is our locality)(b)identity -who we are in Christ , (c)where we are going - we are meant to be on top and fly even you smallest and humblest family will become as great as a powerful nation when the right time comes I will make this happen quickly I am the lord **(Isaiah;60;22)**For God loved the world so much that he gave his only son that everyone who believe in him may not die but have eternal life ,for God did not send his son into the world to be its judge but to be its saviour **(John3;16;17)**Stop thinking of all the reasons why you should not or cannot make it in life ;Every good gift and perfect gift comes down from God, the Creator of heavenly light who does not change or cause darkness by turning **(James1;17)**(Talents)Value what you have been given to you by God-,Success is all about discovering your Purpose ,and completing it before death , You are supposed to go further than the People who raised you, where you are now is not where you are supposed to be, You are supposed to set a new standard for yourself ,Believe you are a seed of Abraham -Abram was very rich man ,with sheep goats and cattle as well as silver and gold **(Genesis13;2)**-For the grace of Lord Jesus Christ, Though he was rich yet for your sake and me he become poor so that through his poverty might become rich, Jesus said as a result the master of this dishonest manager praised him for doing such a shrewd thing because the people of this world are much more shrewd in handling their affair than the people who belong to the light ,When it comes to money the people of the world are wiser in business than the children of light ,understand it that many Christians today are ignorant of Gods promises and want to assume that Spiritual holiness will make you money ,The holiness of Jesus Christ in Salvation will get you to heaven, because you have lived in peace with everyone and tried to live a holy life, because no one will see the lord without it**(Hebrews;12;14)**But you receive the blessing by having the right altitude -Happy are those who know they are spiritually poor ,the kingdom of heaven belongs to them- Happy are those who mourn God will comfort them- Happy are those who are humble they will receive what God has promised them -Happy those pure in heart they will see God - Happy are those who are merciful to others God will be merciful to them happy are those whose greatest desire is to do what God requires them God will satisfy them full**(Mathew;5;11)**Open my eyes lord that I may see wonderful truth in your law, am here on earth for just a little while do not hide your command from me **(Psalm,119;18;19)**The eyes are like a lamp for the body, If your eyes are sound your body will be full of light, but if your eyes are not good your body will be in darkness,- So if the light in you is darkness ,how terribly dark it will be(***Luke 33;36***)So make a certain then that the light in your body is not darkness- If your body is full of light with no part with darkness your future will be, Bright ,Victorious , Successful , Prosperous, no one lights a lamp and then hides it or put it under a bowl instead he puts it on the lamp stand so that people may see and to succeed I must do the following put**(1)**A hard worker has plenty of food (***Proverb,28;19***) those who work with their hands will have abundant food, but those who chase fantasies will have their filled with poverty, when employees find work in the bad Job market they do all they can to keep it even in the wrong economic down turn ,there still practical rules that increase like hood you will keep your Job and earn promotion ,what's taught in God word ,God first in every your plan, he wants you to succeed in life, he is a good father- We succeed by Gods Spirit, Work on your relationship with him - work hard in the kingdom of God drawing close to God, when you do that you will have plenty food, Favour, blessings ,Make peace with God and stop treating him like an enemy ,then if you do then he will bless you, Accept the teachings he gives, keep his words in your heart **(Job;22;21;22)***By deceit the King will win the support of those who have already abandoned their religion, but those who follow fight back(The people that do know their God shall be strong and do Exploits (Daniel;11;32)* Keep this book of law always on your lips meditate on it day and night so that you may be careful to do everything written in it then you will be prosperous and successful **(Joshua,1;8)**Humble yourself before God and he will exalt you **(James;4;10)**Seek your happiness in God and he will give you the desires of your heart**(Psalm;37;4;)**Am wisdom and I have insight I have knowledge and sound judgement **(Proverb;8;12)** reorganise God as your employer ,serve wholeheartedly as if you were serving the lord not men because you know that the lord will reward everyone for whatever good he does**(Ephesians;6;7-8)**A prayer puts a shield protection around you **(Mathew;26;41)**A prayer deals with the devil, The lord is our helper instead of our judge *(Hebrews 13;6)*Work hard and do not be lazy ,serve the Lord with a heart full of devotion ,Let your hope keep you joyful be patient in your troubles and pray all the times **(Romans,12;11-12)**Our prayer room is a changing to the next level of Success , Sing praise to the Lord ,tell the wonderful things he has done **(1Chronicles;16;9)**I will not fear what shall a man do to me, God has good plan for you **(Jeremiah;29;11)**You must trust in the lord for everything *(Philippians;3;8)*In every season you must stay /and consecrate to God, consider everything as Garbage ,so that you could gain Christ, Whatever you Have now in your business is nothing compared to God blessing a head of you -To succeed in life Pray for where seems to be no way ,God to make away for you - God grace is all you need, his Power works in all seasons and think the same way that Christ thought *(Philippians;2;5)* Before you set goals Pray in all your ways acknowledge him and he shall direct you**(Proverb;3;6)**There was a man who was named *Jabez* who was the most respected members of his family his mother had given him the name Jabez because his birth had been very painful **(Pain and sorrow)** But Jabez prayed to the God of Israel, Bless me God and give me much land ,be with me and keep me from evil things, that might cause me pain and God gave him what he prayed for **(1Chronicle;4;10;Jabez prayed;1Chronicles,4;9)Oh God bless me indeed** "and enlarge my territory ,About this time king Hezekiah fell ill and almost died the prophet Isaiah son of Amoz went to see him and said to him "the lord tell you that you are to put everything in order because you will not recover get ready to die Hezekiah turned his face to the wall and prayed remember Lord that I have served you faithfully and loyalty and I have always tried to do what you wanted me to and he began to cry buttery but before he left the courtyard of the palace the lord told him to go back to Hezekeziah ruler of Gods people and to say to him I the lord of David have heard your prayer and seen your tears ,I will heal you and in three days you will go to the temple ,I will let you live 15 years longer , I will rescue you and this city of Jerusalem from the emperor of Assyria ,I will defend this city for the sake of my own honour and because of the promise, I made to my servant David then Isaiah told the kings attendants to put on his boil a paste made of figs, and he would get well King Hezekiah asked what is the signs to prove that the Lord will heal me and that three days later I will be able to go to the temple ?Isaiah replied the lord will give you a sign to prove that he will keep his promise now would you prefer the shadow on the stairway to go forward ten(10) steps or go back ten steps (10)Hezekiah answered it's easy to make the shadow go forward ten steps make it go back ten steps Isaiah prayed to the lord and the lord made the shadow go back ten steps on the stairways set up by king Ahaz(**King Hezekiah illness and recovery;2kings 20;11**)Some people want signs to see that God can bless them and succeed, but dear fellow Christians when you pray God is touched by your prayers ,and he will make you succeed ,don't wait for signs ,Do not worry of anything but in all your prayers ask God for what you need ,always asking him with a thankful heart and Gods peace which is far beyond human understanding will   keep   your   heart   and   mind   safe   in   union   with   Christ Jesus(**Philippians;4;6;7**)Even your smallest and humblest family will become as great as powerful nation, When the right time comes, I will make this happen quickly am the Lord **(Isaiah,60;22)** Hunt for the word of God and the key is the fear of God, but to the Lord said to him pay no attention to how tall and handsome he is I have rejected him ,I do not judge as people judge ,they look outward appearance, but I look at the heart **(1 Samuel;16;7)** people judge before the outcome, but you pay attention to your God he judges the heart for your success to the next level **,_Pray for favour_** for the right people to come to your way, many people have visions but because no right people to favour ,resources will come from all direction ,God will make a way to reach people who will help you and reach your destiny ,we need people who are patient and love to do things of God ,if it pleases the king and if your servant has found favour in his sight so the door which are closed they will be open **(Nehemiah;2;5)** Nehemiah needed an army to protect him ,and resources to build ,so he prayed ,help may not come from the people you expect God will give you connections, God used a penniless widow to feed Elijah it's not wrong to set goals, it's just wrong to set them without consulting God, pray to God to show you what career to pursue, call on me and I will answer you(**Jeremeiah;33;3**)You cannot accomplish things on your own, when God favours you nothing can stop you- you become unstopped pray for influence other than affluence ,pray for protection God to keep you away from harm ,so that you will be free from pain ,God to guide you and me and give us discernment about people who are jealous ,envious hateful, vindictive ,who have secret agendas, people who don't have good interest in your business ,pray that God will protect your, business job, Ministry, from any distractive attack like ,snow, storms, theft and any other calamity ,that can destruct it ultimately, Pray for grace - for I know the grace of our Lord Jesus Christ that though, he was rich yet for our sake he become poor that through his poverty might become rich (**2Corinthians;8;9**) *Believe*-The Lord your God will bless you in the land that he is giving you, not one of your people will be poor ,if you obey him and carefully observe everything that I command you today (**Deuteronomy;15;4**)While others are doubting he wrote I have fought good fight of faith(*1Timothy6;12*)He knew it was not enough to be strong in faith, you must also be strong in fight ,sometimes fear, criticism and past failure, dedicate our direction, and we drift aimlessly through our days ,the future encroaches on us looking more like the past , we oil the wheels that squeak the loudest, hoping life to favour us, but it does not work- succeeding and graduating with highest honour you have to be focused ,and focus does not just happen ,you have to direct it to ,have faith is to know that with God nothing is impossible, everything is possible with God ,it is by faith we understand that the world was made by God , To have faith is the key to pleasing God, when mixed with the word of God we see the results ,faith is the key to overcome ,obstacles, faith brings Jesus close to us to love us ,and act on our behalf, many people in the bible who did greater things had faith Abraham ,Moses left Egypt with Gods people and crossed the red sea when you rely on God you can do everything through him who strengthen you(*Philippians; 4;13*)**Pauls(faith)** was not ashamed of the gospel neither you ,I have complete confidence in the gospel-Its Gods power to save all *(Romans1;16)*It was by faith that Noah made Noah ark, God was warning about things in the future that many could not see ,but Noah obeyed God and build the boat in which his family were saved, as the result the world was condemned and Noah received from God the righteousness ,that comes by faith, Noah's faith didn't only save him but saved his household ,it took many years but he did it, and by Gods grace you can also do the same ,you can make a different for the future generation ,The eyes of the lord searches the whole earth ,in order to strengthen those heart are committed to him(**2 Chronicles,16;9**)don't look at what you cannot do, look at what you can do, God is looking for people who are will partners with him, to fulfil his purpose on earth ,to qualify you must be willing to stand out of the crowd, Noah believed in his vision when nobody else did, people in the world who make a different are different ,they are not afraid of anything, for the first time don't allow the words stop you, obey your God ,people told Noah it's not raining who needs boat? but they were wrong and Noah was right you must endure the rain **(Pain)**In order to see the rain bow ,believe in God for God what he promised he will perform **(Jeremiah1;12)**You can succeed at anytime -Age-stop putting yourself down because of Age ,finances, **Noah was 500years** ,when he started building the Ark, It's not over till when God say it's over ,In order to succeed you have to believe it, that you can do it, create a climate of confidence around you ,speak words of faith, victory blessings, favour, anointing, open opportunities ,open doors, doubt will never take you anywhere, remind yourself of the sufficiency of God there is nothing in us that allows us to claim that we are capable of this work the capacity we have comes from God **(2Corinthians 3;5)**Believe in what you are doing to make our own destiny, It springs from within us believing in ourselves, **You must refuse to let your beginning dictate your end** ,George washing-ton he spent his early years shuffled between foster homes until it is thought Maria Watkins a washer woman found him asleep in her barn she did not just take him in she took him to church and introduced him to Jesus ,when he eventually left her home he took with him the bible she had given him Maria left her mark on his life and George left his mark in the world this father of the modern Agriculture was a friend to three Great President as well as Henry ford and Ghandi, he is credited with over three hundred different inventions and the remarkable thing despite his advantages he never become bitter or spent so much as a moment getting even instead he went to into his Laboratory, Every morning and prayed open my eyes that I may see .How could God fail to bless someone with such attitude ,follow his example God will bless you as well ,refuse to be anything but success, decide commit yourself Success and excuse, do not work together, if you want to succeed forget about excuses, practice mind management ,when your thinking is controlled by sinful self ,there is death, but if is controlled by the spirit there is life and peace**(Romans8;6)**In life you are a no lack person, God put in you everything needed to fulfil your destiny talents ,ideas, creativity ,wisdom ,dreams, visions, strength determination, God crowned you with favour and has given you a successful life ,don't see yourself as a failure or lack person, if you are to live a successful life you have to live as a no failure and lack person, how you see yourself will determine the kind of person you live ,if you go out thinking ,I will never go out and accomplish my dreams, visions , will never have enough, I will never own a house children, I will never pay my bills ,I will never clear my debts ,I will never get of the bad addiction, all this will set a limit to your life of success and accomplishing your dreams and destiny ,those who trust in the lord will never lack nothing ,deep in you trust in the lord that nothing is too hard for God ,for you to succeed connect to your God your almighty God ,has already breathed in your plans and empowered you to flourish, get rid of the failure and lack mentality, you might have difficulties but it's not a surprise to God, your dream is not so big you have the ideas to fulfil your dreams and visions to succeed not fail ,You might be struggling in finances but you are not a poor person, trying to get a head you are a successful person fighting poverty, you might be fighting sickness but you are not a sick person ,you are a normal person trying to regain back your strength and health, you might be fighting Addiction of gossiping, lying, adultery ,for years don't see yourself as an addicted don't see that image coming deep into you are not addicted person you are trying to get free, you are a free person fighting an addiction, freedom is your normal stake, God didn't make us addicted, insecure depressed that's not your portion ,God made you a master piece, get new ideas seeing yourself ,strong health, rich, successful blessed, and highly favoured, accomplishing dreams, visions, living large successful, In his abundance, people of Israel in their history what they had in their mentality was lack, defeat, sickness, God brought them as they were leaving ,God called their captors Egyptians to give them their Gold and Silver, Jewels they didn't leave empty handed they lived with riches Why? What was God doing to leave them to go with all these treasure they were going in the wildness, where no stores and warehouse, God wanted to develop into them a new mentality inside of success, they had been pushed for years not to amount anything ,but their image had start to change to get rid of a slave mentality, that they are successful head not tails, parents who had wrong thoughts ,lack mentality and they cannot overcome the journey obstacles they never reached their destination, but those with a successful mentality reached the promised land change the way you see yourself and level some of you came from poor family addiction all you see is problems no future in your life if you change, your life to a successful mentality strong ,valued, confidence talented, a child of God as your provider, protector, counsellor, and you have the image of abundance ,God will take you places and place, level after level, you never rise any higher than the image you have for yourself, see yourself as a successful person, sometimes we don't realise what gifts ,talents we have ,think of yourself as not being average ordinary, Your creator is the creator of the universe ,he didn't give you a weak brain, a second class paid job ,he gave you everything you need to fulfil your destiny , you have the talents ,determination, looks, blessing to overcome all the storms and obstacles in your life, God put all the potentials in you , are not a failure or lacking person ,you might have problems in the past, but you have the power to speak to yourself in faith that am not settling here ,am a child of the most high God, David to win Goliath he didn't think of the military experience, education, equipment--

David understood one principle that the lord is my shepherd, I shall not lack even though Goliath was much stronger, David didn't fear him, he run towards Goliath, because he knew the greatest power in the universe is backing him, Christians don't run away from the universe, thinking it's too hard,, God is behind you don't run away from the managerial job and promotion, blessed you with fearing critics and challenges ,God is backing you don't run away from the family you married into, because they have a bad reputation of addiction, poverty ,God is backing you and your presence will make a change in this family ,when you take faith a head of you- You win battles ,you are not doing things by yourself God is with you the size of your battle to success is the indication of your success, if you have a big problem don't be upset ,you have a big future ,What made David a king was Goliath was put into his path not to defeat him but to promote him, stop saying it's too hard for me ,I can't take it anymore when you go through obstacles difficulties ask God to make your day saying that you know what's on the other side is ,promotion, success abundance, increase ,new levels of Gods favour, take a move and believe you are a worrier winner not a loser ,don't put defeat mentality in your mind, David with no experience defeated Goliath what you need is wisdom and determination ,Paul said am ready for anything through Christ who strength me, anything that comes your way say am ready for it ,am equipped for it -it may look impossible but you are equal to it ,no problems big for you victory on your way, you have the DNA of success people problems are not a big deal to you-Every Adversary is being temporary don't accept it as permanent, Everything change, you will be on top, get well, rich, things which are seen are subjected to changes, you may be turned down on several occasions but things are turning better than expected, the person you are going to meet could be the one of your dream, the next time you persist fighting an addiction could be the time you are going to be freed, God still can bring your vision ,dreams right person, right Job, heal you from depression, restore you ,God cannot leave anyone out of his plans of success, and accomplishing what he created him to be ,you are anointed blessed ,victorious full of talents, approved by God, don't stay where you are, God doesn't want us to be failures ,lack, borrow ,unable, dependants of left over, break the box of failure ,lack, have big visions dreams of success and victory in all your aspect of life, set new standards for your family **(4)Ask God for a Plan** -because only the plan he will bless is the one he has given you ,many are the plans of man(**Proverb;19;21 Proverb;16;1**)Only a plan he has blessed is the one that will make you succeed ,our dreams may be real but our plans need to be given a breath and work on it, If you don't have a daily objective in life you are a dreamer ,His word will be in your heart like fire(**Jeremiah;20;9**)When God puts a desire for it you can't stop, It God will show you the right path turn darkness into light(**Isaiah,42;16**)God will work out your plans (**Psalms;138;8; Psalm 23;1-5**)If you want to something you will find a way of doing it, Plans are methods needed to success and a goal without a plan is like a road to nowhere ,first the goal-plan the process these methods you must   employ them and stay with them , Write down your plans and establish deadlines, make a detailed list of required activity and set check points ,guard your mind and prioritise your time use your head make use of every opportunity ,you have because these are the evil days don't be like fools then but try to find out what the lord wants you to do not get drunk with wine, which will only ruin you instead ,be filled with the spirit ,speak to one another with words of psalms hymns and sacred songs ,sing hymns, and psalms to the lord with praise in your heart, in the name of our Lord Jesus Christ ,always give thanks for everything to God the father(**Ephesians;5;16;20**)Plan while others are playing after a plan you need to be single minded, not double minded (**James1;8**)People with double mind are unable to make up their minds and undecided in all they do must not think they will receive anything from the Lord Jesus said man shall not live on only bread but with a word that comes out of Gods mouth(**Mathew 4;4**)Build yourself on the word of God before the devil attack you **;<u>Your Plan should be of God</u>** ,make it and all its finishing according to the plan that I will show you, this was a sacred tent Moses had to build that God will live among them is realities, God told Moses he must build a tabernacle and its finishing according to Gods plan (**Exodus25;9**)He prepared Joseph to feed the Egyptians seven years in advance of famine- without Gods plan the best you will do is guesswork estimated things and saying am educated, if you start on your own you won't finish unless if you start according to God's plan ,you won't finish right on your own, if God has called you then he has a plan for you and you are special, if any of you lack wisdom ask God and he will give it to you (**James1;5**)God promised to be with his people Moses said to the lord it's true that you have told me to lead your people to that land but you didn't tell me who you should send with me now if you are tell me your plans so that I may serve you and continue to please you remember you have chosen this nation to be yours the lord said I will give you victory to accomplish greater things call on the lord to lead you (**Exodus;33;12;13**) God promised people of Israelites he will do greater things such he never done before(**Exodus34;10**)Start on your plans they replied let us start building so they began the work (**Nehemiah2;18**) Nehemiah started and finished 5out of 10 people have dreams but fear to start anything people of Israeli were afraid to cross the river Jordon God said ,if you step in the water it will roll back God may give you a plan to do greater things but there should be always obstacles people not wanting you to succeed but what you have to do look at Nehemiah those who carried materials did their work with one hand and held a weapon in the other hand your weapon is prayers fasting and meditation on the word of God preserve in faith people will send threats to you to intimidate you and what you have to say to them you are doing a big project (mission spreading the word of God and you can't stop why should you stop and step down on whatever ever your enemies say when they talk of failing you talk of success from God in your ,business, Education Ministry, or anything and tell them they don't have any share any claim to it it's a winning altitude ,Set realistic goals and work towards it, one priority at a time, many things in life fail for one reason broken focus avoid distraction a double minded man is unstable**(James;1;8)***(2)Understand that Hard work is a blessing-* God created paradise ,then he created us, then he put us to work saying by the sweat of your bow you will eat your food**(Genesis;3;19)**Give in your work a menial one your best pleases him and ultimately he is not your boss who controls your future but God; **Work while others are Wishing-Those who used to rob must stop and stat working ,in order to earn an honest living for themselves ,and to be able to help the poor (Ephesians 4;28)Hard work will give you power, being lazy will make you a slave people who are good at work skilled workers are always on demand** and admired, they don't take a back seat to anyone **(Proverb12;24)** Do you see a man who excels in his work ? he will stand before kings ,he will not stand before unknown men **(Proverb,22;29)** Christians should work so that they don't become a burden to church body, if any one does not provide to his relative and especially his family ,he has denied the faith and is worth than unbelievers**(1Timothy5;8)**Paul was a Tent maker and other disciples they did this to be an example to others and their followers whoever refuse to work is not allowed to eat**(1Thessolonian 3;6;15)**Paul working making tents because he earned his living by working **(Acts18;1;3)**Surely you remember brothers and sisters how we used to work worked and toiled, we worked day and night, so that we would not be any trouble to you ,as we preached to you the good news about the gospel **(1Thessolonian;2;9)** Work hard and do not be lazy, serve the lord with a heart full of devotion ,let your hope keep you Joyful, be patient in your troubles, and Pray all times**(Romans;12;11;12)**I will just take a nap he says, I will fold my hands and rest a while but while, he sleeps poverty will attack him ,like an armed robber**(Proverb 6;10;11)**if your axe is blunt and you don't sharpen it you have to worker harder to use it ,it is sensible to plan a head **(Ecclesiastes10;10)**Do you see a man diligent in his business he shall stand before kings **(Proverb;22;29)**Work and you will earn a living if you sit around talking you will be poor **(Proverb ;14;23)** A farmer whose is too lazy to plough his field at the right time will have nothing to plough**(Proverb;20;4)**They joined together constantly in prayers along with the woman and Mary the mother of Jesus and with his brother after Jesus went to heaven the disciples continued in Prayers **(Acts1;14;Luke11;5;9; ;Isaiah;65;1;16)**Be ye strong therefore and do not let your hands be weak ,for your work shall be rewarded **(2Chronicles 15;7)**Pursue your work with compatible with your gifts, if anyone serves, he should do it with the strength God provides, so that in all things God may be praised **(1Peters 4;11)**Learn everything about your job ,let the wise listen and add to their learning **(Proverb;1;5)**Be thankful for the hard times you have gone through, it's because of the hard time you managed to make it ,We have always to go through tests to have testimony, but you must be strong and not be discouraged, the work that you do will be rewarded **(2Chronicles;15;7)**The blessing of your Job In life always see work as a gift not a punishment ,when God gives man wealth and possessions and enables him to enjoy them, to accept his lot and be happy in his work this is a gift from God**(Ecclesiastes;5;19)**- Someone who will not learn will be poor and disgraced ,anyone who listens to corrections is respected **(Proverb;13;18)** Lord your God will bless your work and fill your barns with corns he will bless you in the land is giving you **(Deuteronomy;28;8)** See the Lord as your work partner ,Stay Christ conscious throughout the day as you perform your duties, and the Lord will command the blessings on you and in all to which you set your hands, Dear Parents prepare your children well if you don't they will have a life of grief, and create a life of grief for others, bosses don't pay workers who don't work ,before you give your children allowance give them some work to do like, cleaning house ,taking out rubbish , helping around the house fetching water ,teach them to do their home work on time and how to get better grades , reward without responsibility is indulgence and if you love your children you won't do that, Teach your children that now means now and finish means don't turn on playing game (Video game) do the job until is finished , children's many times give excuses Mummy or Dad give me a minute(break) but be serious on them don't start buying it or you will be paying forever - A lazy person cannot live in the Whitehouse- If you want to live in the White house you have to work hard ,if you don't work hard you end up in the Poor house of lazy people)when you work hard you achieve your dreams and goals, your work should be of helping others as well who need help, **Have a need(Love)why you are doing something** ,Nehemiah was a waiter in the kingdom not even a builder but when he heard this he cried and wept prayed and fastened (when I heard this I sat down and wept walls of Jerusalem is broken down and its gates burned to fire God is calling you to do something action is needed he will give you the resources needed don't worry love what he is calling you to do fall in love with your work nurses Doctors Teachers Engineers; people lazy people always have excuses it is better to be short handed than to live with lazy people - better to have no body than having a lazy person -a lazy person wastes everyone resources and his resources too-What a lazy person does will take twice as long as long to finish, and will either have to be done over or overthrown out -a lazy person His presence at work is worse than his absence - the lazy person is irritating to one who hires him, like smoke into your eyes , A lazy person sees obstacles in every opportunity though he can hold down on the job, when he looks out the front door of life he doesn't see the brighter ways or high ways of success ,what he sees is only one big barrier patch ,there is always a good excuse like the pay is too little ,people are demanding ,the job is too hard ,Hours are too long, it is too cold hot wet dry to work ,he will not plough because its winter ,They always give excuses like this saying "There is a lion outside I shall be slain in the street(**Proverb 22;13**)His favourite today is tomorrow ,the lazy never does today what he can put off until tomorrow, God is asking why we slumber -A lazy person doesn't just weaken the team ,he destroys the Spirit and diminishes the will to win ,he doesn't just hold the organisation back but destroys its Motivation- The lazy mans words are One day am going to own my business ,and one day am going to make it, Lazy Pastor doesn't just limit Church he destroys its Enthusiasm, its passion to win Souls ,and meet needs before long ,everyone must do more to compensates for the negative influences - The lazy Person is wiser in his ways (eyes) than seven who answer sensibly, The lazy person is the one who is going to get around doing the job ,but never gets around to doing the job ,but never gets around to getting around (**Proverb;26;16**)I never knew a man who was good at making Excuses who was good at anything else (**Franklin Benjamin**)Lazy Men /Woman would rather make an excuse than making a living ; lazy people who refuse to work are only killing themselves ,all they do is think about what they would like to have the righteous however can give and give generously (**Proverb;21;25**) Passionate of what you are doing makes people to connect to you, love of what you are doing makes you famous (singer, business man/woman pastor, minister, doctor, nurse director fashion designer, writer,, chef)Passionate makes you to go places you have never been before, - You can turn your passion to the source of income, , the love of what you doing can make and change you from an ordinary person to Extra Ordinary person , passion can make you go extra miles , Be passionate with what God has called you to do, don't give up, Michael Jordan did give up on Basket ball though he had oppositions Opreh-Winnifried ,Nelson Mandela did not give up, because he had a passion for freedom to free his people ,Jesus did not give up because he had a passion to save the world passion is the a catalyst that drives Vision , all famous people do, what they are passionate about , Success follows Vision and passionate is the energy of Vision - **Vision** -you should have a vision ,what people think of you is opinions ,but God has a bigger vision and plan for your success**,** Many people are taking a wrong direction and they end up missing their destination, you can't arrive where you meant to go at a wrong direction ,where there is no vision people perish **,To Succeed you must do more than you think ,you are capable of**- The poet William Arthur wrote , I will do more than I belong , I will do more than fair ,I will do more than I dream, I will participate , I will do more than I care , I will do more than I forgive I will work I will do more than I learn I will do more than I teach I will do more than I give, I will enrich , I will do more than I live, I dream more than others, if you can dream it you can do it ,I will triumph ,you can't do things in easiest way and reach your goal, you must do more and you must do whatever it takes to achieve your success ,living unselfish life will help you to succeed in life and graduate with the highest honour in life , there is no greater obstacles to live a selfishness life than a life God designed you to live which is unselfishness ,Self -promotion /centred and selfish egos pollute our souls, and destroy our relationship ,we should live a goodly love life, Give generously and graciously towards others give and shall be given to you, good measure pressed down and shaken together and running over(**Mathew;5;48**)Don't just say Hello to only those who say Hello to you to succeed in life , Christians stop expecting to bring you success , don't wait for flower to arrive , God gave you a seed start growing them ,pay careful attention to your work, for then you will get the satisfaction of a job well done, and you won't need to compare yourself to anyone else(**Galatians;6;4**)And besides when you are less needy you will become more attractive to others, But you should remember that success is not comparing/measuring yourself with others what they have or what you have done and every one of us was created and gifted by God different ,look at your fingers on your hand, they are not of all the same size, success is measured of what you have done compared to what you should have done, ***Enjoy the work*** - you do, renew your altitude on the job solicit ,feedback on how to grow ,demonstrate love and grace to those you work with you ,if your work and ethic is poor you have trouble with God ,It's you who make your work important and even what you do in your home /house is important as at your work place , Cooking, bathing children ,feeding them ,teaching them good morals ,God one day will say well done to parents who care after their children ,the father of the righteous child has great joy , A man who fathers a wise son/daughter rejoices in them (**Proverb ;23;24**)Thank you lord amen *how do you stay positive at work when your boss is not?* Take God with you at work, you are like the salt for the whole human race, but if it loses its saltiness there is no way to make it salt again, It has become worthless so it is thrown out and people trample on it, you are like light for the whole world a city build on the hill cannot be hidden though you are not a leader in any, organisation, church, society (*Mathew;5;13-14*)Focus on being the best ,and bringing out the best in the people you work with, tune out negativity and negative comments ,remember you can't control what other people say and do, but you can control how you react 80%of the population vibrates to negative frequency, It is all around us, stay above the fray and quote, ***never wrestle with a pig because both you will get dirt,*** **and the pig will enjoy** , Jesus

60

said you are the light of the world a city set on ,the hill cannot be hidden(**Mathew;5;14**)Make up your mind to be the beacon, that shines in your work place, people don't enjoy being negative ,but because of stress, fear being busy ,and people surrounding them ,and they really need a call to break out of that rut and contrary to ,what you think you can be an instrument of a change as Jesus said you are the salt of the earth and remember salt has to purposes, adds taste and flavour and preservation ,you as a Christian preserve .reconcile and give hope to those around you, and those you work with, take God with you teach them scriptures in the bible -Christian remember that promotion comes when you have passed through the school of trials and graduated with a flying colours ,the higher the value the more the price -If you focus on what you are going through you may miss where God is taking you, God labels you not according to what you are, but what you shall be, you must be strategically positioned ,to receive what you believe God for, when you do not know why you are where you are ,doing what you are doing ,for what purpose then you have not fulfilled the will of God for your life ,and in life this is what I have found the best thing anyone can, *do is to eat drink and enjoy what he has worked for during the short life/Long- time that God has given* him this is the man fate, if God gives a man wealth and property and lets him enjoy them, he should be grateful and enjoy what he has worked for , it's a gift from God- God has allowed him to be happy , he will not worry too much about how short life is(**Ecclesiastes 5;18;20**)Develop passion for your work **(Collossian3;25)** And wrong doers will be paid for wrong doings ,because God judges everyone by his standards, Paul wrote and said "don't just do minimum that will get you by but do your best ,passion for our work is not usually a subterranean volcano waiting to erupt, it is a muscle that gets strengthened a little every day as we show up ,as we do what is expected of us ,and then work from heart for your real master, for God that you will get paid in full when you come into inheritance ,keep in mind always that the ultimate master you are serving is Christ, being Christian does not cover for bad work for God sake, do your best for some reason because you represent Christ in the work place, second when you are faithful in small things God will promote you to greater things(**Mathew;25;21**)Come on and share my happiness*(3)Accept Reality*-Wishing away your present circumstance while feeling entitled to better will just make you feel worse and get you know where our God turns the curses into blessing (*Deuteronomy23;5*) He gives beauty for ashes(*Isaiah;61;3*)In hard times God raises up people with fresh ideas that actually make the future better than the past not only for themselves but for others as well and you can be counted one of those people*(4)*__Confidence__-confident workers trust their God given abilities And where to get this confidence? From God than to trust in human beings Man/woman(*Psalm;118;8*)Confidence in God gives you the assurance that you can do all things through Christ who strengthen you(*Philippians;4;13*)Be confident of this everything that he begun a good work in you will perform it until the day of Jesus Christ (**Philippians;1;6**)Everything that happens to us will be of our own good to them who love God who are called according to his purpose (**Romans;8;28**)<u>We should not Fear</u>- Fear denies us so many things ,but if you get rid of fear in your life, you can do more things, For God has not given us the spirit of fear, but of power and of love, and of a sound mind (**2Timonthy1;7**)Do not be afraid am with you am your God, let nothing terrify you, I will make you strong and help you, I will protect you and save you (**Isaiah 41;10**) The greatest enemy of success is the fear of failure, many people are afraid of trying something in life ,because of the fear of failure , determination is success - fear is a spirit it's an attitude that makes you pull back or freeze in a place or give up , that spirit does not come from God, so resist it ,don't be afraid to take a prayed over risk or accept responsibility for an outcome(**6)Wisdom**- To be wise you must have first reverence for the lord, if you know the Holy one you have understanding ,Wisdom will add years to your life you are the one who will profit ,If you have wisdom and if you reject it you will be the one to suffer (**Proverb;9;10**) But the wisdom that comes from heaven is first of all pure, then peace, loving ,considerate ,submissive, full of mercy ,good fruits ,impartial and Sincere,(**James,3;17**)Those who are sure of themselves do not talk all the time people who are calm have insight (**Proverb;17;27**)n *Curiosity*-get wisdom and understanding curiosity is eagerness to know learn and understand more, Curios workers are interested in what is not obvious others presume that a solution does not exist or is too difficult so they quit at that point at which they should be starting but when others are saying it is a way beyond me the curious employees says there is an answer, there is a better way we just need understanding ,every boss wants curious workers(*Proverb;4;7)*The beginning of wisdom is get wisdom ,though it cost all you have get understanding ,Wisdom is better than rubies or pearls and all your desire cannot compare (**Proverb;8;11**) Wisdom is more than facts ,Wisdom is taking that knowledge and apply it into your life (Action),In life you need right approach ,good ideas ,its" not enough to have the right answers-Wisdom means saying right things at the right time, in the right way ,doing the right thing at the right time, Jesus said you will know the truth and the truth set you free (**John;8;32**) Pay attention to what you are taught and you will be successful, trust in the lord and you will be happy (**Proverb;16;20**) *Remember in life Education is our Passport to the future -tomorrow belongs to the people who prepare for it -without Education you won't have knowledge how to solve the challenge of the Future- Knowledge is nothing unless is put into practice- Knowledge is a treasure of a wise man -When God put Wisdom into your life he gives* *it to you to succeed what separates a Banker Manager from a Cleaner -* *it's what they he/she knows one of them gets a higher pay- God can make you know something that will change the course of your life -In life don't waste your time, Initiative* –think outside the box ,better still throw the old box away and ask God for a new one, just IQ intelligence is more than IQ average, employees with initiatives will always excel over the graduate without it, if you don't have it read history ,education alone won't make you productive but the spirit and the word of God will make you- Paul wrote let the spirit renew your thoughts and attitudes (**Ephesians ;4;23)**I have written to stimulate you to wholesome thinking(**2Peter;3;1)Let** God stimulate your mind with ideas that makes you to be on demand (Employee) Buy more books than seeking for money wisdom teaches you how to use money and how to invest but money you just only spend it any how never stop learning if you know what you are talking about you have something more valuable than and Gold and Jewel(**Proverb 20;19)(Listen while others are Talking** -We need education to fill the empty space anyone to succeed need wisdom if you listen to me you will know what is right just and fair you will know what you should do you will become wise and your knowledge will give you pleasure your insight will protect you from wrong doing God created the world by his wisdom offer you long life wealth and honour stupid people don't respect wisdom the wisdom of the world is jealous bitterness selfishness demonic but to progress in life you need Godly wisdom which is pure peaceful gentle and friendly, it is full of compassion and produces harvest of good deeds ,it is free from prejudice and hypocrisy ,look for knowledge as you look for silver and gold or some hidden treasure, obey the lord and refuse to do wrong beg for knowledge and plead for insight (**Proverb 2;9-)**The Psalmist wrote and said" The fear of the Lord is the beginning of wisdom he gives sound judgement to all who obey him his commands he is to be praised for ever (**Psalm111;10)** God said to human beings to be wise you must have reverence for the lord to understand you must turn away from evil(**Job;28;28)**Jesus grew both in body and in wisdom gaining favour with God and people(**Luke2;52)**Wisdom is the key that opens all the hidden treasure of Gods wisdom and knowledge(**Collossians;2;3)**To get wisdom keep company with the wise and you will become wise, if you make friendship with stupid people you will be ruined(**Proverb;13;20)**Get all the advice as you can and you will succeed, without it you will fail (**Proverb;15;22)** Stupid people always think they are right wise people listen to advice(**Proverb;12;15)**A nation will fall if it has no guidance many advisers mean security(**Proverb;11;14)**Get rid of some people you move with some are there to bring you up move with people who fertilise your mind some people are there to bring you down in life, Moses had the wisdom of the Egyptians and he become greater in words and deeds (**Acts;7;22;29)**King Solomon asked for wisdom and God said I will give you more wisdom and understanding than anyone has ever had before or will ever have again king Solomon was richer than any other king and the whole world wanted to come to and listen to the wisdom that God had given to him everyone who came to him came with a gift **(2Chronicles1;11;12;Kings 3;12)Share wisdom with friends-** make friends in unusual places, Iron sharpens Iron so one person sharpens another person**(Proverb;27;17)**Understand that God wants you to work smarter not just harder if you are intelligence you will be praised if you are stupid people will look down on you a man shall be rewarded according to his wisdom not on effort it does not mean on his hard work**(Proverb12;8)** The blessing of Abraham are yours as a younger Christian who wants to prosper Pray for wisdom if any of you lack wisdom let him ask of God that gives to all men generously and willingly and shall be given You must invest in yourself and get a degree God has given you power to get wealth everyone has a talent and abilities that when developed will make them successful younger/old women /men if you are willing to pay for football match which lasts for only 1hour30 money why not in books may be you value a football match instead of books it may be you value your short time joy than your long time joy invest in yourself and get a Degree/Diploma graduates are paid higher don't leave college before you finish don't build a house and establish your home until the fields are ready and you are sure you can earn a living understand and prepare that you establish your career before get married and build a house prepare your work outside and make it ready for yourself in the field then build your house 40%of divorce in Canada are over lack of finances Isaiah Paul and Luke were educated give in faith and wait God will bless you according to your ability so you must be eager to be open to God leading on how you will be a specialists and prosper/such succeed in life **(Proverb;24;27)**When you graduate from university pray in the Morning afternoon evening Everyday day and get a witness inside that you can get a job at a good pay in your field of graduation apply and get started in your Job**(James;1;5)**Reorganise that specialist get paid well the generalist does not intelligence wins respect but those who can't be trusted are on the road to ruin**(Proverb;13;15)**Stay informed a wise man will hear and increase in learning **(Proverb 1;5)**Observe read and grow ,**Discipline-** When it comes to success prayers is not a key but discipline, though we have been redeemed to reign on the Earth but indiscipline can rob any believer of his throne to another level of success , Country is in trouble ,when its king is a youth and its leaders feast all night long , but a country fortunate to have a king who makes his own decision and leaders who eat at the proper time who control themselves and don't get drunk **(Ecclesiastes 10;16;17)**Daniel was disciplined -Daniel made up his mind not to let himself become ritually unclean by eating the food and drinking the wine of the royal court, so he asked Ashpenaz to help him **(Daniel,1;8)** Reading the bible everyday and speaking in the tongues is not discipline ,but now to continue -the son who will receive his father's property is treated just like a slave while he is still young even though he owns everything**(Galatians,4;1)**but when the time came God sent his own son ,he came as a son of human mother and lived under the Jews law **(Galatians,4;4)**You cannot succeed to the next level until when you are disciplined -Discipline is possessing a sense of mission in the pursuit of any task ,Someone will say I am allowed to do anything ,yes but not everything is good for you ,I could say that am allowed to do anything ,but am not going to let anything make me its slave **(1Corinthians,6;12)**If you are not disciplined others will discipline you or God ,Discipline is acting as been commanded not as convenient ,Discipline is becoming a law to yourself ,we are allowed to do anything so they say ,that is true but not everything is good, we are allowed to do anything but not everything is helpful**(1Corinthians,10;23)**Daniel and Joseph are good example, **Use Criticism as your advantage** - make it work for you because someone who will not learn will be poor and disgraced anyone who listens to corrections is respected **,*Empathy*** always show consideration for others situations ,needs ,feelings and perception try to understand what it takes to walk in their shoes by doing this you increase your motivation ,improve the working environment and improve the productivity level clothe yourself with passion .compassion kindness humanity gentleness and patience you are supposed to wear these qualities to your place of work every day **(8)Humour-** start seeing others and yourself around the world with sense of enjoyment, refuse to take yourself too serious, look for the humour hidden in life serious moment and you will find it people who are dispenser of misery just drug everybody down ,Gods word says a cheerful disposition is good for your healthy (***Proverb;17;22***) being cheerful keeps you healthy it is slow death to be gloomy all the time a sense of humour improves things in your life and makes your work place a better place for everyone/body **Flexibility**-it is your capacity to adapt , adjust and advance in an environment driven by economic difficult and downsizing rigid and re -active employees are often the first to be made reluctant or fired learn to roll with the punches Paul did that I have learned to be content in whatever situation I can do everything through him who gives me strength **(Philippians;4;11-13)**when the winds blow flexible people bend rather than break they live to stand again and even get promoted ***Respect*** - Always consider the right and needs of others treat them sensitively kindly and within the limits of the law do what you are told by your earthly masters do your best work from the heart for your real master for God when you become such a worker God guarantees your financial security and professional success Slaves obey their earthly master in everything and do it heartily not only when their eyes are on you but with sincerity of heart and reverence for the lord, Therefore as Gods chosen people holy and lovely clothe yourselves with compassion kindness humanity gentleness and patience **(Colossian;3;12)**On your job Your value in a job is determined by the value you add to the job when a Christian goes to work each day God holds then accountable for adding enhancing and improving things in their work place the story of the three men to those who use well what they are given even more will be given to them and they will have in abundance and those who waste even the little will be taken from them **(Mathew;25;16)To succeed in life ,you Don't wait for Perfect conditions or** everybody to agree with you David and his brother David's brother discouraged him not to a shame the family but went ahead to defeat Goliath who was the giant by then Qualification don't matter well done is better than well said small deeds done are better than greater deeds planned and not meet don't be wise in words be wise in deeds the secret of getting a head is getting started talk does not cook rice Stop expecting others to bring you success God gave you a seed grow it**(Galatians 6;4)**Take hold of opportunities, God opens doors but you have to take a move and ambitious, if you wait until the wind and weather is are just right you will never Sow anything and harvest anything, God made everything and you can no more understand what he does than understand how life begins in the womb of a pregnant woman **(Ecclesiates11;4;5)**You should each judge your conduct, if it is good then you can be proud of it ,Enjoy yourself what you have done without comparing ,Each of us has his own load to carry ;*You must start* - that may seem obvious, but many of us find ourselves stuck in the starting point /blocks, waiting for something get us going what God has called and equipped you to do ? step out and do it, and he will empower you with his blessing, glory, wisdom and open your eyes to see greater things you will never find until you try; Begin while others are Procrastinating, first people will ask you why are doing, it then later how did you do it Visualise yourself attaining your goal, think and talk of success ,Moses did, he had his eyes on God, no one can see and he kept on going it was by faith that made Moses to leave Egypt without being afraid of the kings anger, as though he saw the invisible God **(Hebrews;11;27)Start small**- the angels told me ,to give Zerubbabel this massage from the Lord ,you will succeed not by military power or by your own strength but by my Spirit ,obstacles as great as mountains will disappear before you- you will build the temple and as you put the last stone in place, the people will shout beautiful-beautiful, another massage came to me from the lord, he said Zerubbabel has laid a foundation of the temple and he will finish the building ,when this happens my people will know that it is ,I who sent you to them, they are disappointed because so little progress is being made but they will see Zerubbabel continuing to build the temple and they will be glad **(Zachariah4;6;10)**;*You must refuse to sit down /around waiting for tomorrow* -opportunities you have to arise and do something do something" **Well done is better than well**

Said" The Bible is a promising book gives courage to be determined so that you as a Christian of today you can be able to accomplish greater things like people in the past King David in all his battles was determined David had just won a couple of military victories but when he returned home he found his home being destroyed by the Amalekites and his family taken captives he was heart stick he and his men fell to the ground and wept until they couldn't weep anymore but didn't stay down David two wives Ahinoam and Abigail had been taken away David was in great trouble his men were bitter at him losing their children and wives and were threatening to stone him but the lord his God gave him courage David acquired of the Lord saying shall I pursue this troops? Shall I over take them? and he answered him pursue for you shall surely over take them and without fail cover all **(1Samuel;30-6- David war against the A male kites determination)**David determination and courage coupled with Gods protection let him to victory learn to talk to God and Pray Weeping may endure for night but Joy cometh in the morning **(Psalm,30;5)** But their insult cannot hurt me because the sovereign lord gives me help **(Isaiah;50;7)**I brace myself to endure them I know that I will not be disgraced-Nelson- Mandela passionate to free his people (read;**John;18;37)** Nothing will ever be achieved without greater men and men are great only if they are determined to be so **(Charles de Gaulle)**The difference between the impossible and possible lies in personal determination(**Tonny-lasorda**) God will never quit on you when you pass through deep waters I will be with you your troubles will not over whelm you when you pass through fire you will not be burnt the hard times that comes will not hurt you for am the Lord your God the Holy God of Israel who saves you **(Isaiah;43;2;3)**I have fought ,I have finished the race, I have kept the faith(**2Timothy 4;7**)Jesus said to him no one who puts his hand to the plough and looks back is fit for the kingdom of God(**Luke9;62**)Obstacles don't have to stop you, if you run into a wall don't turn around and give up ,figure out how you climb it, go through it, work around it(**Michael Jordan**)If you are not determined you will either find a way or make one**(Hamibal)**Winners in life are ordinary people with extra ordinary determination, Jesus himself was determined to save the world, he did not give up, Christians if we are to achieve what God has designed us we have to be determined, and be able to achieve our main purse and goals For whatever was written in former days (Past)was written for our instruction, that through endurance and through encouragement of the scriptures ,we might have hope(**Romans15;4**) What destroys you makes you stronger ,biggest battles brings the biggest victories -Your weakness can be your Discovery point, you never know before or had Joseph said "**God turned into good into what meant Evil** (**Genesis,50;20**)God still does, God controls your destiny not man ,he can turn your pain into gains Your scars into stars ,But their insults cannot hurt me ,because the sovereign lord gives me help(Determination) I brace myself to endure then I know that I will not be disgraced **(Isaiah;50;7)**Whoever is of God hears the word of God the reasons the why you do hear them is that you are not of God**(You are not determined to hear the word of God)** Christians if you are determined to read his word and do his will you will come to understand that heavens and Earth will pass away but his word (God) will not pass away**(Mark;13;31)**But you Brothers and Sisters must not get tired of doing good**(2Thessolonia ;3;13)**And let us not grow weary of doing good in a due season we will reap, if we do not give up **(Galatians;6;7)**What does it take to be a champion, Desire ,Dedication Determination, Concentration, Faith and the will to win**(Patty-Berg)** Decision and Determination are the engineer and fireman of our great opportunity and success, Determination gives you a the resolve to keep going in spite of the road blocks that lays before you**(Denis-Waitley)** A dream does not become a reality through magic it takes sweat -(determination)and hard work**(Colin-Powell)** In life there is always ways of getting almost anywhere you want to go, if you are determined **(Langston-Hughes)** They say love will find a way, I know determination will **(Ronnie Milsap)**Determination is the wake up call to the human will (Anthony Robbins)Self determination is fine but need to be tempered with self control Failure will never over take me if my determination to succeed is strong enough in everything I do Serving God listening to his Word Doing his Will Believing in my life time **Amen** we have the power to do many things because our God is the pushing power only what we need determination*)Get over -yourself* -Don't remind yourself of the past repent and then move on God says he will not remember your sins (*Isaiah 43;25)* there is only one reason to remember the *past is to learn from it and grow wiser* and learn these dear Christians Jesus said this at the end of his life I have glorified you on earth I have finished the work which you have given me to do (**Jesus prayed**) he did not try to compete with John the Baptist or model himself after some old testament prophets he knew what success was and he gives you the above lesson you can adopt to succeed in life *Purpose* many people have a wrong idea about what constitutes happiness true happiness is not attained through self-gratification but through fidelity to a worthy purpose Jesus said the son of man did not come to be served but to serve(*Mark,10;45*)don't pray for generous heart but practice being generous and your heart will fall into line with your action as long as you are a sowed God will give you a divine seed (*2Corinthians 9;10)*Remove the obstacles out of the way **(Isaiah 57;14)** As you run to win in life you have to forgive un forgiving attitude is bad if you don't forgive neither your God will not forgive your trespasses**(Mark11;26)**Pray father forgive as you forgave me whatever I ask for myself in blessing I ask them in double , triple ,measures when you retaliate you deny God the right to

BELIEVER'S BOOK

show you mercy and deal with the situation his way forgive those who hurt you hatred hinders healing and it's not a Christianity way of living - ***Run in such a way to get the prize*** (*1Corinthians 9;24)*Surely you know that many runners take part in race but only one wins the prize run in such a way to get the price and these are some of things you have to do to succeed in life Prepare while others are day dreaming-***You must give it all*** - do it with one heart and use all you power energy /time Divers in the Olympic don't save all their energy for their final dive but they give in every effort they have increasing their chances for Gold medal don't wait for mediocrity at any single stage **(11)Smile while others are frowning-Persist while others are quitting**- you have to press on toward the goal to win for the prize for which God has called you for and to graduate with the highest honour (*Philippians,3;14*) Great achiever stay focused on their Goal they are so single focused and are often considered fanatics focusing on one thing forgetting the past and looking forward what lies ahead of them Paul calling was of his obsession he pressed on to reach the end of the race and receive the heavenly prize for Gods calling permitted nothing and no one to slide-track him down from winning when you lose something today don't stay in one place wake up the next day and start business as usual blessed is the man who preserve under trial because, when he has stood the test he will receive the crown of life , without persistence when the storm of life come you may be swept away, Believe and act according to the promises, if you can everything is possible for him who believe **(2Corinthians;1;20)***Perseverance*-What is it ? It is the energy desire to achieve its motivation, determination ,and commitment, faithfulness patience ,resilience in the face of difficult and willingness to work hard, those who avoid too chose the easy way are costly to employ ,decrease morale, reduce quality ,and lessens the company productivity-Paul wrote challenging his readers to persevere here is my advice ,you should finish what you started, let the eagerness you showed in the beginning be matched now,(*2Corinthians;8;10-11*)For this reason make sure every effort to, add to your faith, goodness and to goodness knowledge, and to knowledge ,self-control and to self-control ,perseverance and to perseverance godliness and to godliness mutual affections and to mutual affections love**(2Peter;1;5;7)**Christian must persevere /focus on Christ and the eternal prize, as for we have this large crowd of witness round us so then let us rid ourselves of everything that gets in the way and of sin which holds you on to us so tightly and let us run with determination the race that lies before us ,let us keep our eyes fixed on Jesus on whom our faith depends ,from the beginning to end ,he did not give up because of the cross on centrally, because of the joy that was waiting for him ,he thought nothing of the disgrace of dying on the cross ,and now seated at the right hand of Gods throne (**Hebrews;12;1;3**) Think of what he went through ,how he put up so much hatred from

69

sinners, so don't let yourself be discouraged and give up even in storm, Persevere All the promises of God belongs to you in Jesus name(**Romans;8;16**)Be alert stand firm (Persevere)in faith be brave ,be strong do all your work in love (**1Corinthians;16;13**)Even if I go through the deepest darkness ,I will not be afraid Lord for you are with me your shepherd rod and staff protect me(**Psalm;23;4**)Love never gives up never lose faith -Faith is always hopeful and endures through every situation (**1Corinthians;13;7**)The lord is good to those who depend on him so it is good to wait patiently quietly for salvation from the Lord (**Lamentation;3;25;26**) As you know we count as blessed those who have persevered you have heard of Jobs perseverance and what finally what the lord finally brought about the lord is full of compassion and mercy(**James;5;11**)The wicked run when no one is chasing them but an honest person is as brave as a lion(**Proverb;28;1**)*To get a lion share you need a lion heart to succeed to next level ,you have to be bold enough in life,* I know your deeds your hard work and your perseverance I know that you cannot tolerate wickedness people that you have tested those who claim to be apostles but are not and have found them false you have persevered and you have endured hardship for my name and have not grown weary (**Revelation;2;2;3**)Amen fall seven times stand up Eight success is a sum of small effort repeated day in a day out success is a matter of hanging on after others have let go-the man who moves a Mountain begins by carrying away small stones it always seems impossible until it is done Great work are performed not by strength but by perseverance- (**Samuel Johnson**) Don't stop when am tired I stop when am done (**Marilyn -Man** more Just because you fail once it doesn't mean you are going to fail at everything (**Marilyn Monroe**)Am Slow walker but ,I never walk back people who are failures are the one who don't know how closer they were to success when they gave up and didn't persevere there is no failure unless when you stop trying (**Elbert Hubbard**)Victory is always possible for those who refuse stop fighting (**Napoleon Hill**) Rivers knows this there is no hurry we shall get there someday (**Milne**)Trees that are slow to grow bear good fruits(**Moliere**)God will witness to your heart (**Romans;8;17**)It will lead you to prosperity(**Galatians;3;14**) Understand that the lord promised to supply your needs and with all his abundant wealth through Jesus Christ my God will supply all my needs (**Philippians 4;19**)The father wants you to prosper so you can have your needs and do not seek what you will eat and drink and do not keep worrying ,seek his kingdom and all things will be added to you ,the father has gladly chosen to give you the kingdom(**Luke12;29;32**)People who persevere in faith in Christ are those who will enter the kingdom of heaven, true child of God you have to persevere in prayers suffering and trials, the snail to reach the top of tree, persevere builds characters and a closer relationship with the lord, persevere in praying a strong spirit is capable of praying with all persevere until the answer comes and with faith ,we need to persevere in prayers to achieve success, healing, guidance, protection ,peace, love ,We should not stop knocking on the door, we should not lose hope, we can pray for weeks months years for something the more we draw closer to our God the quicker he answers our prayers ,in days, months, years *Discern what really success is* When others feel good about you -you are popular- But when you feel good about yourself you are successful- Your life highest level of joy is within you ,*__You must not quit__*-The bible say run in such a way to get a price if you quit you will never win anything just keep going He struck three times and stopped then Elisha told the king to take the other arrow and strike the ground with them the king struck the ground three time and stopped this made Elisha angry and said to the king you should have struck five or more times and then you would have won complete victory over the Syrians but now you will only defeat them only three time(*2Kings13;18)*This a story of a partial winner /victory of might have been if the King had struck the Ground more than five or six times you see it is not only the opportunity it's the attitude that meets the opportunity that determines the outcome God will give you Chances to succeed /win but it is your commitment that determines the size of your victory Paul wrote serve whole heartedly as if you were serving God not men(**Ephesian;6;7**)The clock meant nothing to Paul because he was on a mission, I consider myself life worth nothing to me if only ,I may complete the task the Lord Jesus has given me(*Acts;20;24*)To do which is to declare the Good news about the Grace of our God -People of great impact live with such mindset so here the question Perseverance must finish its work so that you may be mature and complete not lacking anything(**James1;4**)As a Christian who wants to succeed in life (**Is your heart in what you doing ?Are you giving it all?** The secret of my success is that I bit more than I can chew and chewed as fast as I could Vision the bigger the price tag the secret to fulfil your vision and ambition is don't give up / keep going / keep-chewing   pay whatever price it takes to walk with Jesus doing that may be not easy and you will start saying no to certain things and run away from pleasing people but this is the only way you will be at peace with your God and be in the position what he is saying to you nobody has ever said the Christian walk is easy and this is the most lasting important thing and more rewarding our busy days today leads to spiritual bareness being part of the chase can be exciting and rewarding but leaving no time for God is nothing refuse to be carried away by worldly things-Today we are told to succeed we must hit the floor running at a hundred miles an hour and keep it up until when we collapse in the sack at night No matter how much a lazy person may want something he will never get it a hard worker will get everything he wants(*Proverb13;4*)Elijah was depressed that he prayed he might die I have had enough Lord he said take up my life am no longer better than my ancestors he lay down under the tree and fell asleep suddenly an angel touched him and said wake up and eat he looked around and saw a loaf of bread and a jar of water near his head he ate and drank and lay down again the angle returned and woke him up a second time saying get up and eat or the journey will be too much for you Elijah got up ate and drank and the food gave him strength to walk 40 days to Sinai the holy mountain (**1Kings19;4;8**)When Elijah was strengthened by Gods grace, he emerged from depression to a new man, with a new mission in life, Let us look at Peter, who build the new covenant testament church, as he was forgiven in spite of his weakness he was restored and become an Apostle Simon ,Simon ,listen Satan has received permission to test all of you, to separate the good from the bad ,as the farmer separates the wheat from the chaff ,but I have prayed for you Simon that your faith will not fail and when you turn back to me you must strengthen your brothers (**Luke;22;31;32**)Peter is a proof that God takes us when we are weak and speaks and acts through us in ways that brings glory to him alone ,he chose what the world looks down on and despises and think is nothing in order to destroy what the world thinks is important (**1Corinthians;1;28**) The word diligence includes qualities like, honesty, hard work, persistence and striving for excellence ,the bible again says lazy people want much but get little those who work hard will prosper ,Experts says success does not come from being a hundred percept better than your competition, but from being one way syndicated ,one wrote /columnist Dale Dante says if you want to become creative in your company Job or your life it all comes down to one easy Step the extra one when you encounter a familiar plan you just question *What else could we do?* when you lose something today don't stay in one place ,wake up the next day and start business as usual, blessed is the man who perseveres under trials because when he has stood the test he will receive the crown of life ,But the lord says ,do not cling to the events of the past or dwell what happened long ago watch for a new am going to do its happening already you can see it now I will make a road through wildness and give you streams of water there(**Isaiah;43;18;19**)Where you failed in life start again and God will restore you, Perseverance in prayers shows seriousness, God answers prayers in days ,weeks ,and years ,be ye strong therefore Gods time is the best Success does not come to you -you go for it, the difference between the possible and Impossible lies in a person determination ,Christians today we should be determined to serve God, teaching the Gospel and about Salvation serving him ,Praising and worshiping him, doing his will, many people today are determined to make ,fame ,earning wealthy, and other things ,but all these things perish, the only thing that do not perish is the fight to enter the eternal kingdom, many people give up when trials and pain surface the man who can drive himself further once the effort trials and pains gets painful is the man who will succeed ,**You must know to decide what is important in your life** the story of a farmer in one country they decided to move from urban area to rural area to raise Goats on the firm and one day they brought in a rich man because they wanted financial support from him and this rich man asked them what they were going to use the money for and they said they wanted to set up a Goat firm and gave them time to set up but the family had one problem naming the firm one of the children said Mum wanted it to be called SEQ=P but Dad wanted it to be called special Goat=F and the son wanted it to be called the most Loving Firm =H and the daughter Preferred it to be called one Firm in the world =G So they compromised and called it SEQ=P special Goat=F most loving firm=H one firm in the world =G RANCH so when the rich investor meet them after a while he asked them their progress to borrow the money they said they failed to come up with a suitable name to name their firm ,Dear Christian the name was not the issue but what we should focus on most, important things first decision is important if you want to succeed un decided heart Paul wrote and said am still not all I should be but am bringing all my energies together to bear on this one thing forgetting the past and looking forward to what lies ahead I strain to reach the end of the race and receive the prize (**Phillipians;3;13-14**) a decided heart is the result of a made up mind it is what separates the winners from the losers pour your life into something more than self-interest commit a purpose that will outlive keep your eyes on your vision and priorities put into writing because it is not yet time for it to come true but time is coming quickly and what I show you will come to pass(**Habakkuk ;2;3**)But I bless those who put their trust in me (**Jeremehiah;17;7**)(5)**Prioritise your time** ,too many of us are like the car washer who got himself busy trying to keep the place Clean where he clean cars that he forgot to Open the front door for the Washing bay the reason is that why you are in business? Is it not you to Serve customers and make profits? do not get distracted by Secondary things base your life on priorities there is time for everything refuse to wait for tomorrows opportunity the world is blessed by those who are doing something in the right place right time right season success is simple do what is right the right way at the right time - Time is precious commodity and limited resource and make every day of your life count God knew you even before you were born and every day you live is counted in his book God has laid a track for you to live on or run on let us run with endurance the race God has set before us(**Hebrew;12;1**)God will reward you for how you have lived so make every day count (teach us how short our life is so we may be wise (**Psalm ;90;12**) and if you need help figuring out what they are ask God to give you wisdom from his mouth comes knowledge and understanding **Learn to motivate yourself** - Strong and successful people should be applauded and encouraged In life most time no one will do it for you when tragedy struck him David encouraged himself in the lord (*I Samuel; 30;6)*You need to learn how to do so Jude wrote building up yourself you need to Pray in the holy Ghost and open your door to succeed ,To succeed in life do not rejoice over me my enemies when I fall I will arise again when I sit in darkness the lord will be my light to me (**Micah7;8**)*You must refuse to settle for yesterday accomplishment* if what you did yesterday still looks big to you today you probably haven't done enough today Paul celebrated his accomplishment but he focused on what God had for him in future forgetting the past and looking forward to what lies ahead of him (***Philippians3;13-14)***Learn to wait** So let us not become tired of doing good for if we do not give up the time will come when we will reap the harvest due season is when God knows the time is right not when you think it is time (man)God has set time to accomplish everything wait for the lord be strong and take heart and wait for the lord (**Psalm27;14**)In the morning God you hear my voice in the morning ,I lay my requests before you and wait expectantly (**Psalm 5;3**)the lord will fight for you -you only need to be still (**Exodus14;14**)Do not forget in life dear friends there is no difference in the lords sight between one day and a thousand years to him two are the same (**2Peters3;8**)You cannot hurry the seasons or shorten it its only by God (**James;5;7;8**)-(***Don't rely on one person*** you need to have substitutes (**spare tyres**)In order to succeed in life you have to choose your travelling companions ,if you give your life to those who are not worthy of it you ruin your life be more selective choose your friends from among those who share your values ,understand your God given purpose and those who strength you Must be willing to give as Christ told his disciples give money to the poor provide for yourself that don't wear out and save your riches in heaven where they will never decrease because no thief can get them and no moth can destroy them as a younger Christian who want to succeed in life(**Lk;12;33;34**)**Give in Good measure**- Out of your first fruit by faith and shall be given to you in good measure give to others and God will give you indeed you will receive a full measures a generous helping poured into your hands(**Luke 6;38**)As believer who wants to succeed in life remember that it's the lord your God who gives you the power to become rich he does this because he is still faithful today to the covenant that he made with your ancestors never forget the lord your God or turn to other gods to worship and serve them if you do then I warn you today that you will be destroyed (**Deuteronomy;8;18**)whoever who is faithful in small matters will be faithful in large matters whoever is dishonest in small matters will be dishonest in large ones (**Luke;16;10**) bring the full amount of your tithes to the temple so that there will be plenty of food there put me to test and you will see that, I will open windows of heavens and pour out on you abundance all kinds of good things I will not let the insects destroy your crops and grapes vines will be loaded with grapes (**Malachi;3;10;11**) the lord reward those who are faithful and righteous (**1samuel;26;23**)give to the poor and you will never be in need if you chose to close your eyes to the poor many people will curse you (**Proverb;28;27**)if you want to be happy be kind to the poor it is a sin to despise anyone (**Proverb;14;21**)if you give food to the hungry and satisfy those who are in need then the darkness around you will turn to brightness of noon and I will always guide you and satisfy you with good things I will keep you strong and well you will be like a garden that has plenty of waters like a spring of water that never runs dry(**Isaiah;58;10;11;Mat;5;42;Lk12;33**)*There is happiness in giving than in receiving* - Whenever you possibly can do good to those who need it never tell your neighbours to wait until tomorrow if you can help them now(**Proverb;3;27;28**)Some people spend their money freely and still grow richer others are cautious and yet grow poorer be generous and you will be prosperous help others and you will be helped (**Proverb;11;24;25**)If you want to be happy be kind to the poor it is a sin to despise anyone(**Proverb;14;21**)Do not let kindness and truth leave you, bind them on your neck write them on the tablet of your heart, then you will be good Favour with God and man (**Proverb;3;3;4**)People will always forget what you said what you have done but will never forget how you made them feel when you are kind to others they will also be kind to you , If you get rich by charging interest and taking advantage of people your wealth will go to someone who is kind to the poor (**Proverb;28;7**)To succeed in life you must **To succeed in life reach out to others** By love serve one another as for you(**Galatians,5;13**)Dear Christians we are called to be free but do not let this freedom becomes an excuse for letting your physical desire control you instead, Let love make you serve one another, if you are stronger you have to help the weaker side, Spiritually and economically ,be passionate about creating opportunities for others- don't be defined by anything other than the quality of your work and the professionalism with which you treat those above and below you- You won't succeed in life unless you are connected to the right person ,and those who enable you always to succeed ,people who will help you won't come to you usually you must go for them, why do you think there is a newspaper seller on every corner, and soft drink machine on every hotel or citizen advice centres ,success won't come knocking on your door ,you have to go and look for it, Jesus did not set up a throne in the middle of each town ,and say this is the only place you can meet me, no he went to market places, to the boats of fishers, to synagogues, to the homes of people, he went through towns teaching the gospel and healing everywhere,(**Luke;9;6**)what is keeping you reaching out to others fear of rejection until your dream becomes more important to you other than your fear of rejection you will never succeed if you don't reach out successful people dread rejection too the difference is that they believe their goals are worth it   there two kinds of people in your life**(1)**Those who already know you have something they need and**(2)**Those who don't know yet so start a people list the law of relationship says that every person is only four people away from the person they need this simply means that you know **Henry** who knows **Jane** who knows **Steven** who know **Peter** the person you need or you want to get to ,you are already connected follow the dots and you will get to your destination, victory or succeed ,always begin somewhere at some moment ,with someone ,the secret is you must reach out to others that's why God created us make a choice of people to move with unhealthy relationship "**Paul wrote and said** "bad company corrupts good characters (**1Corinthians;15;33**)In the ministry choose people God has chosen for you, but in this you have to pray for it ,look for those God has given the same purpose with you(**Exodus;31;6**)Wisdom have the right skills have the same spirit don't stake on one person help others to become successful whatever good that any man doeth the same shall receive of the lord(**Ephesians;6;8**)Don't be self -centred become interested in others , **In life to move to next level of success you need a prophetic word and honour the word of your religious leaders** - from your pastor the lord sent a prophet to rescue the people of Israel in Egypt and take care of them **(Hosea 12;13)**The sovereign Lord never does anything without revealing his plan to his servants the prophets **(Amos;3;7)**Honour your religious leaders **-Honour your Mother and Father**-respect your father and mother as the lord your God commands you so that all may go well with you so that you may live a long life time am giving you (**deuteronomy5;16**)**Obedient** to your God if you obey him the lord will keep all the promises he made when he told me that my descendants would rule Israel as long as they were careful to obey his commands faithfully with all their hearts and soul(**1Kings;2;4**)**Tear down your barriers**- by praying fasting giving your tithes and doing what the authority wants and don't repeat the past mistakes you will be successful in all your plans visions and what God has called you to do learn to laugh at your failures and shortcomings ,don't be held back by the your failures For God's grace is sufficient for thee for my strength is made perfect in weakness **(2Corinthians;12;9)**- **Diversity your life**- Invest in several areas not one investment many places in fact because you never know what kind of bad luck you are going to have in this world no matter in which direction a tree falls it will lie where it fell when the clouds are full it rains **(Proverb11;2;3)***To succeed in life you have to reduce on Debts*-Poor people are slaves of the rich borrow money and you are a lenders slave because of the interests charged on you(**Proverb;22;7**)Don't promise to be responsible for someone's debts if you should not be able to pay they will even take away your bed **(Proverb;22;26)** **Turn away from Greed**-greed can suck your life make you take People lives ruin your spiritual life family life when you indulge yourself in high interest loans credit cards pay day loan scheme if you try to make profits dishonestly you will get your family in trouble don't take bribes and you will live longer **(Proverb;15;27)**Robbery always claims the life of the robber this is what happens to anyone who lives by violence **(Proverb1;19)** <u>**Chose your words wisely -the power of life and death are in the tongue and that love it shall eat its fruits (Proverb18;21)**</u>Words have the power to build or destroy words we speak are like planting a seed the words we say determines the kind of fruits we harvest are your words positive encouraging of love kindness forgiveness or are negative words full of lies gossiping slander hatred before you speak ask yourself is it kind is it true is it necessary and does it improve be mindful what comes out of your mouth better to be silence if you don't have positive words to say,<u>** To succeed in life you must have time for relaxation**</u>(leisure time)If you rush you must have time to rest **(Mark 6;31)**There were so many people coming and going that Jesus and his disciples didn't have even time to eat so he said to them let us go off by ourselves to some place where we will be alone and you can rest for some time no one has got a greater assignment than Jesus and no one was busier not even you Jesus knew the importance of leisure he understood the balance between work and rest which is why he was able to accomplish so much in little time the more successful the more demands on your time and energy will be people are wonderful but they can be draining as your career and calling grow this will only become so renewing yourself will require constant attention, if you do this you can be sure those around you won't work hard but play enthusiastically schedule it take one day off a week and have total relaxation focus on something other than work ,if you do this your mind will be clear you will make better decisions you will see life in different directions(eyes) and you will accomplish far more stop and answer this question how often do you schedule time for leisure ?what do you do to rest your mind at work? At home? If you had a full day off from work to yourself what would you do? If you struggle to answer this question these are some of the answers reading your bible /church hospital to visit the sick visiting friends listening to gospel music watching Television plays and involving yourself into other activities like ,Gym Mat- making ,if you can't do this you need to pray and ask God to teach you how to rest and ask him Lord teach me how to rest ,show me how I can turn towards you and be restored and renewed, Why people keep themselves busy in life? To earn living help others cover up their laziness development and some because of greed if they make **$20 dollars** today it is not enough for them they want **$50 dollars** greed is not only the aspect this can involve greed for power, praise, prestige, position ,and security And why we are here because we are ambassadors of Christ called to a world -wide mission of making disciples of all nations starting from east to west and to represent the saviours to glorify God and enjoy him forever good quotations that will empower you to be successful in life All our dreams can become true if we have the courage to pursue them(*Walt Disney*) Good things come to those people who wait but better things come to those who go out and get them Things work out best for those who make the best of how things work out(**John wooden**)If you want to achieve greatness stop asking for permission from man only your God(*Anonymous*)If you do what you always did, you will get what you always got(*Anonymous*) don't be afraid to give up the good to go for the great (*John,d-Rockefeller*)Great minds discuss ideas average minds discuss events small minds discuss people(*Elbert*)Opportunity don't happen you create them(**Chris Grosser**)What is the point of being alive if you don't at least try to do something remarkable (anonymous) In life Everyone wants or loves to stay on the Job longer**(1)Favour and Grace of God (2)Because is Valued with Equal Opportunity(3)Loved by his employer and employees (4)Encouraged and challenged Positively (5)Promoted (6)Increase in wages(7) Given opportunity of training and learning new skills (8)Appreciated with small and big gifts**-Life is not about finding yourself life is about creating yourself(*Lolly- Daskal*)The road to success and the road to failure are almost the same(*Colin R Davis)*It's not what you look at that matters, it is what you see(*Anonymous*);**Amen**

Keys to success -(summary)

-**Know yourself -,** Decide what you want to make out of life ,then write down your ,goals, visions and how to reach them, **Amen**

Use the greatest power you can tap through ,-Faith in God the hidden energies of your soul and your subconscious mind ,**Amen,**

Love others and love to serve them ,Amen

Develop positive traits of character and personality ,Amen

Work put your life plan into determination action -, go after what you want with what's in you , **Amen**

QUESTION?

SHOULD CHRISTIANS BE RICH?

RICH means Wealthy

A Christian is not born again to be poor, is not redeemed to be poor ,the word redemption refers to be delivered from sin and freedom from captivity **(Poorness is captivity)** You know the grace of our Lord Jesus Christ ,Rich as he was ,he made himself poor for your sake in order to make you rich by the means of his poverty **(2 Corinthians 8;9),Amen**

The bible says "Warning to the rich and now you rich people listen to me weep and wail over the miseries that are coming upon you, your riches have rotted away and your clothes have been eaten by months, your Gold and silver are covered with rust ,and this rust will be a witness against you

,and will eat up your flesh like fire ,you have pilled your riches in this last days you have not paid any wages to those who work in your field, listen to their complains the cries of those who gather in your crops have reached the ears of God ,the Lord almighty your life here is full of luxury and pleasure you have made yourself fat for the days of slaughter you have condemned and murdered innocent people, and they do not resist you **(James;5;16)**Riches are not bad and God does not say that we should be poor but all depends how we**(1)Acquire our riches and wealth (2)How we use our Riches and Wealth (a)**How we have acquired riches in the last days means making s much money (*Hoarding wealth*) as we can and keep it for Ourselves many Christians through dubious ways not saving little by little through .lies ,gambling .killing ,cheating workers their wages ,and many people are crying against you their cries have been heard by God if its acquired through honest way its good and God is happy with you if you pay wages of those who work for you before the sunset its good because the poor are counting on it do not cheat poor or need hired servants whether fellow Israelites or foreigners living in one of your towns each day before sunset pay them for that day's work they need the money and have counted on getting it if you don't pay them they will cry out against you to the lord and you will be guilty of sin **(Deuteronomy;24;14;15)**Christians you shouldn't favour others at work over the others especially when you are their employee- **Do not take advantage of anyone or rob him (Leviticus 19;13) (b)**At the end of every seventh year you are to cancel the debts of those who owe you money, this is how to be done all those who have rent money to a fellow Israelites are to cancel the debt they must not try to collect the money the lord himself has declared the debt cancelled you may collect what a foreigner owes you but you must not collect what your own people owe you the lord your god will bless you in the land that is giving you not one of your people will be poor ,if you obey him and carefully observe everything that I command you today the lord will bless you as he has promised you will lend money to many nation but you will not have to borrow from them you will have control over many nations but no nation will have control over you **(Deuteronomy,15;1;6)(c)Interest free loan**-if you lend money to any of my people who are poor do not act like a money lender and require him to pay interest **(Exodus;11;25)Leave excessive food in the field for the Poor-**When you harvest your fields do not cut the corn at the edge of the field and do not go back to cut the ears of corns that were left do not go through your vineyard to gather the grapes that were missed or to pick up the grapes that have fallen leave them for the poor and foreigners am the lord your God **(Leviticus;19;9;10) Do not steal or cheat or lie do not make a promise in my name ,**If you do intend to keep it that brings disgrace on my name, Am the Lord your **God(Leviticus 19;11;12)(2)How to use your money if you are given riches -**If in any of the towns in the land that the Lord your God is giving there is a fellow Israelites in need then do not be selfish and refuse to help him instead be generous and lend him as much he needs do not refuse to lend him something just because the year when the debts are cancelled is near do not let such an Evil thought enter your mind if you refuse to make the loan he will cry to the Lord against you and you will be held guilty give him freely and unselfishly and the lord will bless you in everything you do there will always be some Israelites who are poor and in need and so I command you to be generous to them **(Deuteronomy;15;7;11)**Meaning there will always be people in need, not only in Israel those Christians who are poor must be glad when God lifts them up ,and the rich Christians must be glad when the lord brings them down, for the rich will pass away like the flowers of a wild plant ,the sun rises with its blazing heat and burns the plant and its flower falls off and its beauty is destroyed, In the same way the rich will be destroyed while they go about their business**(James;1;9;11) Help those who are in need instead of acquiring all the riches for yourself** -Those whose life are full of luxury and pleasure you have made yourself fat for the day of slaughter ,You have condemned and murdered innocent people and they do not resist you **(James 5;5;6)**Those who are rich and you don't help it's not worthy at all ,God bless you to use you as a vessel ,and bless others to but when you hoard it for yourself it's not worthy- ,The Pharisees who loved money heard all this and were sneering at Jesus ,he said to them "you are the ones who justify yourselves in the eyes of others ,but God knows your heart ,what people value highly is detestable in Gods sight **(Luke,16;14;15)** the issue is not about being rich but the heart attitude towards money that concerns the Lord **Abraham ,Isaac ,Jacob ,King Solomon** were said to be the richest king in the world as a gift from God , **Joanna** whose husband Chuza was an officer in Herods court and **Sussan** and many other women who used their own resource to help Jesus and his disciples **(Luke 8;3)**when Jesus died on a cross for our sins wealthy and well connected men asked for his body and buried it at their expense , the early church shared their resources rich and poor to take care all **(Acts)**When it comes to Earthly riches God never condemns riches but warns that sin enter the equation when becomes the ultimate goal the main pursuit of life ,But those who desire to be rich fall into temptation into snare into many senseless and harmful desire that plunge people into ruin and destruction "For the love of money is a root of all kinds of Evil some people eager for money ,have wondered from faith and pierced themselves with many grief's**(1 Timothy;6;9;10)** No one can serve two masters for either ,he will hate one and love the other or he will be devoted to the one and despise the other , you cannot serve God and money **(Mathew,6;24)** For God uses the poor and the rich for his work on Earth -The Lord makes poor and the rich ,he brings low and exalts **(1 Samuel 2;7)The Lord**

warns us not to be arrogant when using money -Command those who are rich in the things of this life not to be proud but to place their hope not in such an uncertain things as riches but in God who generously give everything for our enjoyment **(1Timothy 6;17)** Rich and poor we all have the same responsibility to keep our priority to the work of God to avoid wasting our lives on things that won't last into eternity , to be good Stewart **, martyrs heroes ,rich and poor ,**What made them distinctive were not their bank account ,properties but how they obediently used their resources to further the work of God on earth,**A road to your Success should or is achieved by Management-**Everything above we have seen needs management ,Time , Resources, Wisdom , Abilities ,Talents, "The bible states it clear that" *to whom much is given of him shall much be required"***(Luke,12;48)**Some people act as if they is no tomorrow ,but it's just the beginning ,what God has given you and has much in store for you ,what you have seen is nothing to what he has in store ,so don't be much carried with the little and assume that you are on top, if you do what he wants he will make certain each step you take, but mismanagement of his resources will lead to your downfall; *Keep falsehood and lies far from me give me neither poverty no riches but give me only my daily bread (Proverb 30;8),*Obey faithful all the terms of his covenant so that you be successful in everything **(Deueteronomy,29;9),**There something that the Lord our God has kept secret but he has revealed his Law and we our descendant are to obey forever **(Deuteronomy,29;29)Amen**

THERE TWO CLASSES OF RICHES THE BIBLE TEACHES US;

First class - You say am rich and well off ,I have all I need ,but you do not know how miserable and pitiful you are! you are poor naked and blind, I advise you then go buy gold from me ,pure gold in order to be rich ,buy also white clothing's to dress yourself and cover up your shameful nakedness, buy some ointment to put on your eyes so that you may see **(Revelation,3;17;18)**I was afraid of you because you are hard man you take what is not yours and reap what you not sow ,he said to him you bad servant ,I will use your own words to condemn you **(Luke,19;21;22)** know what I am hard man taking what is not mine and reaping what I have not shown Then Jesus said to his host when you give lunch or dinner ,do not invite your friends or your brothers and your relatives or your rich neighbours ,for they will invite you back and in this way you will be paid for what you did when you give a feast invite the poor ,the crippled ,the lame and the blind ,and you will be blessed because they are not able to pay you back ,God will repay you on the day the good people rise from death(**Luke,14;12;14)**There was chief tax collector there named Zacchaeus who was rich he was trying to see who Jesus but he was little and could not see Jesus because of the crowd so he run a head of the crowd and climbed a Sycomore tree to see Jesus who was going to pass that way Jesus came to that place ,he looked up and said to Zacchaeus hurry down Zacchaeus because I must stay to your house , Zacchaeus hurried down and welcomed him with great Joy all the people who saw it started grumbling "this man has gone as a guest to the home of the sinner Zacchaeus stoop up and said to the "lord listen Sir I will give a half my belongings to the poor and if I have cheated anyone I will pay back four times as much, Jesus said to him salvation has come to this house today for this man also is a descendant of Abraham , the son of Man came to seek and save the Lost **(Luke,19;2;8) Second class of rich people the bible tells us-** he has filled the hungry with good things and sent the rich away with Empty hands **(Luke,1;53)** And Jesus concluded "this is how it is with those who pile up riches for themselves but are not rich in Gods sight **(Luke,12;21)** for it by our faith that we are put right with God "It's by our confession that we are saved **(Romans,10;12)** Do you already have everything you need ? have you become rich ? have you become Kings ,even though we are not well , I wish you really were kings so that you could be Kings together with you **(1Corinthians ,4;8)** I know your troubles ,I know that you are poor but really you are rich .I know the evil things said against you by those who claim to be Jews but are not they are a group that belongs to Satan **(Revelations 2;9)Amen**

 <u>Note</u> **,Remember-** Money can buy a **Bible** but cannot buy you **Salvation** , Money can buy **Food** but cannot buy give you **Appetite**

POVERTY SIDE /EFFECTS

Our grandparents , mothers and fathers some of us were poor, but we need to change the generation of Poverty/Failure in our family, country , community , and set a new generation of Success , because poverty humiliate, leads to demotion , makes a handsome man look old, woman look ugly, Rich people are always finding new friends but the poor cannot keep the few he has **(Proverb,19;4)**The rich man make many friends but the poor is separated from the few he has (Family , spouse,) if you are poor women will be-little you and undermine you ,you are a problem because of poverty **everyone is looking for value added** , Even the relative of a poor person have no use for him no wonder he has no friends ,no matter how hard he tries he cannot win any **(Proverb,19;7)** Brothers of a poor man hate him Money gives you a voice poor man has no voice in the family meeting, he dance on the tunes of the rich, you cannot give opinion and advice in meetings , when they have a gathering they don't invite you , because you have nothing to offer , a poor man children miss a lot of opportunities, they cannot attain good education not because they don't have knowledge, It's because their parents cannot afford taking them to good schools-,There was a little town without many people in it a powerful King attacked it, he surrounded it and prepared to break through walls, someone lived there who was poor but so clever that he could have saved the town, but no one thought about him , I have always said that wisdom is better than strength but no one thinks of the poor as wise or pays any attention to what he says **(Ecclesiastes,9;14;17)** <u>Note</u> The most important thing in life is to make it to your destiny you protect your future by living righteous **,Amen**

PRAYER FOR SUCCESS AT WORK

Lord I thank you for the way you made me, for the many Gifts and Talents you placed within me ,to change the word according to your Divine wisdom ,and I trust that am the best for your work ,you deserve my Glory am grateful for each and everything you put in place for me ,people I work with, the one I like even the one I don't like, particularly or understand Lord ,I ask you that my focus on earth would be to accomplish the goals you have set forth for me ,to perform during my time on earth and the position or calling you positioned me, give me wisdom and discernment on the things job even in the midst of hostile environment ,help me to learn what you want to teach me, give me patience as you prepare me for great things, help me to do my best and always remain positive ,please quite the complains and disappointments of my heart with your perfect peace ,and allow me to trust in you with my tasks, dress me in your garment of praise add righteousness of Christ that I may bring you glory in everything I do ,allow me to know my identity to walk in your favour to seek you ,and please you more than people I work with**, Amen**

(1)Where there is Contention -**Let me be at Peace**

(2)Where there is Deceit -**Let me speak the truth**

(3)Where there is Fear -**Let me bring Faith**

(4)Where there is Darkness -**Let me bring Light**

(5) Where there is Sadness- **Let me bring Joy and happiness**

These things I ask in Jesus name, **Amen**

BELIEVER'S BOOK

THE -HOLY SPIRIT-

God is Spirit- without the Holy Spirit you cannot relate to him ,- Every time we say that I believe in the Holy -Holy Spirit we mean that we believe in the living God, able and willing to enter human personality, and change it, when we get saved the Holy spirit becomes a **Resident** (dwells in us, because you have received him)when you get filled he becomes a **President**-he controls you, so that you don't do things you used to do, Man is a Spirit who has a soul and lives in the body ,the true man identity is determined by**(a)** the Spirit man,**(b)** Inner man ,**(c)**the hidden man the holy Spirit has given us life ,he must also control our lives ,we must not be proud or irritate one another or be jealous of one another **(Galatians;5;25)** If you want to accomplish the goals and vision of your life you begin with the Spirit ,What I say is this let the Spirit direct your life and you will not satisfy the desire of the human nature **(Galatians;5;16) The fresh verses Spirit - *To set the mind on the fresh is death ,but to set the mind on the Spirit is life, and peace (Romans;8;6) For Gods kingdom is not a matter of eating and drinking but of the righteous , peace and Joy which the Holy Spirit gives* (Romans;14;17)The Holy spirit can be offended -Do not grieve the Holy Spirit -the good news bible says "Do not make the Holy Spirit sad for the Spirit of God mark Ownership on you, a guarantee that the day will come when God will set you free (Ephesians,4;30)** There two kind of Spirit possession -**(1) Evil possession Spirit -(Taken away by human desires and world desires) (2)Godly spirit -Holy spirit -**all Christians should long to posses this spirit because if you know Jesus you are filled with the Holy spirit   When the Holy Spirit enters You/Me we cannot live like the World, Holy Spirit is the break through Spirit, when he comes upon a man he began to see deliverance, he empowers us to break through, the holy Spirit is the solution to the barriers of anything, We can be filled with the Spirit numerous time -and they were all filled with the Holy Spirit and begun to speak with other in strange tongues as the Spirit was giving Utterance **(Acts;2;4)**We need the power of Holy Spirit and the word, to heal and deliver ,given to believers to minister to another ,you cannot minister to another or do the work of God without with the Holy spirit, the word of God and the holy spirit is needed to have the results ,The role of the Holy Spirit is to empower to preach the word of God ,the spirit gives life to the word, and the word becomes life, while Peter was speaking the Holy - Spirit fell on the hearers (meaning it fell on those who believed and those who were prepared for the Holy Ghost) God owned Peters words and bore witness to Peter ,words in other wards was sent by God himself - without the Spirit of the Lord the word remains, Inactive, meaningless and destructive, the attack of the Devil is easy without the Spirit ,Today many

85

people minister with only the word to preach about prosperity, blessings ,and favour because they are talented in using their natural talents ,but the Spirit is a gift and a few have this gift, The holy spirit is not complete without the word of God, and the word is not complete without the Holy Spirit to receive the holy Spirit you have **(a)**to be thirst of him, **b)**You have to be prepared to receive the holy spirit **(Colossians,3 Ephesians 5)** **(c)**You must be sure that can be ,you must desire -If you want to see your personality to be taken over by Jesus start to see your days as the last days the spirit is like Jesus The word is God speaking to you but you have to use it with the Holy Spirit to heal ,to bless and anoint ,now concerning what you wrote about the gifts from the Holy Spirit I want you to know the truth about them my brothers and sisters ,you know that while you were still heathen you were led astray in many ways to the worship of the idols, I want you to know that no one is led by Gods Spirit can say a curse on Jesus, and no one can confess Jesus is Lord without being guided by the Holy Spirit **(1Corinthians 12;1;3)**Each one as a good manager of Gods different gifts must use for the good of others, the special gift he has received from God, whoever preaches must preach Gods massage ,whoever serves must serve with the strength God gives ,so that in all things praise may be given to God through Jesus Christ to whom belong glory and power forever and ever. **amen,** Every human created in the image of God has natural talents**(Playing, football, dancing ,singing)**that make him different from others and don't confuse **talents and gifts(Encouraging , teaching)**When they finished praying the place where they were meeting was shaken they were all filled with the Holy Spirit ,and begun to proclaim Gods massage, with boldness when we gather together and pray the Holy Spirit is in the midst of us, to fill us ,to Convict us, teach us, rebuke us, lead us, give us wisdom understanding and knowledge ,guidance **(Acts;4;31)**-Even if he is a resident in our body if we don't pray we are not filled Johns father **Zechariahs** was filled with the Holy Spirit and spoke Gods massage **(Luke;1;67;Zechariahs Prophecy)** Jesus returned from the Jordan full of the Holy Spirit and was led by the Spirit into the desert where he was tempted by the Devil for 40-days in all that time he was nothing so that he was hungry when it was over **(Luke;4;1;2)**It does not mean you necessary that you have to Speak in tongues to be filled with the Holy Spirit the Holy spirit is already with you as a resident, but to be filled up you need to draw from him in Prayers ,Confession ,Repentance ,and Fasting ,Worshiping and Praise-Those who are led by the Gods Spirit are Gods Children **(Romans 8;14)**those who are born again ,What gives life is Gods Spirit -human power is of no use at all the bible say do not live as human nature tells you to instead you live as the Spirit tells you, If in fact Gods Spirit lives in you the spirit is life for you, whoever does not have the spirit of Christ does not belong to him but if Christ lives in you the spirit is life for you, because you have been put

86

right with God even though your bodies are going to die of sin**(Romans;8;9-10)**Whoever does not have the Spirit that comes from Gods Spirit such really do not understand them they are nonsense to them because their value can be judged only on spiritual basis whoever has the spirit however is able to judge the value of everything but no one is able to judge him as the scripture says who knows the mind of the Lord? Who is able to give him advice? we however who have the mind of Christ **(1Corinthians 1;13-15)**If you repent and receive Jesus as your Lord and saviour get baptised you will receive the Holy Spirit all believers have the Holy spirit as we have faith**(Acts;2;38)The Holy Spirit Is :(1)-Holy Spirit is flowing river Of Joy--**On the last and most important day of the festival Jesus stood up and said in the loud voice "whoever is thirsty should come to me and whoever believe in me should drink as the scriptures says "streams of life giving water will pour out from his inside Jesus said this about the Spirit which those who believe in him were going to receive at that time the Spirit had not been given because Jesus had not been raised to glory **(John;7;37-39)**The words I have Spoken to you brings Gods life giving Spirit yet some of you don't believe (Jesus knew from the very beginning who were the one that would betray him this is the very reason I told you that no one can come to me unless the Father makes it possible for him to do so**(Mathew 6;63;65)**He offered rest and comfort to all of you but you refused to listen to him that is why the lord is going to teach you letter by letter line by line lessons by lessons then you will stumble with every step you take you will be wounded trapped and taken Prisoner**(Isaiah;28;12 Isaiah and the drunken prophet of Judah)**Now go home and have feast share your food and wine with those who haven't enough ,today is holy to our Lord so don't be sad the joy that the Lord gives you will make you strong **(Nehemiah 8;10)**Fields don't be afraid but be joyful and glad because of all the lord has done for you **(Joel;2;21) (2)Holy Spirit is the New wine-**Do not get drunk with wine which only ruin you instead be filled with the Holy Spirit speak to one another with the words of Psalms hymns and scared songs sing hymns and psalms to the Lord with praise in your heart **(Epheians;5;18;19)**Nor does anyone pour new wine into used wineskin for the skin will burst ,the wine will pour out and the skin will be ruined Instead new wine is poured into fresh wineskins and both will keep in good conditions **(Mathew;9;17-Mark;2;22;Luke;5;37)**From Phrygia and Pamphylia from Egypt and region of Libya near Cyrene some of us from Rome both Jews and gentiles converted to Judaism and some of us are from Crete and Arabia yet all of us hear them speaking in our own language about the great things God has done they kept asking each other "what does this mean ?but others made fun of the believers saying they are drunker**(Acts;2;10;13) (3)The Holy Spirit is a Consuming Power -**they were filled with the Holy- Spirit and began to talk in other language as the Spirit Enabled them to Speak

(Acts;2;4) Was it not like a fire burning in us when he talked to us on the road and explained the scriptures to us **(Luke;24;32;The walk to Emmaus with Jesus)** I baptize you with water to show that you have repented but the one who will come after me will baptize you with holy spirit and fire he is much greater than I am and am not good enough to carry his sandals **(Mathew;3;11)** *The Holy Spirit is the revelation of the word*-when whoever the holy spirit comes who reveals the truth about God he will lead you into the truth ,he will not speak on his own authority but he will speak of what he hears and will tell you things to come **(John;16;13)**but as for you Christ has poured out his spirit on you as long as his spirit remain in you -you do not need anyone to teach you for the spirit teaches you everything and what he teaches is true not false ,obey the spirit teachings the, remain in union with Christ **(1John;2;27)***The holy Spirit is the creative power of God- The holy spirit is the yoke destroyer*-when that time comes I will free you from the power of Assyria and their yoke will no longer be a burden on your shoulders **(Isaiah;10;27)***Its is the Holy- Spirit(Person) who anoints us (not the anointing Oil)* - Then Jesus returned to Galilee and the power of the Holy spirit was with him, the news about him spread throughout all territory he taught in synagogues and was praised by everyone,**(Luke 4;14)***The Holy spirit of guidance*- Without the Holy Spirit ,We can't do nothing we are as ships without wind- We are useless Don't you know that your body is the temple of the Holy Spirit who lives in you and who was given to you by God/you do not belong to yourselves but to God he bought you for a Price, So use your body for Gods glory **(1Corinthians;6;19;20)**Christians who neglect the Holy Spirit they are like a lamp that is not plugged in because they are not connected to the   Light source of transmission, As the Sun can be seen only by its own light so Christ can be known only by his own Spirit , The Holy Spirit Voice is as loud as your willingness to listen , Holy Spirit you are welcome to this place flood this place and fill the atmosphere when we are in the tunes of the Spirit we see many Miracles happens in our life ,The Holy spirit comes where he is invited loved, where he is Expected, The primary role of the Holy Spirit is to glorify Christ ,The Holy Spirit is here trying to find somebody to work through and when it finds somebody to work through it can do good ,it is not the Strength of the body that counts but the strength of the Spirit Jesus appeared to his disciples and said "to them again Peace be with you as the father sent me so I send you then he breathed on them and said receive the Holy Spirit if you forgive peoples Sins they are forgiven if you do not forgive them they are not forgiven**(John;20;21;23)**While Peter was still Speaking the holy Spirit come down on all those who were listening to his massage The Jewish believers who had come from Joppa with Peter were amazed that God had poured out his gift of the Holy Spirit on the gentiles also for they heard them speaking in strange tongues and praising Gods greatness Peter spoke up these people have received the holy Spirit just as we also did can anyone then stop them from being Baptised with Water? In the name of Jesus Christ then they asked him to stay with them for a few days **(Acts;10;44)** In the same way all of us Whether Jews or Gentiles Whether Slave or free have been Baptised into the one body by the same Spirit and we have all been given the one Spirit to Drink **(1Corinthians;12;13)** ***Follow always the Holy Spirit directions*** Show God your faith and he will show you his faithfulness, When you are filled with the Holy Ghost you have everything you need in life ,Healing, Forgiveness ,Hope A man/Woman filled of your Spirit God cannot fill you because you are full of yourself with ,Self Pride, dishonest, and other filthy of the world ,God wants his people to be ablaze with the Holy-Spirit activity ,No amount of time front of the mirror, that will make us as attractive as does the having the Holy Spirit ,Now where the Lord is the Spirit and where the Spirit of is there is freedom **(2Corinthians 3;17)**The Spirit of the Lord has made me and the breath of the Almighty gives me Life **(Job;33;4)** Jesus said I have told this while am still with you the helper the Holy spirit whom the father will send in my name will teach you everything and make you remember all that I have told you**(John;14;25;26)**for the reasons below he will interact on with you when you are interested enough to ask question when the learning process begins your question don't bother God if they really come from a hungry heart) Jesus said ask and it shall be given to you **(Mathew;7;7)**There is only one Holy spirit but many functions -It's like electricity has many purpose ,Light, Cooking Bathing floor, Computer work, Ironing purpose. and if you put on the wrong plug you can be killed - The Holy Spirit is there to be active in your body and not to be dormant or Idle , It is ok to be inquisitive God does not want you to be passive and just accept everything that comes into your life **(a)**He wants you to question him so that you find clarity and direction **(b)**He wants you to grow by following the steps of Jesus Christ the word disciples is our translation which refers to learners or students in Jesus days disciples not only learned from the teachers lectures but observing and experiencing every life of the teacher and come time when he said to them the works that I shall do shall you do also **(John;14;12)** Peter James and John the inner circle had more intimate relationship with Jesus Christ was not because he loved them more but that he had a particular plan in mind for them what is God plan for you dear God ,I pray that your holy Spirit will teach me your wisdom will guide me and your love will move me let us be guided by the holy Spirit allow him to speak to our hearts and he will tell us God is love In life the Holy spirit ,Jesus Christ , and our Heavenly father they are all in one accord ,they speak the same language and have the same thought ,and none of them will never say anything contrary to the Bible, the Holy Spirit speaks to your/ my Spirit personally , The Holy Spirit speaks God word ,when he speaks, he speaks of Faith and build you up in Faith, he Speaks of Gods Promises because God will never fail you ,he addresses your needs so that God can supply them ,He will say what is fair ,honourable because is no respecter of Persons ;**Amen**

HOW DO WE ENCOUNTER /EXPERIENCE WITH THE HOLY SPIRIT?

HOW TO RECEIVE THE HOLY SPIRIT?

Do not get drunk with Wine, which will only ruin you instead be filled with the Spirit, instead speak to one another with the words of Psalms, hymns, and sacred songs, sing hymns and to the Lord with praise in your heart, in the name of our Lord Jesus Christ, always give thanks for everything to God the father **(Ephesians 5; 18; 20); Amen**

Through the word of God - the word and the Spirit are inseparable they are intimately linked together those whom God has set apart to become like his Son so that the Son will be the eldest brother in the family **(Romans;8;29)**So then my brothers and sister because of Gods great mercy to us I appeal to you offer yourselves as a living sacrifice to God dedicate to his services and pleasing him this is the true worship that you should offer do not be conform yourselves to the standards of this world but let God transform you inwardly by complete change of your mind then you will be able to know the will of God what is good and is pleasing to him and is perfect **(Romans;12;1;3)**Paul placed his hands on them and the holy Spirit came upon them ,they spoke in strange tongues and so proclaimed the Gods massage they were about Twelve men in all **(Acts;19;7)**The one whom God has sent speaks Gods words because God gives him the fullness of his Spirit**(John;3;34)**Jesus said to them again ,peace be with you as the Father sent me so I send you then he breathed on them and said receive the Holy Spirit **(John,20;21-22)** If you want to live ,talk ,smile ,sleep, eat ,in the spirit keep in the word and become ,abide in the word and become totally saturated with the scriptures ,the more you read the bible turn it and meditate on it over in your heart you will be filled with the Holy spirit, if you are not grounded in the word there will be nothing for the Spirit to remind of you **(John;14;26) Amen**

Through the Gospel-this hope does not disappoint us for God has poured out his love into our hearts by the means of the Holy Spirit who is a gift to us for when we were still helpless, Christ died for the wicked at that time God chose, it is difficult thing for someone to die for the righteous person ,it may even be that someone might dare to die for a good person but God has shown us how he loves us it was while we were still sinners that Christ died for us**(Romans;5;5-8)** The Spirit will be released to you to the degree ,measure and extend ,you stand in reverence honour of the word ,and if you are not filled with the holy spirit you cannot obey the word ,**Amen**

To be filled with the Spirit abide in Jesus -Eat, with Jesus sleep with Jesus dance, Jesus ,sing Jesus ,dream Jesus ,act Jesus, **Amen**

Pray to God-Speak in tongues **(Acts;2;4)**Those who speak in strange tongues do not speak to others but to God because no one understand them they are speaking truth by the power of the Spirit **(1Corinthians;14;2;but read up to verse 25)**In the same way the Holy spirit also came to help us weak as we are for we do not know we ought to pray the holy spirit himself pleads with God for us, in groans that words cannot express and God who sees into our hearts, know what the Spirit pleads with God on behalf of his people and in accordance with his will **(Romans;26;27)**Speak in tongues the Lord is my light and my salvation ,I will fear no one the lord protects me from all dangers, I will never be afraid **(Psalm 27;1)**The lord is my shepherd, I have everything I need he lets me rest in the fields of green grass and leads me to quite pools of fresh water **(Psalm23;1-6);Amen**

Ask-in prayers, And so I say to you ask and you will receive and you will find knock and the door will be opened for you for all those who ask receive and those who seek will find and the door will be opened to anyone who knocks ;Bad as you are you know how much more then will the father in heaven give the Holy Spirit to those who ask him **(Luke11;9;10;13)**This hope does not disappoint us for God has poured out his love into our heart by means of the holy Spirit who is God's gift **(Romans;5;5)**but remember my friends what you were told in the past by the apostles of our lord Jesus Christ they said to you when the last days come people will appear who will mock you people who follow their own godless desires these are the people who cause divisions who are controlled by their natural desire who do not have the Spirit but you my friends keep building yourselves up on your most sacred faith pray in the power of the Holy Spirit and keep yourselves in the love of God as you wait for our Lord Jesus Christ in his mercy to give you eternal life **(Jude 1;17;21)**For this reason I fall on my knees before the father from whom every family in heaven and on earth receives true name I

ask God from the wealth of his glory to give you power through his Spirit to be strong in your inner selves, and ,I pray that Christ will make his home in your hearts through faith I pray that you may have your roots and foundation in love so that you together with all Gods people may have the power to understand how broad and long how high and deep is Christ love and so be completely filled with the very nature of God to him who by means of his power working in us is able to do more than we can ever ask for even think of **(Ephesians 3;14;20);Amen**

Through singing and praising-Sing to yourself any spiritual songs that touch your heart, and connect to the Spirit realms make melody in your heart to the **Lord; Amen**

Speak to your heart -the heart means mans spirit ,to receive the massage with all your heart , you heart must be free, give your heart assignment control your heart , a pure heart does not hold grudges past pains -,Listen to the Lord with your heart without a heart that holds offenses or pains of the past if you can control your heart the sky is the limit the Spirit start moving when you start speaking to yourself , the fruitful prayer is the one which comes from the heart ,speak to yourself , in hymns songs and Psalms, **Amen**

Through the community of the church- while they were serving the Lord and fasting the holy Spirit said to them set a part for me Barnabas and Saul to do the work which I have called them **(Acts ;13;2)**

Thank Giving -thank God for all he has done for you- Instead of blaming and complaining I praise you Lord because you have saved me and kept my enemies from gloating over me I cried to you for help, O lord my God and healed me you kept me away from the grave I was on my way to the depth below but you restored my life **(Psalm, 30; 1-3); Amen**

Through-Gifts/gifting -The Spirit gives one person a massage full of Wisdom while to another person the same Spirit gives a massage full of Knowledge**(1Corinthians;12;7-8)**In other wards the Holy Spirit distributes all those gifts -he alone decides which gift each person should have **(1Corinthians;12;11);Amen**

Repent of sins- if you repent and receive Jesus as your lord and saviour get baptised you will receive the Holy Spirit**(Acts;2;38)**before people were baptized with water but we hear in the book of Acts John says in the few years you will be baptized with the holy Spirit**(Acts;1;5)Jesus was baptised by John the Baptist-**Repent means change of one mind or change of your flesh desires to Godly ways of doing things)Peter said to them each one of you must turn away from your sins and be baptizes in the name of Jesus Christ so that your Sins will be forgiven and also become Gods people when you heard the massage the good news that brought you **Salvation** you believed in Christ and God put his stamp on ownership on you by giving you the Holy Spirit he had promised the Spirit is the guarantee that we shall receive what God promised his people and this assure us that God will give complete freedom to those who are his ,let us praise his glory **(Ephessians;1;13)**And you will receive the Gods gift the holy Spirit for God promise was made to you and your children and to all who were far away all those God calls to himself Peter made his appeal to them and with many other words he urged them by saying save yourself from the punishment**(Acts;2;38;42);Amen**

Tell to others how easy it was- by telling them what happened to you pray for them so they can be healed and receive gods spirit (Mark; **16; 15; 20); Amen**

Through his Sovereign control over circumstances -I will stay here in Ephesus until the day of Pentecost there is a real opportunity here for great worthwhile work even though there are many opponents **(1Corinthians; 16; 8); Amen**

In our Spirit Acts -Many ambitions have been to proclaim good news ,in places where Christ has not been heard of .so as not to build on a foundation laid by someone else **(Romans; 15; 20)**

Through the holy Communion; Amen

Expect God to keep working in your life -may have been healed of Illness and addiction and other problems of all sort at the time of receiving the Holy spirit when you receive the Holy spirit you receive the love of God and the power of God to help you and heal your life and others look at my hands and my feet and see that it is I myself feel me and you will know the ghost does not have flesh and bones as you can see I have**(Luke;24;39)**And when the holy spirit comes upon you- will be filled with power and you will be witnessed in Jerusalem in all Judea and Samaria **(Acts 1;8);Amen**

Live a Christian life - (Gal5; 22; 25 Rom; 12; 9; 21); Amen

;Afterwards I will pour out my Spirit and Everyone your sons and daughters will proclaim my massage, you Old people you will have dreams and your younger people will see Visions, at that time, I will pour out my Spirit, even on servants both Men and Women **(Joel;2;28;29);Amen**

QUESTION?

HOW YOU CAN LEARN TO FELLOWSHIP WITH THE HOLY SPIRIT?

Linger in his presence, share your heart with him, speak affectionately slowly ,softly, and briefly with short phases, pause listen to his small voices, journal your thoughts and what you believe is saying to you

The Formula = Trust,

Thank him for his presence-Sing to the lord all the world ,worship the lord with Joy, come before him with happy songs, acknowledge the Lord that is God, he made us and we belong to him, we are his people, we are his flocks ,Enter the temple gates with thanks giving, go into his courts with praise ,the Lord is good ,his love is Eternal and his faithfulness lasts for Ever**(Psalm ;100;1-5) Amen**

Release revelations- ,ask him to reveal to you his heart and Open your Eyes to the realms of his glory **(Ephesians 1;17;19)**Pray to the Holy Spirit to open your eyes to see the realms of Gods glory open the eyes of my understanding give me the Spirit of wisdom; **Amen**

Use me-ask the Holy Spirit to use you more put, your sail up and expect him to use your everyday -pray thank you Holy Spirit for realising your Power through my life use me fully for your glory **Amen**

Strength me -ask him to strength your mind will Emotions, so that you may contain more of his wisdom fruits and gifts **(Ephessians;3;16)**thank you for your love, patience, joy, Increase my capacity to contain more of wisdom fruits and gifts **Amen**

Teach me- about Gods word and ways make me a vessel -Ask him to manifest his leadership in Every area of your life ,he will order your steps and give you new ideas the helper the Holy spirit whom the father will send in my name will teach you everything and make you remember all that I have told you **(John;14;26)**When however the Spirit comes who reveals the truth about God he will lead you into all the truth he will not speak on his own Authority but he will speak of what he hears and he will tell you things to come, he will give me glory because he will take what I say and tell it to you ,all that my Father has is mine- that is why I said that the Spirit will take what I give him and tell it to you **(John;16;13-15)**Pray Holy Spirit I need you more than the word I say, more than the Air I breath, more than the food I eat , more than the prayers I say, more than the song I sing, more than friends and parents, circumstance, more than my understanding ,Let me see what you see, feel what you feel release it with your power through my life**; Amen**

THE WORK OF THE HOLY SPIRIT;

The Holy Spirit work for those who are thirsty to receive him, and desperate for him: the Spirit is- Pure Gentle ,Wise, Holy, Truth is like Jesus and father **Amen**

(1)The Spirit of Truth -When the spirit of truth reveals its self will guide you and show you the truth The Spirit speaks the truth not facts Jesus said there Spirit of lies and are very easy to notice they never agree with that Jesus is lord Never agree that Jesus is the only way The spirit of Truth agree that Jesus is lord For as many are led by the spirit of God these are the sons of God**(Romans;8;14)**"However when the Spirit of truth has come he will guide you into all the truth**(John;16;13)**He guides us in the truth whatever he shall hear that shall speak and shall show you things to come-The bible says the truth will make you free-but you have to first understand exactly what the truth is before it can work for you to make you free If you allow the realms of the Holy Spirit to enter into you he will allow you to see things from his point of view so you can see what the real truth is on many different matters in your life and once you get to know the real truth is on certain matter you may be dealing with then you will know how to properly handle it ,If God calls you to be a Pastor in this life but he doesn't guide you how to reach that specific goal then you will never make it, you will face many challenges and the only Holy Spirit who will know exactly what steps you will need to make it into your Divine calling ,the Holy spirit will not only guide you into your Divine calling for the lord also guide you as to who God will want you to Marry and people to favour you in the ministry, rather than Man and his reasoning ,We have a supernatural guide in the form of God indwelling Holy Spirit ,You/I can Preach trust but only the Holy-Spirit can impart the truth, the Spirit speaks about your Potentials when the Spirit Speaks he Increases your confidence in God- when he speaks to you /me peace will cloud my mind not confusion the devil is the Author of confusion **(2)The Holy Spirit anoints us with his Divine Power**-It will tell you where you going and where you it's our **GPS** calling us for him God is calling you to be evangelist Teacher Pastor Doctor an attorney the holy spirit will anoint you with his divine power so you can be good in a specific calling and this will be Gods Divine power flowing and operating through you not your own limited and imperfect power God can anoint you with his Divine power to witness to unbelievers ,to cast out demons to heal to be a good spouse for your marriage mate to disciple and mentor newborns to be a good parent to children that's why he is called the helper and there is nothing that he cannot give you a hand on if you will be open to receive this kind of help from him "For the kingdom of God is not in word but in power **(1Corinthians;4;20)**"For our gospel did not come to you in word only but also in power and in the holy Spirit **(1Thessollonians;1;5)**But you shall receive power when the Holy Spirit has come upon and you shall be a witness to me in Jerusalem ,and all in Judea and Samaria and to the end of the world **(Acts;1;8)** **(3))Gods Spirit joins himself to our Spirits to declare that we are Gods children** -Enables God children to address him as Abba the spirit you have received do not make you slaves so that you live in fear rather the Spirit you received bring brought about Your adoption to Son ship and by him we cry **Father -Abba** the Spirit himself testifies with our spirit That we are Gods Children **(Romans;8;15;16)** because you are his son God sent the Spirit of His son into our hearts the Spirit who calls out Abba *Father* so you are no longer a slave but Gods children and since you are Gods Children God has made you also an heirs **(Galatians;4;6)**For the eyes of the Lord run to and fro throughout the whole earth to show himself strong on behalf of those whose heart is royal to him **(2Chronicles16;9)**"but the people of God who know their God shall be strong and carry out great exploits(**Daniels 11;32**)"behold I give you the authority to trample on serpents and scorpions and all over all the power of the enemy and nothing shall by any means hurt you(**Luke**;**10;19**)In mighty signs and wonders by the Power of the Spirit of God(**Romans;15;19**)"truly the signs of an apostle were accomplished among you with all perseverance in signs and wonders and mighty deeds **(2Corinthians;12;12)**God also bearing witness both with signs and wonders with various miracles and Gifts of the Holy Spirit **(Hebrews;2;4)** "and they went out and preached everywhere the lord working with them and confirming the word through the accompanying signs

(**Mark16;20**)"and with great power the Apostles gave witness to the resurrection of The lord Jesus and great grace was upon them all (**Acts;4;33**)"but by the anointing which you have received from him abides in you (**1John;;2;27**)but you have an anointing from the Holy one and you know all things (**1John 2;20**)"Then the fear come upon every soul and many wonders and signs were done through the apostles (**Acts;2;43**)"this is the word of the Lord to Zerubbabel "not by mighty nor by power but by the Spirit says the lord of Host (**Zechariah;4;6**) God anointed the Apostles with his divine power he can do the same with you so that you can be able to fully accomplish the assignment he has for you ,**(4)The Holy Spirit is our Personal Teacher**-So we can learn everything the lord will want to teach us in life Not only The Holy Spirit open up the Bible for us and help us to understand what all the different scriptures and verses mean and how they can be applied to our lives but he can also give us knowledge on anything in our lives **Satan-**is always trying to take you away from your loving God but don't accept listen to your loving teacher the Holy spirit -Who will bring you close to your Father God (**c**) A Good teachers goal is to create in you (**1**) hunger for knowledge (**2**) An ability to seek out more understand things why they happen why they will happen and why they happened when he is no longer around (**3**)A good teacher wants you to put what you have learnt into practice *You say how can I really know if I have* **learnt?** Continue to live Christ as he taught you but as for you Christ has poured out his spirit on you as long as his Spirit remains in you do not need anyone to teach you for his Spirit will teach you everything and what he teaches is true not false obey the spirit teachings then and remain in union with Christ (**1John;2;27**)So when I came to you I was weak and trembled all over with Fear and my teachings and massage were not delivered with skilful words of human wisdom but with convincing proof of the **Power of Gods Spirit ;*Your Faith then does not rest on human wisdom but on Gods Power*** ,(**1Corinthians;2;3-5**)Yet I do Proclaim a massage of Wisdom to those who are Spiritually mature ,but it is not the Wisdom to this World or to the powers that rules this World,- Powers that are losing their Powers, The wisdom I proclaim is Gods hidden wisdom which he had already chose for our glory even before the world was made , none of the rulers of this world knew this wisdom ,if they had know it they would not have crucified the Lord of glory, However as the scriptures say "What no one ever say or heard "What no one ever thought could happen is the very thing God prepared for those who love him-but it was to us that God made know his secret by means of his Spirit the Spirit searches everything even the hidden depths of Gods purpose it is only the Spirit within the people that knows all about them, in the same way Only Gods Spirit knows about him we have not received this worlds Spirit instead we have received the Spirit sent by God ,so that we may know all that God has given us ,so then we do not speak in words taught by human Wisdom but in words taught by the Spirit as we Explain Spiritual truth to those who have the Spirit, Whoever does not have the Spirit cannot receive the gifts that comes from Gods Spirit ,such people really do not understand them ,they are nonsense to them, Because they value can be judged only on Spiritual basis, Whoever has the Spirit however is able to judge the value of everything but no one is able to judge him as the Scriptures says "Who knows the mind of God ?Who is able to give him advice? We however have the mind of Christ (**1Corinthians,2;6;16**)- All that belongs to the father is mine (**John;16;15**)That is why I said the Spirit will receive from me what I will make known to you the Holy Spirit who is your wonderful teacher wants you to search for Gods directions he does not want you to be Passive and simply accept what is being taught to you or what comes into your life he wants you to turn to his word for wisdom to find Divine solutions to human problems you facing in today -today life he wants you to stand on his words instead of lying down and start saying I guess this just things to be Gods word the Bible is a Weapon and true direction that will never allow you to go a wrong side it is everything in life you need to win and manage your life mediate in it day and night morning afternoon and evening do according to what is written in it for then you will have Victory- Success, be Blessed (**Joshua 1;8**) Each time you come to the Bible ask the Holy Spirit to open the eyes of your heart , Holy Spirit guides you to study the word ,and seek understanding it - God wants you us to grow in his knowledge in this life, he wants us to grow in his knowledge because you cannot grow spiritually grow in the Lord unless you first seek after the knowledge that will cause this spiritual growth to occur in the first place, The holy spirit needs something to work with to grow with to spiritually grow us in this life and that something is knowledge and that knowledge is the word of God, We need both the Word and the Spirit working together to cause any kind of true Spiritual growth to occur in this life "But God has revealed them to us through his Spirit for the spirit searches all things yes the deep thing of God for What man knows the things of man except the Spirit of the man Which is in him ?Even so no one knows the things of God except the Spirit of God ,now we have received not the Spirit of the world, but the Spirit of God who is from God that we might know the things that have been freely Given to us by God, In life ask Gods spirit to guide you, give you wisdom to know, to know things you don't know ,and reveal to you the thoughts of God in your life ,Happy are those who finds Wisdom and the man who gains understanding for her proceeds are better than the profits of Silver and her gain than fine Gold she is more precious than Rubies and all the things you may desire cannot compare with her .Length of the days is in her right hand in her left hand riches and honour her ways are ways of pleasantness and all her paths are peace she is a tree of life to those who take hold of her and happy are those who retain her **(Proverb;3;13)**How much better is to get Wisdom than Gold and to get understanding is to be chosen rather than silver **(Proverb;16;16**There is Gold and multitude of Rubies but the Lips of knowledge are precious Jewel**(Proverb;20;15**)If you start seeking the knowledge of God for your life the Holy Spirit will also start to Increase your intelligence levels and when you add more and more knowledge into your mind and brain you will be able to get smarter and more intelligence the mind and brain are like muscle -use it or lose it **(5)The Spirit of Wisdom and Knowledge** -Only the Spirit can reveal to you knowledge and understanding of things and how to be handled when you are led by the -he takes what Jesus wants you to hear and know and reveals it to you - Holy Spirit you will get to know how to apply Knowledge effectively he opens your understanding about things that are to come-The Spirit does not only inspires the scriptures ,he also caused it to be inspiring all the scriptures are God breathed and is useful for ,teaching ,rebuking, correcting and training righteousness **(2Timothy3;16)** Whatever the Spirit does will line up with scriptures because the Spirit inspired scriptures to begin with the two will always agree On earth the Holy spirit is the most busiest person but many people are ignorant about his work and doubt of him, The spirit of God lead people to the Word of God to submit to the word of God we are living in the age of Spirit today yet most people are ignorant about the spirit and most churches don't know him and don't know the Holy Ghost is the only person you hear at the end of your trinity prayers **(Father Son and Holy Spirit)**People don't know his work personality, Characters and his assignment what he was what he is assigned to do if you don't agree with the Holy spirit it means you don't agree with Jesus because Jesus Christ talk about Holy spirit and all his works the holy spirit Teach you and Guide you ,Helps you, and Comforts , Anoint you with Divine Power ,Regenerate or Human Spirit, Rebuke you Convicts you ,but winds don't if you don't believe in the Holy spirit it means that Jesus was a liar ,When he spoke about him about someone who will come after him It means that Jesus promised something that will not happen ,if you don't believe in the Holy spirit as a person who has an identity better disagree with Jesus Holy spirit has names And everyone knows names describe personality and description of Characters Once the Holy spirit enters in on the side of each believer, some very powerful and profound things will start to happen in their lives, if they will open themselves up some works The Holy spirit has names why? because they are other spirits which are not Holy even the demons have names -Once you understand what the Holy Spirit can do you won't live a single day without his help**(6)The Holy Spirit exalts Jesus-**the Spirit has come that we might be deeply impressed with the person of Jesus Christ and go away excited about his work the gifts are necessary to thrust us into the mission and work of Jesus the purpose of The spirit is to exalt Jesus and let him be lifted Before the death of Jesus Christ the Holy Spirit could not enter into human body Jesus and God had all the Power, Jesus Spoke about the Holy Spirit as a gift from the father and Jesus goes ahead to say **"For John-Baptised in water**, but in the few days you will be Baptised with the Holy Spirit- *The Holy Spirit is important in Baptism***(7)The Holy Spirit has the work of drawing the unsaved sinner to Jesus**-he has the power to make us the unsaved to find and accept him as our personal lord and saviour so we can be truly saved and born again The Holy Spirit Testify of Jesus not of his own self and the reason why he does so is so that he can get as many people saved as he can The Holy Spirit and his power is right there by your side when you step out to witness to other unsaved people in life we are not alone when and we are reminded to be open to be used by the Lord to witness to other people so God can personally use you to save as many people as he can before it becomes too late on earth we have a short life time and God command us to Win Souls as possible about the gospel of our Lord and Savoir Jesus Christ and the Holy Spirit is too Eager and willing to work with us together so we can win souls on this ministry of wining souls and bringing Back the lost to God, It's the Holy Spirit work to lead us to our lord and Saviour Jesus Christ "But when the helper Comes Whom I Shall send to you from the Father the Spirit of the truth who Proceeds from the father he will testify of me ,and you also bear witness because you have been with me from the beginning **"(John 15;26-27)**"No one can come to me unless the father who sent me draws him and I will raise him at the last day **(John,6;44)**"And no one can say Jesus is lord except by the Holy Spirit (**1Corithians12;3**)While Peter was still speaking these words the Holy Spirit Fell Upon all those who heard the word **(Acts;10;44)**These verses tells us that God draws the unsaved sinners to his Son through the Holy Spirit-**(8)The Holy Spirit provides conviction of Sin**- To all people believers and unbelievers he has to show us the errors of our ways ,and that we are all sinners in the eyes of God unbelievers they cannot get saved unless they are first convicted by the Holy Spirit, if they cannot see that they are sinners in the eyes of God then they will have no reason why they get saved, and accept what Jesus done for them ,with his sacrificial death on the cross, Born again we all need the conviction of the holy Spirit time to time, day after day ,year after year, months after months ,so we can be shown the errors we have made in life ,and when the Holy spirit does convict us from time to time it's of our own Advantage, if he doesn't show us where we are going wrong we could easily get knocked off the path that God has set up for our lifetime , What the Holy Spirit Convict of us is the Sin, Believers and unbelievers Every Single Man and Woman, has sinned and fallen short of His Glory, Every single person on earth needs to receive the conviction of the Holy Spirit, so we can know the true truth regarding our fallen sinful state before the Lord "nevertheless ,I tell you the truth it is your advantage that I go away for ,if I do not go away the helper will not come to you, but if I depart I will send him to you and when he has come he will convict the world of sin and righteousness and of judgement of Sin, because they don't believe in me of righteousness because I go to my father and you see me no more of judgement, because the ruler of this world is judged **(John;16;7;11)** When the Holy Spirit comes he will convict the world concerning sin and Righteousness and Judgement, Invite the Holy Spirit to lead your decisions and emotions today, we follow, So that we can be very good at the position that God will be, Those whose heart are pure are temple of the Holy spirit, Do not follow your heart always follow the convictions of the Holy Spirit, As Oxygen is to blood so is the holy Spirit to Your Spiritual walk when you doubt in your salvation he will confirm that you are truly Gods redeemed child**(Romans;8;16)**When the Holy Spirit speaks he convicts of Sins never condemn you because his passion is to correct you and the holy Spirit speaks to you with love, He speaks of your Future not your Past, **(9)The Holy Spirit regenerates Us-(meaning of regeneration (Radical Spiritual change) In** which God brings an individual from a condition of Spiritual defeat and death to a renewed condition of life ,An Act of God through the Holy Spirit resulting in an inner personal resurrection from Sin to A new life in Jesus, -Spiritual reborn -Spiritual rebirth starting a new life -Being restored after a decline to a low class New birth begetting a new life Renewal of Moral and Spiritual nature ;The rebirth of the human Spirit to a restored relationship with God Renewed to life and salvation by faith in God) when the Holy Spirit Speaks to you, he gives you wisdom to your mind and Emotions Speaks to your heart ; God had formed man from the dust of the ground and breathed into his nostril the breath of life and man became a living being now ,Jesus breathed a new order of life into his disciples (Eternal life) After the holy Spirit has entered on unbeliever and has led them into eternal salvation through Jesus Christ the next thing to do is enter in on the inside of their human spirits he will then regenerate their human spirit and once have been full regenerated they will now be truly born again in the lord The holy spirit regenerates everyone who is willing to accept Jesus as their personal lord and saviour "But when the kindness and the love of God our Saviour towards man appeared not by works of righteousness which we have done but according to his mercy he saved us through the washing of regeneration and renewing of the holy Spirit whom he poured out on us through Jesus Christ our Saviour that having been justified by his grace we should become heirs according to the hope of Eternal life**(Titus3;4;7)**any time you bring unbeliever to Christ they receive the Holy Spirit on the inside of Then and the Holy Spirit Get down into their Spirit and Fully regenerate them and God is rejoicing a reward is waiting on you in turn**(10)The Holy Spirit help us draw closer to God**-After being born Again and the Holy Spirit has now entered into our Human Spirit and fully regenerated us then he start to draw us Closer to the Lord and have a intimacy relationship with God after accepting Jesus as our Personal Saviour we get to know both him and God the father much better and the Holy Spirit himself will help draw much closer to both of them Through the Holy Spirit we have direct access to Both God and Jesus in heaven and it is by the Holy Spirit that you will have direct access to both God and Jesus the Holy Spirit will also help work you closer to both God and Jesus in your own personal relationship with them "For through him we both have access by one Spirit to the father (**EPhessians;2;18**)"And by his we know that that he abides in us by the Spirit whom he has given us"**(1John;3;24)**"No one has seen God at anytime if we love one another God abides in us and his love has been perfect in us By this we know that we abide in him and he has given us of his Spirit **(1John,4;12)**We have direct access to God the father by one Spirit the lord abides in us by the Spirit he abides in us because he has Given us his Holy Spirit in other words God cannot abide in us unless the Holy Spirit is living on the side of us he does not only live on the side of us but is also able to connect us to both God and Jesus in heaven and due to this Divine connection that he has now set up between us and the Lord both God and Jesus are now abiding in us just like the Holy Spirit is**(11)The Holy Spirit will sanctify us**-in the Lord When you get saved and welcome Jesus as your saviour that the beginning God will accept you to spiritually grow in his knowledge and grace once you grow Spiritually he is going to Sanctify you he will set you apart for himself he will start to renew your mind he will transform you into the express of image of his son Jesus The bible tells us that God is the potter and we are his clay When God start this process of Sanctification he does it by the Word and the Holy Spirit as we read the word want to Change you and the Holy Spirit will start the process and the kind of the person God wants you The Holy Spirit will real move into this sanctification process and what you have to do is to give him something to work with and this something is knowledge and faith and this knowledge can be obtained by reading the bible if you don't spent time reading the bible what you want God to change into you then the Holy Spirit is not going to do anything into your life and sanctify you to the degree that God would like in this life time that why your true sanctification is accomplished by both the word and the Spirit working together "because God from the beginning chose you for salvation through sanctification by the spirit and belief in the truth **(2Thessalonians;2;13)** and such were some of you but you were washed but you were sanctified but you were justified in the name of Jesus and by the spirit of our God **(1Corinthians;6;11)** "For if you live according to the flesh you will die but if you live by the Spirit you put to death the deeds of The body you will live **(Romans;8;13)**Elect according to the to the fore knowledge of God the father in sanctification of the Spirit for obedience and sprinkling of the blood of Jesus Christ grace to you and peace be multiplied **(1Peter;1;2)** God will sanctify you by his word in the following Verses "Sanctify them by your truth your word is the truth **(John;17;17)**that he might sanctify and cleanse it with the washing of water by the word that he might present himself a glorious church not having a spot or wrinkle or any such thing but that it should be Holy and without blemish **(Ephesians**;**5;26)**You are already clean because of the word which I have spoken to you**(John**;**15;3)"**and receive with meekness the implanted word which is able to save your soul**(James;1;21)** 2how can a young man cleanse his way? by taking heed according to your word with my whole heart I have sought you oh let me not wander from your commandments your word I have hidden in my heart that I might not sin against you blessed are you O lord teach me your statutes**(Psalm 119;9;12)**for this reason we also thank God without ceasing because when you received the word of God which you heard from us you welcomed it not as the word of men but as it is in the word of God which also effectively works in you who believe **(1Thessalonians;2;13)the** Holy Spirit lives in us we are charged to be filled with the Spirit we need our full consent and Cooperation before he will do his work at a times it can be painful once God starts to take out the bad behaviours that he doesn't want in us friends live your sometime even family members **(12)The Holy Spirit help us in our Prayers-**Believers are exhorted to pray in the spirit "On all occasions with all kinds of prayers and request with thus in mind be alert and always keep praying for the lords people pray also for me that whenever I speak words may be given me so that I will fearlessly make known the mystery of the gospel**(Ephesians;6;18;20)**In difficult situation when you don't know what to say he will give you the right words to say at the right time **(Acts,1;8)**Do not get drunk on wine which leads to debauchery instead be filled with the Spirit Speaking to one another with, Psalms, Hymns and songs, from the spirit ,sing and make music from your heart to the Lord**(Ephesians;5;18;20)** Sometimes we don't know what to pray for the Holy Spirit, makes intercession for all us believers as we have different needs in our day lives, since the holy spirit is God and Lord himself he will be able to see perfectly into our future and what we will need from our Lord ,before we will know it, the Holy spirit is a head of us and intercede s us to the God the father ,There is time to be quite in the presence of the lord a time to hear the word of God ,be still and know that am God**(Psalm;46;10)**but there is also time to praise the Lord with an un praised voices ,there is time to say from the depth of the inner man Hallelujah For God almighty reigns **(Revelation;19;6)**the Spirit incites us to that kind of worship ,The Holy Spirit inspires us to pray in Tongues "and they were filled with the holy Spirit and they began to speak in other tongues as the spirit gave them utterance**(Acts;2;4;**holy spirit comes at Pentecost as they were together) "For I pray in tongues my spirit prays but my mind is unfruitful so what shall I do? I will pray with my spirit but, I will also pray with my understanding ,I will sing with my Spirit but, I will also sing with my understanding**(1Corinthians;14;14;15)**"Likewise the Spirit also help in our weakness for we do not know what we should pray for we ought but the Spirit himself makes intercession for us with groaning which cannot be uttered now he who searches the hearts knows what the mind of the Spirit is because he makes intercession for the saints according to the will of God**(Romans;8;26-27)**The holy Spirit helps us to know what to pray for how to word your prayers to God what scripture verses to use in your prayers the timing factor when to pray for something the correct battle strategies to use the correct angle and point of view to use with the lord How many time to pray for the request how long to stay with a prayer request To call other believers to pray in agreement with you or not whether there is anything else that you will need to do on your end before God will grant the prayer request if you can be a friend to the Holy spirit in your personal prayers to the lord you will increase your chances of getting your personal prayers answered by him we need to learn to pray in the Spirit especially on some of our heavier prayer request to God the father**(13)The Holy Spirit is our helper and comforter in life** - He does not only help you in smaller thing that occurs to us but also in bigger things that you will need help in the Spirit helps how to solve bigger problems and minor problems at home misplaced item school problems or work place problems we are really helpless in getting accurate guidance and direction unless the Spirit works with us ,The spirit is present and active in our life, especially when we are making vital decisions that are going to affect us for years to come ,when we open ourselves to God the Spirit works in us ,with power and we can rest in his creative work ,we need plenty of comforting in life from time to time due to all the tragedy and misfortune that can hit us at anytime ,helping and comforting the difference is small the bible says "And I will pray the father and he will give you another helper that may abide with you forever**(John;14;16)** "nevertheless I tell you the truth it is to your advantage that I go away for if I do not go away the helper will not come to you but if I depart I will send him to you **(John;16;7)** "but when the helper comes whom I shall send to you from the father the Spirit of the truth who proceeds from the father he will testify of me **(John;15;26)**"but when the helper the holy spirit ,whom the father will send in my name, he will teach you all things and bring to your remembrance all things that I have said to you**(John;14;26)**The Holy Spirit will give life to our mortal bodies ,this is the work of the Holy Spirit that is yet to come ,but the promise of that work is connected incredibly with the resurrection of Christ himself, if the spirit of him who raised Jesus from the dead is living in you he who raised Christ from the dead will also give you life to your mortal bodies ,through the spirit who lives in You **(Romans;8;11) (14) The Spirit Of promises-**

When two or more come together and whatever you agree on will be given to you The spirit of Promises will give it to you the word of God is so rich it gives the answer Water your Word in life speak life and good about your life not negativity When you come to pray in Church come with Answers the Holy spirit is the work of God, Set people free is called the Spirit of Grace he takes the grace of God and brings it to us he judges the wicked he has the power of God release the energy Of God he convicts you other than to be judged ***The Lords servants*** God has called you and given you power to see that Justice is done on Earth through you I will make a covenant with all people through you I will bring light to the nations you will Open the eyes of the blind and set free those who sit in the dark Prison**(Isaiah 42;6;7)**Holy spirit is the Spirit of Burning many times we feel something inside us and burning into us to do something like Singing in the Spirit in church above what you can control and some time when the Spirit is with us the Preacher of the Day he feels it within him it is called the Spirit of Fire)**(15)The Holy Spirit gives us Gifts**-To receive them you should go to God in sincere and heart -felt prayers and ask him to release them to you any time, some are can be actual lifesavers as sometimes the Holy Spirit will manifest these gifts to save some one life "but the manifestation of the Spirit is given to each one for the profit of all "for to one is given the word of wisdom through the Spirit to another the word of Knowledge through the same Spirit, to another faith by the same Spirit to another gift of healing by the same Spirit to another the working of miracles ,to another prophecy to another discerning of spirits to another different kinds of Tongues to another interpretation of Tongues but one and the same spirit works all these distributing to each other individually as he wills **(1Corinthians;12;7;11)**We have divine attributes and qualities that will be coming to us direct from the holy Spirit not from ourselves and this will be God, love ,joy, peace ,that will start to flourish and operate in us not our limited and imperfect ,love, joy and peace ,**The fruits of the Spirit that the bible talk about are ,Love, Joy ,Peace ,Endurance, Kindness -goodness -Faithfulness Gentleness ,Self -control (Galatians;5;22)** The purpose of the Spiritual gifts is to build up, edify-knowledge , exhort ,encourage and comfort the church and many other gifts are needed in the church , Once this kind of Divine qualities start flowing through your life from the Holy Spirit then you begin to become the truly sanctified saint that God is calling you to become in him in this life ,In the Old Testament God said I will give you a new heart and put a new spirit within you, I will take the heart of stone out of your fresh, and give you a heart of fresh, I will put my Spirit within you and make you to walk in my statutes, and you will keep my judgements and do them **(Ezekiel,36;26)**God was talking about Salvation in Jesus Christ receiving of holy Spirit ,and once this occurs their hard heart of the stone was going to be replaced by the heart of the flesh, A heart of flesh is a tender and compassionate type of heart we need the Holy Spirit to tenderize our hearts ,so the Bible tells us in the latter days, that the love of many will be growing cold and when the love of many grows cold, their hearts are going to turn into the hearts of stone which will be the heart of no love for God, Each other, Compassion, but for themselves ,The Holy Spirit has a major role to play here to turn our hard hearts into the heart of the fresh, so that we can start to feel sympathy and Compassion for other people- When you miss the opportunity to have the Holy Spirit in your life you miss a lot, he is powerful than the, **United nation Organization -European Union and African union(16)-The Holy Spirit seals Believers**-His presence in your life is a mark that you belong to God the holy Spirit is the down payment that guarantees that you are completely Christ or Christ owns (**2Corinthians1;22**)And you also became Gods people when you heard the true massage the Good news that brought you to salvation you believed in Christ and God put his stamp of Ownership on you by giving you the Holy spirit he had promised The Spirit is a Guarantee that we shall receive What God has promised his people and Assures us that God will give complete freedom to those who are his let us praise his glory (**Ephesians;1;13;14**)you when you have sinned it's certainly not the devil who is telling you that you are Gods Child there is still a small voice that says "Even though you have failed there is mercy God loves you That's the Holy Spirit whose acting because he has sealed you and has given a deposit of his presence ,The Spirit really has many functions HIS Essential in prophesying of the coming of Jesus Sealed the Baptism of Jesus Mary Conceived Jesus Christ by the Holy Spirit, His crucification was in the Spirit was raised by the Spirit and many On Earth seek of him and then you will find knock and then the door will be open up for you, if you do not seek you will never find their Spiritual laws that are operating in the Gods kingdom and if we do not put effort to seek after God and all his ways his not going to resurrect us back to his kingdom ,the more you seek of God the more he will come and seek after you, and once he starts showing himself to you in a variety of areas and ways you will never remain the same and your life the quick the better -If you find out quickly that God wants to walk .talk work and fellowship with you in life you will enjoy his blessings, guide you ,help you ,teach you, he will Model you, and shape you, into a new image through the sanctifying work of the Holy Spirit, and everyone close to you will begin to wonder those who used to laugh at you will have no one to laugh at -The Holy Spirit here so that he could help us in our walks and Divine destinies with him if there is one thing that can cause you to take off like a rocket at a high speed in your own life walk with the lord ,It has to be your effort to be used and making direct contact with the Holy Spirit - We need to be open to this ministries that is capable of giving to you and they are all ready available to you if they are will to go to God the father in sincere heartfelt prayers and ask him to open up this realm for them because God uses the available committed and ready to be used The Holy Spirit does not do things Twice Amen only the Holy Spirit of the lord that can transform us; **Amen**

WE MUST KNOW:

It's only by the Holy Spirit we are born again "Scriptures say that unless one is born again of water and the Holy Spirit he cannot Enter the kingdom of God **(John; 3; 5); Amen**
No one can say Jesus is Lord -Except in Holy Spirit **(1Corinthians 12; 3)**
Only by the Holy Spirit ,we can put to death the deeds of the body - and without the work of the Holy Spirit we perish **(Romans; 8; 13), Amen**
It's through the Holy Spirit we can pursue our Salvation-We must thank God at all the time for you brothers and sisters you whom the Lord loves for God chose you as first to be saved by the holy spirits power to make you his holy people and by your faith in the truth**(2;Thessalonians 2;13)try to be at peace with Everyone and try to live a holy life because no one will see God without it(Hebrews;12;14)**it is only possible through sanctification by the Spirit
The Holy Spirit is the Spirit of Wisdom - and ask the God of our lord Jesus Christ who will make you wise and reveal God to you, so that you will know him **(Ephessians;1;17)**In this life without his ministry we will waste our live on trifle without this Spirit of Wisdom, Each believer is given the Manifestation of the Spirit, for the common Good **(1Corinthians; 12; 7)-(**The Spirit presence is shown in some way in each person for the good of all);**Amen**
If the Spirit of him who raised Jesus from the dead dwells in you-He who raised Jesus from the dead will also give you life to your mortal bodies through his Spirit who dwells in you
Without the Holy Spirit
(a)No new birth
(b)No Victory over Sin
(c)No Spiritual Wisdom
(d)No Spiritual Gifts
(e) No resurrection
I will ask the father and he will give you another helper who will stay with you forever, he is the spirit who reveals the truth about God, the world cannot receive him ,because it cannot see him ,or know him but you know him ,because he remains with you, and is in you **(John 14;16;18)** Pray for the Holy Spirit to come into your life to do what he can do **,like a consuming fire)** with fresh oil anointing ,healing ,and move mountains in our Family, Business, Ministry**, Amen**
THE PURPOSE OF BAPTISM OF THE HOLY SPIRIT

- When you are Baptised in the holy Spirit you have the Authority to deal with the devil heal the sick, and do the Impossibilities ,**Amen**
- **Demonstrate and manifest the work of God-** And my teaching and massage were not delivered with skilful words of human wisdom, but with the convincing proof of the power of Gods spirit Your faith then does not rest on human wisdom but on Gods wisdom (**1Corinthians2;4-5;**demonstration-Power of Love ,Salvation, Healing; Praying ,Preaching) **Amen**
- **The Baptism of the Holy spirit empowers you/me** -to go and do the work of the ministry (The disciples before Jesus left he empowered them with the Holy Spirit) God never sent us to open up churches without demonstration of his character the massage that lacks demonstrations will lack credibility because all the demonstration of the gospel Proves Jesus is alive he heals and is coming back ,**Amen**
- **The Baptism of the Holy Spirit ,Anoints with supernatural power   (Divine Authority)**To do the impossible ,do miracles ,overcome poverty, -Listen to these words fellow Christian Jesus of Nazareth was a man whose Divine Authority was clearly proven to you by all the miracles and wonders which God performed through him , you yourselves know this for it happened here among you ,whoever believe and is baptised will be saved ,whoever does not believe will be condemned believers will be given power to perform miracles ,they will drive out demons , in my name ,they will speak in strange tongues ,if they pick up snakes or drink any poison they will not be harmed ,they will place their hands on the Sick ,who will get well   (**Mark 16;16;18**)*If you are called to be a prophet where are the wonders and miracles ?Why Jesus had to perform miracles and wonders it's a prove that God was with him* Amen,
- **Remember -a Prophet-** is someone who has received revelations from God is the person being in contact with Divine being and is said to speak on that entity behalf serving as intermediate with humanity and delivering massages and teachings from the supernatural source to people   ,**Amen**

WE HAVE DIFFERENT KINDS OF SPIRIT IN LIFE

(1) A fearful spirit-(Luke8; 24) The disciples went to Jesus and woke him up saying master –master we are about to die what is in this scripture a fearful spirit no matter how often God blesses you and answer your prayers you will still give in to fear especially in crisis you never faced before if you could ask yourself who told the disciples to get into the boat? Jesus in the first place Jesus faith does not exempt you from life storm it equips you to get through them and when you are in the will of God no storm however severe can take you under so don't be afraid of anything in life**(2)An- Undiscerning spirit-(Luke8;45)** Who touched Jesus can understand and tell the difference between the indiscriminate touch of the cloud and the touch of faith drains his power and brings results the last thing a dress maker makes on a dress is a hem so the hem represents a finished work the same back that bore the cross which takes away our sins also bores the stripes which takes away your sickness and by his stripes we are healed (**Isaiah,53;5**)what do you need today forgiveness of sins healing ? reach out in faith and touch Jesus and you will be made holly again**(3)A self- seeking spirit** – (**Luke 9;46**) an argument broke between disciples as to which of them was the greatest Jesus knew what they were thinking so he took a child and said whoever welcomes this child in my name welcomes me and whoever who welcomes me also welcomes the one who sent me for the one who lest among you all is the greatest a self-seeking spirit as long as your motives for serving is to make you look good you will never enjoy Gods approval and his well done is the only which accounts the ability to serve behind the scenes and do it with joy comes from the knowledge that ultimately your service will be re-organised and rewarded by only whose opinion counts when you have finished learning you are finished ,when you can't be told God will have nothing more to tell you the heart of the discerning acquires knowledge the ears of the wise seek it out(**Proverb;18;15**) Children always trust when you promise a child something they believe you act on it and expect it to be so it's better to trust in the Lord than in man (**Psalm,118;8**)a child is a tender hearted finally let us all be tender hearted(**1Peter;3;8**)the holy spirit is symbolised in scriptures as a gentle dove so keep your heart tendered and receptive to his dealings amen (**4**) **A Judgement Spirit (Luke;9;55)**We don't know what manner of spirit Christians we have Jesus went into a Samaritan village and was not well received so the disciples said lord do you want us to command fire to come down from heaven and consume them just as Elijah did? But he turned and said (rebuked them) you do not know what manner of spirit you have (You are) of the son of man did not come to destroy men lives but to save them there is a lesson to learn here a judgement spirit many non-believers view Christians as too judgemental so you can be sincere but to severe -When you mix a mingle only with those who share your views and values you can communicate with others in ways that attack than attract let us be clear never has it been more important to know the truth of God word and stand for it but if you have a right doctrine and the wrong spirit you will drive more people away from Christ than to bring them if Satan has his way he will drive his holiness out of our hearts imagine Christ disciples wanting incinerate those who did not agree with them They weren't even aware of the spirit that was at work within their own heart Jesus said you shall love your brother as yourselves (**Mathew;19;18;19**)that includes your non- Christians you don't have to defend Jesus or sell him all what you have to do is to introduce him the (**Psalmist** said" Taste and see the Lord is good (**Psalm;34;8**)Happy are those who find safety in him -**The peaceful kingdom** -the royal line of David is like a tree that has been cut down but just as new branches sprout from a stump so as a new king will arise from among David descendants The Spirit of the Lord will give him wisdom and knowledge and skills to rule his people he will know the Lords will and honour him and find pleasure in obeying him he will not Judge by appearance or hearsay he will judge the poor fairly and defend the rights of the helpless at his command the people will be Punished and the Evil person will die he will rule his people with Justice and Integrity wolves and sheep's will live together in peace and Leopards will lie down with younger goats Calves and lions will feed together and little Children will take care of them Cows and bear will eat together and their calves and cubs will lie down in peace Lions will eat straws as cattle do Even baby will not be harmed if it plays near a Poisonous snake On Zion Gods sacred hill there will be nothing harmful or Evil the land will be as full of Knowledge of the Lord as the seas are full of water (**Isaiah;11;2;9**)**Its good not to be Spiritual blinded because the Bible warns us** "says In their case the god of this world has blinded the mind of unbelievers to keep them from seeing the light of the gospel of the glory of Christ who is the image of God(**2Corithians;4;4**)"Hear you deaf and look you blind that you may see(**Isaiah;42;18**)But if your eye is bad your whole body will be full of darkness if then the light in you is darkness how great is darkness (**Mathew;6;23**)But blessed are your Eyes for they see and your Ears for they Hear(**Mathew;13;16**)Whoever who hates his brother is in darkness and walks in the darkness and does not know where he is going because the blindness has blinded his Eyes (**1John;2;11**)The Light shines in the darkness and the darkness has not overcome it(**John;1;5**),**Amen**

SPIRITUAL BREAK-THROUGH

And the lord will rescue me from all evil and take me safely into his heavenly kingdom to him be the glory forever and ever (**2Timothy;4;18**)Even if I go through the deepest darkness I will not be afraid Lord for you are with me your Shepherds rod and staff protect me (**Psalm;23;4**)Seek your happiness in the Lord and he will give you the desires of your heart(**Psalm;37;4**)This is the day of the Lords victory let us be happy let us celebrate save us lord save us give us success o Lord may God bless the one who comes in the name of the Lord from the Temple of the Lord we bless you the Lord is God he has been good to us with branches in your hands start the festival and match around the altar give thanks to the lord because is good and his Love is Eternal **(Psalm;118;24;29 ;Psalm 63;1;1;)**Day and Night your gates will be open so that the Kings of the nations may bring you their wealth but nations that do not serve you will be completely destroyed **(Isaiah;60;11;12)**The Holy God of Israel the Lord who saves you says am the Lord your God the one who wants to teach you for your own good and direct you in the way you should go if you had listened to my commands then blessings would have flowed for you like a Stream that never goes dry victory would have come to you like the waves that roll on the shores your descendants would be numerous as grain of sand and I would have made sure they were never destroyed **(Isaiah;48;17;18)**But I will gather you together all you people of is real that are left I will bring you together like sheep's returning to the fold like pasture full of sheep your land will once again be filled with many people God will open the way for them and lead them out of exile they will break out of the city gates and go free their king the lord himself will lead them out **(Micah;2;12;13)** Amen-**Jesus Christ brings Spiritual breakthrough** -If you are in Union with him -For the full content of Divine nature lives in Christ in his humanity and you have been given full life in union with him His supreme over Spiritual rulers and Authority**(Collossians;2;9;10)**-Because Jesus Christ did what God wanted him to do we are all purified from Sin by the offering that he made of his own body once and for all **(Hebrews;10;10)**Dear brothers and Sisters don't be distracted by Spiritual distraction that the blood of bulls and goats can take away sins ,the bible states it clear" For the blood of bulls and Goats can never take away sins**(Hebrews;10;4)**Because the Lamb who is the centre of the throne will be their Shepherd and he will guide them to springs of life giving water and God will wipe away every tear from their eyes**(Revelation;7;17)**So Jesus answered them am telling you the truth the Son can do nothing on his own, he does only what he sees his father is doing ,what the father does the son also does **(John;5;19)**Now that we have been put right with God through faith we have peace with God through our Lord Jesus Christ **(Romans;5;1)Prayers brings -Spiritual breakthrough** -Jesus said to his disciples ,this is how you should pray, Our father in heaven may your name be honoured may your kingdom come may your will be done on earth as it is done in heaven give us today the food we need forgive our wrongs we have done as we forgive the wrong that other have done to us do not bring us to hard testing but keep us safe from the Evil one **(Mathew 6;9;13);Amen**

THE COST OF A GOD GIVEN DREAM

The definition- of dreams can be found in the book of **(Job;33;15)**When people are asleep at night God speaks in dreams and vision he makes them listen to what he says and they are frightened at his warning God speaks to them to stop them from sinning and to save them from becoming -Proud he will not let them to be destroyed he saves them from death itself there several kinds of death in life-*Spiritual death Emotional death, Physical death, Economical death-* We are always dreaming when we are sleeping we remember sometimes the true story of the dream right before we are awake ,Sometime we remember the full story when we are awake ,Men always remember the dream that awake them up there *several cause of dreams* it could be a multitude of Physical and Emotional, Tiredness another cause could be though your body settles in rest your mind can keep right on working and thinking sometimes We wake up *Scared- Happy Mad and Sad*-the book of Isaiah Speaks of dreams as all the nations that assemble to attack Jerusalem will be like a starving person who dreams he is eating and wakes up hungry or like someone, dying of thirst who dreams he is drinking and wakes up with a dry throat**(Isaiah;29;8)The purpose of dreams(1)Give us Warnings** and being warned of God in dream that they should not return to, Herod they departed into their own country another way God appears to wise men to warn them, God appeared to Joseph to warn him to flee to Egypt God spoke to Abimelech and warned him that he taken another man's wife**(2)God use dreams to encourage-** God encouraged Gideon to go to the battle with a few number of Armies of only 300 and in the same God instructed Gideon that, if he is afraid he will go with him upon of hearing this dream,Gideon was strengthened and he worshipped God the purpose of the dream was to encourage Gideon there is no different between the dreams of the past and today, God can visit you in dreams to encourage you to share your vision with others, help the needy, to start a business, build an hospital ,church to encourage others ,what you have to do believe it **(3)*God uses dreams to prophecy to us*- Joseph-** dreamed a dream about his brothers bowing down to him, his dream told about the future but it took years ,**Nebuchadnezzar-** had dreams that had prophecy in them read the book of **(Daniel)l** people have had dreams and many have come to pass .as they lean on God not on their understanding ,for Everything and many have wondered what they thought cannot happen, with God everything is possible ,hope God will give man dreams about his kingdom in heaven and his will to man and turning back to him Everyone shall be glad, many time God has given us dreams and vision but because they don't fit into our human desires we end up burying them ,Sometime it's hard to keep dream alive and many times our dreams remain just day dreaming in life -Shall prophesy and younger men shall see vision and your old men shall see dreams **(Act;2;17)**afterwards I will Pour out my Spirits on everyone your Sons and daughters will proclaim my massage your old people will have dreams and your young people will see vision**(Joel;2;28)**Now hear what I have to say when there are Prophet among you I reveal myself to them in vision and speak to them in dreams it is different when I speak with my servant Moses I have put him in charge of all my people Israel so I speak to him face to face clearly and not in riddles he has even seen my form how dare you speak against my servant Moses?**(Numbers;12;6;8)**Have I not commanded you to be strong and courageous do not be afraid do not be discouraged for the Lord your God I will be with you Whenever you go **(Joshua;1;9)**God wants you to pursue your dream after dreaming big the dream that he has put in your heart No matter where you are from your dreams are still valid**(Lupita - Nyongo)**God still speaks to us in dreams and there is no clear scriptures in the bible that prohibit God from speaking to us in Dreams you may Ask yourself this **Question does God still speak to us in dreams ?** these people are not drunk as you suppose it's only nine o'clock in the morning instead this is what the prophet Joel spoke about this is what I will do in the last days God says will pour out my spirit on everyone your sons and daughters will proclaim my massage your younger men will see visions and your old men will have dreams yes even on my servants both men and women I will pour out my spirit in those days I will perform miracles in the sky above and wonders on earth below there will be blood ,fire and thick smoke the sun will be darkened and the moon will turn red as blood before the great and glorious day of the lord comes and ten whoever calls out to the lord for help will be saved **(Acts 2;15-21)But in most common ways God speaks to us through his word**-in the past God spoke to our ancestors many times and many ways through the prophets but in these last he has spoken to us through his Son he is the one through whom God created the universe the one God has chosen to posses all things at the End **(Hebrews 1;1;2 ;Gods word through his Son)your dreams should be supported by scriptures** -God will always make a dream clear to you if it's from him God spoke to Joseph and made it clear and he said get up take the child and his mother and go back to the land of Israel because those who tried to kill the child are dead so Joseph got up took the child and his mother and went back to Israel**(Mathew;1;20;21 return of Jesus, Mary Joseph from Egypt**)So as Joseph woke up he married Mary as the angles of the Lord had told him to do but he had no sexual relationship with her before she gave birth to her son and Joseph named him Jesus **(Mathew;1;24)**they answered "each of us had dream and there is no one here to Explain what the dream mean it is God who gives the ability to Interpret dreams Joseph said "tell me your dreams**(Genesis;40;8** ;Joseph interprets the prisoners dreams) God will send someone to make it clear to

you but you have to do your part and pray over your dream, God is not
God of Disorder may our God our father and Lord Jesus Christ give you
grace and peace **(1Corinthians;1;3)Every dream is not intended to be
shared**- because some other people won't understand it so don't share your
dream to everyone One night Joseph had a dream and when he told his
brother about it they even hated him more **(Genesis;37;5)**God gave Joseph
another dream and said to his brother "I had another dream in which I saw
the sun ,the moon and Eleven stars bowing down to me he also told the
dream to his father and his father scolded him what kind of dream is that?
Do you think your mother your brother and I are going to come and bow
down to you? Joseph brother were jealousy of him but his father kept
thinking about the whole matter**(Genesis;37;9)** When Joseph dreamed big
his brother Envied him here comes the dreamer they said to each other
come now let us kill him and throw him into one of these cisterns and say
that a ferocious animal devoured him then we will see what comes of his
dream**(Genesis;37;19;20)** this dream was far bigger than the first-
Sometime those closest to you will resent your dream the most not
everybody would like to celebrate your Success, relative people who are
close to you would be the least to celebrate you and you wonder some
people may not hate you because of the shoes you put on or the
expensive car dress but because of your dream when Jesus fame began
to Spread the first people to reject from the town he was born the
scriptures says "and so they rejected him Jesus said to them a prophet is
respected everywhere except in his home town and by his own family
because they did not have faith he did not perform many miracles there
(Mathew;13;57)be wise who you tell your dreams-**Many times God
takes it serious when we speak on his behalf Prophets or Interpreters
of dreams-** May promises a miracle or wonder in order to lead you to
worship and serve gods that you have not worshipped before even if what
the promise come true do not pay attention to them the Lord your God is
using them to test you if you love the Lord with all your heart follow the
Lord and honour him obey him and keep his commands worship him and
be faithful to him but put to death any interpreters of dreams or prophets
who tell you to rebel against the Lord who rescued you from Egypt where
you were slaves such people are evil and are trying to lead you away from
the life that the lord has commanded you to live they must be put to death
in order to rid yourselves of this Evil **(Deuteronomy;13;1;5)**Listen to
what I the lord say am against prophets who tells dreams that are full of
lies they tell dreams and lead my people astray with their lies and boasting
I did not send them or order them to go and they are of no help at all to the
people I the lord have spoken **(Jeremiah;23;32),Amen**

Many times God give us big dreams and end up not unaccomplished because of:

(a)*Fear ,(b)Doubt and not believing on what God says about our life, (d)Past mistakes (e)Discouragements (f)settling for average(g)Low self esteem(h)Friends we share with our dreams*(I) disappointment ,(1)**Settling for average**-for we are Gods handiwork created in the image of Christ to do good works which God prepared us to do (**Ephessians;2;10**)we are not created to be average, but we find ourselves in a comfort zone and we fail to do what more God has for us, but God is good he will make sure he will stretch us so we can fulfil his dreams he has put in us, we can't remain in the comfort zone and kill our God given dreams ,we have to be confidence that we can do all things through him who gives me strength(**Philippians 4;13**)the things outside of our comfort zone may seem impossible but we can do them when we trust God– (2)**Discouragement kill dreams** –Joseph had two dreams and the second one was bigger than the first in both dream he dreamt of being in a position of great authority but his brother didn't like to be told these dreams they even hated him all more because of his dream and what he said ,they threw him in the pit sold him like a slave and pretended was dead Joseph may have thought he had misheard Gods dream he may have felt discouraged but these things led Joseph to the right place of Gods given dream to be fulfilled it might seem that our dreams is gasping its last breath but we need to keep believing God can't let discouragement kill our God given dreams(3)**Disappointments kills dreams** –disappointment is the gap between expectations and reality when something goes wrong or does not turn out the way we want it or think we give up and say I will never do it again and results in our dreams being killed and the desire to reach our potential we tend to forget that experiment failure is the price we have to pay to achieve success ,When we don't accomplish our dreams(4)**Lack of faith/doubt** With God all things are possible(**Mathew;19;26**)By faith Moses when he had grown he refused to be known as the son of Pharaohs daughter, he chose to be mistreated along with the people of God because, he was looking for a reward a head to his reward he persevered because he saw him who is invisible (**Hebrews;11;26-27**)By faith Abraham saw his children he counted them every time he looked up at the star(**Genesis ;15;5**)Jesus said whoever say to this mountain be removed and cast into the sea "and does not doubt but believes that those things he say will be done he will have whatever he says(**Mark;11;23**)When God gives you a dream you will be able to see things which are invisible to others remember there two kind of people in the word the realists and the dreamers the realists know where they are going the dreamers have already been there God gave you the gift memory to re-play the future Moses saw the promised land long before he got there

God does not make a mistake when he gives you imagination because of it ,you can stand on in the middle of your dream and envision it before it comes to pass even when others are doubting so if you are dreamer who has been already in your imagination trust God and put you dream to the test if you come from a discouraging family or don't think of yourself as an especially imaginative person don't lose hope you can still discover and develop your dream God has put the ability within you, Line up your word with God's word and the mountain will become your servants, **(5)Lack of confidence**-We find it very hard to fulfil our dreams because its known dreams are fragile and they are at a great risk when they are new to us when the people we love and respect don't encourage and approve us and without past records of success to follow up we slide back but we must know people who know their God shall be strong and carry out great exploits(**Daniel;11;32**) We must know God by ourselves and have a relationship with him trust him and believe that he is always on our side to help us to move forward in our dreams Caleb shows us that it's not about the age it's about our faith we have in God with God we can face everything we think we can't, fear holds us back we can step into our calling even when things around us are telling us we can't Caleb had a different Spirit and followed God wholeheartedly God brought him into the promised land he wanted with his and his descendants inherited it (**Numbers;14;24**)God don't give up on us your dream may be buried but the good news it's still alive if you arise and pursue it, God will breath into it, believe you are a child of destiny, if God is for you who can be against you, don't fall apart -God controls the universe, remember Gods promise come to pass he knows how to bring out what he promised you, it's never too late to became what he created you to be in the universe, God commands us to be strong and courageous there will always be obstacles but you need to discover your faith deep in God and yourself our faith moves God to accomplish our dreams -sometimes God gives a dream sometimes the circumstances required to fulfil it won't be to your liking Joseph as an example he faced betrayal and false imprisonment but that is what took him to get to the throne of Egypt The indispensable first step to getting the things you want out of life is this decide what you want (**Ben-Stein**)Be Miserable or motivate yourself whatever has to be done its always your Choice (**Wayne- Dyer**)Start where you are, Use what you have, Do what you can(**Arthur Ashe**)Never limit yourself because of others limited imagination never limit others because of your limited imagination(**Mae Jemison**) What is not started today is never finished tomorrow(**Johann-Wolfgang-von-Goethe**)The only thing worse than starting something and failing is not starting something (**Seth -Go din**) A year from now you may wish you had started today(**Karen Lamb**)Much of the stress that people feel doesn't come from having too much to do it comes from not finishing what they started(**David Allen**)Do not be embarrassed by your failure learn from them and start again **(Richard Branson)**The only thing that will stop you from fulfilling your dream is you **(Tom Bradley)**The best years of your life are the one in which you decide your problems are your own you do not blame them on your father the Economy Political Leaders you realise that you control your own destiny You don't have to see the whole stair-case just first take the first step**(Martin Luther king)**A journey of a thousand miles must begin with a single step **(Lao-Tzu)**When you encounter obstacles you discover things you never knew in life ,Obstacles are calls to strengthen you not to surrender to your purpose ,God has called you to do in life when your dream look impossible trust in the Lord and act as though it's impossible to fail Jesus looked at them and answered this is impossible for human beings but for God everything is Possible for God**(Mark;10;27)**Believe in winning don't listen to those who discourage you or those who are saying you are taking a big chance ignore the impossibility in life and focus on what God say can be done Keep away from people who try to be little your ambitions Small people always do that but the really great make you feel that you too can become great you are fully loaded with everything by God that can make your dream come true Every Great dream begins with a dreamer   always remember you have within you all the strength Patience, Talents, Opportunities, Favour ,friends, anointing ,Grace ,Passion to start to change the world- When you look back in life you see many things you would have done but because of doubt , Fear you failed yourself there is only one thing that makes a dream Impossible to achieve the fear of Failure **(Paulo-Coelho)**The future belongs to those who believe in the beauty of their dreams**(Eleanor Roosevelt)**To accomplish great things we must not only act ,but also dream ,not only plan, but also believe **(Anatole- France)**If you take responsibility for yourself you will develop the hunger to accomplish your dreams **(Les Brown)**Remember you have something into you some can't even handle what God put into you is beyond their imaginations, Believe and trust in God and thank him for your dream he will remove all the forces of darkness on it and help you fulfil it obstacles that looks permanent are going to change , always put this in mind the enemy always distract people who have great dreams when you are a big dreamer you are a threat to the Enemy and the enemy always will work tooth and nail to put you down when God gives you a big and great dream it doesn't mean you won't have problems opposition betrayal but you have to know they are pushing you forward to a higher level and they are temporary-Not only those things I reckon everything as complete loss for the sake of what is much more valuable the knowledge of Christ Jesus my lord for his sake I have thrown away everything away I consider It all as refuse /garbage so that ,I may gain Christ **(Philippians;3;8),**Stop worrying about temporary things quit losing your sleep over night -Don't let something small steal your Joy it's easy to remember the opposition, betrayal, discouragement but forget about them and remember the dream God put in you-The more you worry the more likely to have bad dreams and the more you talk the more likely to say something foolish**(Ecclesiastes;5;3)**The prophet who has had a dream should say it is only a dream but the prophet who has heard my massage should Proclaim that massage faithfully What good is straw compared to Wheat?**(Jeremiah;23;28)**Your dream will never be fulfilled unless you are willing to pay the price that comes with it and that price is not paid once but over a life time first there is an initial cost you will have to make Personal sacrifices and sometimes painful you may have to walk away from personal attractive options and valued relationship because some of them may not be fitting into God plan for you in life leaving things that have given you your security and your identity will requires grit and grace that only God can provide, Paul wrote being of the tribe of Benjamin a Hebrew of Hebrew Pharisee Paul once had wealth and status scholars reckon that when he committed his to Christ as was customary his friends and family would have held a funeral service and consider him dead to them from that point forward Pauls calling was to cover Asia with the gospel Paul wrote a half of the New Testament but great assignment call for great sacrifice and Paul was not alone By faith Moses when he had Grown up refused to be known as a son of Pharaohs daughter he chose to be mistreated along with the people of God rather than enjoying the pleasure of sin for a short time he regarded disgrace for the sake of Christ as of a greater value than the treasure of Egypt because he was looking ahead for his reward*(Hebrews;11;24;26)*The question is has God gives you a dream do you have faith and fortitude to fitful it ? Have you counted the cost and are you ready to for it ?*(2 Corinthians;11;23)*Are they servant of Christ I sound like a mad man but am better servant than they are, I have worked more much harder I have been in prison more times, I have been whipped much more and I have been near to death more often all successful people have paid a price for their success in life and its on-going which we don t want to pay they paid initial and continue to pay every day, and Paul brings it clearly the true story behind his success worked much harder been in prison more frequently ,been whipped , and exposed to death, beaten with rods one day stoned three times ,spent day and night in open sea, and been constantly on the move, been in rivers ,dangers in bandits danger from his countrymen ,went without sleep ,he knew hunger and thirsty and gone without food, been cold and naked ,beside everything else ,I face the pressure of my concern for all the Churches most of us have a vague notion that same day ,we will have to make a sacrifice but the price will have to be paid sooner than we think not expecting that many of us become discouraged some of us table our dreams putting them on hold others have abandoned them entirely the question you must answer is *27 years* from now what will I wish I had done today that's the cost of a God given dream stop and listen careful to what some of the people around are saying many of them express regret because they backed off from their dreams of earlier years a career not pursued an opportunity left unsealed a relationship left to break and die decades later they come back to it and think more about it but for some is too late they cannot achieve their dreams at any price for others the dream is possible but the price is now much higher than before one writer said put your dreams to test **Dr John Maxwell-** wrote going after a dream is climbing a mountain ,We will never make it to the summit ,if we are carrying too much loads /weight as we enter each new phase of the climb we face a decision do we take on more things to carry lay down things that won't help us exchange what we have for something else or stop climbing altogether, Most people try to take so many things with them when successful people climb they let off things think of many things do one or start changing in order to reach a higher level the price for reaching your dream never stop the journey continues only if you continue paying the price the higher you want to go the more you must give in your energy and time the greater the price the greater the joy you feel when you finally reach your dream ,If you are not willing to risk the unusual you will have to settle for the Ordinary**(Jim Rohn)**A Task without a vision is drudgery a vision without a task is day dreaming but a task with a vision is the pathway to victory and achievement Inspiration Quotes about dreams Nothing happens unless first a dream**(CarlSandburg)**Reach higher for the stars lie hidden in your soul Dream higher for the stars lie hidden in your souls dream deep for ever dream precedes the goal **(Pamela Vaull Starr)**Go confidently in the direction of your dream live the life you have imagined **(Thoreau)**Trust in dreams for in them is hidden the gate to eternity **(Kahil Gibran)**How much better to know that we have dared to live our dreams than to live our lives in a lethargy regrets **(Gilbert Caplin)** When you stop chasing your dream your dream start chasing you**(Dez Del Rio)**The best reason to have a dream is that in dreams no reasons are necessary**(Ashleigh Brilliant)**It is better to risk starving to death then surrender if you give up your dreams what is left **(Jim Carrey)**be careful with what you water with your dreams water them with Optimism and solution and you will achieve success always be on the lookout for ways to turn a Problem into a solution or opportunity to Success always be on a way to nurture your dreams**(Lao Tzu)**keep your dreams alive understand to achieve anything requires faith and belief in yourself vision hard work determination and dedication remember all things are possible for those who believe**(Gail Devers)**Let go of your expectations the universe will do what it will sometimes your dreams will come true sometimes they won't sometimes when you let go of a broken dream another one gently takes its place be aware of what is not what you would like to be taking place **(Melody Beattie)** We may place blame give reasons and even have excuses but in the end it is an act of Cowardice to not follow our dreams (**Steve Maraboli**)What you can do or dream you can do begin it boldness has genius ,Power and magic in it (**Johann Wolfang Von Goethe**)The biggest adventure you can ever take is to live the life of your dream (**Oprah Winfrey**) As soon as you start to pursue a dream your life wakes up and everything has a meaning (**BarbaraSher**)Find yourself and express yourself in your particular way express your love openly life is nothing but a dream and if you create your life with love your dream becomes a masterpiece of art (**Don Miguel Ruiz**) Throw your dream into space like a kite and you do not know What it will bring back a new life a new friend a new love a new country (**Anais Nin**)Do not spoil what you have, by desiring what you have not remember that what you have was once among things you hoped for (**Epicurus**)You are never too old to set another goal or dream another dream (**C.s Smith**) A man is not old until regrets take the place of Dreams (**John Barrymore**)Never give up on a dream because of the time it will take to accomplish it the time will pass away (**Earl Nightingale**) I have had dreams and I have heard nightmares I overcome the nightmare because of my dreams(**Jonas Salk**)Father we thank you for the sweet dreams and wisdom to know the cost of dream to fulfil your calling to serve you fully (to you and me now when God gives us one dream we should ask him for another dream God to lift our sight cause us to aim higher but remember before God gives you another dream he will first see what you did with the first do not despise the small beginning for the lord rejoice to see the work begun-The angels told me to give Zerubbabel this massage from the Lord you will succeed not by military mighty or by your own strength but by my spirit obstacles as great mountains will disappear before you will build the temple and as you put the last stone in the place the people will shout beautiful- beautiful another massage came to me from the lord he said Zerubbabel has laid the foundation of the temple and he will finish the building when this happen my people will know that is I who sent you to them they are disappointed because so little progress is being made but they will see Zerubbabel continuing to build the temple and they will be glad (**Zechariah 4;6;10 Gods promise to Zerubbabel**)So what God promised he will fulfil it great Ending always start with humble beginning in the same way you younger people must submit to your elders and all of you must put on the Apron of humility to serve one another for the scriptures says "God resists the proud but show favour to the humble yourself then under gods mighty hand so that he will lift you up in his own good time leave all your worries for him because he cares for you (**1 Peter,5;5;7**) if your dream is to become true it is in harmony with God -**If your dream is to prosper financially-**remember that it is the lord your God who gives you the power to become rich he does this because he is faithful today to the covenant that he made with your ancestors**(Deuteronomy;8;18)**honour God with your tithe **(Malachi; 3;8;10) Practice Fiscal discipline** rather than squandering what God gives you on extravagant spending and impulse buying's ;**Amen**

PRAYER AS A WEAPON IN LIFE

MOUNTAIN MOVING PRAYERS- Whatever begins in prayer ends in victory, when you fail to pray, you plan to fail ,A Prayer is nothing else than being on terms of friendship with God-Minutes invested in prayers yields greater returns than hours we spend in useless things like ,Gossiping, What's up, Face book, Magazine - Prayer is divided into different kinds **(1) -Vocal prayers** - Sing and spoken words -loudly -**The second one is(2) -Spirit prayers** (Praying in tongues)**(3)- Mental prayers-** meditation and contemplations - **Prayer of Adoration- (Psalm,105;Psalm 106)** thanking God*(for all he has done for us)* whatever you get by prayers you sustain it in prayers . ,**Worshiping and ,Praising***(Giving glory because God is good-Adoration*) Petition - requesting for help From God*(favour ,blessings, Anointing ,Wisdom ,Protection)* **Prayer of Petition -** *The Bible states it clear "First of all then I urge you that-Petitions ,Prayers ,Requests and thanksgiving be offered to God for all people for the Kings and all those who are in Authority, that they may live in quiet and Peaceful life, with all Reverence toward God ,and with Proper Conduct-this is good and it pleases God our Saviour-***(1Timothy,2;1;3),**Presenting your request to God ,praise God with all your heart, allow God to rule in your heart , Don't worry about anything ,but in all your prayers ask God for what you need, always asking him with a thankful heart ,and Gods peace which is far beyond human understanding, will keep your heart and mind safe, in union with Christ **(Phillipians,4;6;7) Prayer for the word of God -** I pray that your love will keep on growing more and more together with true knowledge and perfect judgement ,so that you may choose what is best , then you will be free from all impurities and blame on the day of Christ your lives will be filled with the truly good qualities which only Jesus Christ can produce for the glory and praise of God**(Philippians,1;10;11)** We have courage in God's presence ,because we are sure that he hears us if we ask for anything that is according to his will he hears us whenever we ask him and since we know this is true ,we know that he gives us what we ask from him **(1,John;14;15)** May my words and thoughts be acceptable to you ,O lord my refuge and my redeemer **(Psalm,19;14) Prayer of Forgiveness -** Be merciful to me O lord because of your constant love ,because of your great mercy wipe away my Sins and make me clean from my sins**(Psalm,51;1;19 David prayer) Prayer for Faith -** Jesus Answered have faith in God, I assure you that whoever tells this hill to get up and throw itself in the sea and does not doubt in his heart ,but believe that what he says will done for him , for this reason I tell you when you pray and ask for something believe that you will receive it ,and you will be given what you have asked for **(Mark 11;22;24 Mathew 20;20;22)**

Intercessions-**prayers** (Praying for your ,family ,friends Nations ,Jobs , Leaders ,Politicians ,Sick-**James;5;14;15** standing in the gap for others,(**Ezekiel,22;30, Jesus prayed for his disciples, Peter and all Believers John 17)** - their eyes to be open to the Gospel God to save them from the forces of darkness ,and send labourers into their path) **Prayer for Blessings-** As he came up to kiss him Isaac smelt his clothes ,so he gave him his blessings ,he said "the pleasant smell of my son is like the smell of a field which the Lord has blessed ,May God give you dew from heaven and make your field fertile ,may he give you plenty of Corn and Wine may nations be your servants and may people bow down before you ,may rule over your relatives and may your mother descendants bow down before you ,may those who curse you be cursed and may those who bless you be blessed **(Genesis 27;27;29;Isaac blesses Jacob)**The Lord commanded Moses to tell Aaron and his Son to use the following Words in blessing the people of Israel ,May the Lord bless you and take care of you ,May the Lord be kind and gracious to you, May the Lord look on you with favour and give you peace , And the Lord said ,If they pronounce my name as a blessing upon the people of Israel, I will bless them **(Numbers 6;22;27)Prayer for ,Spiritual Strength (Sinners)**The prayer made in faith will heal the sick ,the lord will restore them to health and the sin they have committed will be forgiven **(James;5;15-16)** Forgive us the wrongs we have done, as we forgive the wrongs that others have done to us **(Mathew 6;12)** Jesus said forgive them they don't know what they are doing **(Luke 23;34)**Suffering- Are any of you in trouble ? you should pray Are any of you happy ? you should sing ,praise Are any of you ill? you should send the church elders leaders who will pray for them rub oil on them in the name of the Lord **(James;5;13,** Soaring everything is well-**)The Prayer for Supernatural-Power-** Elijah was the same kind of person as we are , he prayed Earnestly that they would be no rain and no rain fell on the land for three years and half **(3-Years 1/2)** , Once again he prayed and the sky poured out its rain and the Earth produced crops(**James;5;17;18 Prayer for Straying people running away from Church** - My brother and Sister ,if any of you wander away from the truth and another one brings them back again ,remember this whoever turns a sinner back from his or he wrong will save that sinners soul **James-5;19;20)Prayer for emotional healing** -to set you free from emotional wounds ,**Prayer for healing and anointing with Oil -** Laying hands on the sick ,**Prayer of Concentrations** -To do God's will, **Prayer of Co-operation (unity) -** to work together in one Spirit as Sons and daughter of the most high God serving one God, **Prayer of the commanding Power using the name of Jesus (Authority),** We need to give full time to Prayers and the work of preaching **(Acts;6;4)** Who wants everyone to be Saved and come to know the Truth, for there is one God who brings human beings together the man ,Christ Jesus who gave himself to redeem

Everyone that was the proof at the right time that God wants everyone to be Saved**(1Timothy;2;1;6) Prayer to Speak in Supernatural tongues ,Led by the Holy Spirit-** The person who speaks in strange tongues ,then must pray for the gift to Explain what is said ,for if I pray in this way my Spirit prays indeed but my mind has no part in it what should do I do then? I will pray with my Spirit but I will pray also with my mind ,I will sing with my Spirit but I will also sing with my mind ,when you give thanks to God in spirit only how can ordinary people taking part in the meeting say" Amen" to your prayer of thanksgiving? they have no way of knowing what you are saying Even if your prayer of thanks to God is quite good other people are not helped at all , I thank God that I speak in strange tongues much more than any of you ,but in church worship I would rather speak five words that can be understood in order to teach others ,than speak a thousand words in strange tongues **(1Corinthians 14;13;18)**Those who speak in strange tongues do not speak to others ,they speak to God because no one understand them ,they are speaking secret truth by the power of the Spirit ,but those who proclaim God massage speak to people and give them help , encouragement and comfort ,those who speak in strange tongues help only themselves but those who proclaim Gods massage help the whole church I would all of you to speak in strange tongues but I would rather that you had that gift of proclaiming Gods message ,for the person who proclaim Gods massage is of greater value than the one who speaks in strange tongues ,unless if there is someone present who can explain what is said so that the whole church may be helped so when I come to you my brothers ,sisters what use will I be to you if I speak in strange tongues ? not a bit, unless if I bring you some revelation from God or some knowledge or some inspired massage or some teaching **(1 Corinthians 14;2;6) - A prayer of Praise and Thanks giving - (Luke,1;46-55)Touches God to ,Bless, Anoint , Protect, Favour ,Strength, Heal us , give you Joy and peace ,**We must acknowledge ourselves who is the Source of our Strength , God hears Prayers, heeds Prayers, Answers Prayers, and Delivers by Prayers,**(Em-Bounds)**Be a Man/Woman of Prayers- *(1)Prayers brings us into line with God Will,(2)Prayers Changes Circumstances for Every believer for good, heals sickness and disease (3),Prayers changes Characters ,(4)Prayer purifies our Wildest thoughts and Elevates our Whole life (5) Prayer soothes our Troubled Spirits calms our unbridled instincts ,(6) Prayer is natural function of the Soul-(7),Prayer is the appropriation of Our heritage ,(9)Prayer brings God to our Aid because prayers brings God near to us it brings the supernatural power of God in our life ,marriage, business ,education ,prayer shows you mighty great things that you don't know (10)It brings results (James 5;16)(11) Prayer is a live Privilege of fellowship with God, (12)Prayer brings Joy and Happiness (13)-Prayer is Vital for Christianity maturity (14) Prayers and the Word of God are*

123

food for our Soul (John 14;13) prayer does not need proof but needs practice , The lord is near to all who call on him to all who call him in truth(**Psalm 145;18**)I prayed to the lord and he answered me he freed me from all my fears the oppressed look to him and are glad they will never be disappointed ,the helpless call on him and he answers he saves them from all their troubles ,his angles guards those who honour the lord and he rescue them from danger, find out yourself how good the lord is honour the lord those who obey him have all they need even the lions go hungry for lack of food but those who obey God lack nothing (**Psalm;34;4;10**)Because you answer prayers People everywhere will come to you (**Psalm;65;2**)Seek the lord while he may be found, call on him while is near(**Isaiah;55;6**)Hear my cry O God, listen to my prayers in despair, and from far from home, I call to you take me to a safe refuge (**Psalm 61;1;2**)Praise awaits you our God in Zion, to you our vows will be fulfilled ,you who answers prayers to you all your people will come (**Psalm;65;1-2**)The lord is far from the wicked, but hears the Prayers of the righteousness (**Proverb;15;29**)Call upon me in the days of troubles I will deliver you and you will honour me (**Psalm ;50;15**) Answer me when I call to you my righteous God give me relief from my distress have mercy on me and hear my prayers then in their troubles they called to the lord and he saved them from their distress he calmed the ragging storm and the waves became quite they were glad because of the calm and he brought them safe to the port they wanted (**Psalm,107;28-30**)The lord has heard my cry for mercy ,the lord accepts my prayers(**Psalm;6;9**)Every morning Lord ,I tell you what I need ,and I wait for your answer ,I pray to you in the sunrise ,I offer my prayer and wait for your answer (**Psalm5;3**) Hear my prayer Lord listen to my cries for help do not be deaf to my weeping I dwell with you as a foreigner a stranger as all my ancestors were (**Psalm,39;12**)Hear my Prayers lord listen to the words of my mouth listen to my players ,do not ignore my plea(**Psalm;54;2;1King 8;45; 1Kings;8;49**)Then from heaven your dwelling place hear their prayer and their pleas and uphold their cause and forgive who have sinned against you(**2Chronicles;6;39**)Every morning We ask God for, Mercy. Wisdom ,Protection from enemies wars, Success, Favour, Jobs, Children, Direction, Deliverance from Sins ,Victory, Blessings ,Status in different countries he answers, I call on you God for you will answer me, turn your ear to me and hear my Prayers(**Psalm;17;6**)**Isaac**- prayed to the lord on behalf of his wife, because she was childless the Lord answered his prayer and his wife Rebekah become pregnant (**Genesis 25;21**)**Moses**- replied when I have gone out the city, I will spread out my hands in prayers to the lord the thunder will stop and there will be no more hails, so you may know the world is the lord (**Exodus;9;29**)Lord almighty God of Israel you have revealed this to your servant saying's will build a house for you "so your servant has found courage to pray this prayer to you

(2,Samuel;7;27)David- built an altar to the lord there and sacrificed burnt offering and fellowship offerings then the lord answered his prayers in behalf of the land and the plague on Israel was stopped **(2,Samuel;24;25)**The lord said to him I have heard the prayers and the plea you have made before me I have consecrated this temple which you have build by putting my name there forever my eyes and heart will always be there**(1Kings;9;3 ;2Chronicles;6;35)** May your eyes be open towards this temple ,night and day, this place of which you said "my name shall be there "so that you will hear the prayer your servants prays towards this place**(1King,8;29 ;2Chronicles;6;19)**The lord appeared to him at night and said, I have heard your prayers, and I have chosen this place for myself as a temple for sacrifice**(2 Chronicles;7;12)**Yet give attention to your servants prayer and his plea for mercy, Lord my God hear the cry and the prayer that is praying in praying in your presence this day **(1Kings,8;28 ; 2Chronicles;6;19) Nehemiah prayer-**they said to me those who survived the exile and are back in the province are in great trouble and disgrace ,the wall of Jerusalem is broken down and its gates have been burned with fire when I heard these things I sat down and wept for some days I mourned and fasted and prayed before God of heaven then I said the God of heaven ,the great and awesome God ,who keeps his covenant of love with **those** who love him and keep his commandments ,Let your ears be attentive and your ears open to hear the prayer your servant is praying before you day and night for your servant the people of Israel I confess the sins we Israelites including myself and my fathers have committed against you**(Nehemiah;1;3;6)**Lord let your ear be attentive to the prayer of this your servant and to the prayers of your servants, who delight in revering your name give your servants success today by granting him favour in the presence of this man I was cupbearer to the king**(Nehemiah;1;11)**The Priests and the Levites stood to bless the people ,and God heard them, for their prayers reached the heavens ,his dwelling place**(2Chronicles;30;27)**A prayer is an effort of will ,the Psalmist said" Listen to my voice in the morning lord **(Psalm;5;3)** God always wants to Speak to us in the morning, after all he can speak to us any time ,he chooses he wants us to have the first place of him in everything we do in life ,wants to be number one priority for the day, before you do anything turn on what's-up turn on your television, reading news paper ,we need God to give us insight for the day, what's important for the day ,we need solutions, and creative ideas and a clear sense of guidance, his promises are true ,the steps of man and woman are ordered by the lord**(Psalm;37-23)**God wants you to give him your first time**(minutes and hours of the days)**before you are being occupied by other things of the day we are important to God and God is important to us he wants to speak to us as a first priority and if we lose this chance we lose many things it's a big loss if we fail to hear what he say to us and his guidance in our mind the secrets of strength ,victory ,success ,healing, is morning prayers in order to succeed you must put God first in your daily morning routine in the book of(**Isaiah;50-4**)Isaiah says The lord has given me his words of wisdom, that I know how to comfort the weary morning by morning he wakens me, and open my understanding to his will ,the lord has spoken to me, and I listened I have not rebelled or turned away, this is not only for Isaiah God does it for you every-morning ,be in his presence ,your day will be different from other people, who don't have time for him in the morning, God will give you understanding ,how to do your things, what to say before you get into the situation, he said am the lord who teaches you what is best for you ,who directs you in the way you should go (**Isaiah;48;17**)Even if you are in the right place spiritually not listening or not in realms, God will work with you every-morning by morning until when you recognise and respond to his voice(**Oswald Chambers**)It is a shield to the soul a sacrifice to God and a scourge to Satan (**John Bunyan**) It takes time but eventually the sheep grow familiar with the voice of their shepherd and learn to trust him for everything they need Your needs moves Gods heart and your faith moves God to action (**Luke11;5;11**)Jesus said to his disciples suppose one of you should go to a friend house at midnight and say friend let me borrow three loaves of bread a friend of mine who is on a journey has just come to my house and I haven't got any food for him ,and suppose a friend should answer from inside don't bother me the door is already looked and my children already in bed I cannot get up and give you anything but I tell you this though he won't do it for friendship sake if you keep knocking enough he will get up and give whatever you need because of your shameless persistence ask yourself Prayers are not answered by repeating words again and again When you pray do not use a lot of meaningless words as pagans do who think that their god will hear them because their prayers are long(**Mathew;6;7**)A prayer has two parts(**1**)**For Gods benefit (2)human benefits** ,Honour the first and the second part will be guaranteed ,Whatever is rooted in prayers cannot be uprooted by the hands of man, battles are won on knees , Blessings that are rooted in prayers no man can uproot them , Marriages ,family, studies , calling, Anointing ,Business, Children Church , Friendship , that are rooted in prayers no man can uproot them , If you are not praying you are praying with your destiny, if you want to go to next levels don't sympathise in prayers , a Prayerful woman she is a powerful woman, a powerful life is full of prayers , whatever planted in prayers cannot be uprooted ,   **Prayer** is a meeting point between **Divinity and humanity,** One day after they had finished their meals in the house of the Lord at Shiloh ,Hannah got up she was deeply distressed and she cried bitterly as she prayed to the Lord ,meanwhile Eli the priest was sitting in his place by the door , Hannah made a Solemn promise ,Almighty look at me your servant ,see my trouble and remember me ,don't forget me ,if you give me a son, I promise that I will dedicate him to you, for his whole life and that he will never have his hair cut ,Hannah continued to pray to the Lord for a long time and Eli watched her lips ,she was praying silently her lips moving ,but she made no sound , so Eli thought she was drunk and said to her stop making a drunken show of yourself ,stop your drinking and sober up no I am not drunk sir" she answered I haven't been drinking Am desperate and I have been praying out my troubles to the Lord Don't think I am a worthless woman I have been praying like this because I am so miserable   Go in peace Eli said and may the God of Israel give you what you have said him for, may you always kindly think of me she replied ,then she went away ate some food and was no longer sad ,the next morning Elkanah and his family got up early and after worshiping the Lord ,they went back home to Ramah ,Elkanah had Intercourse with his wife ,Hannah and the lord answered her prayer so it was that she became pregnant and gave birth to a son she named him Samuel * and explained "I asked for him **(1Samuel 1;10-20),** Sometimes we burst in tears ,and our tears goes un noticed by friends family members, mothers and fathers, pastors ,but God answers our prayers , when he see us in sorrow and reward us with tears of Joy **-Hannah prayed-** ,the lord has filled my heart with Joy ,how happy I am because of what he has done ! I laugh at my enemies ,how joyful I am because he has helped me ,no one is holy like the Lord there is no one like him ,no protect like our God**(1,Samuel,2;1-2I)**then my favour will shine on you like the morning sun ,and your wounds will be quickly healed ,I will be with you to save you, my presence will always protect you on every side ,when you pray ,I will answer you ,when you call to me I will respond , if you give food to the hungry and satisfy those who are in need then the darkness around you will turn to brightness of noon ,and I will always guide you and satisfy you with good things I will keep you strong and well , you will be like a garden that has plenty of water ,like a spring of water that never runs dry ,your people will rebuild what has long been in ruins ,building again on the old foundation, you will be known as the people you rebuilt the walls who restored the ruined houses , the Lord says if you treat the Sabbath a sacred and do not purse your own interest on that day, if you value my Holy day and honour it by not travelling working, or taking Idly on that day ten you will find the Joy that comes from serving me I will make you honoured all over the world and you will enjoy the land I gave to your ancestor Jacob I, the lord I have spoken **(Isaiah 58;8;14)** If your marriage is breaking up pray , if your business is slow pray , If your life looks to be hopeless and meaningless pray ,Lord heal me and I will be completely well ,rescue me and I will perfectly safe you are the one I praise **(Jeremiah,17;14)**Don't settle for less pray God is not limitless ,he will answer your prayers and all your ,mockers and enemies their mouth will be shut when God remember Hannah gave her a son Samuel and Samuel was a judge in Israel and you don't hear anywhere of Peninnah children motioned and the bible no anywhere mention of Peninnah name again pray that God will give you blessings ,favour Grace , protection , Joy , anointing ,that will shut the mouth of your enemies *A prayer less Christian is a weak Christian , A Prayer- less church is a weak church ,A Prayer-less Christian is a miserable Christian , A Prayer less nation is a defeated nation A Prayer less family will be a defeated Family , A family prays together stays together ,somebody prayed for you who do you pray for? God cannot answer Prayer until you have Prayed ,what you bide on earth I will bide in heaven* , God says I have given you the power of my Authority the sanctity of my blood I have given you the word when are you going to use the word ,power and the blood and announce that Christ is the Lord -*Why God will answer your prayers?* To protect his reputation, as one who makes covenant and keeps them ,if my people who are called by my name will humble themselves and pray and seek my face and turn from their wickedness then ,I will hear from heaven and I will forgive their sins, and I will heal their land(**2Chronicles7;14**)So how can you become familiar with the voice of the lord, Don't pray when you feel like it, have an appointment time with the lord, and keep it, a man is powerful on his knees (**Corrie Ten Boom**)(1) Give God your walking thought with your head on the pillow and eyes still closed, offer God a prayer and say to him thank you lord for good night rest today and I belong to you ,the moment you wake up every morning, all your wishes and hopes for a day rush at you like wild animals in shoving them all back in listening to that other voice taking that other point of view letting that other larger stronger guitar life come flowing *(2)*Give God your waiting thought ,the matured married couples has learned the treasure of shared silence they don't need to fill the air with constant chatter just being together is enough /sufficient try being silent with God(*Psalm46;10*)Says stop fighting and know that am God, awareness of God is the result of stillness before God -Jesus prayed that they may be one father just as you are in me ,and am in you may they also be in us so that the world may believe When are you most deeply aware of Christ presence in you as he promised? To what degree have you consciously invited him to be more and more at your home in your heart? How has your practice of Intimacy with God developed in the last few days week's months and years?(**3**) Give God your whispering prayer Christians have learnt the value of belief sentence prayers these Give God a whispering thought these are prayers that can be said anywhere in any setting frame ,Lauibach sought unbroken communion with God by asking him every two or three minutes, Christians pray am I in your will lord am I pleasing you lord ,Imagine giving every moment as a potential time of communication with God, by the time your life is over you would have spent five months on the traffic lights ,eight months on junk mail, opening a year and half looking for a lost stuff ,and a whooping ,five years standing waiting in various queues, why don't you give these moment to God by giving God your whispering, the common becomes uncommon, simple phrase like thank you lord father or I stand on your word or my desire is to please you, can turn a commute into a pilgrimage, you don't need to leave your office or kneel in the kitchen, just pray where you are, let the kitchen become a cathedral, and the classroom become a chapel ,Give the lord your warming thought at the end of the day, let your mind set be on him, Conclude the day as you begun it, talking to God ,Thank him for the good deeds, question him about the hard parts of the day, seek his mercy ,seek his strength as you close your eyes, take assurance in the promises he who watches over **(Psalm121;4)**-The protector of Israel never dozes or sleep ,if you fall asleep you pray don't worry what a better place to doze off then in the arms of your lord God -Lord teach me how to pray (***Luke11;1***) Jesus one day was praying when he finished, one of his followers said to him lord teach us how to pray ,just as John taught his disciples , none can teach like Jesus how to pray, pupil need a tutor who knows his work, who has a gift of teaching ,who is patient and love and this will help the students -Jesus is all this and much more -Jesus loves to teach us how to pray if you **(a)** are ***not sure God is really listening to you when you talk to you***(b) *Don't understand why some **prayers seem to go unanswered (c) wonder if you are praying right or generally feel frustrated in prayers (d) are eager to know what to do to feel more secure and connected to God and gain confidence*** that your prayers make a difference say lord teach me how to pray although there some principles of prayers that apply to everyone God will lead every /each of us differently /individually he wants to take you the way you are and help you to discover your own self rhythm of prayers to develop a self- style of prayer that maximises your relationship with him ,He wants the prayer to be easy natural life giving way of communicating as you share your heart with him ,and allow him to share yours with you, prayer is simple is nothing more than talking to God and taking time to listen to what he has to say to you ,God has a personalised prayer plan for you to communicate most effectively with him ,so begin by saying lord teach me how to pray Jesus spent night praying (***Luke,6;12***)He went to the mountain and spent the night praying and those who had come to hear him ,and be to be healed of their diseases ,those troubled by the evil spirit were healed ,those who tried to touch him for power was going out from him and healing them all, Jesus spent hours in prayers ,he even prayed all night showed his incredible success flowed out of the rich relationship with the father, he made deposits each morning so that he could withdraw all day long one bible teacher writes I have gone from labouring and striving to pray for few minutes every few days to enjoying beginning my day with prayers then to praying throughout the day as things come to my heart and finally ending my day communicating with the lord as I feel asleep, I have moved from sporadic irregular prayer life to regular times of prayers that are disciplined without being legalistic where I one thought was fulfilling an obligation to God by praying ,I now realise that I absolutely cannot survive a day and be satisfied ,if I do not pray ,I realise a prayer is a great privilege not a duty ,I no longer approach God in fear, wondering, if he will really hear me and send an answer to my prayers ,I now approach him boldly as his word says to do and with great expectation, some people preach about it in churches ,bible study and go for weeks, days without taking time to pray every morning and evening he hears my voice *(Psalm,55;17) (1)Jesus prayed when pressure of life had increased*-healing the sick *(2)Prayed when important decision had to be made choosing his friends* -At that time Jesus went up a hill to pray and spent the whole night there praying to God when day came he called his disciples to him to chose twelve of them whom he named apostles Simon he named Peter and his brother Andrew James and John Philip Bartholomew Mathew and Thomas James son of Alphaeus and Simon (who was called the patriot)Judas the son of James and Judas Iscariot who became the traitor *(3) You should always pray so that the Holy God of Israel the lord who saves you, says am the lord your God the one who wants to teach you for your own good and direct you in the way you should go* (Isaiah 48;17)*(4)Before you do anything pray for* (Investment, Start a Business ,Marry ,Form Partnership ,Start driving Lessons or a Course in education)formulate a plan discuss with God listen to his voice, don't rely on your own understanding **(Proverb 3;6)(5)***Before you start on a journey or in the morning, before Sunday service (Church leaders you need to pray)*Jesus very early the next morning, long before day light he got up and left the house ,he went out of the town to a lonely place where he prayed ,but Simon and his companion went out searching for him ,they said everyone is looking for you ,but Jesus answered we must go on the other village round here I have to preach in them also because that's why I came so he travelled all over Galilee preaching in the synagogues and driving out demons **(Mark1;35;39)**I cry out in distress and hears my voice God is far too creative to insist that every person interacts with him in exactly the same way he designed each of us differently there are prayer principles that apply to all of us, but God leads us each differently as individuals ,we are all at different place in our walk with him ,we are all at different level of spiritual maturity , we all have different type of experience in prayers yes we need to learn the fundamentals of prayers and we need to move beyond intellectuals knowledge about how to pray and take those principles to the lord and say teach me to apply this to my life (heart) in my situation show me how this idea is supposed to work for me ,God am depending on you, teach me how to Pray to make me effective in Prayer to make my relationship with you, the most rewarding of my life, when you ask Lord to teach me how to pray you are asking him to teach you to pray ,in distinctly personal way and enable your prayer to be easy, natural expression of who you are, you need to go before God just the way you are, and give him the pleasure of enjoying the company of the original, that he made you to be ,you need to approach him with your personal strength ,weakness ,uniqueness and your heart and soul and everything else you need in life so wonderful distinguishes you from everyone else God enjoys meeting you where you are developing a personal relationship with you and helping you to grow to become everything he wants you to be (*Psalm 33;15*)He forms all their thought and knows everything they do ,he fashioned our hearts individually, so your prayer should be consistence with the way God designed you, can learn from other people who are more experienced in prayers than you are but you need to be careful not to make them your standard or become **clone** it is very wrong to force yourself to do what other do if you are not comfortable with it in your spirit don't try to keep with someone else copy their prayer style and don't feel compelled to work every prayer principle you have learned every time you pray ,Most of us are afraid not be like others ,We are more comfortable following specified rules than daring to follow the leading of -*Gods spirit* ,-When we follow Manmade rules ,we please people, But when we step out in faith and follows Gods Spirit, we please him- you don't need to be pressured to pray a certain way or for a certain length of time ,or to focus on certain things ,because other are doing ,so let the God Spirit take the lead and you will be in a lot of surprise in life ,you need to be determined to be yourself refuse to spend your life guilty because you are not like somebody else ,the bible says ___he fashioned their heart individually___ so when it comes to prayer the massage for you today is be yourself , praying with the right mind set, you do not receive because you ask a miss (**James;4;3**)You don't receive because your motives are bad you ask for things to use for your own pleasure some times in our prayers we are me centred and see God as a genie to be conjured up to fulfil our every wish then when we don't get them we think he does not exist ,he does not hear us, does not care, James said you don't receive because you ask a miss that you may spent it on your pleasure selfishness is at the root of many unanswered prayers the first part in the lord prayer is hallowed be your name second your kingdom come and the third will be done (**Mathew 6;9-10**) Our first concern in prayers should be what God wants not we want from God when we are praying with a right mind set we should **Ask- God(1)** *cleanse us with his blood to* because you can't come into his presence tainted by sin ,you must confess and ask him to forgive you (**"2)Ask-God-***to slay your sinful nature* -as a new creature in Christ we wrestle daily with our daily old nature and as long as that nature has the upper hand our prayer will be hindered (**3**) **Ask- God** *to fill you with the Holy Spirit the indwelling of Gods*- divine spirit   enables you to overcome temptation and live according to his will- God is spirit and is worshipped and praised in the spirit**(4)Ask- God** *to guide your steps* God plan for our lives is always better than anything you can think of in life **(%) ask** him to use you for his glory, make yourself available as a servant with a willing heart to do whatever he ask of you, king Solomon did **(1Kings 3;9)**asked Lord give your servant an understanding heart ,that I may discern between the good and evil ,that's why God made king Solomon the richest man in his day ,God said because you have not asked life for yourself but have asked for understanding I have given you a wise and understanding heart so that there has been not been anyone like you before you, nor shall any like you arise after you and I have also given you what you have not asked both riches and honour so that there shall not be anyone like you among kings all your days before you as God for material thing s ask God for wisdom when you have wisdom God will trust you God can trust you with material success because he knows you will use them to glorify him understanding is wisdom and knowledge ability to interpret life as God to see what he sees in a situation understanding is the ability to see through Gods eyes hear through his ears think through his mind and feel through hid heart what is the answer to the lonely rejected parental care-business problem political conflicts in our prayer we need to pray for understanding as king Solomon did getting wisdom is the most important thing you can do whatever else you get insight love wisdom and she will make you great embrace her and she will bring you honour she will be your crowning glory**(Proverb;4-7;9)**When you pray with the right mind set you will get your prayers answered ,pray from your heart, Look to the Lord and his strength, seek his face always **(1Chronicles,16;11)**When you search me with all your heart you will seek me and find me **(Jeremiah;29;13)**God is not moved by the multiplicity of your words ,he is moved by the heart that spills, the burden of days across the altar exposing all the pains to the power of our God who can what? Can do whatever you have the Faith to believe him for whatever things you ask for ,when you pray believe that you will receive them , and you will receive them**(Mark,11;12)**Ask God to do the things which are impossible for you, because for him there is nothing impossible for him, healing , wisdom supernatural powers, peace , nothing is impossible for those who believe , open your mouth you are not talking to human beings , you talking to the creator of heaven and earth he own everything ,he moves mountains shuts the mouth of the lions ,heals the sick ,makes a way where there is no way, Your confidence in prayers is not based on your ability, how much you speak, but on Gods ability to hear and understand , he knows what you are trying to say , the old hymns goes in season of distress and grief, my soul has often found relieve and often escape the tempers snare by the thy return sweet ,hour of prayer either learn how to pray or become a worrying good at worrying ,what you give to God ,he handles , Spiritually when everything is going out and nothing is coming in you collapse under the weight of all, is that where you are today ,a prayer is your answer, it restores life -What life depletes when you are praying you are saying , I believe God you are more competent to deal with this than myself , and I trust in you to do it , my heart and my soul is in your hands , my family, my career .my finances ,my worries. my investments are in your hands -God is ready to intervene on your behalf ,just pray for your heart , commit your way to God and trust him and shall bring to pass(**Psalm37;5-6**)**Pray** Seth had a son whom he named Enoch it was then that the **people began using the Lords Holy name in Worship** (*Genesis 4;26*) **So how often do you call on the name of the lord?, (a)Only when you are in church? (b) Only when you are in trouble? (c) Occasionally? Never?(d)Or you say but you Don't know what to say-**Do not-Pray for easy lives pray to be stronger Woman /men- Do not pray for tasks equal to your power pray for power equal your tasks ,you don't tap into Gods resources until you attempt that seems humanly impossible I can do everything God asks me to do with the help of Christ who gives me the strength and power **(Philippians 4;13)All** progress involves risks, David was attending his sheep there came a lion but in Gods strengthened him he defeated it plus the bear and later a giant Goliath if he had feared and run away he would have missed the chance to become a king of Israel when you have faith it's an opportunity from God to move you from one level to another and conquer but fear steals your opportunities(**1Samuel;17;34**)The Bible states it that Samson prayed only when he was in trouble(1)**When he thought he was dying of thirsty-**then Samson became thirsty so he called to the Lord and said you gave me this victory ,am now going to die of thirst and be captured by these heathen Philistine? then God opened a hallow place in the ground there at Lehi and water came out of it ,Samson drank it and began to feel much better so the spring was named Hakkore it is still there at Lehi,**(Judges;15;18;19 Samson defeats the Philistines Judges 15;9;20) (2)The second time when Samson prayed -**When he was put in prison kings met together to celebrate their victor over him ,they offered a great sacrifice to their god Dagon they sang that their god had given them victory over Samson God, Samson was called to entertain them and they made him stand between the pillars, when the people saw him they sang praise to their god, Our god has given us victory over our enemy who devastated our land and killed so many of us! the building was crowded with so many people Men and Women on the roof watching Samson entertain them ,Then Samson prayed "Sovereign lord remember me, please give me strength just once more so that with this one blow, I can get even with the philistines for putting out my two eyes ,so Samson took hold of the two middle pillars holding up the building putting one hand on each pillar ,he pushed against them and shouted let me die with the philistines, he pushed with all his might and the building fellow down on the kings and everyone else,

Samson killed more people at his death than he had killed during his life **(Judges,16;23;30)***If you don't know what to say*-**Adore**- you build your Intimacy in relationship by focusing on the other person so change your prayer pattern get up tomorrow morning and ask God is there anything I can do for you today Adoration is to Worship ,Praise Honour and Exalt him in other wards to respect God for wonderful things he has done for you blessings protection and provisions **(Psalm,103;Psalm,145) (1)Ask**- (Supplication) most of the time Gods will is already revealed in his word, so read it when you know you are praying you pray with confidence and faith Gods greatest desire is to believe in spite of the circumstances, your feelings and all opinions is nothing Jesus said whatever you ask for in prayers believe that you have received and it will be yours(*Mark11;24&Mathew;7;7;8)Bad as you are you know how to give good gifts to your children how much more then will your father in heaven give good things to those who ask him (Mathew;7;11)* I will do whatever you ask in my name so that the son will bring glory to the father you may ask me for *anything in my name and I will do it (***John 14;13;14***)Keep speaking Gods words over and over your situation ,my word shall not return to me void, but it shall accomplish what I please and prosper in the things for which I have sent (Isaiah;55;11)anyone who wants his prayers should keep speaking his word, Asking seems to come naturally to Children, we can freely talk to him ,and ask him anything like any caring father (Parents)he will say yes to some and he will say no to some, you have to wait (2)***Accept**-God told the prophet Habakkuk the vision is yet for an appointed time though it takes time wait for it (***Habakkuk;2;3)***put it in writing because it is not yet time for it to come true, but the time is coming for it to come true, and time is coming quickly and what I show you will come true, it will certainly take place and it will not be delayed, God understands your sense of Urgency, but he always work in his best and interest, not your own one ,his willingness to answer your prayer ,is not the question when you pray according to his will*(John5;14)*but his answer is determined by the condition of your heart and your readiness to handle what he wants to give you, Instead of pestering him like a child grow up and say lord you promised it, I believe it and that settles it your word let us pray (***Ephesians;6;18)***It is through Jesus Christ that all of us Jews and gentiles are able to come in one spirit into the presence of the father, nothing can take the place of prayer not money ,not even relationship or food you eat and water you drink ,the truth is we do greater things after we pray, but we cannot do great things until we pray in the spirit at all times and on every occasion with all kinds of prayers and request with this in mind, be alert and always keep praying for Gods people (***Ephesians,4;28)***those who used to rob and steal must stop and start working in order to earn an honest living and be able to help the needy, Because you answer prayers people everywhere will come to you(*Psalm65;2)*Jesus got up every morning and prayed made deposits each morning ,so that he could make withdrawals throughout the day (*Mark;1;35)*So many of us give different excuses ,we are busy to pray and so we are so busy to have power ,when you pray your life transform- if you want to know God better start praying ,Your father in heaven will give good gifts to those who ask (**Mathew;7;14**)Pray the largest prayer you cannot think of, A prayer so large that God in answering it will not wish that you have made it large, when we love our children we want to be generous with them and that how God feels about us, If you then thought you are evil know how to give Good gifts to your children how much will your father in heaven give you good gifts to those who ask him, Some of us have difficulties in accepting the gifts God gives us particularly material gifts No body voice sounds sweeter to him than yours, nothing in the world keeps him from directing his full attention to your request, so come to him in your prayer, Pray continually (*Thessalonian;5;17)Pray continually* -If you can worry continually you can pray continually you just need to change your focus (*Exodus;17;8;9)* here there is a lesson if you are willing to invite God to involve himself in your daily life you will experience his power in your home, your relationship ,your Job, and whenever else its sobbing Its hard for God to release his power in your life to you Lord I lift up my soul (**Psalm 25;1**)Hear my voice, I pray to you lord in the morning, at sunrise, I offer my prayers and wait for your answer(**Psalm5;3 &Ps;55;17**)) Answer me when I call to you O my righteous God give me relief from my distress ,be merciful to me and my prayers (**Psalm 4;1**)When you Just put your hands in the pocket and say I can have this on my own, if you do that don't be surprised you will get a nagging feeling that the tide of battle has shifted against you ,and that you are powerless to do anything about it to experience Gods power in life you must pray continually *(Psalm91;15)* When they call on me, I will answer them, when they are in trouble ,I will be with them, I will rescue them and honour them ,we are limited we cannot handle much God on the other hand, he never get tired his ear is always open to our ears and he has unlimited capacity to help ,You will never hear him say due to an usually high call volume am un able to answer or to take your call massage at this time please leave your massage or call back latter ,the bible says he shall call upon me and I will answer in trouble ,I will deliver and honour him the desire of the righteous will be granted (*Proverb;10;24)*the prayer of the righteous is his delight (*Proverb;15;8)* call to me and I will answer you and show you great might things which you don't know(*Jeremiah;33;3)*If you abide in me and my words abide in you will ask what you desire and shall be done for you For we do not know what we should pray for(*Romans; 8;26)* In the same way the spirit also comes to help us weak as we are, for we do not know how we ought to pray, the spirit himself pleads with God for us in groans that words cannot express and the lord who sees into our heart s knows what the thought of the spirit is, because the spirit pleads with God on behalf of his people ,with his will and the spirit makes intercession for us with a groaning which cannot be altered now, who searches the heart knows what the mind of the spirit is, because he makes the intercession for the saints according to the will of God ,and we know all things work together for good for those who love God and to those who are called for his purpose, Prayers work like 999 all you need is dial and you are instantly connected to an operator who is trained to keep calm emergency situation, and able to connect with emergency service required to send help straight away ,you might not be able to say what the problem is perhaps a loved one has died or had a heart attack and you are so out of control all you can do just scream into the telephone no problem, The operator does not need all the details, he knows where the call is coming from, and help is on the way ,there is times of desperation and pain, when we pray *999* prayers we are overwhelmed sometimes we don't know the words to say speak ,but God hears he knows our names our situations ,and knows where the call is coming from, help is on the way, he has already began to bring a solution, likewise the spirit also help in our weakness in prayers ,it is better to have a heart without words than words without a heart ,**John Bunyan said"-;** You will ask what you desire and shall be done, why does it take you so long to ask, let God be your first option before you do anything , Prayer moves God and when God moves, people and situations Change ,Jesus said to Peter that Satan has asked for you that he may shift you like wheat ,but I have prayed for you that your faith should not fail you ,and when you have returned to me strengthen your brethren and God answered that prayer, there is no distance in prayers, you can protect yourself into any situation at anywhere anytime on earth claiming the promises ,whatever you ask in prayers believe you have received it, and it will be yours **(Mark;11;24) Samuel prayed when his people were in the dry season and it rained-**On that same day the lord sent thunder and rain ten the people of became afraid of the lord and Samuel people went on to ask Samuel to pray for them to the lord so that they won't die ,after realizing that besides all other sins they had sinned against God by asking for a king Samuel said don't be afraid even though you have done such an evil thing do not turn away from the lord, but serve him with your heart ,don't go to other false gods ,they cannot help you or save you, for they are not real, the lord has made solemn promise, and he will not abandon you, for he has dedicated to make you his own people**(1Samuel;12;18;23)**Lesson to learn here even when you have done Bad things- repent to God of your evil ,he will forgive you**,** Some of us we don't pray, because we think we have blown it already in life -When the Philistine were about to annihilate Israel Samuel said I will intercede with the lord for you **(1Samuel,7;5)**and the result?;; the lord thundered against the philistine ,God comes by invitation- your prayers open doors for him any time you pray in Jesus name the holy spirit is authorised to go to work accomplishing things on your behalf that cannot be accomplished any other way, if someone says that he is praying for you leaves you ignorant about the incredible power and potential of your own prayers, if someone says he prays for you this shows you have given away your greater expression and love for your God -you know better than anybody what you want and God knows what you want from him you have to do it yourself and other follow, make a prayer a habit ,He knelt down three time's day and prayed *(Daniel;6;10)* Peter whom God used to build the church and John God used to write the book of revelation made time in their daily schedule life for prayers Peter and John went up together to the temple at the hour of prayers the ninth three hours *(Acts;3;1)*In the afternoon the hour of prayers the apostle Paul who wrote much of the new testament said never stop praying *(1Thessalonians;5;17)*Daniel habit of praying was well known that his enemies used it to trap him, he knelt down on his knees three times a day and prayed and gave thanks to God as was his custom since early days ,then these men assembled and found him praying *(Daniel;6;10)* Daniels prayers shut the mouth of the lions, and caused the heathen King to say men must tremble and fear before the God of Daniel ,for he is the living God his kingdom is the one which shall not be destroyed ,he delivers and rescues, and works signs and wonders in heaven and on the earth, who has delivered Daniel from the power of the lions ,so Daniel prospered the Psalmist wrote" he who dwells in the secret place of the most high shall abide under the shadow of the almighty*(Psalm;91;1)*Be still before the lord and wait patiently for him *(Psalm;37;7)*Once you identify your secret place and begin to use your regularly a kind of aura surrounds it you will grow to love it and eventually it will become the important place in your life the power of the prayer defies calculations nothing lies beyond the reach of prayer except that which lies outside the will of God *(Psalm;66;19)*The Psalmist wrote" God has really surely listened and has heard my prayers ,if I heard cherished Sin in my heart the Lord would not have listened and has heard my prayers the character flaws you are working on and your tendency to stumble from time to time don't disqualify you from God blessing the sin you cherish does that in prayers the first thing God will want to talk to you about usually the last thing you want to talk to him about namely the sin you don't want to let go of it will actually keep you from the place of prayers when Adam sinned he hid from God saying I heard your voice and I was afraid because I was naked*(Genesis;3;10)*Christians should have an appetite for prayers, Christians should not be forced to pray- you don't need to force a healthy child food, so it is with those who are spiritually healthy they have appetite for the word of God, and for prayer , a little Girl committed a certain offence and when her mother discovered it, she began to question her daughter immediately the child lost her smile and cloud darkened, her face as she said mother I don't feel like talking, so it is with us ,when our fellowship with God is broken by sin in our lives we do not feel like talking to him, so if you don't feel like talking ,praying to him today it is probably a good indication that you need it, when you fail to pray in life you set yourself to fail, Jesus prayed so that he should not fail Satan is at work to take prayers out of our homes churches schools work place Government debating about prayers in public places but Satan won't win and he knows it his ways is trying to convince us that he will win because he has little time but he won't ,we thank you Lord for this opportunity to seek from you the habit of prayer ;**Amen**

The prayer that touches God(1)Continued prayer -Pray and believe until God answers**(2)Heartfelt prayer-**Prayer that comes from the heart **(3)Mockery immune prayer-**Prayer made despite the risks of mockery **(4)Emotional prayer-**Prayer made out of genuine deep rooted desire for a change **(5)Open prayer** -the prayer that opens the heart and pours the heart out ,<u>**Hannah; Prayer;(1Samuel;1;12;20)**</u>Hannah made a solemn promise Almighty Lord look at me your servant see my trouble and remember me don't forget me if you give me a son I promise that I will dedicate him to you for his whole life and that he will never have his hair cut Hannah continued to pray to the lord for a long time and Eli watched her lips ,she was praying silently her lips were moving but she made no sound so Eli thought she was drunk and said to her stop making a drunken show of yourself ,stop your drinking and sober up, No, am not drunk sir ,she answered I haven't been drinking I am desperate and I have been praying ,pouring my troubles to the Lord ,don't think I am a worthless woman I have been praying like this because I am Go in peace Eli said "and may the God of Israel give you what you have asked may you always think kindly of me, she replied ,then she went away ate some food and was no longer sad ,the next morning Elkanah and his family got up early and after worshiping the Lord, they went back home to Ramah, Elkanah had intercourse with his wife Hannah, and the Lord answered her prayer ,so it was that she became pregnant and gave birth to a son she named him Samuel and explained I asked the Lord for him **(1Samuel;12;19)** A woman of prayers is a powerful woman a great woman is the who makes others greater , teach your friends , family members, children ,mothers, fathers, community , to pray let the generation of prayer warrior start from you, be a role model to them , A Church rooted in prayers is a powerful Church , A Preacher /Pastor rooted in prayers is a powerful Servant of God , Children and Marriages rooted in prayers are powerful ,Families ,Jobs , Education ,blessings ,Financiers rooted in prayers, no man can uproot them , if you are not praying you are playing with your destiny , Pray for wisdom ,Visions , healing ,protection ,favour, change , faith ,blessings , mercy ,grace   **Amen**

PRAYER POINTS

My Father Arise and let- my ways be open in Jesus name; **Amen**

Jehovah the story changer Arise -let my story change in Jesus name; Amen

God of suddenly Arise in the thunder of your Power appear in my situations in Jesus name; **Amen**

By the power in the blood of Jesus Christ O God Arise and disappoint my Enemies in the name of Jesus Christ; **Amen**

Any Evil power mandated to destroy our calling**,** church, families business, destiny ,catch fire in the name of Jesus Christ , **Amen**

Any secret plans of the devil secreted to destroy our family catch fire , in Jesus name , **Amen**

Any gathering which is not of God in my career ,business , family, relationship ,either in the Sea , Earth, forest, dark places , scatter and catch fire in Jesus name ,Amen Whoever attacks you does it without my consent ,whoever fights against you will fall **(Isaiah 54;15),Amen**

Any gathering upon my life I over turn the table in Jesus name **,Amen**

Any conspiracy against my life I turn it to my up-liftment in Jesus name, **Amen**

God of 24hours miracle where are you appear now in my situations now in Jesus name; **Amen**

God Arise Visit me in your Favour in Jesus name; Amen

Empower my Angles of blessings to break through now in Jesus name; **Amen**

Where is God of Elijah divide my Jordan by fire in Jesus name; **Amen**

God of 24 hours miracle Arise locate me by fire in Jesus name; **Amen**

Pharaoh of my Father house let me go in Jesus name; Amen

Miracles that will wipe out my past ridicule manifest in Jesus name; **Amen**

Uncommon and Extraordinary testimony Locate me by fire in Jesus name; Amen

My father do what will make me forget the past years of pain in Jesus name; Amen

My past labour Arise become testimonies in Jesus name; Amen

I shall not see shame in the name of Jesus Christ; **Amen**

I shall not see demotion in the name of Jesus Christ; Amen

I shall not see defeat in the name of Jesus Christ; Amen

Voices speaking against my raising up shut up in the name of Jesus Christ; Amen

Satanic barriers to my breakthrough catch fire in the name of Jesus Christ; Amen

Every -Evil power behind my stagnant die in Jesus name; Amen

Every Evil power using my Glory to shine die in Jesus name; Amen

As- You speak these words with faith, they are not mere words but with Power these Gods word will prepare you for a better future ,and change your life in this life and after when you leave this world -the more you meditate on the word of God upon your life the word will sustain you, and direct your Spiritual life, ,Encourage yourself and others to feed on the word of God it is a nourishment for the Soul , And take care of your words and the words will take care of you In Jesus name; **Amen**

QUESTION?

WHAT HINDER OUR PRAYERS TO BE ANSWERED BY GOD?

(1) Un-confessed Sin -your sin have hidden his face from you so that he will not hear(*Isaiah 59;2)*It is because your sins that he does not hear you it's your sin that separate you from you when you try to worship him (**Isaiah;56;2)**I will bless those who always observe the Sabbath and do not misuse it I will bless those who do nothing evil as a Christian God expects you to walk in obedience What does God requires of you?*(1)***To act justly-** love, mercy and walk humbly with your God(*Micah6;8)* these are the basic requirements and if you don't meet them you are wasting your time praying unless it's a prayer of repentance you must seek God forgiveness and then he will hear your prayers-**(2) Failure to pray** people don't read the bible yet the bible is a book of prayers ,our daily problem are being solved , we spent a lot of time talking about prayers and we fail to get down to mean business of praying -Prayers realises the energy of God the goal of the prayer is not to overcome, Gods reluctance but is to believe him and take hold of his willingness ,his word says you do not have because you don't ask , no praying woman/man accomplish so much with so little expenditure of time ,until when you learn to pray in faith and wait on God for the answer you will get *nowhere- if you don't learn to pray , believe and wait on God you will get nowhere* -**(3)Failure to care** when the Israelites complained that God was not answering them their prayers he told them fairly share your food with the hungry clothe those who are cold and don't hide from those who need your help if you do these thing God will answer you **(Isaiah58;6-9)** self-centeredness you can pray for years /weeks /months and days, asking God for certain things and end up in frustrations, if you only think about yourself , stop think again focus on other people's needs to, God will answer you **(4)Unresolved conflict** –Husband /wives children be considerate as you live together treat each other with respect so that nothing will hinder you prayers there is no point of praying if you are always fighting each other anyone who claims to be in light but hates his brother /sister is still in darkness(*1John;2;9)*God will answer you when you are in light deal with things which drive you to a part and amend your relationship now sometimes it's not possible to make amends live in peace with everyone(*Romans;12;8)*sometimes one would like keep the issue alive than accept your apology ,when that happens look into your heart do you really want to restoration or would you rather place blame and let things faster you of the gracious gift of life so that nothing will hinder your prayers, if your attempts have been whole hearted and honest God won't let a broken relationship stand in the way of your prayers ,but if your attempts have been half hearted and self -serving try again this time for real (*James;4;2*)you do not have because you don't ask, you desire but you don't have ,you covet but you cannot get what you want so you quarrel and fight you do not have so you should not fight and you should solve unsolved conflict, God don't answer your prayers when we pray because we don't persist , we are supposed to stay attached to him, to answer you involves, patience, faith ,persistence, Jesus gives us a parable of a Woman who kept pleading with a hard hearted judge to grant her petition, when she finally wore him down, he gave her what she asked, Jesus had only one reason for this parable to show you that you should pray and persist and don't give up(*Luke;18;1*)the point is not persistence but co-operation and that's what God wants from you, don't quit when you persist he will answer you **Before you ask adore**– any prayer that starts with asking can be described as a self- centred prayer and shallow ,enter his gates with, thanks giving ,and his courts with praise (**Psalm;100;4**)Gods love and faithfulness are/is your starting point you are lifted out of yourself your spirit is lifted for connecting to God the content of your prayer becomes more scriptural and you earn the results When God puts you on hold be patient in trouble and prayerful always, (**Romans;12;12**)be joyful in, hope, patient in affliction ,faithful in prayers we have been dubbed in a microwave generation for good reasons we change through life like we are on fire ,but God has his own time –table and cannot be rushed , and when he puts you on hold watch your words like a small rudder on a big ship ,what you say determines your direction and helps to stop the wrong thoughts from infiltrating your mind **Weldon" *said my mind is my Garden, my thoughts are seeds, my harvest will be either flowers or weed,*** ask God to help you control your emotion, Paul said be glad for all God is planning be patient in troubles and prayerful always complaining magnifies the problem prayers turns negativity into a powerful force for good look for the humour in it Solomon-said he who is a merry heart has a continual feast (**Proverb15;15**)Laughter's dispels tension lightens the burden and fills your soul with joy, appreciate the chance to learn the Chinese views problems as prospect in their culture, Solomon said the diligent make use of everything they see (**Proverb12;27**)Learn from your experience regardless of how hard it is, and remember some of the world greatest discoveries and breakthrough resulted from crisis ,love unconditionally problems are caused by people and under pressure, it's tempting to lash out the bottom line is we all do mistakes and nobody is beyond redemption **Are you glad about that ?**Learn to see people through Gods eyes overcome evil with Good(**Romans;12;21**)Be courteous and maintain your dignity when you are under pressure (**Luke;21;19**) stand firm and you will win in life when God puts you on hold make peace your priority don't let your inner man/woman controlled by your outside pressure when you go to war everybody suffers but when peace that comes from Christ controls your thought (**Colossians;3;15**)It restores your perspective and creates an atmosphere that is conducive to solutions ,look for a breakthrough, from an expected source when you commit thy way unto the Lord (**Psalm;37;5**)don't be surprised when the people and circumstance he sends into your life are not the one you expected ,he spoke to Balaam through a donkey (**Numbers22**)and he used the burning bush to get Moses(**Exodus 3**)Don't be in the hurry even notice the faster you go the more behind you get Jesus said by your patience possess your soul as Henry black observes, God timing is the best ,he may be withholding your directions to cause you seek him more intently, don't try to keep the relationship away from him, and get on doing ,God is much more interested in your relationship, than what you want don't be too proud to ask for help ,Solomon said with humility comes wisdom (**Proverb11;2**)If the people you turn are not immediately available be patient and don't give up ,God designed us to work together and somewhere up to the road you will be called to help somebody, by sharing what you have, learning right now through hard times and before you know it he brings us a long side ,someone else so that we can be there for that person(**2Corinthians1;4**)Amen- **Key to unanswered prayers** -ask and you will receive that your joy may be full (**John16;24**)if your prayers are not being answered ask yourself(**1**)**How is my relationship with my God-** if I regard iniquity in my heart the lord will not hear me (**Psalm 66;18**)anything that adversely affects your relationship with God also affects your prayers ,friendship gives you favour ,intimacy gives you access, Jesus said you abide in me and my words in you will ask and receive what you desire and shall be given to you (**John;15;7**) *We must belong to God, and One Mediator between God and Man* -The man Jesus Christ (**1Timothy 2;5**)because Jesus is the mediator between God and Man ,we must give him our total Allegiance before I yield the control of my life to Jesus Christ the control of my life Jesus, Christ I would pray but I was not sure if God was listening or would Answer, After I asked him to be the Lord of my life I have the confidence that God was hearing my prayers,(**2**)*When we pray to the Father (God)in the name of his Son Jesus Christ* ,**God answers our prayers**, only the name Jesus Christ gives us the credibility with The Father not ours , Education or Wisdom ,Wealth ,Wives ,Children ,Church background, Job Position, for the full content of divine ,nature lives in Christ ,in his humanity ,and you have been given full life in union with him, he is supreme over every spiritual rulers and

Authority **(Philippians 2;9;10)**Only Jesus Christ name "he said if you ask anything in Jesus name I will do it *(John 14;14)But Peter said to him I have no money at all ,but I give you what I have in the name of Jesus Christ of Nazareth ,I order you to get up and walk, then he took him up at once the man's feet and ankles become strong ,he jumped up, stood on his feet and started walking around ,then he went into the temple with them, walking and jumping and praising (Acts,3;6;8)* **(3)How strong is your Faith** -without faith it is impossible to please God for he who comes to God must believe that he is the giver of those who diligently seek him(**Hebrews11;6**)and note these things Believe Gods deepest longing is to be believed, regardless of the circumstances, and emotions, We must pray in Faith "Jesus said And Everything you ask in prayers believing you shall receive it **(Mathew;21;23)** ,the fact is that you are asking God for your needs demonstrate your Faith and Hope ,There many times God has answered my Prayers as soon as I pray, and other times I have to wait for them to be answered, some of my requests have been on my prayers request for years, and Am still waiting but I know God will answer them in Jesus name- Diligently when you pray put your heart and soul into it Paul speaks of labouring in prayers **(Colossians4;12)** Am God is not some force out there, his your heavenly father who knows that you need all these things **(Mathew6;32)**Your highest priority should not be getting what you want /needs but building your relationship with him-**(4)**-We must have a forgiving Spirit "Jesus says whenever you stand praying forgive, if there is anything against anyone so that your father also who is in heaven may forgive you your transgressions *(Mark;11;25) th*is verse makes it clear that you can't carry ,Anger hatred or bitterness in our heart towards anyone, if we expect God to forgive us and hear our prayers--We must have a clean heart -if I had ignored my sins the Lord would not have listened to me but God has indeed heard me he has listened to my prayers I praise the Lord because he did not reject my prayers or keep his constant love from me **(Psalm,66;18;20)**It is very important to keep a Clean heart ,before God, someone said confess them as you do them, don't bunch them until you go to Church on Sunday ,Christmas, Easter or Crisis arise in your life, confess your sins as soon as you become aware of them, any altitude or Action that is not pleasing to God admit it that its wrong ,and ask God for his Mercies and forgiveness God is faithful and forgives and cleanses us from all our wrongs *(read 1John;1;9)***(5)Patience** are you showing patience until Gods time finally comes see How God tested Patience **(Psalm105;19)until** what he had predicted came true the word of the lord proved him right Joseph was tested by the very promise God gave him can't you hear Satan whisper I thought the dream said you were supposed to be a Prime- minister what are you doing in prison ? But it only looks like a prison in reality it is the place of destiny Joseph saw Gods promises fulfilled in his time and you will have to wait for Gods time when we pray all these are achieved(**Jeremiah;32;27**)his love is unconditional ,has no limit power to do what we can't do-They will be done on earth as it is in heaven(**Mathew;6;10**)Gods will is never questioned nor should it be in your life -God is more concerned about our life on everyday basis ,he multiplied food for the hungry, healed all those who were sick (**Mathew;8;16**)and he will meet our needs if we pray, do not worry about what to eat, drink, trust him for today through your prayers and faith(**Mathew;6;31**)When you ask and you don't receive it means you are asking with a wrong motive ,that you may spend what you get to your pleasure(**James;4;3**)In churches we have the ministry of Intercessor (intercedes for us it's a powerful ministry)(**Job;16;21**)I want someone to plead with for me as one pleads for a friend the bible says so Joshua fought the Amalekites and Moses .Aaron and Hur went to the top of the hills as long as Moses held up his hands the Israelites were winning but whenever he lowered his hands the Amalekites were winning when Moses hands grew tired Hur and Aaron held his hands up so Joshua overcome the Amalekites army(**Exodus;17;10-13**)this story truly illustrates the power of intercessory prayer far from the Crowd but seen by the eyes of God are Men and Women who hold up their hands of Ministries in prayers and God is looking for more of them ,Job wrote and said my intercessor is my friend on behalf of a man he pleads with God as a man pleads for his friend (**Job;16;20;21**)Pray with your mind spirit sing with your spirit, and mind (**1Corinthians;14;15**)pray in the spirits in all occasions ,with all kinds of prayers, and requests keep praying for all saints, pray for me also ,that whenever I open my mouth words may be glorifying the lord ,so that I will fearlessly make known the mystery of the gospel (**Ephesians;6;18-19**)(6)**Fasting during your Prayer Season** -God to answer your prayer fasting is important in praying to achieve something Ezra leads the people in fasting and prayers ,So we fasted and prayed for God to protect us and he answered our prayers (**Ezra;8;23**) though the ministry of intercession is not written nowhere in the bible everyone is meant to pray without ceasing in life, praying for the ,Sick ,Peace, those without faith ,Winning soul ,Wicked(sinners)praying for Children ,Leaders ,Marriages ,Singles (**a**)Praying is a sacrifice which calls you away from the pleasure and comfort of life ,Praying is an identification in which you have to stand with others (**c**)A Prayers move the hand of God on behalf of others , Today to pour his blessing, favour anointing on us, the lord /God who said I sought for a man among them that should stand in the gap before me for the land (**Ezekiel,22;30) is** looking for intercessor you can be one of them in the book of (**1Timothy2;8**)Men everywhere lift up holy hands in prayers without anger or disputing, let us approach the throne of Grace with confidence ,so that we may receive mercy, and find grace to be in our time of need (**Hebrews4;16**)Is any of you in trouble ? he should pray, is anyone happy let him sing songs of praise, is any of you sick he should call on elders in the church to pray for him and anoint him with oil in the name of the lord and the ,Prayer offered in faith will make the sick person normal again, lord will raise him up, if he has sinned he will be forgiven ,therefore confess your sins to each other and pray for each other so that you may be healed ,the prayer of a righteous man is powerful and effective (**James 5;13;16**)When we ask we must believe and don't doubt, because he who doubts is like a wave of the sea blown and tossed by the wind that man should not think ,he will receive anything from the lord(**James,1;7**)Devote yourself to prayers being watchful and thankful(**Colossian;4;2**)Do not be anxious of anything but everything in by prayers, and petition with thanks giving present your request to God **(Philippians;4;6)**And as he taught them he said" it is not written " my house will be called a house of prayers for all nations(**Mark,11;17**)This the confidence we have in approaching God, that if we ask anything according to his will he hears us and ,if we know that he hears us whatever we ask we know that we have what we have asked of him **(!John 5;14;15)We should keep feeding our faith and starving our doubts,** There is nothing great you can accomplish in this world without having prayed, keep Praying for big things, and small things ,Thanking ,Worshiping ,and Praising God pray until something happen as a change in your life , **Amen;**

HOW CAN WE BE STRONG IN PRAYERS!

To know who you are speaking to God - his promises comes to pass and are all yes ,nothing is too hard for him ,has all the power ,**Amen**
Ask for Gods will - his will and choice is the best ,**Amen**
Pray for the holy Spirit -to lead you, teach you, and open your insight ,and see beyond your insight see the hidden treasure of God ,Amen
Say what you need, (Mark11;22;24) Amen
Thank God for everything -(1 Thessalonians 5;18),Amen
Ask for forgiveness of yours sins- and forgive others , **Amen**
Pray with a friend, and don't be self cantered- pray for others ,Amen
Pray the word - Abraham - prayed In his faith did not leave him ,and he did not doubt Gods promises ,his faith filled him with power ,and he gave praise to God, he was absolutely sure that God will be able to do what he promised,(**Romans 4;20;21;Abraham did not stagger at Gods word Amen**
Memorise scriptures and meditate on them ,Amen
Pray in faith ,without doubt God will answer your prayers ,(Mark 11;20-24 2;Corinthians 4;18; Hebrews 11;1) After you have prayed don't doubt- It is true that we live in the world but we do not fight from worldly motives ,the weapons we us in our fight are not of the world weapons, but God powerful which we use to destroy strong holds we

destroy false arguments, we pull down every proud obstacles that is raised against the knowledge of God ,we take every though captive ,and make it obey God **(2 Corinthians 10;3-5)**

POWERFUL PRAYER DECLARATION

DECLARE -means
-make known formally or officially
- To make or make manifest flow.
God spoke (declared all things into existence ,he declared and the word come into existence hence we are created in his own image, he has given us Authority and power or declare over our own life (lives) Closed mouth =Closed destiny, are mouth is a spiritual weapon for conquest "this will be your chance to tell the good news, make up your minds beforehand not to worry about how you will defend yourself because ,I will give you such words and wisdom that none of your enemies will be able to refute or contradict ,what you say(Luke;21;13) God is always going to meet you at the point of your decree, you will succeed in all you do and light will shine on your path .we have to declare things in our lives Faith - Praying ,Reading Scriptures ,and Fasting is not enough declare it, and God will do it, speak it the lord is my Counsellor, Protector , I call on the Lord for help and from his sacred hill he answers me ,I lie down and sleep and all night long the Lord protects me**(Psalm;3;4;5)**Declare all the promises of God ,You declare over your life without even knowing,(have you ever said am so fat and ugly- These are negative declarations, that bring negative results into your life. We must learn to declare positive words over our lives and you will begin to see positive results.-positive declaration touch Gods heart ,Amen
Faith comes by hearing and hearing the Word of God. (**Romans 10:17**)This is a powerful scripture we should use in our daily lives/Declaration. When faith is being released is when blessing are released by God ,What you keep saying -You move towards it or break through, If you change the way how you see things -things change replace negative things with positive things circumstances change - Despite of the situations you are going through believe in unexpected or unseen; **Amen**
Ephesians 1:17-23
Asking our glorious Father and his loving son Jesus Christ to give me the spirit ,and insight so that I grow in my knowledge of God. I pray that my will be flooded with light ,so that I can understand the confidence and hope he has given me.
I also pray that I will understand the incredible greatness of God's Power and believe in him. This is the same mighty power that raised Christ from the ,Dead seated in the place of honour at Gods' right hand in the Heavenly realm, far above any ruler or authority in power or leader but also in the world to come.

God has put everything under his authority in Christ and he has head over all things for the benefit of the church- The church is his body and is made full and complete by Christ who fill all things everywhere with himself.

Ephesians 3:14-21

I pray that from his glorious unlimited resources, he will empower me with strength through his spirit. Then Christ will make his home in my heart as his roots will grow down into God's love and keep me stronger and give me supernatural power to understand his stead love. All God's people should know how wide, how long and how deep this love is. May I experience the love of Christ though it may be too slow to understand fully now, then I will be made complete with all the fullness of life that comes from God.

Now all the glory to God who is able through his mighty power at work within me to accomplish infinitely more than I might ask or think. It is written I believe therefore I have spoken since we have that same spirit of faith we also speak and believe (**2Corinthians 4; 13**)these are the things we received when we got saved and we should praise God -we praise God for financial and material Spiritual blessings

Declare who you are in JESUS CHRIST.

Christ is enough for me, **Amen**
God you are bigger than a mountain any disease and powerful
I am a child of God, **Amen**
Am redeemed from the hands of the enemy
Am forgiven, **Amen**
Am justified ,**Amen**
Am sanctified ,**Amen**
Is a new creation in Jesus Christ, Amen
I am a partaker of God's divine nature, Amen
Am redeemed from the curse of the law
Am delivered from the power of darkness
Am led by the Holy Spirit., Amen
Am kept in safety everywhere I go. **Amen**
Am getting all my needs met by Jesus. **Amen**
Am strong in the Lord and the filled with his mightiness, **Amen**
Am doing all things through Jesus Christ who strengthens me, **Amen**
Am an heir of God and a join heir of Jesus Christ, **Amen**
Is an heir to the blessings of Abraham, **Amen**
Am observing and doing the Lords commandments. **Amen**
Am blessed coming and going out. **Amen**
I have eternal life. **Amen**
Am blessing with spiritual blessings, **Amen**
Am healed by the stripes of Jesus Christ.

Am excising my authority over the enemy. **Amen**

Am more than a conqueror. **Amen**

Am establishing God's word here on earth, **Amen**

Am an over comer by the blood of the lamb and the word of my testimony. **Amen**

Am daily overcoming the devil. **Amen**

Am walking by faith and not by sight. **Amen**

Am casting down wrong imaginations. **Amen**

Am bringing every thought into captivity in Christ Jesus.

Am being transformed by renewing my mind.

Is a labourer together with God ,**Amen**

Am righteous of God through Jesus Christ.

Am the light of the world ,**Amen**.

My children will fulfil their destiny, **Amen**

When people tune me on their television and radio channels will never turn me off when am preaching, **Amen**

Am blessing the Lord forever and I will continue praising him with my own mouth , **Amen**

Am the head and not the tail. Am above only and not beneath am increasing, **Amen**

Am putting on the mind of Jesus Christ. **Amen**

There is a continuous blessing to my brother , family and sisters friends in Christ, **Amen**

Am free from all kinds of bondages.

The bondages that are destroying the anointing I render them powerless for God resides in me, therefore I am bondage free.

I have what it takes to fulfil my destiny and purpose, **Amen**

3-years or days - from now are going to be more than I am today successful wiser my youth is being renewed

I have decided to follow Jesus no turning back all I need is in you salvation, joy, and break through breaking the forces of darkness and releasing overflow for me

HEALING DECLARATIONS

Jesus has redeemed me from curse and therefore I forbid sickness or diseases to come upon my body. **Amen**

Every disease and virus that touches my body dies instantly in the name of Jesus Christ. I declare every organ and every tissue in my body to function as God created it to do and I forbid any malfunction disease in me through the name of Jesus Christ. **Amen**

Heavenly father through your word you have imparted your life into me which restores my body and every air I breathe and every word I speak I am so thankful. **Amen**

Father you word has become part of me- it is flowing in my blood stream and in each cell of my body, restoring and transforming my health. Your word is strength and fresh for you' are sent it to heal me. My immune system is growing stronger every day and I speak life to my immune system, forbidding confusion and any kind of ill health. The Holy Spirit who raised Jesus Christ from the dead dwells in me and stores the word of God in me which guards my life. **Amen**

The spirit of God dwells in me permanently. Therefore, I stand against every cell that does not promote life and health in my body and declare to be cut off source. There's no space for tomorrow growth that will live in my body because the greater one lives inside of me than the one in the world and his name is Jesus Christ. **Amen**

My body is the temple of the most high and the Holy Spirit. I command my body to release the right chemicals of functioning and my pancreas to release the amount of insulin for life and health in the name of Jesus Christ. I forbid my body to be affected by any virus or disease that might word against my health. Every cell of my body supports life and health in the mighty name of our God. **Amen**

I speak to my muscles, bones and joints and I call them to be normal in the name of Jesus Christ. They will not respond to any diseases for God promised in **(1Peter2:24),** that he carried away all our sins in his own body while on the cross so that we can be dead to sin and live. For what is right. I have been healed by his wounds and God's promises permits and grant every part of body a full package of life and health by the power of the Holy Ghost, **Amen**

Jesus Christ bore my sicknesses, carried away all kind of pain and made me free till now for his word healed me completely. ,**Amen**.

DECLARATION
;
We should believe and say what we are in God and what he says we are.
-We should believe and declare that we can do what God says we can do.
We should believe and say that God is who he says he is.
We should believe and say that God will do as he says.

Here are scriptural statements that every Christian and believer can boldly declare;
Am a new creation in Christ and my old life has passed away **(2 Corinthians 5:17),Amen**
All my sins have been forgiven in Christ
Am redeemed, sanctified and made righteous in Christ **(1Corinthiians1:30),Amen**
I have been transformed (transferred to the kingdom of God, Son the king of light **(1Colossians; 1:13)**

I have become the righteous in the kingdom of God in Christ. **(2 Corinthians 5:21),Amen**

God has prepared good works beforehand for me to walk in. **(Ephesians 2:10),Amen**

I can do all things through Christ who strengthens me. **(Philippians 4:13),Amen**

I overwhelmingly conquer in all things through Christ who loved me. **(Romans 8:37),Amen**

My God supplies all my needs per his riches in glory in Christ **(Philippians 4:19),Amen**

Am called to be a saint **(I Corinthians 1:2)** Holy people who belong to him in union with Jesus Christ together with all people who worship our God lord Jesus Christ ,their God and ours.

Am a child of God **(John 1:12) (John 3:1:2)**

My body is the temple of the Holy Spirit **(I Corinthians 6:19)** who lives in you and who was given to you by God. You do not belong to yourself but to God. He brought you with a price so use your body for God's glory.

It's no longer that I who lives but Christ lives in me **(Galatians2:20)**.This life I live now is by faith in the son of God who loved me and gave his life for me.

I have been delivered from God from Satan's authority. **(Acts26:18)** You are to open their eyes and get them from darkness to light and from the power of Satan to God so that through your faith in me they will have their sins forgiven and receive their place among God chosen people.

God's love has been shed abroad in my heart by the Holy Spirit. **(Romans 5:5)**.This hope does not disappoint us for God has poured out his love into our hearts by the means of the Holy Spirit who is God's spirit to us.-the same spirit that he powered in his Son is in us

Greater is he who is in me than he {Satan} who is in the world. **(1John4:4)**.But you belong to God my children and have defeated the false prophets because the spirit who is in you is more powerful than the spirit of those who belong to the world.

Am blessed with the spiritual blessing in the heavenly place in Christ **(Ephesians 1:3)** before we were born, God had already chosen us to be his through union with Jesus Christ so that we would be holy and without fault before him.

Am seated with Christ in the heavenly places far above all of Satan spiritual forces. **(Ephesians 2:4-6)**. Also, God's mercy is abundant and his love is greater that while we were spiritually dead in our obedience, he brought us to life with Christ. It's by God's grace that we have been saved in union with Christ Jesus; he raised us to rule with him in the heavenly world.

Because I love God and am called per his purpose he is causing all things to work together for me **(Romans 8:28)**

If God is for me, who is against me (**Romans 8:31**) - certainly not God who did not even hold his son but offered him for us. – He gave his son – will he not also freely gives us anything? Who will accuse God's people? God himself declares them guilty who then will condemn them, not Christ who died for them. Nothing can separate us from Christ's love (**Romans8:35-39**) can trouble, hardship, persecution, hunger or poverty neither things of the world will ever do.

Is a friend of God (**Revelation 1:6**) He made us a kingdom of priests to serve his God and father. To Jesus Christ be the glory and power forever and ever! Amen.

Being that I am his child; God is leading me by his spirit. (**Romans 8:14**)Those who are led by the spirit are God's children ,for the spirit that God has given you does not make you a slave, and cause you to be afraid, instead it makes you God's children. By the spirit's power we cry out to the father, God himself to declare that we are belong to God.

We will possess all the blessings he keeps for his people because we belong to him with Jesus Christ his son. For when we share his suffering, we share his glory.

As I follow the Lord, the path of my life is getting brighter and brighter. (**Proverbs 4:18**) until the day has come but the path of the wicked is dark as night – they fall but they cannot see what they have stumbled over.

God has given special gifts to use for his service. (**1Peter 4:10-11**)Preachers must preach \God's messages whoever that serves must serve with strength that God has given him or her so that in all things, praise may be given to God through Jesus Christ to whom glory and Power belongs forever.

I can cast out demons and lay hands on the sick to heal and recover (**Mark 16: 17- I8),Amen**

Believers will be given power to perform miracles, drive out demons in my name, they will speak in tongues and if they pick up snakes or drink any poison they will not be harmed, they will place their hands on the sick and get well. God always leads me in triumph in Christ. **Amen**

Am an ambassador for Christ (**2Corinthians 5:20**).Here we are speaking for Christ us through God himself were making his appeal through us we were plead on Jesus behalf. Let God change you from enemies to friends. I have eternal life (**John3:16**) For God loved the world so much that he gave his only son so that everyone that believes in him many not die but be **Saved by having eternal life**.

Everything I ask in tongues and believe I shall receive (**Mathew,27:22**).If you believe you will receive whatever you ask in Jesus name.

By Jesus' stripes am healed (**1Peter 2:24**) Christ himself carried our sins in his body so that we are free of sin and live in righteousness. It is by his wounds that you have been healed, **Amen**

BELIEVER'S BOOK

Am the salty of the earth and the light of the world (**Mathew5:13:14**).You are like the salt of the earth for the whole human race, but if salt loses its saltiness, there's no way to Make it again for it has become worthless, so it is thrown out and people trample on it. You are like light for the whole world, a city built on a hill that cannot be hidden. No one lights a lamp and hides it under a bank instead he put out the light on the lamp stand where it gives light to everyone in the house and so in the same way you light must shine before people.

Am an heir of God and joint heir with Jesus Christ (**Romans8:17**) since we are his children we will possess the blessing he keeps for his people and we will possess with Christ what God has kept for him if we share Christ suffering we share his glory too. As am part of the chosen race, a royal priesthood, a holy nation and people for God's own possession (**IPeter2; 9**) chosen to proclaim the wonderful acts of God who called you out from darkness into his marvellous light. At one time, you were not God's people but now you are his people at one time you did not know God's mercy but now you have received mercy. **Amen**

Am a member of the body of Christ (**1Corinthians 12:27**).All of you are Christ body and each one is part of the church. God has out all in place, firstly apostles, prophets, teachers and those who perform miracles power to heal.

I cast all my cares upon the Lord because he cares for me. (**1Peter,5:7**) Leave all your worries with him because he cares for you. **Amen**

I resist the devil and he flees from me (**James 4:7**) - so then submit to the Lord God and resist the devil will run away from you. Come near to God and he will come near you. **Amen**

The Lord is my helper; I will not be afraid (**Hebrews 13; 6**) - Let us be bold and say the lord is on our helper, I will not be afraid. What can anyone do to me? **Amen**

Christ bore my sickness and carried away my sins (Isaiah 53:4-5)-but he endured the sufferings that should have been ours, the pain that we should have borne but he thought of us and took this punishment on himself sent by God. We are healed by the punishment and made whole by the bowls he received. – All of us were like sheep that the Lord made the punishment fall on him yet we all deserved to be in his place.

My citizenship is in heaven (**Philippians3:20**) we are however the citizens of heaven and we are eagerly waiting for our saviour the Lord Jesus Christ to come from heaven. Her will change our weak mortal bodies and make them like his glorious body using power by which he us able to bring the things under his race. **Amen**

For me live is Christ and to die is again (Philippians 1:21) - Christ has the title and above authority in both heaven and earth. **Amen**

God will complete the work he has begun in me (**Philippians1:6**) and so is sure that God began this goodness in me and will finish it well. **Amen**

God is at work with me (**Phillpians2:13**) For God is always at work in you to make you willing and able to obey his own purpose. **Amen**

I have been redeemed from the curse of the law. (**2Corinthians3:13**).But by Jesus becoming a curse for us, we were redeemed and now free from the curse of law. Anyone who is hanged on the tree is under God's curse. Jesus died so that the blessing God promised to Abraham might be given to the gentiles and through faith we may receive the spirit promised by God. **Amen**

Am the Lord's bond slave(**1Corinthains 7:22**).For a slave who has been called by God is free for the Lord and in the same way a free person who has been called by Christ is a slave – so God bought us with a price and shouldn't e a slave for human beings. Every one of you should remain in union and fellowship with God in the same condition you were called.

Am finding my life by losing it for Jesus' sake. (**Mathew 16:25**). For whoever wants to save his life will lose it but whoever loses his life for my sake will find it. – will people gain anything if they win the whole world and lose their life, of course nit there's nothing they can gain in life for the son of man is about to come in God's glory of his father with his angels. Then he will reward each and every one accordingly to his deeds.

The lord is my defence of my life will I fear? (**Psalms 27:1**). The lord is my light and my salvation I will fear no one for the lord protects me from all dangers. I will fear not. **Amen**

The lord is my shepherd I shall not want (**Psalms 23:1**).The lord is my shepherd; I have everything I need he lets me rest in the field of green pastures and leads me to a pool of fresh waters. **Amen**

The lord will satisfy me with long life (**Psalms 91:14**).The lord says I will save those who love me – and those who acknowledge me as lord when they call to me, I will answer them. When they are in trouble, I will save them, I will rescue them and honour them, I will reward them with long life and I will save them. **Amen**

DECLARATIONS TO SPEAK OVER MY/YOUR LIFE;

-As I live in God my love grows more perfectly, and I can face him with confidence on the Day of Judgment ,because I live like Jesus here in the world. (**1John 4:17**),**Amen**

-I receive an abundance of grace and the gift of righteousness I rein in life through Jesus Christ. (**Romans 5:17**),**Amen**

-Wives as a wife, I submit myself to my husband as a fitting in the lord. My husband love me like Christ loved the church, and gave himself up for her. (**Colossians3:18, Ephesians 5:25**) (**Job; 22:8, Isaiah 60:1**),**Amen**

I declare God's word about who I am, what I have and what I can do in Christ Jesus ,who gives me strength. Am established as his son, daughter in all ways and I shine in his light **Amen.**

Husband as husband I love my wife as Christ loved the church and gave himself up for her. **Amen**

-Wives the heart of husband trust in me. He has no lack of gain,(**Proverbs31; 11)**-Husband express belief in my life and encourage her, I have no lack of gain. **(Proverbs 31:11- 28).**

Wives I do my husband good and not evil ,all the days of my life. **(Proverbs 31:12).**Husband – I cover my wife with the word to present her holy and blameless before the Lord. **(Ephesians 5:26).** My kind and tender hearted to others. I forgive them as God in Christ had forgiven me. **(Ephesians 4: 32),Amen**

I can do all things through Jesus Christ that strengthens me. **(Philippians 4:13),Amen**

I ask God to set a guard on my mouth. He helps to watch over the door of my lips **(Psalms141:3).** I let the peace of Christ rule over in my heart as a member of one body. Am called to peace and am thankful. **(Colossians 3:15)**

God loads me daily with benefits. He is my salvation **(Psalms68:19),Amen**

Am God's servant and he keeps pleasure in my prosperity **(Psalms 35:27),Amen**

God has not given me a spirit of fear. He gives forever love and self-discipline **(2Timothy;1: 7),Amen**

I walk in the manner of worthy of the lord pleasing him with all respect. I bear fruit in every good work and am increasing in knowledge of God. **(Colossians 1:11)** Am being strengthened with power and his mighty. I have great endurance and patience. **Amen**

I meditate on God's word day and night. Am successful and prosperous **(Psalms 1:2-3) (Joshua 1:8)**

God makes all grace bound toward me so that I always have all sufficiency and abundance for every good work. **(2 Corinthians 9:8),Amen**

I honour the lord with my wealth and the first fruit of all my labour. Then the barns will be filled with plenty of vats and overflow with new wine. **(Proverbs3:9-10),Amen**

I bring the whole truth into the store house. He opens the window of heavens for me and pours out a blessing so great that I don't have enough room for it. **(Malachi 3:10),Amen**

I prosper in all things I remain in health just as my soul prospers. **(3John 1:3),Amen**

God abundantly blesses my provisions **(Psalms132:15),Amen**

I give and receive God measures pressed down shaken together running ever will it be put into my help **(Luke 6:28).**

Jesus Christ is generous in his grace and though he is rich, he lay down for my sake to be poor. So through poverty, he could make me rich. **(2Corinthians 8:9)Amen.**

I experience all blessings as I obey the lord my God (Deuteronomy **28:2),Amen**

Am blessed in the city and in the county **(Deuteronomy 28:3)**

I am blessed from the front of the body, am blessed with equivalent of production growth of herds, my cattle and the offspring of my flock **(Deuteronomy 28:4),Amen**

Am blessed when I come in and when I go out **(Deuteronomy 28:6),Amen**

The Lord causes my enemies who rise against me to be defeated before my face. They come out against me one way and flee before me seven ways. **(Deuteronomy 28:7)**

The Lord commands his blessing on my store house and in that is at my hand to do and he blesses me in the Land that he is giving me. **(Deuteronomy 28:8),Amen**

The lord established me as a holy person to himself; I keep his commandments and walk in his way. **(Deuteronomy 28:9),Amen**

The Lord grants me with plenty of goods yield and also increase of livestock and the production of my ground. **(Deuteronomy 28:11),Amen**

All the people of the earth see that am called by the name of the Lord **(Deuteronomy 28:10),Amen**

The lord opens to me his good treasures, the heavens to give them to my land in its season and to bless the work of my hand. **(Deuteronomy 28:12),Amen**

I will lend too many nations but I will not borrow **(Deuteronomy28:12),Amen**

The Lord makes me the head and not the tail. I am therefore above and not beneath .**Amen**

I am my father's daughter and son and all he has is mine. **(Luke 15:3),Amen**

God blesses me and surrounds me with favour as a shield. **(Psalms 5:12),Amen**

My ways should please the lord and my enemies are made at peace with me **(Proverbs 16:7),Amen**

Am in Christ Jesus he became my wisdom, my righteousness, sanctification and redemption. **(Corinthians 1:30),Amen**

The God fills me with all joy and peace in faith ,so that I bound in hope with the power of the Holy Spirit. **(Romans 15:13) Amen**

The Lord of peace is peace in every way, he always gives me is peace **(2Thessalonians),Amen**

Am steadfast in mind, he keeps me in perfect peace for I trust in him **(Isaiah 26:3),Amen**

I do all things without grumbling or complaining to be blameless and innocent. I appear a slight in the world **(Philippians 2:14; 15),Amen**

I press on that u may lay hold of that which Christ has also laid of me forgetting those things which are behind and reaching of reward to those things that are ahead. Press towards the good for the prizes of the upward call by God in Christ Jesus **(Philippians 3:12-14),Amen**

God instructs me and keeps me as the apple of his eyes **(Zachariah,2:8)Amen**

I speak God's word and his angels do the voice of his word. **(Psalms 103:30),Amen**

The lord has given me the tongue of the disciples. I know how to speak a word in due season to those who are weary**. (Isaiah 50:4)Amen**

The Lord God awakens me every morning to fellowship with him and he opens my ears to hear as the learned. **(Isaiah 50:4)**

(Proverbs 11:30) Righteousness gives life but violence takes it all away. **Amen**

You must live with consequences of everything you say for it preserves life and destroy it .**Amen**

You will have to live with the consequences of everything you say for they preserve your life or destroy you. **(Proverbs18: 20),Amen**

Your reward depends on what you say or do- You will get what you deserve **(Proverb12; 14),Amen**

God forgive all my inequities and heal all my diseases. **(Psalms,103:3),Amen**

God redeems my life from the past. He crowns me with loving kindness and compassion **(Psalms 103:4),Amen**

God satisfies my mouth with good things and renews my strength like of an eagle **(Psalms 103:5),Amen**

Like a sheep that lost its way, I have been brought back now to follow the shepherd and keep the law of the most high that reigns for ever more. **(1Peter2:4-5)**Speak life in your life when it comes to declare things and Promises God made to be yours, though you have not seen them yet, but will come to pass, God does not change or lie as you declare his promises and declarations it will become real to you -you will walk in favour and victory of God, I declare to be a blessing to my family, friends, village ,country, where they have not reached i will set a record in history **(In Serving God , Business, Education, loving others), Amen**

I declare to build, hospitals ,schools , churches, orphanages, dams bridges , roads , in my village, country, where they have not reached to start a new generation of Change, **Amen**

I declare to start a new generation of self independent and I rebuke the *syndrome of dependence ,Amen*

QUESTION?

SHOULD DO WE ASK OR PRAY TO GOD FOR THE ABILITY TO SPEAK IN TONGUES?

The word of God (bible) is very clear and does not teach that Christians can or only will speak in tongues-God has given us many gifts to be victorious not only speaking in tongues that can make us victorious in life! The person who speaks in strange tongues then must pray for the gift to explain what is said **(1Corinthians;12;13)**Because if you don't do it ,how when you give thanks to God in spirit only how can ordinary people taking part in the meeting say "**Amen** "to your prayer of thanksgiving they have no way of knowing what you are saying even if your prayer of thanks to God is quite good other people are not helped at all,-I thank God that I speak in strange tongues much more than of you but in church worship I would rather speak five words that can be understood in order to teach others than speak a thousands of words in strange tongues **(1Corinthians;14;16;18)**If they want to communicate to God the confusion is only in the book of**(Mark 16;17;18)** says" believers will be given power to perform miracles, they will drive out demons in my name they will speak in strange tongues, if they pick up snakes or drink poison they will not be harmed, they will place their hands on sick people who will get well "and the book of Corinthians states they are not all apostles or prophets or teachers to work miracles or to heal diseases or to speak in strange tongues or explain what is said set your heart on more important gifts**(1Corintians 12;29;30)**Other gifts are helping, encouraging, administration**(2)**The person who speaks in strange tongues then must pray for the gift to explain what is said **(1Corinthians;14;13)**The Spirit presence is shown in some way in each person for good of all the spirit gives one person a massage full of wisdom while to another person the same spirit gives a massage full of knowledge one and the same spirit gives faith to one person while the other the power to heal**(1Corinthians;12;7-11-)Amen**
(3) Be eager to pursue gifts that edify the body of Christ such as **prophecy (1Corinthians; 14; 5; 6)** Speak, Faith, Gods, word-Instead of pursuing tongues; **Amen**
(4) Focus more on the gifts God has given you rather than the one he has not given you like those in **(1Corinthians;12;7;11)**Use the gifts God has given and be faithful but -If you want God to bless you with the Spirit of speaking in tongues God has no obligation and Limitations he can answer your prayers since you are eager to have the gift of the Spirit you must try above everything else to make greater use of those which help to build the church**(1 Corinthians;14;12)Amen**

THE IMPORTANCE OF SPEAKING IN TONGUES

Speaking in tongues is thanks giving to God -when you give thanks to God in the spirit only how can ordinary people talking part in the meeting say amen to your prayers of thanks giving ? they have no way of knowing of what you are saying even if your prayer is quite good other people are not helped at all, **(1Corinthians 14;16;17)Amen**

Tongues gives you personal edification (Strength ,tongues are power a charger) you do good for yourself to speak in strange but those who proclaim goods massage help the whole church **(1 Corinthians,14;4)**

Keeps our prayers in line with God- and God who sees into our hearts ,knows what the thought of the Spirit is because the Spirit pleads with God on our behalf of his people and in accordance to his will **(Romans,8;27),Amen**

God keep his love in us - this hope does not disappoint us, for God has poured out his love into our heart by means of the holy spirit who is the Gods spirit to us **(Romans 5;5),Amen**

Tongues stimulates faith - but you my friends keep on building yourselves up on the most sacred faith pray in the power of the Holy spirit and keep yourselves in the love of God as you wait for our Lord Jesus Christ , in his mercy to give you eternal life **(Jude 1;20;21),Amen**

Tongues helps you to be freed from the forces of Darkness- but if no one is there who can explain then the one who speaks in tongues must be quite and speak only to himself and to God **(1Corinthians,14;28),Amen**

Tongues helps to be self Conscious - those who speak in strange tongues do not speak to others but to God because no one understands them they are speaking secrets truths by the power of the Spirit **(1 Corinthians 14;2 1Cor14 6;19),Amen**

Tongues are supernatural prayers -for unknown situations ,Amen

Tongues are supernatural in the Baptism of the Holy spirit, (help to release the supernatural)they were filled with the Holy Spirit and begun to talk in other language as the spirit enabled them to speak **(Acts,2;4)** Paul in Ephesus- while Apollo's was in Corinth ,Paul travelled through the anterior of the province and arrived in Ephesus there he found some disciples and asked them ,did you receive the Holy Spirit when you become believers? "we have not even heard that there is a Holy Spirit ,they answered ,well then what kind of baptism did you receive ? Paul asked ,the baptism of John was for those who turned from their sins and he told the people of Israel to believe in the one who was coming after him -that is in Jesus ,when they heard this they were baptised in the name the Lord Jesus ,Paul placed the hands on them and the holy spirit came upon them they spoke in strange tongues and also proclaimed the Gods message they were twelve men in all **(Acts,19;1;7)**Tongues open door to the Supernatural **(Acts,19;6) ,Amen**

Tongues gives power to perform signs and wonders - whoever believe and is baptised will be saved ,whoever does not believe will be condemned ,believers will be given power to perform miracles ,they will drive out demons in my name , they will speak in strange tongues ,if they pick up snakes or drink any poison they will not be harmed ,they will place their hands on sick people ,who will get well, **(Mark.16;1618),Amen**

There is no who should stop us from speaking in tongues because they are important as we encounter the Spirit of God in Spirit and in Mind in understanding who God is and what he can do in our life, Tongues gives us access to speak to our God as individuals,**(Spirit)** and as a group when we speak to him in the language of day life**(Mind),Amen**

MAKE YOUR CHILDREN PROUD OF YOU!

Grandparents are proud of grandchildren, just as children are proud of their Parents (**Proverb;17;6**)Children are crown to the age and Parents are the pride of their children, your children is already in the process of becoming the kind of person he or she s going to be, so to bring them right and make them proud of you live by these examples(**1)Assure them your love-** they need to know your love is a given and it will never be withdrawn because of their appearance .achievement and actions let them know they are loved for who they are and that their worth in your eyes is never a question Be their guiding light let your light shine (**Mathew;5;16**)Before others that they may see your good deeds and glorify your father in heaven, Every child including mine and yours are born lost into a world of moral and spiritual darkness /decay so parents it is your responsibility to be their guiding light , the bible says Ahaziah son of Ahab did evil in the eyes of the lord because he walked in the ways of his father and mother (**1kings22;51-52**)Our children may not follow our advice ,but they will follow your example weather good or bad, we are called to be the sign post at their cross road map in their confusion, Paul encourages his spiritual children saying follow my example as I follow Christ (**1corinthians11;1**)You don't need a degree in parenting to shine at home , embracing and living on Christ teaching each day qualifies you to be a good parent , you can be a righteous man who walks in his integrity how blessed is his son and daughters after him (**Proverb;20;7**)-(2)**Build a strong character and Godly values** direct your children onto the right path and when they are older they will not leave it involve your children in church family and family when they are younger regularly attending bible study believing church (**Hebrews10;25**) study the word with them and allow them to do it themselves(**3)Establish clear boundaries and be consistent in maintaining them-***Do children like rules?* No but your first goal is not to make them happy it is to teach them responsibilities and happiness will follow them (**4)Help them to discover their potential** that means by observing, listening ,and once their talents are identified helping to develop we have different gifts according to Gods given grace (***Romans;12;6***)So we are to use our different gifts in accordance with the grace that God has given us (**5)Encourage them to pursue their life vision** you younger women and men shall see vision(***Joel;2;28***) afterwards I will pour out my spirit on every one your sons daughters will proclaim my massage your old people will have dreams and your young people will see visions don't pour cold water on the fire of their enthusiasm bring it out get out of the critic state and become their greatest supporter in every activity like football singing dancing preaching .if you do o you will make them proud of you (**6) Don't try to duplicate yourself to them** God gave each of your children their unique make up and personality so don't try to make them something that God and the rest of us don't need one more of As God wants us to pray for our children let us look at an example of how Timothy $Paul prayed for other **(1Timothy 1;2; Paul Colossians 1;9;13)Prayers for your Children** as a loving parent you have to pray for your children for *(1)Wisdom (2)Grace and Favour (3) Mercy (4)Peace (5)Walk Spiritually (6) God give them power and Strength to fulfil his purpose and their destiny ,* <u>*When the Mother Prays for her Children*</u>-For this child I prayed and the lord has granted me my petition I prayed for the child and the lord has granted me what I asked of him(**1Samuel;1;27**)Parenting can be difficult and challenging task but at the same time can be the most rewarding what parents have to do first pray for their children God has blessed with them because they are a gift from God and a real blessing of Gods promise to man and woman God blesses with many children with abundant crops with many cattle and sheep(**Deutoromy;28;4**)(And parents have the responsibility to teach them about God and his word the–Bible should be the foundation taught day and night in homes and the truth to be taught ,Worshiping God constantly ,Sunday ,morning, afternoon ,and evening prayers ,to be a daily routine in homes Husband and wives must be respectful to each other(**Ephesians5;21**)Because they are Gods examples to the children being a good parent is all about raising children who will follow your example in obeying and worshiping God- Every terrorist was once a child so was a missionary difference from them It is often the influence of the parents Samuel the prophet led the nation of Israel for 40 years and guided king David in some of the very crucial decision making but who was behind his leadership his mother listen therefore I have lent him to the lord as long as he lives he shall be lent to the lord (*1Samuel;1;28*)While you have children hold them love them care for them and empower them but understand that you are a steward you don't own them they belong to God some day they will grow up and leave make sure that when they do they have a spiritual anchor because life will give them lots of storms never underestimate the power of a parent pleading with God on behalf of a child who knows how many prayers are being answered right now because of the faithful pondering of a mother 20 /40 years ago ? if what you are doing in this fast paced society is taking you away from Praying time for your children you are doing too much there is nothing more important special precious than the time a parent spends interceding with God on behalf of a child it's not too late for the child who bought tears think of Jesus mother who had to watch her son crucified but also had the joy of seeing him raised from death you may go to your grave wondering but don't stop praying why? Because when mother pray God listen we thank you lord for our caring loving precious mother who Prays on our behalf and you listen to them ***How to pray for your children*** ;(I will pour out my blessing on your children*(Isaiah44;3)* Lord am blessed and grateful for the wonderful gift of children you have given me ,to care and love , enjoy and celebrate , thank you for being good to them ,teach me the responsibility of lifting them , keep them in the centre of your love, and designed purpose ,bless them with wisdom and knowledge of knowing you let them put their trust in you enable them to recognise the gifts and calling on them , you must pray claiming Gods promises over your children *are such prayers effective* ?Yes God says am already to perform my word, we serve a Promise making God so shall my word be that goes forth from my mouth it shall not return to me void but it shall accomplish what I please it shall prosper in the things for which I have sent it*(Isaiah;55;11)*So pray for your children each day and stand on those promises ,I will pour my spirit on your descendants and my blessing on your off springs*(Isaiah;44;3)*And this is my covenant with them, say the lord my spirit will not leave them neither will these words ,I have given you they will be on your lips and on the lips of your children and your children forever I the lord I have spoken*(Isaiah;59;21)*Now this is what the lord says don't weep any longer for I will reward you says the lord, your children will come back to you, from distant land of the enemy there is hope for your future says the lord your children will come back to their own land*(Jeremiah;31;16-17)*The Posterity of the righteous will be delivered*(Proverb11;21)*Blessed is the man who fears the lord who finds greater delight in his commands his children will be mighty in the land the generation of the upright will be blessed*(Psalm;112;1-2)*Believe in the lord Jesus Christ and you will be saved you and your house hold *(Acts16;31)*Thank God for your family-Children are a blessing from the Lord off springs a reward from him ,the Sons the man has when he is younger are the arrows in a soldiers hand happy is a man who has many such arrows he will never be defeated when he meets his enemies in the place of judgement*(Psalm;127;3-5)* God use my children for your glory ,make your face shine upon them ,your grace on them and your love on them ,Parent you have to pray for them in faith for Wisdom is and let them know the fear of the Lord is the beginning of wisdom, he gives sound judgement to all who obey his commands ,he is to be praised forever**(Psalm111;10)**Happy is anyone who becomes wise who gains understanding there is more profit in it than there is silver it is worth more to you than wisdom is more than jewel nothing you could want to compare with it Gold it offer you long life as long as wealth and honour can make your life pleasant and lead you safely through it those who become wise are happy wisdom will give them life the lord created the earth by his wisdom his wisdom caused the river to flow and the clouds to give rain to the earth **(Proverb 3;13;19 - to vs. 35)**for this reason we have prayed for you, since we heard about you ,we ask God to fill you with knowledge of his will with all the wisdom and understanding ,that his spirit gives then you will be able to live as the lord wants, and you will do what pleases him your lives will produce all kinds of good deeds and you will grow in the knowledge of God ,may you grow in the strength which comes from his glorious power so that you may be able to endure everything with patience ,and with Joy ,give thanks to the father who has made you fit to have your share of what God has reserved for his people in the kingdom of light **(1Collosians3;12)** Pray for your Children for the wisdom from above which is pure full of peace .gentle and friendly its full of compassion and produces a harvest of good deeds, its free from prejudice and hypocrisy and goodness is the harvest that is produced from seeds the peace makers plant in peace , but the wisdom of the world is, foolishness, jealousness ,bitterness ,selfishness boasting of the wisdom which is unspiritual and demonic where there is disorder, jealous ,selfish there is every kind of Evil protection because we cannot allow or afford to allow Satan to snatch or take them his ways ,it is a Privilege to pray for them, Prayer for children as they were babies they depended on their parents to do everything for them ,but as they grow up we must continually release them to God praying for them in faith trusting to do his great work in them, You pray for them for mercy   because of God's mercy we are not consumed because his compassion fail not they are new every morning great is your faithfulness **(Lamentation 3;22;23)**The peace of God can sustain us through the worst circumstance and different from the peace of the world offer ,the world offer temporary peace, but the peace of God which transcends all understanding, will guard your heart and mind **(Philippians;4;7)Lord your word says** "You lord give perfect peace to those who keep their purpose firm and put their trust in you **(Isaiah;26;3)**Peace I leave with you my peace I give you do not let your heart be troubled and do not be afraid **(John14;27)** We thank you that your light shine on them on the same way your light shines before others that they may see the good deeds and glorify you in heaven **(Mathew;5;16)**Lord we thank you that you have blessed them throughout the day may the lord make his face shine on them and be gracious to you, the lord turns his face to you towards you and give you peace **(Numbers;6;24;26)** Lord we thank you for the spirit of love, power and sound mind because the spirit you gave us does not make us timid but gives us power love and self discipline **(2Timothy 1;7)** The Lord gives strength to his people and blesses them with peace **(Psalm ;29;11)**Father we thank you because they will not be anxious about anything but in every situation by prayers and petition with thanks giving present your request to God **(Philippians, 4;6)**Teach them to pray to God regularly with their request both small and big, God to prepare for them for the future without worries of unrest in the word, We pray for them so that they will know that you are with them ,let them be strong and courageous not to be afraid or terrified because of them for the lord goes with them he will never leave you nor forsake you **(Deuteronomy;31;6)**

Father we thank you that they will grow in grace and knowledge of our saviour Jesus Christ to him be glory both now and forever **(2Peter;3;18)** Grace means unmerited favour, you will never need to struggle with whatever you are failing , God who gives all the grace will make everything right, he will make you strong, support you and keep you from failing **(1Peter 5;10)**The more they know and meditate and apply Gods word in everyday life, they will grow spiritually and become greater influence over those God has placed around them ,Father we thank you that they will stand for what is right ,stand firm with the belt of truth buckled around your waist with the breastplate of righteousness in place(**Ephesians 6;14)**Father I/we thank you that they will know Jesus Christ more intimately ,to know the power of his resurrection and participation in his suffering becoming like him in his death and so somehow attaining to the resurrection from the dead **(Philippians 3;10;11)**Let the spirit lead them guide them ,so that they may know Jesus themselves and eventually learn to recognise his voice speaking to their hearts ,Father we/I thank you because you will call them and no one hinders them from coming because the kingdom belong to them **(Mathew19;13;15)** Pray for them , God to deliver them from generation of curses, to serve the Lord all their days of life , pray for them to live longer and fulfil their purpose in life , Spirit of ultimately death not to locate them, not to bury them when they are young , God to separate them from other children of the world, who are not Godly , pray for them their anointing and calling to be fulfilled, and their dreams to be fulfilled , the blessings of God to be on them ,and become the plight of the nation , to be protected by God, walk in higher places as sons and daughter of God , Father we/I pray that they honour and respect parents both fathers and mothers so that they may live longer children obey your parents in everything for these pleases God ,**Amen**

PARENTS TEACH YOUR CHILDREN,

God expects you to enable your children to make wise decision, by teaching them on different issues of life like, Religion (Bible principle and foundation) ,Marriage ,Relationship ,Sex, Money, Work ,It's is the Job of the parents to teach them how to go through life ,your Availability ,Disciplining - Spiritually teaching is important in their life, train your children because - if you are not Available you cannot give direction, your discipline will be resented and your spiritual leadership will be rejected, If you want your children's to be heroes and if you don't give your children time ,they may pick up a wrong hero, and break up your heart, because you left them for someone to lead them for you, and this someone may be someone you don't like and when that happens the greater problem is not that you won't be around, it is that you will no longer be missed as God is our good father he has never abandoned, if you are not willing to serve him today choose for yourself today whom you will serve, the gods of your ancestors used to worship in Mesopotamia or the gods of the Amorites in whose land you are now but as for me and my house hold we will serve the lord (*Joshua 24;15*)Why God created you in his own image don't leave your children for the Mum or Dad alone, yet before you gave birth to them you were begging him for a child, and when he gave you a child you abandoned them, don't let Love of money steal the love of your children let their joy be in you and let your Joy be in your children first, most fatherless daughter without fathers are likely to marry at their teens and have children out of good marriage, divorce is roaming high because of these girls grew up in a fatherless home, teenagers admitted to Psychiatric hospital it's because of fatherless homes school dropout in most country it's because of the single Parents ,Drugs and Alcohol, Gun crime, attempted suicide ,we see on street. are caused by a single parent homes ,the child you don't pamper or teach today will became a problem to the nation tomorrow, **Parents both Male and Female teach your children's morals and life experiences don't allow your children to be taught by the system charity begins at home** ,But they did not follow their fathers example they were interested in making money so they accepted bribes and did not decide cases honestly(*1Samuel;8;3*)Samson did not win the prize he was meant to win and Samuel a reorganised moral and spiritual giant watched his Sons reject his example and teachings and pursue lives of bribery and shame since Adam children doing their own things have broken their own parent hearts -So what do parents have to do-good decision making is the key to happy life, but good decision making is not a skill some of us are naturally talented and blessed while poor decision making is handicap others are born with courage ,education or age process does not automatically give you a key to better decision making Spending time with good decision makers is wise but it does not rub off on you and the earlier you teach your children the better Poor decision making can earn us a reputation that haunt our prospects indefinitely a person who plans chooses evil will get a reputation as trouble makers (*Proverb;24;8*)When you get a negative reputation it's hard to recover from it(**Proverb;25;10**)The short term benefits of making poor decision leads to long term losses and regrets the person God blesses must exercise self- control live wisely and have good reputation *(2)*How I feel afterwards what outlast our decision are the subsequent feelings of self- respect against shame and positive self- worth against negative self-worth our actions ultimately become history but our thoughts about them continues to shape our future carefully guard your thoughts because they are a source of true life children with self –respect against shame and positive self-worth against negative self-worth our actions ultimately become history but our thoughts about them continue to shape our future children with self -respect are much less to like to indulge in promiscuous Sex ,drinking, drugs, Anti -social and illegal behaviours, self-respect and self-worth ,are internal standards which are loathed to violate –giving in to selfish choices is like abandoning the moral core of our being the sacred soul God gave us ,Teach your children discipline ,bring them in training and instructions of the lord- Gods word is timeless who the lord loves corrects (**Proverb3;12**) It is easier to shape a child ,than to repair an adult ,Teach them Gods way ,train a child in a way he/she should go when they are young and shall not depart from them (**Proverb;22;6**)This is the taste of God when they are still younger and when they are old the world won't be to satisfy their taste   discuss with them how they see the world teach them about the glory of the lord through everyday life I have taught you wisdom and the right way to live nothing will stand your way if you walk wisely you will not stumble when you run(**Proverb;4;11**)Wise children make their fathers proud of them foolish children bring their mother grief(**Proverb;10;1 ;Proverb;15;20**) Younger children if you do not accept teachings from your parents God will use foreigners to teach you letter by letter line by line (**Isaiah;28;9**)A younger man who obeys the law is intelligent one who makes friend with good for nothing is a disgrace to his father(**Proverb;28;7&29;17**)Children for God said respect your father and mother and whoever curses his father and mother is to be put to death(**Mathew;15;4**)Commit them to the Lord speak to them and guide them they will learn the easy way or hard way and if they go astray God promised they will come back Give them to the lord say I have taught them and given an example now I give them to you deal with them accordingly to your will God I have done my best **Children /Women are blessing from God -**For God loved the world so much that he gave his only Son so that everyone who believe in him may not die ,but have eternal life for God did not send him to into the world to be its judge ,but to be its saviour(**John3;16;17**)If some men are fighting and hurt a Pregnant women, so that she loses her child, but she is not injured in any other way the one who hurt her will be tried/fined whatever the amount the women husband demands subject to the approval of the judge(**Exodus;21;22;23**)Jesus said let the children come to me ,and do not stop them because the kingdom of God belongs to them,placed his hands on them and went away(Blessed them) **Mathew19;14**)God blessing the women said ,I will take care of your flocks like a shepherd ,he will gather the lambs together and carry them in his hands /arms he will gently lead them(**Isaiah;40;11**)The work they will do will be successful and their children will not meet disasters, I will bless them and their descendants for all the time to come (**Isaiah;65;23**) The priest and the teachers of the law become angry when they saw the wonderful things Jesus he was doing ,and the children shouting in the temple ,praise to David sons(**Mathew,21;15**)**The** one in the kingdom of the Lord is the one, who humbles himself ,and become like a child, Whoever welcomes a child welcome me, remember who does not receive the kingdom of God like a child will never enter it (**Luke18;17**)Teach them the commandments, repeat them when you are at home, when you are away ,when you are resting and when you are working ,tie them on your Arms, and wear them on your foreheads as a reminder, write them on your door posts, on your house gates honour him your God   ,worship **him and make your promises only in his name(Deutoromy;6;7)**See that you don't despise any of the little ones their angles in heaven, I tell you are always in the presence of my father in heaven When a woman is about to give birth she is sad because her hour of suffering has come but when the baby is born she forgets her suffering because she is happy that a baby has been into the world (Work of the Holy spirit) The day many sacrifices were offered and the people were happy full of Joy because God had made them very happy the women and children joined the celebrations and the noise they made could be heard far a wide(**Nehemiah;12;43,dedicated the city**)When you die and buried with your ancestors I will make one of your sons king and keep all his kingdom strong(**2Samuel;7;12**)Jesus knew what they were thinking so he took a child stood him by his side and said to them whoever welcomes the child in my name welcomes me and whoever welcomes me also welcomes the one who sent me (**Luke;9;47**) -(so teach your children the following(**1**)The consequence's you get as a result of the choices you make let your children know it's not their circumstances but the decision they make about them that govern their lives you may think your children know this but they don't know their wiring problem makes cause and effect difficult to connect until their brain reaches later adolescence asking what were you thinking about will just invite the famous shoulder shrug and blank stare they are not stupid but just need guidance(**2**)You will have options children commonly feel powerless and hopeless when reacting to negative circumstance ,they tend to be either thinker concluding that things are either good or all bad ,teach them thinking frequently produces children who become pessimistic disempowered easily manipulated depressed adults knowing they always have good options prevents circumstances from dictating their lives Another important skill you have to teach your children is in (*Galatians6;7*)Do not make /deceive yourselves no one makes a fool of God, people will exactly reap what they sow, if they sow in field of the spirit from the spirit they will gather the harvest of eternal life ,yard by yard life is fine for their life to go right, your children they must learn to think right so teach them to (**1**)**Ask**- what are their options in different situations but do it with a right attitude if your face is like thunder when you talk to them they will run for cover brain storm with them writing down every option that is offered tell them that there is no wrong answer and no idea that will be judged as silly all suggestions are accepted and valued encourage them to think for themselves **(2)**What benefit comes from each option ,the goal is not to convince them but for them to discover and embrace the truth for themselves ,and that comes through patience, not pressure, ask them to list which benefit seems most important to them**(3)**What negative result comes from each option children can be brutally honest that's okay ,it's just part of learning Gods cause and effect, law of sowing and reaping indeed many adults regrets could have been avoided by following this law = don't preach or rant about how terrible the results are, teach them to question themselves am willing to accept the results *how would they change my life ?(4)* What personal value are involved in this decision valued based decisions leads us to higher road rather than the path of the least resistance suggest some Godly values such as loyalty ,trustworthy faithfulness responsibility compassion friendship self -denial honour ,courage break it down small for younger children but don't miss your opportunity**(1)***Pray for them and give them to God* anxiety and frustrations will only make you the kind of parent they don't enjoy being around and who can't enjoy them you are not meant to carry such a load your heavenly God he want to help you always to carry it for you *(1Peter 5;7)* **(2)Remember that God loves them more than you do** ,he gave his only son to save yours , he knows their heart and how to reach it ,and turn it towards him ,so give your children to him ,at times parents despair over their children's decision and actions, you can do your best to bring them up correct and you fail but you need not to give up failure is a fact of life and of parenting and nobody does it perfectly, if he is not in Christ parents assume heavier load of guilty than they deserve example Isaac ,Jacob and Esau .Aaron struck out completely with Nava lab and Abihu menorahs (c)Realise you are not responsible for their decision they make their own choices condemning yourself just discourage you and it just undermines your ability to be the parent they need the word of God say salvation is of the Lord *(Jonah2;9)*He saves and deliver so it's the parents responsibility to follow the above mentioned strategy to have a happy home and family getting them from childhood to adulthood is a task **(1corinthians;13;11)**When I was a child my speech feelings and thinking were all childish now I have become a man/woman I have no more childish ways you sometimes wonder if your children is ever going to reach maturity ? You are welcome to the toughest phase of parenting when they reach adolescent age they change a lot from excitement to boredom self-confidence to t self- doubt happiness to despair sociability to reclusiveness co-operation to opposition and when you ask them what's happening. They say nothing or don't know and the truth they don't know they are being bombarded by the changing biochemistry the child is a navigating between words of childhood and adulthood needing your understanding and attention patience for them the odyssey of adolescent can feel freakish ,embracing and perplexing Christians children know their roles and rules of their world adults knows theirs children are expected to act like children and adults like adults but teenagers have traits of both yet belong in neither when they are in childhood they are denied adult prevail ages of course you can't you are a child the words of adult and children are relatively distinct, stable predictable places but it's not so in the reality of teens they alternate between two words never certain they are fish or fowl adult or children so they gravitate towards peers who share but also don't understand their experiences what do they need   (1)Parents   who   are   clear   minded   and   self   - controlled(**1Peter4;7**)going from childhood to adulthood is a transition, that requires wisdom and love ,your teens will sometime behave like children /feel- your work is to realise that whatever their status they will become /Men /Women of the world, and they will remain adult ,they need parents who understand them, and their experiences sometimes stress level make them feel out of control **(3)*Parents you have to be their parents not their mates*- they need someone in charge to shepherd them towards maturity ,if you abdicate your role because you are afraid of your children anger –rejection or unhappiness you abandon their own confused ways you are the calm God guide them in the short-term they may consider your values rules lifestyles and moral out-dated expect no less that's par for the course in parenting *(4)You have to be rational* –not re-active your work requires you to be open minded and self- controlled be the growth up you cannot help your child to become adult if you are not hold on these forget becoming cool by lowering your standard that's no win alternative to good and loving parent- teens they will challenge you be yourself maintain your standard they need you to have character yes they will fight you now if you remain cool what you have to do love be consistent resolute they will follow your footsteps and both sides be happy dear Christian read your bible and **learn much how you can bring up your children the same way Jesus Christ was brought up   because they are the future generation for tomorrow (5)Teach your children there is time for silent and time to** speak(Ecclesiastes 3;7) A time to tear and time to mend to speak and time to be silent ,teach your children to ask, decision made in haste are often regretted poor decision, are situation ally driven caused by momentary stress peer pressure .mood swings and temporally emotions like loneliness when situation changes our feelings changes and our decisions often look doubtful can the decision be made later reducing the risk? Pressuring children often increase their desperation and leads to premature decision but assuring them you're that time is on their side lowers their reactivity and like hood of the future regrets helping them to see that God has made everything appropriate in its time (*Ecclesiastes; 3; 11*) Offer them space to think wisely about their options allowing for Gods guidance ask them how they feel about the result if they are pleased compliment them if not say am sorry about that any idea? What will you change next time instead of judging their failure reward their success you can teach your children (**Proverb; 4; 23) Be careful how you think your life is shaped by your thoughts above** all guide your heart for everything you do comes from it teach them to ask themselves about these two question how will people value feel about me after decision? the trust and respect of others is always needed to succeed reputation trumps money even in the secular market place choose a good reputation over great riches being held in high esteems is better than gold or silver(***Proverb;22;1***)We worry much about what a child will become tomorrow yet we forget that he is someone today (**Stadia Tauscher**) Children make your life important(**Erma Bombeck**)I brought a child into this dark world because it needed light that only a child can bring (**Liz-Armbruster**) A child can ask questions that a wise man cannot answer Children need love especially when they do not deserve it (Hulbert-Harold)The world is new as many times as there are children in our lives(**Robert-Brault**)Children make you want to start life over(**Muhammad Ali**)What is a home without children ?Quite (**Henry Youngman**)A Child needs seldom a good talking to as good listening (**Robert Brault**)If we would listen to our children we would discover they are largely self- explanatory(**Robert Brault**)I love these little people and it is not a slight thing they who are so fresh from God love us (**Charles Dickens**)The only thing worth stealing is a kiss from a sleeping child (***Joe –Houlds-worth***)Children need freedom and time to play, Play is not a luxury play is a necessity(**Kay Redfield**)It is easy to build strong children than to repair broken men (***Fredrick Douglas***)Your family is not an important thing but Everything in life -you don't choose yr family and children God gives them as a gift to you as you are to them ;read more about children quotes in other books; **Amen**

CHILDREN GROW LEAVE PARENT HOMES

For this reason a man shall leave his mother and father that's why a man leaves his father and mother and is united to his wife and they become one flesh(***Genesis;2;24***)you will have succeed as a parent when your children are able to leave you and go out and build a successful life on their own you will never cut them off but comes time when you must "cut the Aprons strings and let them stand on their own two feet remember the children you are raising right now belongs to God before they belonged to you The earth is lord and all who live in it (***Psalm,24;1***) you are a teacher you don't own them and your opportunity to teach them is amazing brief your children were born to leave not to stay you cannot control their ticking biological clock your job is to prepare them for a leaving for the next few days ,let's talk about giving your children rots and wings roots before fruits develop ,roots must thrive and healthy roots requires healthy soil with the right elements for feeding ,and protecting plants roots, also depend on attachment to the soil, there two kinds of families the first offers insecure attachment their children attachment is ambiguous ambivalent indifferent or even neglectful making children feel emotionally unprotected uncertain, they are wanted and loved though they desperately need both these things their children lack confidence ,self-worth emotional ,strength and courage to take risks **(2)**The second offer secure attachment the parent and children connection is expressed and consistently reinforced even during necessary absence their children feel safe and securely attached such children become spiritually, socially and emotionally ,capable with the self -worth and courage required to face the challenges life puts in their path, on the journey to adolescent to adult hood your children will experience, insecurity ,contradictions and mood swings, they will send you conflicting signals ,needing closeness, yet distance connection yet independence all at the same time they will pull you in with one hand and push you away with the other ,you must still understand that your children still need to feel securely attached, even while they are distancing from you, when they push you away you must show them maturity ,remembering that it's not personal, It's just how they test their ability to become independent, adult minutes, hours ,days ,weeks ,later they are your children again wanting to be up close, it's the tug of-war of parenting youngster ,and it will resolve its self the right way, if you handle it with understanding ,above all contain your heart and anger ,do not prove engage in contentions debate, and strife ,your children anger irritation ,exasperation, embitterment (***Ephesians;6;4)***the worst outcome of frequent run instinct with your children is that it produces long term discouragement in them ,long after the mop-up your children can lose heart(***Colossians;3;21)***And have a crushed spirit in some cases they give up trying altogether in western culture girls hold onto the parent –child rope longer than boys generally distancing later and with less finality boys tend toward earlier long lasting distancing when you deny your son or daughter the God given need for gradual latitude they will disconnect farther and faster use wisdom ,let out the rope gradually and they will learn adult skills and stay more closely connected ,Another thing you must give your children wings they are born to fly not to stay in the nest by becoming overly protective and stifling in the name of responsible parenting you will end up losing them ,Jesus said children are designed to leave out and go out and build a home of their own, their drive for freedom is God driven ,not assign of ingratitude ,disrespect or rebellion a good carpenter works with the grain not against it ***so what should you do*** ?before your children ask for outright independence teach them how to handle them it wisely give them opportunity to prove their readiness and as they demonstrate trustworthiness increase their autonomy and vice-versa let them know that in life you don't inherit happiness you earn it be flexible but take charge let you children know they can't demand privileges like driving, dating and spending money they have to prove themselves worthy help them to see how they can earn increase autonomy or lose it and how they can give it back make them responsible for their own freedom by letting them know that it's not right or a gift but a reward for showing maturity A mother bird does not push her baby out of the nest until she knows it's ready to start flying the gift of freedom to an unprepared child is not wings it's an invitation to catastrophe do agree to autonomy until they have proven they can handle their agreed upon responsibility you cannot always prevent you children from getting hurt in this world you will have trouble(*John 16;33*)I have told you this so that you will have peace by being united to me the world will make you suffer but be brave I have defeated the world either they will get hurt and learn how to deal with reality or suffocate in your cocoon never becoming mature a hurt much sadder and much more painful and debilitating what s involve in giving your children wings ? realise that without autonomy they will become healthy adults this involves learning thing like clear thinking being responsible for their own decisions learning from bad decisions how to make better ones being free to make mistakes and pay the price of learning what it means to grow up**(2)D***on't treat their need for autonomy* **as** *evidence* you are failing as a parent indeed, if they fail to distance you should question your Parenting style making them independent is biblical and affective Parenting **(3)**don't mistake their distancing as a rejection of you, it is not abandonment of you ,it is advancement for them it is a proof of ingratitude or selfishness and rebellion ,it is their real word opportunity to demonstrate your success as a parent, when they don't want to attend uncle Bert family reunion don't tighten your grip to save the family from disintegrating the family is meant to disengage like cells splitting off and multiply the bible says we are to be fruitful and increase in number and fill the world (*Genesis 9;1*) God blessed Noah and his son and said have many children so that your descendants will live all over the earth, they cannot stay in the nest and fulfil their destiny ,release them and then get a life of your own that your responsibility not endless , parenting let out the rope, trust God and they will be back to see their very cool parents Healthy parenting call for finding the right mix of autonomy with each of your children some children distance sooner some later ,take small tentative steps some leap confidently into the gap there no good or bad children ,when it comes to this jump more or less challenging one as a parent you discover trials and error, what works for you and your family (children) criticising ,controlling, threatening ,preaching ,shaming etc. Are futile counterproductive and a sign you have lost your grip it will only increase their flight instinct or make them feel insecure, as though no one is really at the helm pretending you have got it together as a parent is a well-intentioned but costly game don't be intimidated by the idea of being honest and transparent with your children Its less stressful for you both and that they are imperfect and they know you are too so don't be afraid to say no am learning to parent growing children like you are learning to be one I need your help to be good at it to discover what works for both of us and help you be good at it too, *are you willing to be on a team and learn together?* that kind of honesty draws positive response it is also good role modelling teaching them humanity and co-operation as a coach and prayers united focus on wining and learning to improve not on competing or dominating succeeding or failing as a family is all about learning and growing ,**What** you **owe your children in life** here am I and the children God has given me**(Isaiah;8;18)**We are signs and symbols in Israel from God the almighty who dwells on mount Zion you may not be able to give your children everything you would like and they need but here are some of the things you have to give them in a happy life as a Dad God expects you to lead a family a family of your children and wife without a good leadership the family is headed for a life of trouble most children go astray because most crimes are we see it's not because of unemployment ,Education and Poverty, it's because of the Absence of the father in the family, what a man can teach a boy a woman cannot teach it to a boy ,and what a woman can teach a girl the man cannot teach to a girl, as parents both female and male you must know your responsibility in the family, and understand that if one of you is missing as good parents something is missing in the family, men do not abandon your children and woman for a mere small misunderstanding you can solve in a jiffy**(1)Let them see God in you** four younger girls were discussing their mothers one said my mother Knows the governor another said my mother knows the mayor third one said my mother knows the best singer in the world and confidently the fourth that's nothing my mother knows *God mum dad do you know God?* If you don't commit your life to him today**(2)***listen to them* if some of us paid much attention to our dogs as we do to our children we would be living in a dog patch you will never understand your children until you take time to listen to them to what they are saying and what they want**(3)Believe in them** as a child the great Caruso was told by a music teacher that he had no talent at all parent make sure your voice is the loudest in the home build their confidence give them the faith and self -worth required to overcome the obstacles they face in life **(4)Connect with them** get to know what they want they like ,get near them and know them, their struggles ,their talents ,their weakness their music, their fears, their friends, their visions and ,dreams and if their attitudes are not positive start making changes straight away before long **A word** to **single parents,** love covers over a multitude of sins **(1Peter;4;8)**above all love each other deeply because love covers over a multitude of sins if you are struggling to bring your children alone you have to teach them the following as you do they will be reinforced in you would be surprised how many instructors learn while they teach**(1)Teach them to love imperfect people**- let them know that loving is a risk but its worthy taking hearing you say this will help them to grow up and do not become cynical because of what they have been through explain to them that when you love people you must love what's good and accept what's still in the pipeline it will save them heartache and God is the remedy for all this (*2*)**Tell them that the future is better than the past** ;We are fuelled by the past but fuel only works when its combusted into another form so allow the pain of the past to fuel the future with compassion wisdom and hope many of the people we admire have experienced failures this year winner was last year runner up so learn from your mistakes and seize the new day once you do that all things are possible (**Mathew19;26**)Jesus looked at them straight and answered this is impossible for human beings but for God everything is possible**(3)Show them how to adapt to changes** when you get stuck in the past it is always the expense of the future after the initial shock is over and your anger has subsided start making plans draw closer to the lord God and decide to live again don't get stuck in the stage that was just meant to be part time /part of process this too shall pass let it-**law and order in family** in order to live a happy life with your children discipline them you will be glad they will turn out to be delightful give you peace of mind to live with today we know work has taken much of parent care where both partners live their children look after themselves as a result become a law unto themselves(**Proverb;29;15**)A child left to himself disgrace his parents most of us we are loving parents but our children need discipline and rules to live by love has a backbone it's called law and order without it love is just a waste a refusal to correct is a refusal to love (*Proverb;13;24*)Failure to punish your children or enforce law and order to gain short term popularity with kids always ends up costing us their long term respect expecting your children to work out what's wrong and right for themselves is a burden they should not have to bear their neurological and moral equipment is not sufficient developed yet for such responsibility the bibles says children are prone to foolishness and fads the cure comes through tough minded discipline (*Proverb;22;15*) Your children learn to make good decision from the reward and consequences of dealing with the law and order so don't fail them if you don't punish your children you don't love if you do you love them Children who are of joy don't live a lawless home giving your structure makes them feel cared for and here are a few of them**(a)Enforce the rules consistently** what brings a smile today should not bring outcries tomorrow inconsistency weakness your authority and breeds disobedience in them here are some things to do avoid comparison no child should be just like the other *(b)*A*void hurtful naming* such as you are stupid lazy bad waste of time and space describe their actions don't demonstrate their self-worth*(c)A void idle threats* enforce the rules or drop it**(d)Avoid** *bribes-*

they just breed manipulation and diminish the importance of rules*(e)Don't fear saying no* their future success and happiness depends on learning to deal with it (f) avoid making fun of their weakness and mistakes *(2)***Explain clearly your rules to them-** punishing a child over a rule they don't understand or they ignore just make them resentful the fewer your rules the better just make them understand do able and observable preaching and moralising only creates rebellion and resistance and you should admit your failure though you blow it occasionally you are still responsible what they have to follow your law and order not your lapse or downfall if you don't punish your children you don't love them if you do you will correct them **(Proverb;13;24)**Discipline your children when they are younger enough if you don't you are helping to destroy them**(Proverb19;18)**When we were punished it seemed to us at the time something to make us sad not glad later however those who have been disciplined by such punishment reap the peaceful reward of righteous life **(Hebrews12;11)** Speak the truth in love and use wards to build them not to destructive words and discouraging **(Ephesians 4;15;19)**,**Amen**

FRIENDSHIP

FRIENDSHIP--Can be defined as anyone who lay down his/her life for another-Who does, what God commands her/him to do(***Psalm119;63***)Do not sit active in the part of the ungodly they will Poison you- **Abraham** believed-God and it was credited to him as righteousness, and was called Gods friend**(James;2;23)** It is possible to be a friend of God as Abraham was ,We are the descendants of Abraham, the enemy will try to tell you that you are alone in this world, but understand you are a friend of God ,people may let you down and forsake you, but him he will never forsake you, he is with you always ,thinking of you and never let you down, but people can let you down, When friends leave you ,remember God will never leave you or forsake you ,**Moses was a friend of God**-the Lord would speak to Moses face to face ,as one speaks to a friend ,then Moses would turn to the Camp but his younger Aide Joshua son of Num did not leave the tent **(Exodus 33;11)**,God is a friend forever ,God has already choose people who will encourage us, Inspire us, give us advice ,help us to fulfil our destiny in life, True friendship requires, Time, Energy, Sacrifice and, Investing yourself, and not every so called friend will prove to be one ,When you are acting contrary to God word it's easy to fool yourself that when a slap of a friend can be trusted to help you, Paul couldn't have physically survived many of his trials and persecutions without friends but -God who encourages us the downhearted encouraged, us with the coming of Titus it was not only his coming that cheered us, but also his report of how you encouraged him, he told us how much you want to see me how sorry you are ,how ready to defend me so I am even happier now **(2Corinthians;7;6;7)**Sometime the Solution requires more than Prayers or Counselling, It requires a friend who understands -People you spend your life always have a greater impact, they can assimilate you into their life style so be careful of the people you associate with   We don't meet people by accident they cross our path for reasons, some friends are investment ,others are time wasters , Some people come in your life as a **Blessing** other as a **Lesson, (Burden)Some can be of help or hindrance in your life** -It's sad when Gods people don't spend time making friendship and instead go off on their own, they end up discouraged and bitter, because they don't have anyone to encourage and advice them, *What a blessing to have good friends in life, although sometimes we forget and say there no good friends, We make mistakes even our best friends make mistakes no one is perfect* - **good friends still exist and you can justify them with the fruits they bear in your life,** If you want to know who you are going to be in**(4-Years)**Look at friends you have- if you have People who are Kind, Considerate ,People of excellence, Inspire you, and challenge you -Generous, those Qualities are going to move you places and lift you up- if you can't figure out where you stand with someone it might be time to stop standing and start walking, if you have friends who are compromising ,critical ,indifferent ,moody ,who don't know God, respect their Parents ,Spouse ,unfaithful, hot tempered don't respect others always, this is your wakeup call- You don't read this book by accident you have to make new friends ,you are not going to become who you were created to be by having such kind of friends around you- Life is short to waste your valuable time with those people- don't surround yourself with friends who are sympathizers , you need friends who will take you to another high level -You don't have to be rude to them or go on the top of your flat and announce start distancing yourself from them slowly by slowly give them little time, The Bible warns us before you fall into friendship ,be careful keep company with the wise and you will become wise, if you make friendship with stupid people ,your life will be ruined (*Proverb;22;24;25 ;Proverb;13;20*) Good friends do not keep on doing bad things to you -you can talk to them and they will listen to you Associate with people of ,big Dreams, Vision, people that will Motivate you, Encourage you ,or Bring new ideas, add value to you and bring you wings to soar like eagles - Don't walk with people who are not going your direction ,True friends are concerned about what you are becoming ,they look beyond the Present and care deeply about ,you as a whole person they give you a hand when you are down ,Two friends are better off than one ,they can help each other ,if one falls they can reach out, but those who fall alone it's a real trouble (**Ecclesiastes;4;9;10**) Especially those families which are lonely ,God will bring them in your life when you are in the Spirit you will work for the good of each other, and years latter you are going to be growing stronger ,sharing up downs and ups, praying ,sharing and looking after each other, God always provide godly friends who support us in bible reading ,going to church, giving advices and companionship ,But God who comforts the downcast comforted us by the coming of Titus and not only by his coming but also the comfort you had given him he told us about your longing for me ,your deep sorrow, your ardent concern for me so that my Joy was greater than Ever (**2Corinthians;7;6;7**)God has Eagles for you, but if you hold on chickens you will never go higher , Sit with generous people you will be generous, Kind people you will be kind ,Successful people who are motivated, determined ,people of good qualities ,be selective not all people you work with are friends, not all that are school mates are friends, neighbours, your church mates, if you are to make them your friends make sure they have the qualities you want that make you better, don't spend time with gossiper and talk much ,the law Principle is whatever quality your friends have eventually rub at you, Spirits are transferable you hung up with gossiper you become gossiper compromiser, you become compromiser,   excellent people Excellence rub you   don't sit with worthless people (companion) at lunch time, you might be lonely and desperate to have friends but don't hung around with them ,God is going to bring you people of value -Stop planting flowers in peoples yards who are not going to water them - stop watering dead plants ,You may not be able to control someone behaviours but you can control how long you participate in it ,Some people won't go all the way with you, I got a place for you in my heart- but not in my life - Wrong friends will betrayal you as Judas did to Jesus, be   careful who you trust and who you tell your problems, remember that not everyone that smiles at you is your friend, some will spill on you dirtiness , if you spend time with the wrong people you will never find the right one -Stay away from negative people who are always-Complaining-Compromising- Doubting-Gossiping, they have a problem with Every situation they are going to drag you down those who spend their time looking for faults in others usually spend no time to correct their own - You can't hung up with chickens and expect to soar like Eagles in life - You can trust a friend who corrects you but kisses from an enemy are nothing but lies You will come across friends in your life who will say the right words at all times but in the end its always their action you should judge them by action not words that matters some may inspire you or they drain you ask Gods direction and wisdom to choose wisely-it is better to have nobody than to have who is a half there or who doesn't want to be there When you run from them never go back because they broke you - You have the responsibility to protect what God has given you gifts Dreams, Visions ,Assignment if you expose yourself to them their Spirit will go with you -you need people of greater character people who are not inspiring to reach your dreams Leave them behind God will never let to give up something without ,something better coming in return-When you obey God even if it is difficult a blessing will follow you, a blessing is a tax to obedience, people are stuck where they are because they are still hanging with somebody they are meant to get rid of long time ,the sooner you make changes the better, don't spend time with people that bring the worst in your life ,tempered people ,gossipers ,negative people God has people that will make your seed grow and flourish and rise to a new level, the law of friendship or group people who drink find drunkenness, gossipers find gossipers, negative people find negative people ,Victorious people find victorious people, happy people find happy people ,birds of the same fathers fly together, Daniel had friends of excellence characters the three didn't bow down to the kings idols ,you need people of courage and visions, wrong friends can make you to miss your destiny, Students don't hang out with troublesome friends those who are not focused ,who are not disciplined, and have bad morals can make you to became a chicken yet you were created to be Eagles, don't worry about having a few friends ,what matters is the quality of friends you have ,not quantity and fame or popularity -your friends may call you names, Coward, book warm

,don't worry about the names they call you God has better names for you, In a few years you will be their Manager ,Pastor, select the best out of many true friends are always happy for your achievements ,those who are not for you let them go ,God move people from your way and bring new one ,some may be of your blood family members, let them go some, you have to keep a distance from them, sometime we don't want to hurt their feelings by letting them to go ,but we are doing a mistake after a period of time they cause trouble and conflicts in our life, don't try to please everyone, it's your responsibility to make yourself happy, when you love someone more than they deserve, surely they will hurt you more than you deserve, if you find yourself constantly trying to prove your worth to someone you have already lost your value *,Some of us our life has been ruined because we choose wrong friends who are ,Lairs , Gamblers , Lazy, Addict , Gossipers ,Corrupt , not God fearing , those with all kinds of bad morals, but never is too late to change and change them as well*, The Lord said to Abram leave your country, relatives and your father home and go to the land that am going to show you and his nephew , Lot went with him and all the wealth and all the slaves they had acquired, but in future they had problems and Abraham had to depart from Lot**(Genesis;12 Genesis;13)** How many times do we always encounter problems because we don't obey God, because people they are connected to us and we miss our blessing and calling/destiny, they may be connected to you but don't have your Spirit and calling from God -You need to have people around you who can help you as well with, advice courage you can't reach your destiny on your own, if you are always giving and not receiving ,that unhappy relationship, You gradually need to change, **Amen**

QUESTION?

HOW TO BECAME A FRIEND OF GOD?

(1) Be Holy -because God is holy -for it is written "be Holy because am Holy **(1Peter 1;16;)** Am the Lord your God consecrate yourself ,be holy because am Holy ,do not make yourself unclean by an creature that moves along the ground **(Leviticus,11;44)** Little children let no one deceive you, whoever practices righteousness is righteous as he is righteous **(1,John;3;7)Amen**
(2)Study Gods word ,love God and seek him -I love those who love me ,whoever looks for me can find me **(Proverb,8;17)** You will seek me and you find me and you will find me, because you will seek me with all your heart **(Jeremiah 29;13)Amen**

THE FOUNDATION FOR FRIENDSHIP!

Is royalty and honest , a true friend will always be your defence, lawyer, before he/she becomes your judge, there is no such a fair weather friend ,you don't need friend in fair weather ,a fair friend is not a friend at all-Friendship doesn't require being shy, quietness, reserved or having dynamic personality to have a good friendly relationship you must be a good friend , I do not call you servants any longer because servants do not know what their masters is doing instead, I call you friends because, I have told you everything I have heard from my father, you did not chose me I choose you and I appointed you to go and bear much fruits, the kind of the fruits that endures and so that the father will give you Whatever you ask of in my name, this is what I command you love one another (*John;15;13;15*)Jesus himself is a true friend for he laid down his life for his friends me and you ,become a friend to him by trusting him as your personal saviour being born again and receiving a new life in him The book of(*Romans;5;6;8*)Describe a true friend as for when we were still helpless Christ died for the wicked at the time that God choose ,It is a difficult thing for someone to die for a righteous person it may even be that someone dare to die for good person but God has shown us how much he loves us, Jesus explained it clear that whoever receives one such child in my name receives me, and Whoever receives me receives not me, but the one who sent me (**Mark;9;37**) In the world we live today each and every one of us needs friend at, our Churches, Schools ,Work ,Place, Homes, and Neighbourhood ,Country, we live in and outside- A true friend reaches for your hand and touches your heart What is a friend a single soul dwelling in two bodies (*Aristotle)* friendship is one mind in two bodies (*Mencius)*In my friend I find a second self(Isabel) It's a good thing to be rich and strong but it's good to be loved by many It's good to have a friend who loves you the way he/she loves himself/herself (*Mark;12;31)*A friend loves all the time and a brother is born for adversity(*Proverb;17;17*)Do two people start travelling together without arranging to meet(*Amos3;3)*A friend is the one whom you can be yourself with no fear that she/he will judge you someone you respect and that respect you not based upon worthiness but based on likeness of mind - To stand in the position of a friend you have to be a friend Some friends do not last but some friends are more than royal than brothers (*Proverb;18;24)*And the word become true that said Abraham believed God and because of his Faith God accepted him as a righteous and so Abraham was called a friend of God(*James;2;23)*Listen stand at the door and knock if anyone hears my voice and opens the door I will come in and eat with them and they will eat with me (*Revelation;3;20)*A true friend will bring you back to God if you are running away because of the mistakes you have made knowingly or unknowingly Instead of him blaming you, Come to me all of you who are tired from carrying heavy loads and I will give you rest, take my yoke and put it on you learn from me because am gentle and humble in spirit ,and you will find rest in the yoke, I will give you is easy and the load I will put on you is light (*Mathew;11;28;29*)Do not forget your friends or your fathers friend, if you are in trouble don't ask for a relative for help a neighbour nearby can help you more than a relative who are far away(*Proverb;27;10*)Two people are better than one, for they can help each other succeed, if one person falls the other can reach out and help, but someone who falls alone is in real trouble(*Ecclesiastes 4;9;12*)God used Peter and John to heal the Lame man sitting at the temple gate Adam couldn't make it alone by himself so God said I will make a helper for him(**Genesis;2;18**)A true friend will always make you Laugh there is a saying which states **"If you have no wrinkles you haven't laughed enough "**So make friends whom you will free with crack Jokes, and be stress free, Be friendly to everybody ,but don't have everyone as a friend ,Friendship is the breathing rose with sweets in every fold (**Oliver-Wended-Holmes**)Give time to people -but don't give time wasters ,gossipers , critics, complainers and blamers, An open rebuke is better than hidden love wounds from a sincere friend are better than many kisses ,from an Enemy (*Proverb;27;5;6*)The language of a friendship is not words but meaning *(Henry-David)*Irons sharpens Iron so a friend sharpens friends (*Proverb;27;17*)Put no trust in a neighbour have no confidence in a friend guard the door of your mouth from her who lies in your Arms (*Micah;7;5*)Best friends can tell you things you don't want to tell yourself(*Frances ward welter*) Some people go to pastors clergy and priests others to poetry but I to my friend*(Jesus)*Friends are kisses blown to us by Angles -A single rose can be my Garden a single friend my world*(Leo buscaglia)Only a true friend* will tell you when your face is dirty-A friend is the one who comes in when the whole world has gone out*(Grace Pulpit)A friend knows the song in my heart and sings to me when my memory fails(**Donna Roberts**)*The best I can do for my friend is simply be his/her friend The Godly give good advices to their friends the wicked lead them astray(**Proverb;12;26**)When choosing friends you have to be careful ,don't choose friends who will only bring you down ,and draw you away from Christ- So if your right eye cause you to sin, tear it out, and throw it away, It is better to lose part of your body than to have it all thrown into hell, and if your right hand is leading you to Sin cut it off and throw it away, it is better for you to lose a part of your body than to have all of it go into hell(**Mathew,5;29;30**)/(<u>**Ways how to make friendship (1)**</u>**Put a Smile on your face** -To attract other people attention to respond to us today give a smile to a stranger can only be the sunshine he can see but be careful there some friends who are two faced they smile and laugh with you but they slander you behind your back**(2)Make eye contact-** When you look at them **(3)Call people by their names-** when you meet them friends are known by their names **(4)Talk to each other about their favourite topics, Jesus and God Reading Bible ,Gospel Music ,Football Gospel Conferences(5)Find time to give a word of encouragement -** compliment act of kindness be open and master the art of feedback don't back off helping in difficult issues tell the truth all the time**(6)Let us not love with words but with actions(1John;3;18)**We need to know the common objective of each other just remember this is not a one day job are you both patient enough relationship and friendship takes time **(7)Show appreciations to those who matters in your life -** and let them know that you love them and do it often look for the best in them don't try to turn people into your shoes and don't expect them always to be like you develop Empathy and understanding of them don't take other people for granted respect and value them avoid thinking that you have power over them relationship and friendship is based on respect and mutual trust **(8)Serve gladly-**Service is the only thing we have to sell and exchange but it's very difficult to teach because nobody makes a relationship with friends wants to be a slave **(9)*But Serve other first*** as if you were serving God not Man, Avoid self- centeredness focus on other side of your pattern listen to them and let them listen to you as well **(10)*Forgive those who have wronged you-***Forget and move on take pleasure in other people and their success their success is your success good friendship doesn't only make work more fulfilling and enjoyable it make improved performance if you are friends at work :***Personality who were true friends to each other in the Bible*** -**(1)Elijah and Elisha** time came for the lord to take Elijah up to heaven in a whirlwind Elijah and Elisha set out from Gidgal and on the way Elijah said to Elisha now stay here the lord has ordered me to go to Bethel but Elisha answered I swear by my loyalty to the living lord and to you that I will not leave you so they went Bethel when it come to go to Jericho they went together River Jordan the same **2,Kings2;1;2)-(2)Job** friends (**Eliphaz-Bildad-$ Zophar**)When they heard how much Job had been suffering they decided to go and comfort him while they were still on a long way off they saw Job but did not recognise him when they did they began to weep and wail tearing their clothes in grief and throwing dust into the air and on their heads then they sat there on the ground with him for seven days and nights without saying a word because they saw how much was suffering **(*Job2;11;13)(3)Ruth$ Naomi*(*return to Bethlehem*)** Again they started crying then Orphan kissed her mother in law good bye and went back home but Ruth held on to her so Naomi said to her your sister in law has gone back to her people and to her God go back with her but Ruth answered don't ask me to leave you let me go with you whenever you go wherever you live I will live your people will be my people and your God will be my God wherever you die will die and that where I will be buried may the lords worst punishment come upon me if I let anything but death separate me from

183

you when Naomi saw that Ruth was determined to go with her she said nothing more*(Ruth1;14;18)(4)David $ Nahash* Sometime later king *Nahash of Ammon died and his son Hanun become a king David said I must show you loyal friendship to Hanun as his father Nashash did to me so David sent a massager to express his sympathy (2Samuel10;1;2)(5)David &Abiathar (the slaughter of Priests)*So Saul *said to Doeg you kill them and doeg* **killed 85 priest** *all who were qualified to carry the ephod Saul also ordered all the other inhabitants of the Nob city of priest to be put to death men and women children and babies cattle and donkeys and sheep's they were all killed but Abiathar one of Ahimelech sons escaped and went and joined David he told him how Saul had slaughtered the priests of god David said when I saw Doeg there that day I knew that he would be sure to tell Saul so am responsible for the death of all your relatives stay with me and don't be afraid Saul wants to kill both you and me but you will be safe with me (1Samuel18;23)*David $ Jonathan I grieve for you my brother how dear you were to me how wonderful was your love for me better than even than the love of women (*Jonathan son of Saul hide David*;2Samuel1;26) Once again Jonathan said to him (Promise to love him for Jonathan loved David as much as he loved himself (*1Samuel;20;17;more 1Samuel;20;42*) Then Jonathan said to David God be with you the lord will make sure that you and I and your descendants and mine will never keep sacred promise we have made to each other then Jonathan went back to the town dear Christian choose the friends who are there for you in all situations like David Jobs Abiathar, Naomi and Ruth Elijah and Elisha hold a friend with both your hands friends are Gods way of taking care of us a true friend is the best possession (*Franklin*)Make friends when you don't need one, a friend is the one who knows about you and still loves you, Good friend helps you to find important things when you have lost them ,Your smile courage and hope ,How to improve yourself Remember to love yourself ,what you are doing ,and behave in the way that ensures You will continue to do so, not only will you sleep easier at night but other people will respond to yourself, respect and dignity, When you are to change your behaviours explain to the friends you have, what you seek to achieve and asking for a fed back, if you change overnight without explanation people will be suspicious of your motives particularly, If it is one off change or your behaviours is inconsistent; but remember when the Son of man came, he ate and drank and everyone said look at this man , he is a glutton and a drinker a friend of tax collectors and other outcasts !Gods wisdom ,however is shown to be true by its results **(Mathew;11;19)**
Amen

CHARACTERISTICS OF GOOD FRIENDS AND BAD FRIENDS
BAD FRIENDS

Their words do not co-operate with their hearts -they love to flatter, they fake smile ,and many time compliment you and insult you ,at the same time The scripture say "they his words are smooth as butter ,but in his heart is war, his word are as soothing as Lotion ,but underneath are daggers *(Psalm;55;21)*They smile and laugh with you ,but then slander you behind your back, while he was still speaking a crowd came up and the man who was called Judas one of the *(12-Disciples)*was leading them he approached Jesus to kiss him but Jesus said "would you betray the Son of Man with a Kiss *(Luke;22;47-48)*A gossip betrays a confidence so avoid anyone who talks too much*(Proverb;20;19)*Do not drag me with the wicked -with those who do evil those who speak friendly words to their neighbours, while planning evil in their hearts *(Psalm;28;3)*Even my close friends someone I trusted one who shared my bread has turned against me*(Psalm;41;9)*Smooth words may hide a wicked heart ,just as a pretty glaze covers a clay pot ,people may cover their hatred with pleasant words but they are deceiving you they pretend to be kind but don't believe them they hearts are full of many evils *(Proverb;26;23-25)Be aware of* your friends do not trust anyone in your clan, for every one of them is a deceiver and every friend is a slander *(Jeremiah;9;4)Do not spread* slanderous gossip among your people ,do not stand idly by when your neighbour life is threatened I Am the Lord*(Leviticus;19;16)*
They always gossip about their friends, they always want to know your information and secrets so they can gossip to others, but my enemies say nothing but evil about me how soon will you he die and be forgotten?"they ask they visit me as if they were my friends but all the while they gather gossip and when they leave they spread it everywhere *(Psalm; 41; 5-6)* A gossip goes around telling secrets but those who are trustworthy can keep a confidence *(Proverb; 11; 13)* A perverse person stirs up conflicts and a gossip separate friends *(Proverb; 16; 28)*
They always be little you your talents and your accomplishment
They always make fun of you
When you are alone with each other it's never a problem, but when others are around you they constantly try to make you bad
Everything is a competition to them always trying to wind up you
When they are around others they act like they don't know you ,
When you make mistakes they always gloat and sometimes allow you make mistakes, if an enemy were insulting me I could endure, it if a foe were rising against me I could hide but it is you a man I like myself, my companion, my close friend with whom I once enjoyed sweet fellowship at the house of God as we walked about the worshippers *(Psalm 55;12;14)*

They purposely give you wrong advice so you don't succeed or surpass them in something ,Good friends tell the truth even if it hurts , An open rebuke is better than hidden love, wounds from a sincere are better than many kisses from an Enemy *(Proverb;27;5-7)*

They always take advantage of you, they use you for what you have ,and know the scriptures say "Do not take advantage of each other but fear your God, I am the lord your God *(Proverb;27;6)*Many curry favour with a ruler and everyone is the friend of one who gives gift**(Proverb;19;4)**A poor person is disliked even by his neighbour but those who love the rich are many**(Proverb;14;20)**The poor are shunned by all their relatives how much more do their friends avoid them? though the poor pursue them with pleading they are nowhere to be found*(Proverb;19;6;7)In life* get to know the more you have to offer the more you have to watch out for people using you !,**Amen;**

They are never there when you need them in your time of need and in bad situations they run away they close their mouth when you are in danger, My heart pounds my strength fails me even the light gone away from my eyes my friends and companion avoids me because of my wounds my neighbour stays far away*(Psalm 38;10;11)I am scorned by all my* enemies and despised by neighbours even my friends are afraid to come near me when they see me on the street they run away to the other side *(Psalm 31;11)*

They never build you up and make you better but always bringing you down because they are down they are critical they always see the bad they never see the good in you always remember what you have been taught and don't let go of it keep all you have learned it is the most important thing in life don't follow the ways of the wicked don't do what evil people do and don't follow them stay away from them and keep on going because they cannot sleep until they do evil they cannot rest until they harm someone they feast on wickedness and cruelty as if they were eating bread and drinking wine the ways of the good person is like the light of dawn growing brighter until full daylight but the wicked walk around in the dark they can't even see what make them stumble my Children pay attention to my words listen closely what I say don't ever forget my words keep them always in your mind *(Proverb 4;13;21)*Do not be fooled bad companion ruin good characters come back to your right senses and stop your sinful ways I declare to your shame that some of you do not know God *(1Corinthians;15;33-34)*

Warnings Keep your life free from the love of money and be content with what you have, for he has said I will never leave you or forsake you**(Hebrews13;5)**You adulterous people do you know that friendship with the world is an enemy with God ,therefore whoever wishes to be a friend of the world makes himself an enemy of God**(James4;4)**Therefore encourage one another and build up one another just as you are doing(*1Thessolonia 5;11$Peter4;8;10)* A man is known by the company he shuns as well as the company he keeps its better to be lonely than in a bad company ,forget all the reasons why it won't work and believe ,why it can work good friend still exists have a changed mind that good friends exist in life and make more friends in the world, In life never lose friends we only learn who the true one are "respect yourself enough walk away from anything that no longer serves you grows you ,or makes you happy, Never try to revenge on anyone always continue to love everyone your enemies and friends -Do yourself a favour and read more about friendship and don't forget whatever you learn you will prosper;**(Proverb 19;8)** **Amen**

LONELESS

In the first chapter Genesis Old Testament, it was good to created man alone (Adam) but after he realised it was not good Adam was enjoying great relationship with God but because he didn't have a human companion God said it was not good God designed two voids one is a void he can fulfil himself the second one is a void the right person can fulfil and you cannot fill either void with things like jobs cars money say *what should I do* ?open your eyes today one in three relationship today begins on internet but there dangers there you can be anybody you want to be on the internet yet not be known and loved for the person you really are further more loneliness can blind you to your true needs and another person's lack of characters pray about it when One writer wrote and said am a single the kind of compassion I ache for I don't have it but this feelings drives me to seek God why/am I single I long to love and to be loved / singleness brings you close to lean on God to face an uncertain future without fear**(Psalm;27;1)There some advantages of being Single/Alone and Disadvantages**

Advantages

If you really are going to be a happy single ,you have to stop treating single as the annoying time that you pass between relationship and embrace it, rather than focusing on what you lack focus on what you have you **(Natalie-Lue)**I celebrate myself and sing myself Its better to be alone than in a bad company being surrounded by wrong people is the loneliest thing in the world, a busy Vibrant ,goal oriented woman is so much more attractive than a woman who waits around for a man to validate her existence ,Singleness is no longer a lack of options but a choice to refuse to let your life be defined by your relationship status but to live every day happily and let your ever after work itself out Singleness is not a status it's a word that describes a person who is strong enough to live and enjoy life without depending on others ,it doesn't mean that you know nothing about love sometimes being solo is wiser than being in a false relationship if we seek paradise outside ourselves ,we cannot have paradise in our hearts**(Thomas-Merton)**I don't want to be named labelled as lonely just because I am alone**(Delta Burke)(b)**The best part about being alone is that you really don't have to answer to anybody you do what you want mess up your own room your credit report or even your life ,you can come and go as you please and stay out as late as you want to you live life on your own term without apologies you do not need to ask for opinions before doing something -you sleep fastest who sleep alone**(Richard-Avedond)(c)**Being alone can give you an opportunity to discover who you are and figure out why you are always alone, **(d)**Sometime life is too hard to be alone and sometimes life is too good to be alone **(e)**When we cannot bear to be alone .it means we do not properly value the only companion we will have from birth to death -ourselves **(Eda- Leshan)**We are born alone ,we live alone ,we die alone ,only through our love and friendship can we create the illusion for the moment that we are not alone**(Orson-Welles)**Being alone or isolated at times doesn't always mean that you want to distance yourself from others it simply means that you need some space to see things clearly and nothing can give peace only yourself a man can be himself alone so long as he is alone if he does not love solitude he will not love freedom ,for it is only when he is alone that he is really free , my alone feels so good I will only have you if you are sweeter than my solitude **(Warsan - Shire)**- if you can take care of yourself you can take care of someone else being single sometimes doesn't necessary mean you are unavailable ,sometimes you have to put a sign that says ***"Do Not Disturb "on your heart,*** He who knows others is wise he who knows himself is enlightened**(Lao Tzu)**All our unhappiness comes from our inability to be alone**(Jean De la Bruyere)**-Pray that your Lon less may spur you into finding something to live for ,great enough to die for-What a lovely surprise to finally discover how unlovely being alone can be when you discover how unlovely can be you come to understand the dangers of being alone -Be able to be alone ,lose not advantage of solitude and the society of thyself**(Thomas-Browne)Disadvantage** When we truly realise that we are all alone is when we need others most**(Ronald Anthony)**The most terrible poverty is loneliness and the feeling of being unloved **(Mother-Teresa)**The person who tries to live alone will not succeed as a human being ,his heart withers if it does not answer another heart ,his mind shrinks away if he hears only one echoes of his own thought and finds no other inspiration**(Pearl-Buck)God** Created everything for a purpose Man and Woman being alone wouldn't be the best option in life that's why Adam and Eve was created -God He is our protector provider and saviour whether you have a husband or not have faith Paul says be satisfied with your present situation God will not leave you when we have tested loneliness past what we think we can bear out cry to Jesus he is close to the broken hearted and saves those who are crushed in spirit **(Psalm;34;18)**He knows what it means to long for something ,he is longed for the affection of his loved ones for years authenticity one in a while a man spark my interest then a funny thing happened the more interested I become the more I become someone else - the old fears kick in am I pretty enough ?thin enough ?talkative enough charming ? God made me who Am and years of being single have made me to learn who this woman is? I would rather be single than be with someone who wants me to be someone else- Freedom is nothing but a chance to be better the choice is yours being Married or Single Before you enter into a relationship you have to know these principles-**Evaluate**-can two walk together unless they have agreed (*Amos 3; 3*) *Do two people travel together without arranging to meet?* No a successful marriage is based on two things finding the right person and becoming the right person and the second thing is harder than the first just because two people share the same bed and same name it does not guaranty harmony here are some practical suggestions based on the word evaluate **Enjoy**-do you enjoy the same things may be it is not a big deal now but later when your husband is glued to a big football match on the television and you want a little conversation it will be **Values** –the bible ask can two walk together unless when they agree ? Do you agree on major issues such as school fees for children tilting in church intimacy parenting finances, in law-goals and your relationship with God you may disagree over many things but these are making or break issues **Accessibility-a**re you both emotionally accessible or is a strong silent type who does not communicate or understand you need to love do you really love each other? Not the Hollywood version but the kind that listens to your spouse .opinions and concern overlooks faults and failings value them and expresses itself through kindness **Understand** –as the lord does not make snow- flakes a like he does not make two people a like so can you understand and handle things and each other differences **Appreciations** – your partner can not read your mind so get into the habit of expressing your appreciations for one another **Temperament** –if you are naturally upbeat but they are moody and introverted you may have an oil and water mix how will you handle this **Environment** –if you are from a different back ground are you comfortable in the same social and spiritual settings ? If you want a happy marriage evaluate these things don't rush into relationship don't excite love until you are ready songs of songs(**2;7**)Daughter of Jerusalem promise me women of Jerusalem swear by the swift deer and the gazelles that you will not interrupt our love it so desires when we feel hurt and rejected there is something inside us that wants to prove that we are still worthy and desirable as a result we can end up jump into the next relationship too quickly but just as a child does not go from crawling to driving overnight there is a process involved and if you try to circumvent it you will end up back at square one wondering what happened one writer says a new relationship wont successfully heal you avoid aggravating inflicted wounds or instantly clean a mess regardless of the temporally bliss sooner or later you will end up faced again with your old stuff if this is your situation do things the right way take your time these things cannot be feigned rushed or pursued they will be given to you when you are really ready and not a moment sooner you want the real deal this time and God wants to be your filter so in order to reach the treasure of your heart a person must first pass through him Solomon wrote don't excite love don't stir it up until the time is ripe and you are ready don't be in such a hurry to take the edge off your pain that you run a head of God it takes time for him to make you a person he wants you to become while he is working on you he is preparing the heart of the right person /partner to show up at that right time in the meantime there is a way to fill the emptiness inside work on developing a closer relationship with God and he will fulfil your joy and peace **(Romans;15;13)**But whoever drinks the water I give them will never thirst indeed the water I give them will become in them a spring water welling up to eternal life**(John 4;14)** we all want to be loved and appreciated for who we are and when it does not happen on our time table its attempting to rush into another relationship hoping it will make everything better one Author wrote and said *there is no prince charming to sweep you off your feet and make you happy with yourself* even when the first part of the story seems to go well sleeping beauty wakes up to discover her prince is just a common frog you cannot expect a person to give you what only your heavenly father can provide mere mortals even with good intentions can never come close to you when you pin all your hopes and dreams on someone else you are bound to be disappointed when you sell your Soul in an attempt to attain the unattainable the cost is higher and the potentials for peril is steep don't let obsessive desire lead you down a path of despair obsession is powerful it fuels fantasies and drives you to reckless behaviours you won't find *Love till you Love* and respect yourself enough stop looking for someone or something outside yourself to give you worth one day Jesus met a Woman who had married five times and was pursuing yet another relationship recognising that her need was not for another man but a relationship with God he said no one who drinks the water I give will ever be thirsty again Jesus saw beyond her sin to her real need and restored her sense of self-worth bottom line only the water Jesus gives will quench your soul thirst The true foundation of friendship *(1John;1;7)*but if we walk in the light as he in the light we have fellowship with one another and the blood of Christ his son purifies us from all our sins the word of God says better a nearby friend than a distant family;*(Proverb;27;10)*Sometime it is easier to develop a close friendship with those outside your immediate family circle but there is another kind of blood relative mentioned in the bible brothers and sister s joined together through the blood of Jesus Christ it is a kind of relationship that does not permit you to go and do your self-centred things *(Colossians;3;18)*The peace that Christ gives is to guide you in decision you make for it is peace that God has called you together in one body and be thankful it requires us to work hard getting along with each other treating each other with honour*(James3;18)*It calls for a long term commitment not readily understood by the me generation ,where when the going gets tough its acceptable to bail out a relationship and move on one writer said that today many Christians don't understand the meaning of brotherhood and sisterhood it says find friends like minded like income people who vote like you and have the same uniform these friends work until the bottom fall out of your life you face a pressing problem or a tragic loss ,illness and **suddenly you realise that no one cares much about you** *why?* **Because you** have not in any body life and now when you need to make a withdraw there is no money in the friendship bank Paul wrote and said I have no one like Timothy who genuinely cares about your/welfare all the other cares only for themselves but you know how Timothy has proved himself he and I like a son and his father have worked for the sake of the gospel **(Philippians;2;20;22)remember** alone you can do so little together we can do so much; **Amen**

A HAPPY -MARRIAGE

MARRIAGE- Is defined as the process by which two people make their relationship public ,official and permanent ,joining of the two in a bond that lasts until death- Marriage is when the man leaves his Father and Mother and is united with his wife and they become one *(Genesis;2;24)*A man does well not to marry, but because there so much immorality, Every man should have his own wife ,and every woman should have her own husband- A man should fulfil his duty as a husband and the woman should fulfil her duty as a wife ,and each other should satisfy the others needs - Marriage begins when we marry the ones we love and they blossom ,when we love the one we marry**(Tom-Mullen)**Eliza Abraham servant was sent to find a wife for Isaac he prayed and said" O lord give me success today and God did, and Rebekah become the great history of today in the **bible,** Search from the book of the lord and read ,not one of these shall fail not one shall lack her mate, for your mouth has commanded it, and his Spirit has gathered them **(Isaiah,34;16)**Whoever who finds a wife finds a treasures and receive favour from God **(Proverb;5;15;19)**The Wife is the reflection of the Husband glory ,Marriage is to be honoured by all and husband and wives, must be faithful to each other , God will judge those who are immoral and those who commit adultery**(Hebrews;13;4;7)**A good wife is her pride and joy - A wife who brings shame on her husband is like cancer in the bones **(Proverb;12;4)**;Reach out to others, that they mean taking down the wall you have been hiding behind and building a bridge ,the bible say don't be interested only in your own life ,be interested in others *(Ephesians;4;25) Many family have depression from each side either Woman or Man because they have not received blessings from their partners , your wife ,children and husband, need your blessings*-Philippians 24 there is no perfect relationship or risk free ones ,It is in finding and unmet need and pouring but, If you put yourself into that you conquer loneliness, and discover new life in living, But don't forget God will not leave you alone **(Hebrews;13;5)**The real act of marriage takes place in the heart not in the ballroom ,or church or Synagogue, It is a choice you make on your wedding day, and over and over again, and that choice is reflected in the way you treat your husband and wife**(Barbara De Angelis)**Marriage is not a Contract it is Permanent, It needs total commitment- Marriage is not a ritual or an end, It is a long intricate ,Intimate dance together and nothing matters more than your own sense of balance and your choice of partner**(Amy-Bloom)**Marriage is not a noun Its a verb ,it is not something you get it is something you do, It is the way you love your partner every day, The beauty of marriage is not always seen from the very beginning but rather as love grows and develop over time,**(Fawn-Weaver)**Love is glue that Sticks ,the Husband and Wives together- Marriage is not to think alike ,but to think together, In every marriage more than a week old, there are grounds for divorce ,the trick is to find and continue to find grounds for marriage, Divorce starts in the mind and the devil feeds the mind, never entertain thoughts of getting divorce, never threaten your spouse with Divorce, choose to remain married-God hates divorce for no good reasons; men ought to love their wives just as they love their own bodies, a man who loves his wife loves himself -people never hate their bodies instead they take care of them just as Christ does the church for we are members of his body **(Ephesians ;5;28;29)** A wife is not a master of her own body but her husband is in the same way a husband is not a master of his own body, but his wife is ,Do not deny Yourselves to Each other's unless you first agree to do so for a while in order to spend your time in Prayers ,but then resume normal marital relations in this way you will be kept from giving in to Satan temptation, because of your lack of self control *(1;Corinthians;7-1;5)*In the same way you wives must submit to your husband ,so that if any of them do not believe Gods word, your conduct will win them over to believe it ,will be necessary for you to say a word because they will see how pure and reverent your conduct is*(1Peter;1;2)*For a man was not created from a woman but a woman from a man **(1Corinthians 11;8)** Submit to one another because of your reverence for Christ, wives submit to your husband as to the lord for the husband has authority over his wife just as Christ has Authority over the church ,and Christ himself is the saviour of the church his body -Wives must submit completely to their husband just as the church submits itself to Christ **(Ephesians;5;22;-24)**A woman should always be self controlled and pure and to be good housewives who submit to their husbands so that no one will Speak evil of the massage of God **(Titus;2;5)**Wives submit to your husband for that is what you should do as Christians husband love your wives and do not be harsh with them**(Colossians;3;18;19)**Better to live on the roof than share the house with a nagging wife **(Proverb;25;24)** Do nothing out of selfishness Ambitions in humanity,-Value others above yourself **(Philipians;2;3)**Your speech should always be pleasant and interesting and you should know how to give the right answers to everyone **(Colosians;4;6)** Counselling each other, helping each other giving money to each other- if the woman can give the outsiders, what about the husband or wife you share the same bed, Happy are the poor in Spirit for there is the kingdom of heaven**(Mathew;5;3)Amen**

REASONS FOR MARRIAGE

- **(1)Help-** The lord God "Said it is not good for a man to be alone, I will make a helper suitable for him **(Genesis;2;18)Amen**
- **(2)Procreation -**God blessed them and" said to them be fruitful and increase in number ,fill the Earth , and subdue it ,rule over the fish in the sea and the birds in the sky over all creatures that moves on the ground **(Genesis;1;28)Amen**
- **(3)Honour -**Marriage should be honoured by all and the marriage bed kept pure for God will judge the Adulterer and all the sexually Immoral **(Hebrews 13;4)Amen**

WHAT MAKES MARRIAGE HAPPY WHILE OTHERS SLIDE INTO MISCHIEF ?

Luck ?Hanging and kissing, going out with your Spouse every weekend, Money ,good genes ? The answer is in the word of God *(bible)* Unless the Lord builds the house the builders labour in vain ,unless the lord watches over the city the guards stands in vain *(Psalm,127;1)* At the same time says the Lord , I will be the God of all families of Israel, and they shall be my people *(Jeremiah 31;1)* Jesus said happy are the humble ,happy are the poor in spirit, the humble who rate themselves insignificant pride that is self- promoting and always demanding its right ,bring misery while humility. Self- denial and considering -your friends needs brings happiness **(Mathew19;6)**they are no longer two but one no human being must separate them what God has joined together**(Mathew;19;8;9)**any man who divorces his wife for any reason /cause other than unfaithfulness commits   adultery   if   he   marries   some   other   woman **(Ecclesiastes;9;9)**Enjoy your life with a man /woman you love there something that your spouse cannot live up to but **Solomon** wrote and said catch us the foxes the little foxes that Spoils the vines for our vines have tender grapes **(Solomon;2;15)**and the word tender means when we fail to treat one another tenderly. graciously ,lovingly ,considerately ,and with respect we go astray a neglected partner is vulnerable to anyone who comes along ,resentment wells up and takes over, Marriage doesn't lose its meaning one day ,overnight months and years insensitivity and neglect but it doesn't have to be that way for you, something can be done you can lay aside all the excuses that are causing your marriage to breakdown ,and start again with, Praying together ,Eating on the same table everyday as you began ,a simple kiss ,romance, find something good to say to each other ,Everyday, respect your differences ,Identify your special place, and special songs develop a strong sense of honour ,respect your differences, Marriage takes two this can make a difference if acted on upon, Its between you and your Spouse to see a difference, bring new ideas in your marriage ,between Wife/Husband ,Instead of differences ,Change your marriage and flourish again, the book of revelation tells us "But this I have done against you , do not love me as you did first ,think how far you have fallen, turn from your sins and do what you did first, if you don't turn from your sins I will come to you and take your lamp stand from its place(**Rev;2;4**)If Gods word don't work in your family and marriage then it won't work elsewhere, the secret of finding a good marriage is not just finding the right person but becoming the right person and that can only happen when you make a daily commitment to living by the principle of God word ,demonstrating the fruit of the spirit is Love joy -peace- patience -kindness -goodness- faithfulness- humility and self control,-there is no law against such things as these and those who belong to Christ have put to death their human desire with all its passion the spirit has given us life ,he must also control our lives we must not be proud or irritate one another or be jealous of one another(**Galatians5;22;25**)Marriage is not supposed to make you happy and satisfied, It's your Job to make your marriage happy and satisfying -Yeah people ask the secret of our long marriage we take time to go the restaurant two times a week a little candlelight dinner ,soft music and dancing? She goes Wednesday I go Saturday a good marriage is based on Mutual sacrifice, Adam had to sacrifice something to Eva **(a Rib)** and your wife or husband will know you love her? Him when you are willing to give up those things that is important in order to meet his? Her needs and promote His? Her well being there is no more Lovely ,friendly charming relationship ,Communion or company than a good marriage(**Martin-Luther**)-Many men's wants to be married but still behave like singles even women, especially Men they don't want to sacrifice their ,Time, Money, for the better lives of their Wives ,they want a maid -they want to marry someone they want to Starve, the more you invest in your marriage the more valuable it becomes -The husband determines the Climate and the Wife thrive accordingly ,there is a reason your wife she is still cold and there is a solution the difference between an Ordinary marriage is in giving ,just a little extra every day as often as possible as long we both shall live ,Warm her up and watch her, Melt, When you begin to Love her , Nurture her, Cherish her, Encourage her, Protect her, and know her both Inner Value/Outside value as Christ did the church ,he gave up his life for the church -You will have a different wife /Woman in your arms ,if you treat her good,- The Secret of a happy marriage remains a secret these are just tips ,greatest marriage is not something that just happens, It is something that must be created-Marriage is like an Empty Container, you get out what you have put in -Marriage has a price to pay ,and It's like a bank account, it is the money you have deposit that you withdraw -if you deposit ,Peace, Love, care into your marriage your, marriage account will not breakdown ,and will always be smiling, and Overflow -though we know well that marriage is not about collecting things, the Joys of marriage are not Tangible, you live them that what makes them so special and have this in mind that marriage is not a 24 hour repair shop, your marital partner is not supposed to meet every need ,some of those needs you may have to take care of yourself ,through your friendship or other activities - Marriages you Admire they have issues in their families but they work on their issues and fix them right other than complaining ,blaming and stop being critical to each other- greatest marriage are build on team work ,a mutual respect ,a healthy dose of admiration and a never ending portion of love and grace Your Spouse is the Rose you have, don't cry for what you don't have ,For a married people I have a command which is not my own but the Lords a wife must not leave her husband(**1corinthians 7;10**)The story of one married Christian who said to another, I never knew what real happiness was until I married you, now is too late , God wants you to be holy and completely free from Sexual Immorality, each of you men should know how to live with your wife in a Holy and honourable way, not with lustful desire like the heathen who do not know God (**1Thessalonians;4;3;5**)Getting married is taking a huge risk you cannot predict what will happen in the future ,circumstances may change so leave room for adjustments ,a husband can lose a Job or you may fail to have babies, all these require prayers otherwise you might divorce -<u>**There things that kills our marriage and need s to be solved**</u>(1)Dishonesty ,False Promises. Excuses, Lying -Trust takes time to build but easy to break, Anger, unhealthy- communication ,critical judgement ,the bible states it clear do not use harmful words but only helpful words the kind that builds up and provide what is needed so that what you say will do good to those who hears you(**Ephesians;4;29**)Unforgiveness- breaks marriage -Marriage is a continual commitment ,you have to be kind and tender hearted to one another and forgive one another as God has forgiven you through Christ(**Ephesians;4;32**)<u>**How can marriage problems be solved?**</u>-First we need to know the causes of problems ,the biggest one is <u>**Selfishness motives**</u>-when you spent your life/time doing things your own way it's difficult to give the right and differ to another person some day you do it well other days poorly and other days not at all when we live for our kingdom our decision, thoughts ,plans ,actions and words are directed to our Personal desires and we seek to surround ourselves with people who will Serve our kingdom a marriage of two serving their own kingdom will eventually end in bloody battles but when two submit to the kingdom where Christ reigns and where Peace and Joy found marriage becomes an Opportunity to exist and Spouse begins to enjoy the beauty and the benefits of the kingdom of God our greatest marital problem is ourselves we will always rise to our own defence and be tempted to blame others while believing the best out of ourselves -God uses marriage to reveal the sin of self-righteous marriage can be easily transformed when one person sees the sin and humbly confess ways they have damaged the relationship its only when the two give up their own kingdom and join together as one living the principle of Gods kingdom that love peace joy harmony can be found and these are some principles you have to take in account to have a happy marriage **(1)*Happy are* the are the Peace maker-** the need to be right and win only both lose giving up Personal victory to be a peace maker is ultimate victory and is an important key in marriage you would be eternally lost if our lord Jesus Christ had not willingly surrendered his right for our wrongs the ring is not a sole symbol of Christian marriage but the cross superimposed on the ring Christ like surrender of our crucified self -promotes marital happiness**(2)*Happy are the merciful*-**those who don't injure hurt each other those who don't disappoint one another because we know if you hurt one another and one want to pay back is not good anger rises up and followed by the desire to make them pay back but just as revenge begets revenge mercy begets mercy - Mercy is not letting them get away with it treating your spouse mercifully is reciprocal (important it creates atmosphere where when fail you shall obtain mercy - mercy ends when nothing works**(3)*Happy are the meek*** -the gentle patient and kind handling your spouse struggling with kindness and long suffering is an expression of love that brings healing into the painful chapter of life and marriage ,When there is a storm /problem you have to come together and solve it, two people are better than one, if one falls the other can help to reach out for help (**Ecclesiastes;4;9;12)**When you have problems regarding finances relationship /love children you are couples and if one is being affected / being two make a huge different ,but protect the intimacy in your marriage and don't let anything or anyone come between you, and your spouse tell your spouse what you need sometimes emotions are so overwhelming you don't know what you need do you need space ?Do you want to be alone /around people? Do you want to talk? Listen to your mates feelings because all of us have different needs in life couples to have a happy relationship and marriage**(4)Be willing to compromise to each other**-there is no perfect marriage, there is no ready marriage, marriage is hard work ,volunteer yourself to work daily on it ,marriage is like a car that needs proper maintenance and proper services, if this is not done it will break down somewhere exposing the owner to dangers or unhealthy circumstances Let us not be careless about our marriages there is no marriage without Conflicts, knowing how to disagree and work through anger and disappointment is probably the key to lots of stuff going well is not about getting what you want all the time ,it's not a dictatorship it is not wanting to win all the time because that would mean the other person would lose, all the time may be Ok for you , but not good for the marriage , A great marriage is not when the perfect couple comes together, It is when the imperfect couple learns to enjoy their differences**(Dave-Meurer)**Marriage is more than finding the right person it is being the right person, The secret of successful marriage is to treat all disasters as incidents and none of the incidents as disasters **(Harold George Nicolson)(5)<u>Deal with the core issues-</u>**Marriage is not a place for criticism for abuse in the family Never demean your mate in Public before you Criticise your mate taste stop and remember they picked you, We all have weakness, struggles, fantasies strength, Childhood memories, unspoken needs and logging hidden deep inside if criticism is found there it will ruin any chance of true intimacy or trust and dissolve the hope that once might have existed ,and Remember God designed marriage to be a safe haven in a dangerous World, If you can't trust your spouse who can trust you? Every marriage has a weakness, Only God does not have a weakness, so if you focus on your spouse weakness you can't get the best out of his strength, Everyone has a dark history no one is an Angle ,when you get married or you want to get married stop digging into somebody past, Marriage is not for impatient some of the best stuff takes a while to develop you have to stick around to find out what matters is the Present life of your sweet wife and Husband, Old things have passed away forgive and forget focus on the present and future ,many marriages would be better-A good marriage is the union of two good forgivers If the husband and the wife clearly understood that they are on the same side chains do not hold marriage together it is threads hundreds of tiny threads which sew people together through the years marriage is like finger prints each one is different and each one is beautiful**(6)<u>Always have a shared Goal and Dreams for your family and future-</u>** If you spend too much of your time working making money and focusing on Children and neglect the other side you are making a big mistake you may wake up one day and find your spouse in your neighbours compound, , Work together to bring up your family and remember you are more than children ,Every marriage has its own challenges Marriage is not a bed of roses but you can make it a bed of roses Every marriage has gone through its own test of blazing fire True love proves in times of Challenges fight for your marriage make up your mind to stay with your Wife and Husband in times of need remember the ***Vows For Better For Worse in Health and Sickness*** I will be there for you my Wife /Husband God has a plan for you as you are together if you haven't discovered it talk about it then pray together and ask God to reveal it to you ,Every marriage has its own Level of success don't compare your marriage with anyone else we can never be equal some will be far some behind to avoid marriage stress be patient work hard and with time your visions ,dreams and goals shall come to pass**(8) <u>Get help from other people</u>**- sometimes there is no way to compromise one want to talk and the other don't want to listen find a counsellor ,Pastor or good Christian friend who can help in advice and pray for yourself and find others to pray for you these will make a different spouse encourage and help each other

(**1Thessolonia;5;11**)Instead of walking away/around your neighbours ,grass fertilise yours by looking for the good in your spouse speak encouraging words acknowledge your efforts the bible says Love .Protects trusts ,hopes persevere (**1Corinthians;13; 4and 7**)instead of making comparison ask God to help you see your partner like once you did before a Man does not clip his toenails either and that of woman does rub her husband feet while feeding each other grapes our spouse are the people we feel in love with and often they just need encouragement instead of complaining nurture your spouse/mate in the area they need it most   get to know that marriage is not a science rocket ,the principle of marriage it's based on are really pretty simple respect Loyalty, Kindness - Christians say they didn't know marriage would be hard God designed it that way for the purpose of aligning both your hearts with his kingdom and rescuing you from your own kingdom, let God always guide you in your decision making God cannot give you a complete person you desire he gives you the person in form of raw materials in order for you to mould the person that you desire this can only be achieved through Prayers love and patience- As spouse to get married is declaring when you get married you must declare a war against enemies and some of the mentioned enemies are the above mentioned and their solutions ;**Amen**

QUALITIES A CHRISTIAN MAN WANTS FROM A WOMAN!

- ✓ **Spiritually-Sounding** -Active in Church, using gifts ,God gave her Praying, Ushering involvement in Sunday school teaching ,Involvement in the Choir; **Amen**
- ✓ **Sweet Spirit** -With good altitude you should not use outwards aids to make yourself beautiful such as the way you do your hair or the jewellery you put on or the dresses you wear instead your beauty should consist of your true inner self ,the ageless beauty of a gentle and quite Spirit which is of a greatest value in Gods sight for the devout women of the past who placed their hope in God used to make themselves beautiful by submitting to their husbands like was like that she obeyed Abraham and called him her master you are now her daughter if you do good and are not afraid of anything(**1 Peter;3;3-6**);Amen
- ✓ **Supportive**--then the Lord God created a woman from the Rib of a Man and brought her to a man to be his help mate, in Dreams Visions, Goals, Aspirations to encourage a man ,because he knew man he can do things by himself ,but he needed someone to help him; She does him good not harm with all days of her life (**read; Proverb 31; 11-31**); Amen
- ✓ **Men love women who are selfish less'**-do nothing out of selfish motives in humanity, value others above yourself ,and look out for

one another's interest, not just for your own, the altitude is the one that Jesus Christ had **(Philippians 2;3;5)Amen**

✓ **Submissive** -It is better to live on the corner of a rooftop than to share a house with a contentious woman **(Proverb; 25; 24)**Let your conversation be always full of grace **(Colossians; 4; 6)**Submit yourselves to one another because of reverence for Christ **(Ephesians 5; 22)**

✓ **Men look for Women with Solid friendship-** Someone you can talk with a whole day, talk about everything, Laugh with, and Trust. be yourself around, Share with common interest ,Enjoy their presence A woman who Opens her mouth with wisdom and the teachings of Kindness is on her tongue ,For it is good who works in both too will and work for his good pleasure **(Philippians ;2;13)**

✓ **Sexy Woman** -Every man is looking for a woman he is proud of he can take out in Public; **Amen**

WHAT QUALITIES WOMEN LOOK IN MEN?

In the same way you must live with your wives with the proper understanding that they are weaker than you Treat them with Respect because they also will receive ,together with you God's gift of life ,do this so that nothing interfere with your prayers **(1Peter;3;7)**

women like men who are spiritual-Know God not unbelievers and a good relationship should be build on the foundation of God for both male and female should look for a spouse who knows God

Women like -Un distracted Listeners, Interrupted conversation when you are with them,

Women -like men who understand them, Paying attention to them, men who understand their desires, Dreams, Gifts goals, Fears, and Insecurities; Amen

Women -Love or like Men- who Value them -giving honour shows, value or worth, in business, careers, Ministry, Hobbies; **Amen**

Women- Like Men who give them quality Time -to understand them, Protect them; **Amen**

Women like Protection- Financially, Physically ,Safety, and Strength, and Encouraging them; Amen

Women like men who are Creative-Good planning for family, date out, men who can think of something new in the relationship; **Amen**

Men-If you know what you are doing you will Prosper in your Marriage, and God blesses everyone who trust him -We Human we make plans but It's the Lord who has the Final say /Word-We make plans but the Lord determines what happens ;**Amen**

HOW TO HAVE PEACE IN FAMILY?

Both partners /spouse -Should have affection for God

Truth and transparency-talk the truth to each other -everyone has sinned and is far away from Gods saving presence but by the free gift of God's grace all are put right with him through Jesus Christ who sets them free**(Romans;3;23)**don't hide the truth because you want to marry confess your sins, **Amen**

Financial security of husband/ wife and children -Save today, many challenges we see in family are related to finances **(Mathew; 14; 14; 21)** and agree on how money to be used in the family on one term; **Amen**

Embrace and encourage each other-Praise on your wife/ husband children don't discourage, smile, Amen

Team Parenting- bring children together, play with each other husband /wife and children teach them together children miss something when their parents are singles, what a man can teach a boy a woman cannot teach what a woman can teach a girl a husband cannot teach, Children it's your Christian duty to obey your parents for this is right thing to do respect your father and mother this is the first commandment that has a promise added **(Ephesians; 6; 1; 2) Amen**

Dual counsel -even Jesus knew what to do but he asked his disciples, in life if you refuse to be counselled you won't be able to counsel others even your family members, Amen

Affection and attention - A man should fulfil his duty as a husband and each should satisfy the others needs **(1Corinthians; 7; 3)** so be happy with your wife and find joy with the woman you have married **(Proverb; 5; 18)** teach your children how to greet, hug, Amen

DANGERS OF HAVING SEX OUT OF MARRIAGE OR BEFORE MARRIAGE!

(1)Creates shame (2)Damage your relationship with God (3) Alters your views about Sex (remove my sins and I will be clean wash me and I will be whiter than snow **(Psalm,51;7)(4)**Cause you to make comparison between people who are good in bed ,and those who are not good in bed (6)Ruins your reputation and it can take a while to build it again and cause people to disrespect you,(7)Creates Soul ties always making you to remember your Ex -boyfriend -Ex girlfriend - Use your body for Gods glory some of you will say am allowed to do anything yes, but not everything is good for you, I could say that am allowed to do anything but am not going to anything make me its slave, someone may say food is for the stomach and the stomach for food yes, but God will put an end to both the body is not to be used for sexual immorality, but to serve the lord and the lord provides for the body(1Corinthians;12;13)Since you are Gods people it is not right that any matter of sexual immorality or indecency or greed should even be mentioned among you **(Ephesians;5;3)**God did not call us to live in immorality, but in holiness so then whoever rejects this teaching is not rejecting a human being, but God who gives you his Holy Spirit**(1;2Thessalonians4;7;living in light 1Thessalonians4;3)**What human nature does is quite plain it shows itself in immorality filthy and indecent actions**(Galatians;5;19)**What I meant was you should not associate with a person who calls himself a believer but is Immoral or greedy or worship idols or is a slander or a drunkard or a thief do not even sit down to Eat with such a person **(1Corinthians 5;11)**And he went on say" it is what comes out of the person that makes him unclean for from the inside from a person's heart come the evil ideas which lead him to immoral things to rob, kill, commit adultery ,greedy .and do all sorts of evil things decent ,indecency, jealousy slander pride and folly all these evil things come from inside a person and make him unclean**(Mark 7;20;23)**For all that is in the world the desires of flesh and the desires of the Eyes and pride of possession is not from the father but from the world**(1John2;16)**You shall not commit Adultery **(Exodus;20;14)** Someone else will say food is for the stomach and the stomach for food yes but God will put an end to both**(1Corinthians 6;17)** Avoid immorality any other sin a man commits does not affect his body but the man who is guilty of Sexual immorality sins against his own body **(1Corinthians;6;18) ;Amen**

QUOTES ABOUT MARRIAGE

The bond of matrimony are like any other bond, they mature slowly **(Peter de-Vries)**Marriage is like a garden take time to grow ,but the harvest is rich unto those who wait patiently ,and tenderly care for the ground **(Darlene Schacht)**What a happy and holly fashion, it is that those who love one another should rest on the same pillow**(Nathaniel-Hawthorne)** I love being married ,it is so great to find that one special person you won't annoy, for the rest of your life**(Rita; Rudner)**Divorce is the past tense of marriage ,Success in marriage does not merely through finding the right mate but through being the right mate**(Barnet R Brickener)**More marriage might survive if the partner realised that sometimes the better comes after the worse**(Doug Larson)**Never get married in the morning because you never know who you will meet in the evening **(Paul-Horning)**Long marriage is two people trying to dance duet ,and two solos at the same time**(Anne Taylor Fleming)**Two things are owned to truthfulness lasting marriage and short friendship**(Robert Brail)**Love is a flower, which turns into a fruit at marriage**(Finnish-Proverb)** A dress that zips up the back will bring husband and wife together**(James H Boren)**All marriages are happy it's the living together afterward that cause troubles

(**Raymond Hull**)Our wedding was many years ago the celebrations continues to this day(**Gen-Perret**)Any woman who reads the marriage contract and then goes into it deserves all the consequences (**Isadora Duncan**)A first rate marriage is like a first rate hotel expensive but worth it (**Mignon McLaughlin**)A man wife has more power than the state (**Ralph Waldo Emerson**)Like good wine marriage gets better with age once you learn to keep a cork in it (**Gene-Perret**)I never knew what real happiness was until I got married and by then it was too late,(**Max Kauffman**)Marriage is not a word is a sentence Marriage is three parts and seven parts of forgiveness of sin(**Langdon- Mitchel**)Once a woman has forgiven her man she must not reheat his sin for breakfast(**Marlene Dietrich**)What counts in making a happy marriage is not so much how compatible you are but how you deal with incompatibility(**George-Levinger**)When a man steals your wife there is no better revenge than to let him keep her(**Sacha-Guitry**) Never marry for money ye borrow cheaper (**Scottish Proverb**) A happy marriage is the union of two forgivers (**Ruth Bell Graham**) The problem with marriage is that it ends every night after making love and it must be rebuilt every morning before breakfast (**Gabriel-Garcia**)The highest happiness in the world is marriage (**William Lyon Phelps**) Bachelors know more about women than married women, if they didn't they would be married too (**Hl Mancken**)Marriage is a meal where the soup is better than desert (**Austin O Malley**) It is not that marriage that fails it is the people that fails all that marriage does is to show people up (**Harry Emerson-Fosdick**)being divorced is like being hit by Mack truck ,if you live through it you start looking very carefully to the right and the left (**Jean A Kerr Marry-marry**) A man without a wife is like a vase without flower(**African Proverb**)Husband are like fire they go out when unattended(**Zsa-ZsaGabor**)Getting Divorced just because you don't love a man is almost silly as getting married just because you do(**Zsa-Zsa Gabor**)Love is blind but marriage restores it(**Samuel Lichtenberg**) Marriage is good for those who are afraid to sleep alone at night (**St Jerome**)Any married couple should forget their mistakes no use to remembering the same things (**Daune.Dewel**)There is no more lovely friendly and charming relationship .communion or company than a good marriage(**Martin-Luther**)One advantage of marriage is that when you fall out of love with you it keeps you together until you fall again a successful marriage requires falling in love many times always with the same person(**Mignon McLaughlin**)-Marriage is like a call in the night ,first the ring and then you wake up ,Dear Christians do more research read about quotes that will bring you Joy in your marriage and open your eyes to greater insight to know more about marriage God bless you ;**Amen**

UNITED WE STAND IN GOD-(CHURCH)

United- means the Spirit of togetherness **(integrated, merged, banded together)**for a common purpose or by a common feeling to serve God united **(Under one God father ,Son and ,Holy Spirit)** together we can do more for God, and ourselves in the spirit of togetherness ,To thank God for what he has done ,and what he is about to do in our life ,Let us not give up the habit of meeting together as some are doing, instead let us encourage, one another, all the more since you see the day of the lord is coming**(Hebrew;10;25) Its team work that makes the dream work ,** *We will never change the world by going to church -we will only change the world by being the church- A day in Gods temple (Church) is more important than a thousand days spent somewhere else ,*And may God, the source of patience and encouragement enable you to have the same point of view among yourselves ,by following the examples of Christ Jesus , so that all of you together may praise with one voice, the God the father of our Lord Jesus Christ *(Romans;15;5;6)*Behold how good and how pleasant it is for brethren to dwell together in unity **(Psalm;133;1)** One can chase a thousand but two can chase thousands, **,,Joy is in Church** -God give those who mourn in Zion ,Joy and gladness, Instead of grief, a song of praise instead of sorrow ,they will be like trees that the lord has planted himself, they will do what is right and God will be praised for what he has done ,they will build cities that have been long in ruins**(Isaiah;61;3;4)**Look at the sky we are not alone, the whole universe is friendly to us and conspires only to give the best to those who dream and work together- your coming to church and being united matter - because you come full of Spirit of faith , joy, your dream and vision , testimony ,dress code ,beauty , smile ,voice and words all maters- Being Together we are better stronger, smarter and more powerful ,when we come together in unity there is a blessing ,don't waste your time isolating yourself you will become what you are created to be, when you connect with the right people - Then Jesus went to Nazareth where he had been brought and on the Sabbath he went as usual to the Synagogue he stood up to read the Scripture and was handed the book of the prophet Isaiah, he unrolled the scroll and found the place where it is written the Spirit of the lord is upon me ,because he has chosen me to bring good news to poor, he has sent me to proclaim, liberty to captives, and recovery of sight to the blind to set free the oppressed and announce that the time has come when the lord will save his people, Jesus rolled up the scroll gave it back to the attendant and sat down all the people in the synagogue had their eyes fixed on him**(Luke;4;16;20)**We should value Church as Jesus value church - **(1)Its is a place for prayer-** I will bring you to Zion, my sacred hill give you joy in my house of prayer ,and accept the sacrifices you offer on my altar ,my house will be called the house of prayer for all nations"(**Isaiah;56;7**) and it is said to them "it is written in scriptures that God said my temple will be called the house of prayers but you are making it a hide out for thieves (**Mathew;21;13**)Its is a place to pray for our nations, pray for the peace of Jerusalem may those who love you prosper, may there be peace inside your walls and safety in your palace (**Psalm;122;6;7**)Church is a place we learn at the feet of Jesus in prayers(2)**We meet in church to re-fill our lamps with-food(word)water, oil and life** -the Lord says come everyone who is thirsty here is water come you that who do not have money buy corn and eat come buy wine and milk it will cost you nothing why you spend money on what does not satisfy? Listen to me and do what I say and you will enjoy the best food of all (**Isaiah;55;1;2**)**(3)It is a place to encounter power and strength-**Is the Hospital for the wounded-they grow stronger as they go they will see God of gods on Zion *(Psalm;84;7)* *O God you are my God and I long for you ,my whole body desires you like a dry worn out and waterless land my soul thirsty for you in the sanctuary let me see how mighty and glorious you are (Psalm;63;1;2)* **Come all to me all ye that Labour and are heave laden and I will give you rest (Mathew 11;28)**Leave all your worries to him because he cares(**1 Peter 5;7**)-Go to a church you can be ,encouraged, valued ,where you don't have to pay, God has a solution for everything *(4)It's the place to encounter wisdom and knowledge-*School that trains the Principles of Discipleship,-in days to come the mountains where the temple stands will be the highest one of all towering above all the hills ,many nations will come streaming to it, and their people will say let us go up the hill of the lord to the temple of Israel's God ,he will teach us what he wants to do we will walk in the paths he has chosen for the lord teachings comes from Jerusalem from Zion he speaks to his people *(Micah;4;1;2)(5)It is a place to posses our possessions -*but on mount Zion some will escape and it will be a sacred place ,the people of Jacob will possess the land that is theirs by right the people of Jacob and of Joseph will be like fire ,they will destroy the people of Esau as fire burns stubble no descendant of Esau will survive I the lord have spoken *(Obadiah 1;17;18)(6)The church is where we meet Jesus for healing miracles, signs and wonders-One day when Jesus was teaching some of the Pharisees and teachers of the Law were sitting there who had come* from every town in Galilee and Judea and from Jerusalem the power of the Lord was present for Jesus to heal the sick some people came carrying a paralysed man on the bed and they tried to take him into the house and put him in front of Jesus because of the crowd they could find no way to take him in so they carried him up on the roof made an opening in the tiles and let him down on his bed into the middle of the group in front of Jesus when Jesus saw how much faith they had he said to the man your sins are forgiven my friend *(Luke;5;17;20)* Jesus went all over

Galilee teaching in the synagogues preaching the good news about the kingdom and healing people, who had all kinds of disease and sickness the news about him spread through the whole country of Syria so that people brought him all those who were sick suffering from all kinds of diseases and disorders people with demons ,epileptic and paralytic and Jesus healed them all *(Mathew;4;23;24)* **-(7)The Church set people free-The spirit of the lord is upon me because he has chosen me to bring the good news to the poor, he has sent me to proclaim liberty to the captives ,and recovery of sight to the blind ,to set free the oppressed and the time has come when the lord will save his people through the church that the captive are set free***(Luke;4;18)* the church is about saving lives not taking it , we have been called to be Ministers of Grace , not judge who are always quick to point out the sins of others as if we have achieved it all we are called to love and not to condemn God wants to do great things in our life when we are united We must seek him together , we must let go of self centeredness ,greet hatred and God wants us all us to be Holy , we should not starve our family , friends , Community , Country, the spirit of togetherness invite a friend to church every time you get the opportunity ,we are children of God of God we should set example ,The time has come for judgement to begin and Gods own people are the first to be judged, If it starts with us *,how will it end with those who do not believe the good news from God? (1 Peter, 4;17) The slave trade in long-time history was abolished through the church missionary ,who signed treaties of slavery abolition,-*and And so I tell you Peter you are a rock and on this rock foundation, I will build my church and not even death will be able to overcome it(**Mathew;16;18**)No enemy can prevail in the church-**The Apostles and the followers of Jesus Christ meet** Day after day they met as a group in the temple and they had their meals together in their homes eating with glad and humble hearts(**Acts;2;46**)-(***broke bread* and shared**)they were led by the Power of the holy Spirit they were not a subversive political threat to the Roman Empire and that the Christians Faith was the fulfilment of the Jewish Empire-When the day of the Pentecost came all the believers were gathered together in one place suddenly there was a noise from the sky which sounded like a strong wind blowing and it filled the whole house where they were sitting then they saw what looked like tongues of fire which spread out and touched each person there they were filled with the Holy Spirit and began to talk in other tongues as the Spirit enabled them to Speak **(Acts,2;1;4)We go to church to strengthen our relationship with God and people-**some friend do not last but some friends are loyal than brothers **(Proverb;18;24)** God ,Jesus, and Holy Spirit are our friends**(8)It's a place to the lonely ,**When we gather together always the Holy Spirit is with us (United we stand)It is estimated that there over half a million practising Christians in the world but the church wouldn't even exist today if it hadn't been for a small group of disciples who were sold on Christ the things of God were not of part time interest or a convenience based commitment to those early Christians but their highest priority we should always come on together on Sunday (Sabbath) The Lord" says if you treat the Sabbath as sacred and you do not pursue your own interest on that day if you value my Holy day and honour it by not Travelling ,Working ,or Talking Idly on that day then you will find the Joy that comes from serving me I will make you honoured all over the World and you will enjoy the land I gave your Ancestor ,Jacob I the Lord I have spoken **(Isaiah 58;13;14)**if you want to be serious with God stop and reflect on what they took seriously and why the disciples took it as important to seek God and his kingdom **(1)**Giver of life before God who gives life to all things(**1Timothy;6;13**)The thief comes to steal kill and destroy I have come in order that you might have life in all its fullness(**John10;10**)It is important to seek and be serious - God is the greatest God said" Am who am the one who is called I am has sent me to you tell the Israelites that, Am the lord the God of their ancestors, Abraham, Isaac and Jacob ,have sent you to them this is my name forever(**Exodus;3;14)**In God we find purpose meaning and satisfaction Human was created for relationship with God and with relationship with one another ,that why the **bible say" Love one another -encourage one another -Help one another** - You will seek me with all your heart yes you will find me and I will restore all your land ,I will gather you from every country and every place I have scattered you and I will bring you back to the land from which I had sent you away into exile I the lord I have spoken we seek God because he has invited us to do so knowing God is a privilege- We seek him through Prayers Worship and Praise Reading his word he created us so that we should know him through Jesus Christ ,we should take (1)**church seriously -**as believers of **long** time ago did,believer met together in the temple, And every day when you meet together there is a commanded, Blessing, Victory- Healing- Break through, from the forces of darkness ,When you are united don't isolate yourself by saying you are talented enough strong enough ,Educated enough, favoured, blessed enough, you might be what you have in mind what God has in mind has something bigger, more rewarding that you can't do by yourself-Personally I don't know if you feel the same when I enter Church the prayers , instruments played, Songs and voices makes a change to me, A smile on your face attracts me, and I feel victorious, gives me joy, Your smile keeps me alive, Your smile encouragement breath into other peoples - Your hug keeps me going- Your being together keeps me stronger ,and keeps the atmosphere better- Your faithfulness in giving is what keeps other going in poor nations, your - Your presence enlarge my expectation from God -because the faith we have is more than for one individual **(With 2 or 3 or a thousand)**When we gather together much is expected from God -coming together is not only filling you but helping others, I could have stayed home and pray but there is power in Unification it's good to watch listen at home but our heart misses you, God is bigger than anything and under control, it doesn't matter where you come from, mistakes you have made, nationality ,colour, Jobs you have done before, though we have differences we worship the same God, What broke your heart and stopped you going or coming together, if you continue being united the forces of darkness is going to die, and you experience peace, Until when you go to the house of God then I understand what happen to the wicked **(Psalm;73;17)**When you get united the Spirit of defeat cannot stay because we know we belong to God, there some break through which only comes, When you come together to church, don't go another year flying alone , Penguins' live together because they catch warm together with their fathers, If one live on its own it can die, their protection is because they are united ,they can't live alone by themselves, same with we Christians, we need one another so we can overcome the storms of life ,stay united in faith ,we draw our strength from others ,When we are unite we experience, joy ,break through, restored , Our battery are being charged again- faith is a place of Power God is consistently working in the life of believers when we become together in the ordinary building it becomes **a Health- Arena-** Every ones faith creates Power ,breaks bondage ,Chains ,Healing restoration- Victory - let us magnify God together ,Let always God be your first priority- Connect with others, it's good to pray alone, but there is something special that happen when you are united**(1)By ourselves we are strong--but together we are unstopped(2)Alone I can enjoy but together we can celebrate(3)By ourselves we get through the difficulties out--By together we get through better(4) By ourselves we are blessed -But together we get the full sum of blessings (4(Alone I can smile but together we can laugh (5)When we are connected to each other in the house of the Lord our roots becomes strong winds comes but they won't shake you --Because we are together God is able we cannot fail(6)Alone winds may take you- Together we cannot be defeated (shaken)We are powerful together but weak alone, and the storms can be higher than solutions -But together we shake them up (7)You may feel like giving up -But Church is going to encourage you- it's not about your prayers- But our prayers -(8)Alone we can say - but together we can talk,** When you lost your loved one in the family the Church prayed for you and you felt supported, encouraged ,people helped you to stand when you couldn't stand on your own -you are created to be united the church has something to offer you spiritual ,emotion healing ,counselling meeting new friends bloom you and flourish you ,and enlarging your family ,In God you also have something to offer to the Church encouraging your Pastor and giving him support ,Tithing ,your presence means a lot to the church ,Pastors don't preach to Chairs or buildings ,Churches stand on the Power of God and people ,when you help others God also help you ,people who are successful have a Good relationship with God and their friends, We cannot leave as Islands isolated - God created people to be around Adam and Eva, Abraham was blessed with many children for a reason -What hold you back individually cannot hold you back again ,when you are united- Your faith may not be enough that why you didn't break through, that why God has ordained you to be in church and united, Think better live better, When you are united, it's not only that God protect you but all of you as a group your week will go better, because you prayed as a group ,the house of the lord will prepare you for what you going to meet in the next week the **Bible say** "Me and my family go to the house of the lord to serve him, When you are planted in the house of the Lord with others ,Blessings will follow you- Favour, Levels that you could not reach on your own, Healing, Marriages, Bills, paid, Your children back home ,Birthday celebrations ,will start to crop up in a Godly way,-I love your sanctuary where your glory shines, battles that you could not fight alone like ,temptation ,addiction, struggle ,flooding, accidents ,because you are connected, honouring -God will answer your prayers fast as a group, because he knows and may be not only you ,but other people also have the same problems but hidden, but when you face God in united faith and believe a change will come ,You can be good by yourself but not great by yourself ,My prayer is that our fellowship with you as believers will bring about a deep understanding of every blessings which you have in our life in union with Christ ,your love dear and brothers has brought me great joy, and much encouragement, you have cheered me the hearts of all Gods people **(Philemon 1;6;7)**- Some say they pray at home they don't need Church my request come for others ,your presence of worship creates an atmosphere God to Bless ,Heal, Favour, Protect and grant faith in those who don't know the power of God-Stop complaining have the Spirit as football fans, who are united for their teams and support they give to their players, they give them morale to win trophy , United can defeat their enemies ,and win territory ,Go to church you will achieve much - getting united in the, church helps you to know that the church is the bride of Christ ,then I heard what sounded like a large crowd like the sound of a roaring water fall like peals of thunder I heard them say Praise God for the lord our almighty God is king let us rejoice and be glad, let us praise his greatness for the time has come for the wedding of the lamb and his bride has prepared herself for it she has been given clean shinning linen to wear the linen is the good deeds of the Gods people then the angles said to me write this happy are those who have been invited to the wedding feast of the lamb and the angles added these are the true words of God**(Revelation 19;6;9)**It's good to be united in the church because we contribute something for the church and the church give us something as a group we share Talents, ,Abilities, Testimonies ,Purposes ,gifts ,so it's not a mistake to be united in the church, **The question?** Are you a hit and miss church goers? Do you get upset if the service exceeds an hour, or the minister takes an extra *(10 minutes)* is once a week your limit? Not for this New Testament Christians, So what drew them the temple orchestra and choirs? Cutting edges media or youth programmes did they have more time and less responsibility than we have today? No everything about their life was harder /took longer ,and was less convenient yet their encounter with Jesus so transformed their priorities, that every day they continued to meet they hungered in the presence of the lord, believing his promises where two or five gather together as my followers am there among them**(Mathew18;20)**Taking God seriously involves involvement with other fellow Christians, experiencing this unique aspect of his presence, Hearing his word together and encouraging one another **(Hebrews10;25)** You need those Special dimension of fellowship with God that happens only when his family gather together with him when you are with other people you share burdens of each other and the bible says help to carry one another burden and in this way you will obey the law of Christ **(Galatians;6;2)** When we are united in Church we are able to rejoice, the Bible" says be happy with those who are happy, weep with those who weep ",have the same concern with everyone do not be proud but accept humble duties, do not think of yourselves as wise **(Romans;4;15**)Be united with others in church and rejoice there is no other place in life you will find joy like in the church, because you are in his presence**(God)** and you are rejoicing with him ,with others then king Solomon and all the people there offer red sacrifices to the Lord he sacrificed-**22000,**head of cattle and **120,000.**sheep as a fellowship offerings and so the king and all the people dedicated the temple **(1 Kings 8;62;63)**-dedicate the house with joy-then the people of Israel the priests the Levites and all other who had returned from exile joyfully dedicated the temple **(Ezra6;16)(2)They fellowshipped serious**-Today we are more than common interest based Social-club We are family birth children of our heavenly father blood relatives the cross made it so we have all been baptised by one spirit *(1Corinthians;12;13)* Those early disciples valued their relationship it went beyond merely hymns, and hearing sermons ,they met together shared everything they had sold their property and possessions ,shared the money with those in need*(Acts2;44;45)*Do we have such love caring enough to share everything with our brothers and sisters in need? How many of them shared what they had? All the believers how much did they share? All they had Gods word describe the church as his body its member exist individually but can function properly in connection with one another hands arms shoulder legs extra cannot live separately they must be joined together to a body with the head to accomplish their purpose the early church survived incredible persecution and achieved amazing things *why?* Because they understood the need to value each other and to sacrifice personal interest for the sake of the whole as isolated self- reliant self- promoting, individualism they would have been destroyed by the overwhelming forces of their enemies as a believer you may survive a part from the church but you cannot thrive your God given potential will never be realised until you commit yourself whole heartedly to a local fellowship ,and invest yourself in serving Gods, vision for that church you cannot accomplish all the tasks alone you need company with others **(3) Prayers**(*Acts 2;42)*All believers they devoted themselves in prayers, spent their time in learning from apostles taking part in fellowship and sharing the fellowship meals (breaking bread)and the prayers ,they took prayers seriously, the new testament church was conceived in the womb of the prayers after ten days of united prayers in the upper room every one present was filled with the holy spirit ,*What happened next ?*They launched a church that is still impacting the world after 2000 years did their prayers life diminishes not in the least all the believers devoted themselves to prayers conditioned fellowship it was born bathed and brought to fruition in prayers they bequeathed us the empowering biblical principle that is nothing is important and lasting without a prayer Today if you want to get a small crowd in the church call for a prayer meeting, **Question?** *How much time do you pray? What makes you a stranger to a place of prayers?* Is it the myth that prayer is a hard work it **is not** if your priorities are right do you wear yourselves out worrying about things as though things about to you prayer will make the hard bit of your life easier ,and more fruitful ,consistence praying lift you up to a higher positive place where you learn how to accomplish more while experiencing a deep peace of heart and soul Jesus said *are you tired*? Worn-out burned out on religion? Come to me, I will show you how to take a real rest walk with me watch how I do it learn the unforced rhythms of grace I won't lay anything heavy or ill lifting on you, keep company with me and you will learn to live freely and lightly (*Mathew;11;28-30*) and there can be a better way to live**(4)Don't give up the Spirit of togetherness** meting together(**Hebrews10;26**)the early Christians took Gods word seriously ,they spent their time learning ,they encouraged each other, When we are united in Church we find people who can help us in difficulties were we need help, Spiritual growth, love marriage ideas, decision making, Financial advices, Divorce, loss of our beloved ones, job loss, Intensive professional, counselling through the word of God and our friends , but today you find out that personal bible reading is less common among Christians than prayers instead of a word from God that fortifies us for a challenge of a day we have substitute Exercise ,Football ,Viewing Movies, and Cappuccino or Drinking in Pubs Our bible reading is confined to the Pastor on Sunday sermon ,the early Christians were committed to the word that they invested their Time

Learning and Studying to understand and master the apostles teachings Gods word not only helped them to withstand life challenge but when persecution made them fugitive they took the word with them and planted new churches around the world(*Acts;8;-7)(1)*Being united in the church helps our Children to learn the word of God**-develop their characters and lays a firm solid foundation for them as future citizen of the kingdom of God**(2)Being united in the church helps our children to know the importance of togetherness** ,the value of sharing love, value of baptism ,Lords supper Easter and resurrection Christmas value, The believers who were scattered went everywhere preaching the massage Philip went to the principal city in Samaria and preached the Messiah to the people there crowds paid attention to Philip as they listened to him and say miracles that he performed evil spirit come out of many wit loud cry and many paralysed and lame were healed ,Are you growing in God word so that fortifies you against tough times and prepare you influence your world for Christ ? They stayed continually at the temple praising God and giving thanks(*Luke;24;53*)For many of us the word worship and praising has come to Sunday morning services a place we attend rather than a voluntary act of devoted heart glorifying God, being a spectator at the Sunday service the new testament believer understood David instruction enter his gates with thanks giving and his court with praise (*Psalm100;4*) do you want to be a serious worshipper enter his presence focused exclusively on his goodness and wholeheartedly express to him your appreciations for all he is and what he has done for you in your life we shouldn't forget the value of being united in the church even when the church member , Pastor, a child of your church member , Upset you do not give up they are human being don't isolate yourself from church Every Church has problems ,United we stand , Stand firm live in harmony with Each other Let there be no divisions rather be of one United mind and United in thought sand purpose, Success calls for the death of individual Ago and Self interest ,When mistakes are made refuse to place a Blame ,be Forgiving. don't allow an Offence develop into Bitterness ,and Steal your Joy and Happiness ,Together offer Praise to one Another offer help in Each one Weakness ,Stay focused on bigger, Visions and Goals, when you live together nothing can stop you (**1 Corinthians 1;10**)**Christian conducts** read(**Titus,3;1;7**)I pray for change of story, people to seek for God more than before in good seasons ,and bad seasons , I pray to see a massive influx of people in the church where women and men of influence in the world coming to seek God ,Judges, politicians ,religious leader ,environmentalists ,doctors, lawyers and let the church become the centre of everything, and the fountain of life to everyone in life ,Now shall come to pass in the later days that the mountains of the Lords house shall be established on top of the mountains, and shall be exalted above the hills, and all the nations shall flow to it ,many people shall come and say come and lets go up to the mountain of the Lord, to the house of the God of Jacob ,he will teach us his ways , and shall walk in his paths, for out Zion shall go forth law all the word of the Lord from Jerusalem **(Isaiah 2;1-3;Micah;4;1)** Even Jesus had the Twelve disciples, in life you cannot make it alone you need other peoples help and you -you have to be united in the same Spirit to achieve your goals ,United we stand in, Faith ,Prayers ,Spirit, and Action ;**Amen**

CHOOSING A CHURCH THAT WILL SUIT YOU
-THINGS YOU HAVE TO PUT INTO CONSIDERATION!

(1) Based on sound theology- believing in Jesus ,God ,the Trinity, Heaven , Hell, Believe in Salvation ,Jesus died and rose again -You must not go to church which does teach false teachings on riches, whoever teaches a different doctrine and does not agree with the true words of our Lord Jesus Christ and with the teachings of our religion is swollen with pride and knows nothing -he has unhealthy desires to urge and quarrel about words and this brings on jealousy disputes Insults Evil Suspicions and constant arguments from people whose minds do not function and who no longer have the truth they think religion is a way to become rich well religion does not make a person very rich if he is satisfied with what he has **(1Timothy;6;3;6)** -**(2)**Based on Bible teachings **(3)**Does it have a Clear Vision **(4)**Does it allow you to Exercise your/my gifts and talents too in the building of the kingdom**(5)**Does the choice of the church you have made does it challenge you Spiritually to grow**(6)**Does it the church meet the Season you are or I am ?example if you are a single does it have conferences for Singles and meetings if you are married does the church organise conferences for married couples Sunday school Services for the Children**(7)**Does the church involve the community -Love one another ,Encourage one another- Bear with one another **(8)**Does the church have good Leaders Seen in**(1Timothy 3;1;7)** **(9)**We must be able to choose Churches which are a based on kingdom growth not Empire growth- **Kingdom churches are** ----Churches which help others to grow Spiritual and develop their gifts and Talents and move on to other places but **Empire Churches are---** the one who want you to develop your gifts and Talents within and don't leave to any other area ,**Amen**

SOME REASONS FOR LEAVING A CHURCH

Some churches are throwing away the Bible and Believing in lies yet the Bible is the word of God and we should only believe in God, his Son Jesus Christ and the Holy Spirit and the word of God- because what the bible say is what God is and we must believe it ,if you are in the church which lives like the world lives or act Church which support Homosexuality

,does not support or have sound doctrines and has homosexuals working in the ministry ,support abortion ,prosperity gospel if the church is about business, and not Christ does not believe that Jesus died and rose again you are in a wrong Place , but be careful sometime we want to leave churches for minor reasons example small arguments with someone, small gossip people talk and gossip just ignore them -Whatever the reason you must pray over it and trust God; **Amen**

Reasons for leaving a Church

(1) False Gospel-which is no gospel at all ,Evidently some people are throwing you into confusion and are trying to pervert the gospel of Christ but even, if we or an angel from heaven should preach a gospel other than the one we preached to you let them be under Gods curse a we have already said so now I say again if anybody is preaching to you a gospel other than what you accepted let them be under Gods curse **(Galatians 1;7;9)**If anyone teaches otherwise and does not agree to the sound doctrines or instructions of our lord Jesus Christ and to godly teachings they are conceited and understanding nothing they have unhealthy interest in controversies and quarrels about words that results in envy ,strife malicious talk ,evil suspicions and constant friction between people of corrupt mind who have been robbed of the truth and who thinks that godliness is a means to financial gains **(1Timothy 6;3;5)** I urge you Brothers and Sisters to watch out for those who cause divisions and put obstacles in your way that are contrary to the teachings you have learned keep away from them **(Romans;16;17) (2)False Teachings** -as for a person who stirs up divisions after warning him once then twice have nothing more to do with him **(Titus;3;10)** Watch out for false prophets they come to you in sheep's, Clothing's but inwardly they are ferocious wolves **(Mathew;7;15)**And in their greed they will exploit you with false words their condemnation from long ago is not idle their destruction is not asleep**(2Peter2;3)**For the time is coming when people will not endure sound teachings but having itching ears they will accumulate for themselves teachers to suit their own passion and turn away from listening to the truth and wonder off into myths**(2Timothy;4;3;4)**For such people are not serving our Lord Christ but their own appetites by smooth talks and flattery they deceive the minds of naive people **(Romans 16;17) (3)If they deny Jesus is God in flesh**- I told you that you would die in your sins for unless you believe that am he you will die in your sins **(John8;24)**The Jews answered him it is not for good work that we are going to stone you but for blasphemy because you are being a man make yourself God **(John;10;33)**(4)Elders with un repentant Sin -but those elders who are sinning you are to reprove before everyone so that others

may take warning **(1Timothy;5;20)-(5)When the church is filled with members who are not being disciplined sin running wild in Church** false convert who don't care about Gods word this can lead you to leave a church the bible say if your brother Sins against you go and tell him his fault between you and him alone if he listens to you -you have gained your brother but if he does not listen to you take one or two brothers along with you that every charge may be established by the evidence of two or three witness, If he refuses to listen to them tell it to the Church and, If he refuses to listen to the church ,let him be to you as a gentile and a tax collector**(Mathew,18;15;17)(6)There is Sexual immorality among you-**and of a kind that is not tolerated even among pagans for a man has his father wife and you are arrogant ought you not rather to mourn? let him who has done this be removed from among you**(1 Corinthians 5;1-2) (7)If the church wants to be like the world- it wants to be hip trendy water down the gospel and compromises** - Do not be conformed to this world but be transformed by the renewal of your mind that by testing you may discern what is the will of God what is good and acceptable and perfect**(Romans;12;2)**You adulterous people don't you know that friendship with the world is Enmity with God? therefore whoever wishes to be a friend of the world makes himself an Enemy of God**(James 4;4)(8)The Church which has never preached on Sin** -but encourage one another daily as long as it is called Today" so that none of you may be hardened by Sins deceitfulness **(Hebrews 3;13)**The world cannot hate you but it hates because I testify that its works are Evil **(John 7;7)**Take no Part in   the   unfruitful   works   of   darkness   but   instead   expose them**(Ephesians,5;11)(9) Church were un Holy living is tolerated is not good to stay** -I wrote you my the letter not to associate with sexually immoral people not all meaning the sexual immoral of this world or the greedy and swindlers or idolaters since then you would need to go out of the world but now am writing to you not to associate with anyone who bears the name of brother if is guilty of sexual immorality or greed or is an idolater ,revilers ,drunkard or swindler not even to eat with such one **(1 Corinthians;5;9;11)-(10)Church were people are Hypocrisy-**having the appearance of godliness, but denying its power avoid such people **(2Timothy;3;5)**For it is written the name of God is blasphemed among the gentiles because of you**(Romans;2;24)**This people honour me with their lips but their hearts is far from me**(Mathew 15;8)(11)Using money improperly without accountability ,if the church is passing the offering basket more than necessary in one service there must be a problem, Is the church all about Christ or is it in his name?** He said this not because he cared about the poor but because he was a thief and having a charge of the money bag he used to help himself to what was put into it **(John 12;6)** And we are sending along with him the brother who is praised by all the churches for his services to the gospel what is more he was chosen by the churches to accompany us as we carry the offerings which we administer in order to honour the Lord himself and to show our eagerness to help, we want to avoid any criticism of the way we administer this liberal gifts for we are taking pains to do what is right not only in the eyes of the lord but also in the eyes of man **(2Corinthians 8;18-21);Amen**

FACTORS FOR CHURCH GROWTH

Church growth glorifies God - Everything lives in growth, every church to grow must base its growth on
(1)God the father- God of increase -no one can come to me unless the father who sent me ,draw him to me and I will raise him to life on the last day**(John;6;44)**,God of increase draw men to church there is no difference between the one who sow and the one who waters, I sowed the seed Apollo's watered the plant but it was God who made the plant grow**(1Corinthians;3;6)***People who plant the seed are -Evangelists ,and those who water the seeds are- Pastors and Teachers* ,God will reward each one according to the work done**(1Corinthians,3;8)**It's not by your human power and strategies to make the church to grow) the people who live there will sing ,praise they will shout for Joy by my blessings they will increase in numbers my blessings will bring them honour **(Jeremiah;30;19)**I am the vine and you are the branches ,those who remain in me and I in them will bear much fruits for you,-you can do nothing without me **(John15;5)** Praising God and enjoying the good will of all the people .and every day the Lord added to their group those who were being saved **(Acts;2;47);Amen**
(2)Base on Jesus Christ-master and builder of the church ,and I tell you Peter, you are a rock and on this rock foundation I will build my Church and not even death will be able to overcome it **(Mathew 16;18)** when am lifted up from the earth I will draw everyone to me **(John;12;32)**lifting Jesus draws multitudes and growth of church ,Am the vine ,you are the branches ,he who bides in me and I in him bears much fruits for without me you can do nothing **(John 15;5),Amen**
Base on the Holy Spirit-Lord of harvest ,many of them believed his massage and were baptizcd and about **3,000**people were added to the group that day **(Acts;2;41)**When the Holy Spirit pour out his spirit on them in the upper room and they increased in number ,all the believers continued together in followership and shared their belongs with one another **(Acts;2;44)**But more and more people were added to the group a crowd of men and women who believed in the lord **(Acts 5;14;Miracles and wonders)** Pray to the owner of the harvest that he will send out workers to gather in his harvest**(Mathew;9;38);Amen**

HOW TO PATTERN WITH THE THREE TO SEE GROWTH IN CHURCH?

Pastors and church leaders have to be concern about church growth and God does his part,

(1)Pastors and church leaders have to pray and fast-Seek God first and other things will be added to you , Open my eyes so that I may see the wonderful truths in your law **(Psalm;119;18)**Then my favour will shine on you like the morning Sun, and your wounds will be healed , I will always be with you , to save you my presence will protect you, on every side ,when you pray I will answer you when you call me I will respond **(Isaiah 58;8;9)**And when you ask you do not receive it because your motives are bad you ask for things to use for your own pleasure, **(James;4;3)**Elijah prayed and rain rained*, There forces in Church and can only be broken by prayers and fasting,-*The light shines in the darkness and the darkness has never put it out **(John;1;5)**Pastor have to make flyers come and see what God has done **(testimonies)**

Keep sowing the seed (word of God -Feed the church with the word of God those who are there and you will see an Increase. And some seeds fell in good soil the plants grew and produced corn , a hundred grains each and Jesus concluded listen if you have Ears **(Luke 8;8)**This is what the parable means the seed is the word of God **(Luke 8;11)**To preach the massage .to insist upon proclaiming it (Whether the time is right or not) to convince ,reproach and encourage as you teach with all patience **(2Timothy;4;2)**The group presented them to the apostles ,who prayed and placed their hands on them and so the word of God continued to be spread ,the number of the disciples in Jerusalem grew larger and larger and a great number of the priest accepted the faith **(Acts 6;6;7)**Keep the grass greener the more the grass is greener the more gathering of the sheep - Sheep only follow where the grass is ,He gives me new strength ,he guides me in the right paths as he has promised **(Psalm;23;2)** Whenever there is a dead body the vultures will gather ,but where there is fresh meat the Eagles gather ,Eagles, don't eat dead bodies or yesterday meat they feed on fresh meat with fresh word of God people will come in multitude church leaders have to work hard in the kingdom of God to feed the sheep on fresh word, the bible says I will give you rulers who will obey me and rule you with Wisdom and understanding **(Jeremiah 3;15)**Miracles can gather congregations but the word of God brings growth and keep them ,So he asked the twelve and you would you also like to leave? Simon Peter answered him "Lord to whom would we go ?you have the word that gives eternal life and now we believe and know that you are the holy one who has come from God **(John;6;68;69)** you can't get a word and don't stay and people staying because of the word will lead to church growth ;**Amen**

Be prepared - Jonathan grew powerful because he faithful obeyed the Lord his God **(2Chronicle;27;6)** Stand up and work while the voice was speaking Gods spirit entered me and raised me to my feet and I heard the voice continue **(Ezekiel;2;2)**The elders who do good work as leaders ,should be considered worthy of receiving double pay ,especially those who work hard at preaching and teaching **(1Timothy;5;17)**Do you best to win full approval in Gods sight, as a worker who is not ashamed of his work, one who correctly teaches the massage of Gods truth**(2 Timothy;2;15)**nothing of is important is free study the word of God Labour in the work of God ,**Amen**

Faith is vital in church growth--Anything supernatural is facilitated by faith ,Everyone needs to build his faith to see supernatural growth in church and life ,If a church is not growing is dying ,a kings greatness depends on how many people he rules, without them he is nothing **(Proverb;14;28)** He was not able to perform any miracles there, except that he placed his hands a few people and healed them he was greatly surprised because did not have faith**(Mark;6;5;6)***Faith puts you in command of circumstances - * Faith is a Spiritual force-* you don't need to first see it or touch it ,to see how works - Faith is a dominant force- Faith is universal -is everywhere - * Faith is a catalyst of everything -*you have to build your faith capacity* -It was faith that made the Israelites able to cross the red sea as if on dry land when the Egyptians tried to do it the water swallowed them up, It was by faith that the walls of Jericho fall down after the Israelites had marched round them for seven days, It was faith that kept the Prostitute Rahab from being killed with those who disobeyed God for she gave the Israelites spies a friendly welcome should I go on ?there isn't enough time for me to speak of Gideon ,Barak, Samson ,Jephthan, David. Samuel, and the prophets, through faith they fought the whole countries and won, they did what was right and received what God had promised ,they shut the mouth of lions ,put of fierce fires, esc aped being killed by the sword they were weak but become strong they were mighty in the battle and defeated the enemies off foreigners**(Hebrews;11;29;34)**Am telling you the truth those who believe in me will do what I do -yes they will do even greater things because am going to the father;**(John;14;12)**Those who accept my commandments and obey them are the ones who love me ,my father will love those who love me ,I too will love them and reveal myself to them **(John;14;21)**They should hold to the revealed truth of the faith with a clear conscience**(1Timothy;3;9)**Yes said Jesus "if you yourself can everything is possible for the person who has Faith;**(Mark;9;23)**Jesus healed the boy with possessed by an impure spirit, that robbed him of speech ,whenever it seizes him it throws him to the ground ,he foams at the mouth, gashes his teeth ,and becomes rigid, since from his childhood, the disciples couldn't do it but Jesus did ,In above all this take up the shield of faith with which you extinguish all the flaming arrows of the Evil one **(Ephesians;6;16)**being full persuaded that God had power to do what he promised **(Romans;4;21);**Abraham justified by faith ;**Amen**

GOD IS ABLE

GOD IS OMNIPOTENT- (has all the Power)not equal to anybody or anything- Many people believe that God was only able during the past to fulfil his promises and do miracles but still able even today- Now the Earth was formless and Empty and God said let there be Light and there was light **(Genesis 1;2-3)**His a miracle working God- Who can turn the impossible to be possible ,We serve a powerful God he can make a way where there is no way -Create something out of nothing Open doors that seemed to be closed ,can turn empty places in your life and create something beautiful, can Speak light into your life in your places of darkness ,Can turn your barren and formless dreams and visions and give them a shape ,he can resurrect in your dormant talents and gifts, he can turn your crooked places straight again ,he can take you places you have never dreamed about - When **Abram was 99 Years** old the lord appeared to him and said "**I am almighty God (all power in him)**,Obey me and do always what is right I will make my covenant with you and give you many descendants Abram bowed down with his face touching the ground and God said I make this covenant with you ,I promise that you will be the ancestor of many nations ,your name will no longer be Abram but Abraham because am making you the ancestor of many nations I will give you many descendants and some of them will be kings you will have many descendants that they will become nations I will keep my promise with you and to your descendants in future generations as everlasting covenant , 1 w will be your god and the God of your descendants (**read Genesis;17;1-27)-He is Able** *-God is not limited by-Education Environment -Politics ,Friends ,Economy* -God is able to meet your needs trust in him, Faith is the key to all things Jesus the same ,today, yesterday and forever **(Hebrews;13;8)**He was absolutely sure that God would be able to do what he has promised, Abraham his faith did not leave him and did not have doubt in God, he was accepted because of his righteous by God ,and this righteous was not only written for him alone ,also for us who are accepted as righteous, who believe in him ,who raised Jesus our Lord from death ,God will not do things which are not Holy since he is Holy ,everything he does is Holy and sinning is not his character He is able in everything whose commands brings into being what did not exit(*Romans;4;21*)*You will do everything you have promised ,Lord your love is Eternal ,complete the work that you have begun(Psalm 138;8)*But the lord is still in the city he does what is right and never what is wrong Every morning without fail bring justice to his people and yet the unrighteousness people keep doing wrong who are not ashamed **(Zephanian;3;5)**And am sure the Lord who began his work in you will carry it on until it is finished on the day Jesus Christ you are always in my heart and so it is right for me to feel as I do about you (**Philippians 1;6;7**) He will also keep you firm to the end so that you will be faultless on the day of our Jesus Christ and should be trusted who called you to have fellowship with Jesus Christ (**1Corinthians 1;8**)The lord your God takes care of this land and watches over it through the year (**Deuteronomy11;12**)Planning financial visions and working with God guarantee us profits in return - The lord unfailing love and mercy still continues fresh as the morning as sure as the sunrise (**Lamentation 3;22**) There is no meaning without God he is a friend you can call at night day time afternoon and answer your call- He is the only one who can do no man can do He opens the eyes of the blind ,Raise the dead, Heal the sick Comfort us loves us, God is much concerned about us and providing to us because is our father called **Abba** for the Spirit God has given you does not make you a slave and curse you to be afraid instead the spirit makes you- Gods children and by the spirit of power we cry out to God Father my father Gods spirit joins himself to our spirits that we are Gods children(**Romans8;15;16;Galatians4;6**)**God is our** source and sustain us Created the heavens and hearth by his own power (**Jeremiah;32;17 Jeremiah;32;27**)God is powerful nothing is impossible with God (**Luke18;17**)To him who is able to do exceedingly abundantly above all we ask or think be glory forever (**Ephesians;3;20-21**)**God is called Jehovah, Jireh**-meaning the Lord will provide **In life you can decide to live in a place of (1)not enough (2)Just enough (3)More than enough** ,the choice is yours ,Place of not enough as slaves in Egypt they were forced to depend on Pharaoh for everything when you rely on anyone for everything you are not free until when you come to understand that god is your provider you will live with a not enough mentality Elijah was living by a stream in the middle of famine and ravens brought him meat each day then one day the ravens didn't turn up and the brook dried up Why ?God dried up a temporary source to drive Elijah back to his true source regardless of what or whom he uses God is still the source and Provider **(2)Place of just enough-** in the wildness Israel had just enough, Manna for each day, It's good to appreciate for what we have and this pushes us to trust in God, but we shouldn't be comfortable in just enough seasons we need to move forward for better things or best things other than only good things **(3)**God has a plan for more than enough which is of lacking nothing there will never go hungry or even be in need its rock have iron in them and from its hills you can mine copper you will have all you want to eat and you will give thanks to the Lord your God for the fertile land and that has given you (**Deuteronomy 8;9-10 blessing of Obedience**)and his goal for us is abundance in every Area so that we cannot hoard for ourselves (**2Corinthians 9;8**) don't be intimidated by the size of the problems -don't let circumstances convince you that God cannot help you don't stop believing , God is in control and arranging every good thing for you it's we to bless others and fulfil our assignment in life to him who is able to do exceedingly abundantly above all that we ask or think according to the power that works in us be glory forever**(Ephesians 3;20;21)**It is right for us to praise you in Zion and keep our promises to you because you answer prayers people everywhere will come to you on account of their sins our fault defeat us but you forgive them happy are those whom choose whom you bring to live in your sanctuary ,We shall be satisfied with good things of your house the blessing of your sacred of your temple, you answer us by giving us victory and you do wonderful things to save us, people all over the world trust in you, set the mountains in place by your strength, showing your mighty power, you calm the roar of the seas and the noises of the waves ,you calm the uproar of the people, the whole world stands in the awe of the great things you have done ,your deeds brings shout of Joy from End of the earth to the other ,you show your care to the land by sending rain, you make it rich by sending rain ,you make it rich and fertile ,you fill streams with water, you provide the earth with crops, this is how you do it you send abundant rain on the ploughed fields and soak them with water, you soften the soil with shower and cause younger plants to grow ,what a rich harvest your goodness provide ,wherever you go there is plenty the pastures are filled with flocks, the hills are full of Joy ,the fields are covered with sheep, the valley full of wheat, everything shouts and sings for joy**(Psalm 65;1;13)**The more we depend on God the more dependable we find he is-God doesn't Owe us anything -yet his grace he still gives us good things **(Billy- Graham)** In life don't be afraid, It gives your father happiness to give you the **(benefits of his kingdom)**The bible states it clear" do not be afraid you little flock for your father is pleased to give you his kingdom**(Luke 12;32)God gives you because he is able**-give and it will be given to you a good measure pressed down shaken together and running over will be poured into your lap for with the measure you use it will be measured to you"**(Luke,6;38)**When God gives you because is able give to others bring the full amount of your tithes to the temple so that there will be plenty of food there put me to test and you will see that I will open the windows of heaven and pour on you Abundance all kind of good things I will not let the insect destroy your crops and your grapes vine will be loaded with grapes then the people of Israel will call you happy because your land will be a good land to live**(Malachi;3;10)** Sometime when we are overwhelmed we forget how big God is -God is in the Laughter's ,Sadness ,in the Bitterness and the Sweet there is a Divine purpose behind everything and therefore a Divine presence in everything **(Neale Donald);Amen**

QUESTION?

WHY GOD HAS BEEN ABLE TO PROVIDE TO US

Every good gift and Every Perfect present comes from heaven it comes down from God the creator of heavenly lights who does not change or cause darkness by turning by his will he brought you into being through the word of truth so that we should have the first place among all creatures **(James 1;17;18)**The fact people do not know your name ,you are not highly Educated ,you don't have money ,friends or because of your Colour, Height, nationality does not stop God to do what he promised to do for you and it doesn't stop Gods miracles into your life, *Keep your Soul, Heart and Spirit ,Open to miracles*; *Miracles is always often to see the common in uncommon ;*Amen

If God is for us who can be against us**(Romans 8;31)** -God watched you even before you were born **(Psalm 139;15)**He had a plan and a future for me before my birth**(Jeremiah;29;11)**is the foundation for our life, .**Because he loves us unconditionally(John3;16)**Nothing can separate us from the love of Christ hardship ,hunger, poverty ,danger of death **(Romans;8;35;39)**nothing ;**Amen**

Because God is omnipotent -he has too much he is able to provide to us - Exceedingly abundantly above all that we ask **(Ephesians;3;20)**He is called, Elshaddai all sufficient .God of surplus ,he does not wonder how he is going to provide to you ,how he is going to meet your needs , he has overflow for you and me, he wants to bless you and be a blessing to others , Ask in confidence that is more than able to meet all my needs according to his riches of his glory in Jesus Christ God wants to give to you he can accelerate your harvest of blessing , so you will be sowing with one hand and reaping with the other he can speed up your healing , he is no limited by human limitations ,he is not limited by the enemy Moses told the Israelites the Egyptians you see today you shall see again no more forever**(Exodus,14;13)**When the Israelites left Egypt ,God instructed them to borrow Gold and Silver of their taskmaster That because the Egyptians owed them **400 years back-** pay back with interest and when they obeyed God he broke the chain of lack and they got back what has been stolen from them ,he is not limited by anything only doubt can make you to miss your blessings , whatever Satan has taken from you he can restore it to you greater is that is in you than the one in the world **(John,4;4),Amen**

Because he promised -they are my people and I created them to bring me glory **(Isaiah43;7)** His word does not change ,his word remains forever, if it is promised in God's word it is God's will ,so refuse to settle for small things, ask big, tell him exactly what you and he will do it for you, and be confident believe him, for your desire and needs ,if you are walking in obedience and seeking to please him

God provide to us because he wants-to avoid a bad reputation (created us in his own image he doesn't want us to lack he is our manufacturer) and because of the promises he made he made an everlasting covenant with our ancestors he wants to meet your every day needs in life he wants to inspire faith in us by his spirit

He satisfies my mouth with Good things- So that I stay younger and strong like an Eagle **(Psalm 103; 5)**

Because we are loyal to him-the lord keeps close watch over the whole world, to give strength to those whose hearts are Loyal to him ,you have acted foolishly and so from now on now you will be at war **(2 Chronicles 16;9)**If we are not loyal to him in our, tithes ,offerings and giving, we are to struggle in life ;**Amen**

God always wants us to be successful - he wants to remove mountains in our life, wants to heal your Body, Soul and Spirit**,** heal us financially, spiritually, and emotionally and be successful, Amen

He is able to provide to us-because he doesn't want us to be anxious and lack nothing (Philippians 4;6)do not worry of anything ,but all in your prayers, ask for what you need always asking him with a thankful heart God wants us to be at peace **(2Thessalonian 3;16)**

To believe in only him that he can do all things ,Expectancy is the Atmosphere for Miracles -Miracles are proud creatures they will never reveal themselves to those who don't believe -the person who doesn't believe makes it certain that he/she will never take part in one -Miracles is often the willingness to see the common in uncommon**; Amen**

God is able to provide to us- So that we are not disappointed-to turn to other gods; **Amen**

He is able to provide us because we ask - Ask and you will receive ,seek and you will ,find knock and the door will be open to you, for everyone who ask will receive, and anyone who seek will find and the door will be opened to those who knock **(Mathew;7;7-8)**The lord says Come that who is thirsty here is water come that you who have money to buy corn to eat come buy wine and milk it will cost you nothing why you spend money on what does not satisfy you, Am the bread of life, Jesus told them those who come to me will never be hungry, those who believe in me will never be thirsty **(John 6;35)** come to me all of you who are tired from carrying heavy loads and I will give you rest **(Mathew11;28;30)**Give all your worries to God **(1Peter5;7)**Jesus said how much more shall your father ..give good things to them that ask him ,no good things will he withhold from them that walk upright **(Psalm;84;11)**Do not be afraid little flock for your father is pleased to give you the kingdom **(Luke,12;32)** as a father there is no one would have love to bless as his children same to God ,it gives him pleasure to give his children the kingdom and brings a smile on his face he wants to see us prospering increasing higher and if God say no it is because it would not be good for you, trust him he ,has something better than you think for you - **Jabez** was more honourable than his brother and his mother had named him Jabez saying I gave birth to him in pain **(Jabez- name means sorrowful or sorrow maker)**Jabez cried out to the God of Israel Oh that you would enlarge my territory and bless me,*(Expansion of territory means - places you have never been , business you have never, done before calling you have never had before , open doors, God doing it above expectation and above human power)* Let your hand be with me the hand of God is powerful in business , family affairs , deliverance, strength , finances),and keep me from harm so that I will be free from pain and God granted his request **(1Chronicle 4;9;10)**Jabez asked big, God's blessing Jabez acknowledged that the God of Israel is the source of all blessing ,and he asks God for grace no doubt this request was based at least in part on Gods promises of blessing to Abraham and his descendants **(Genesis22;17)**Jabez asks for victory and prosperity in all his endeavours ,and that his life would be marked by increase ,God granted him an expansion of territory, Jabez asks for the guidance of God and his strength, to be evident in his daily existence the presence of Gods hand was granted,   Jabez asks God for protection from harm Jabes acknowledges God as his defender and this was granted by God (No weapon formed against you to prosper ,**(Romans,8;31,** Every plan of the devil /wicked ,to be scattered ;**Isaiah 54;17)**God granted him whatever he asked ,heavens answered   and his story was changed , Everybody called him sorrow and pain but God changed his name and God can change our story too, if we pray ,Don't believe in what people have named you -**(You are who God say you are ! not pain and sorrow)**Jesus taught his disciples to pray father in heaven deliver us from the Evil one **(Mathew,6;9;13)**Jabez acknowledged that Gods hand would be with him no doubt to provide ,protection and guide, Gods ,protection, guidance ,preservation and deliverance are all provided for us through this scripture ,all the scriptures is inspired by God, and is good for teaching the truth, rebuking errors, correcting faults ,and giving instructions, for right living ,so that the person who serves God may be fully qualified and equipped to do every kind of good deed **(2Timothy 3;16;17)**God heard about Jabez prayers and was set free ,from all these sorrow and pain, blessings over weighed the sorrow of his beginning ,the prayer he prayed overcome the name Jabez and Jabez was successful -***Solomon*** humbled himself prayed for wisdom and was granted to him ,he meet kings and influence people in his place **(1Kings 3;5;14)** ask God big there is nothing wrong with requesting God to bless you ,The psalmist did save your people Lord and bless those who are yours ,be their shepherd and take care of them forever **(Psalm28;9)**If you acknowledge God he will help you find what you can't

-Help you do what you can't God will breath favour in your life he will open doors for you

Because we are patient enough

God is able to provide to us because we are obedient(blessing of obedient)-If you listen to these commands and obey them faithful the lord your God will continue to keep his covenant he made with you and show you his constant love as he has promised your Ancestors love you and bless you **(Deuteronomy ,7;12;13)** And all these blessings shall come upon you and overtake you if you obey the voice of God **(Deuteronomy;28;2)** But if you will only obey me you will eat the good things the land produce ,but if you defy me you are doomed to die I the Lord I have spoken **(Isaiah 1;19);Amen**

He paid a price for you and me- by giving away his only Son to die on the cross so that our sins will be forgiven and have life in its fullness, The thief comes only in order to Steal kill and destroy, I have come in order that you might have life -life in all its fullness **(John 10; 10)**

Because- we thank him, Pray and Ask him, in loud voices -he answers our prayers -God is able to provide to us- life is better because we know our provide , we acknowledge him before anything else ,he honours our prayers ,because his faithful-We know well that without him ,we wouldn't have been alive and wouldn't have been where we are ,and what he created us to be -God is able to provide to us because we thank worship him and praise him in the good and bad situation for our Family -Wisdom -Children- Food- Life and air we breathe, Good service, and Church leaders, Politicians ,Weather, Ministry ,in our Education ,Divine Favour -for forgiveness of our Sins ,Friends Direction ,Cancelled addiction in our life ,Protection ,Strongholds coming down forces of darkness cancelled ; but I call to the lord God for help and he will save me Morning ,noon and night my complaints and groans go up to him and he will hear my voice he will bring me back from the battles that I fight against so many enemies**(Psalm 55;16;18)**Always ask God with a loud voice-never be ashamed to pray in a loud voice never be shy to thank God and glorify him in a loud voice **(Luke;17;11;16);Amen**

He is able to provide to us because he wants to be glorified in giving to us- the more we glorifies him the more he bless us, He provide to us because he wants us to praise him and worship him as only our God-creator and he alone to be praised and worshiped (Worth all and all belongs to him) because he created me and you for a purpose; **Amen**

He wants our joy and peace to be full- as we receive from him; **Amen**

He wants others to see that we are serving a big God- and we are his disciples because much fruits are produced from our prayers God of miracles -God is almighty he is all powerful nothing is too great or too hard for him anything is possible for anyone who has faith; **Amen**

What does God demand of you to do?

Now people of Israel listen to what the Lord your God demands of you - your life goes better if you put God first in life**(1)seek him first**- One thing have I desired of the lord that I will seek him**(Psalm;27;4)(2)Worship him the lord and do all what he demands of you(3)Love him(3)Serve him with all your heart and soul(Deut;10;12;22)if we serve God faithfully he will provide to us(Mathew;6;33)**Trust in the lord with all your heart, never rely on what you think ,you know remember the lord in everything you do and he will show you the right way ,never let yourself that you are wiser than you are, simply obey the lord and refuse to do wrong ,if you do it will be like good medicine healing your wounds and easing your pain **(Proverb;3;5-8)** God to supply your needs look beyond your insight, claim unlimited divine supply, ask God for wisdom, territory listen to Gods calling and obey ,and let go off your fears in life, I prayed to the lord and he answered me he freed me from all my fears ,the oppressed look to him and are glad, they will never be disappointed ,the helpless call on him and he answers, he saves them from all their troubles his angles guards all those who honours the lord and rescues them from all dangers, find out how good the Lord is **(Psalm;34;4;8)** Those people who obey God in everything and always do what is right whose words are sincere ,and do not slander others, they do not do wrong to others friends nor spread rumours about their neighbours, they do what they promise no matter how much, it costs they make loans without charging Interest, and cannot be bribed to satisfy against the Innocent whoever who does the right things will be secure **(Psalm;15)** If you don't obey the law God will find your prayer too hateful to hear **(Proverb 28;9) ,Amen**

WE AT TIMES TEND TO QUESTION OURSELVES WHEN IS GOD GOING TO DO IT FOR ME/YOU?

God is not limited by time sometimes he takes a short time =Some time he takes long to answer your prayers and requests-his thoughts are not our thoughts -How great are Gods riches how deep is his wisdom and knowledge who can explain his decisions? Who can understand his ways? As the scriptures say who knows the mind of the lord? Who is able to give him advice? Who has ever given him anything so that he had to pay back? for all things were created by him and all things exists through him and for him to God the glory forever amen**(Romans,11;33;36)**We are persuaded that God has power to do what has promised ,the reason we don't turn to Gods more often is because at some basic and unconscious level we are not fully convinced he is able and willing to move on our behalf, being able to admit that He has the power to do what he promised,- It is important opens all the door for us- Lack of faith in God will not change your life , until you pray, God help me I say things with my mouth, I don't follow them/ and I don't believe in you ,Lord change me so I can see things how you want me to see them, God open my hears so I can hear your word and will for my life, Lord open my heart so I can love you more than before ,direct my steps ,When you begin to pray that way you can start walking into your word /bible rediscovering that, **God is able to make something out of nothing** in the beginning God created the heavens and earth **(Genesis1;1)**In the beginning there was nothing and God filled the world with everything needed what about now when there is something to start with he can take the empty places in your life and make something beautiful ,he can speak light into your darkness, speak life into your sickness (Healing),he can take your formless dreams and give them shape ,he can resurrect in your dead talents and make them potential ,he can make your crooked places straight , God **(1)Cannot Lie (2)God cannot be Mocked (3)Cannot change what he promised,** And think not to say within yourselves we have Abraham to our father for I say unto you that God is able of these stones to raise up Children unto Abraham **(Mathew3;9)God is able he is able to provide for you when you don't have-** Make a way where there is no way able to provide to you when you are in wildness s *(Ephesians 3;20)* **God is able to give you more than** you need so that you will always have enough for very cause-The bible says he gives generously to the needy his kindness lasts forever and God who supplies seeds to sow and bread to eat will supply you with all your seed you need and will make it grow and produce a rich harvest from your generosity he will always make you rich enough at all times so that many will talk thank God for your gifts which they receive from us **(2Corinthians 9;8;11)God is able to give me and you Eternal life,** My sheep listen to my voice I know them and they follow me and they shall never die no one can snatch them away from me what the father me is greater than everything and no one can snatch them away from the fathers care the **father and I are one** ,then the people again picked up the stones to throw at him Jesus said to them I have done many good deed in your presence which the father gave me to do for which of these do you want to stone me? **(John 10; 27; 30)**Do not fear those who kill the body but unable to kill the soul but rather fear him who is to destroy both soul and the body in hell **(Mathew 10;28)God is able to comfort** us in all our afflictions -so that we can be able to comfort those who are in any affliction with the comfort which ourselves are comforted by God **(2Corinthians 1;4)**For this reason I also suffer these things but am still full of confidence because I know whom I have trusted and I am sure that is able to keep me safe until the day what he has entrusted to me hold firm to the true words that I have taught you as the example for you to follow and remain in the faith and the love that is ours in union with Christ Jesus **(1Timothy 12;13)God give hope** but those who hope in the lord will renewal their strength they will soar like Eagles they will run not grow weary they will walk and not faint **(Isaiah 40;31)** May God of hope fill you with all joy and peace as you trust him so that you may over flow with hope by the power of the Holy Spirit **(Romans 15;13)** <u>**He is able to shelter you,**</u> He is able to defeat your enemies that stand in your ways he is able to go through fierce trials with you and bring you out he is able to promote you where people overlook you God is able to heal your disease God is able to do exceedingly abundantly above all that we demand from him according to the power that he has Whatever it takes to own the word God is able to do it otherwise you won't be able to pray with confidence you will make a few wishes on your knees but you won't be able to preserve in prayers until you know in your heart that God is able and nothing is too difficult for him he is just waiting for you to reorganise that and come to him in faith asking for help he is committed to you (*James 1;18*)He chose to give us birth through the word of truth ,that we might be the kind of first fruit of all he created ,so we might be the most important of all the things he created ,be careful around people who don't value you, and themselves because they are incapable of valuing and themselves ,look for those who enhance you, not inhibit you ,who fertilise your mind, and forty your faith ,when you are with them you will see you best qualities, mirrored and be nurtured by the words that comes from their lips ,when you encounter anyone who says you have nothing to offer be sure to laugh, when God made you he said that's very good and everything he made he was pleased (*Genesis1;31)*Stop entertaining negative options, you have so much potential that the word possibility is written all over you, by God grace you can be everything he desires ,God decides you to give you in life through the word of truth, so we might be the most important of all l things he made , he didn't pick you because of your virtues, while we were sinners Christ died for us **(Romans 5;8)** He is the God of the second chance and third one too Paul wrote and said there has never been the slightest doubt in my mind that he started the great work in you/me would keep at it and bring it to a flourishing finish **(Philippians1;6)** The lord who brought you far will bring you to rest of the ways he has committed to you just make sure you are committed to him let God restore you ,<u>**God is able to deliver**</u>--If the God whom we serve is able to save us from the blazing furnace and from your power he will deliver **(The three friends accused of disobeying the king put in fire** because they dint worship other gods God delivered them **(Daniels 3;17)**King Nebuchadnezzar repented his understanding reason honour and splendour after the seven years had passed and he said I look up at the sky and my sanity returned I praise the supreme God give honour and glory to the one who lives forever he will rule forever and his kingdom will last for life he looks on the people of earth as nothing angles in heaven and people on earth are under his control , when my sanity returned .my honour my majesty and the glory of my kingdom were given back to me my officials and my noble men welcomed me and I was given back my power with even great honour than before Nebuchadnezzar praise and honour the king of heaven everything he does is just and can humble those who are proud *Daniels4;34-36)*God made dry path in the mighty Jordan river to allow the passage of his people he did this so that all the people of the earth might know that his hand of the lord is powerful and so that they may fear him**(Joshua 4;24)**Ah Sovereign Lord you have made the heavens and the earth by your great power and outstretched arm nothing is too hard for you **(Jeremiah 32;17)**Then the lord said to me am the Lord the God of the whole nation nothing is too difficult for me **(People were worshiping idols and behaving bad*; Jeremiah 32;26;27)T*he Angle said to Mary even Elizabeth your relative is going to have a child in her old age and she who was said to be unable to conceive is in her sixth month for no word from God will ever fail *(Luke1;36;37)*Is anything to hard for Lord ? I will turn to you at the appointed time next year and Sarah will have a son "*(Genesis18;14) God is able to save*-Praise the lord who carries our burden day after day he is the God who saves **(Psalm68;19)** Leave all your worries to him because he cares **(1Peter5;7)**Leave all your troubles with the lord and he will defend you he never lets honest people be defeated **(Psalm;55;22)The lord is able to qualify you for something you Fear**-Because of, Education, Colour, Size Ammunitions, Gods odds are not the same as ours-The lord and Gideon The lord said you can do it because I will help you -you will crush the Midianites as easily as if they were only one man **(Judges;6;14;16)Gideon Army of 300 defeated 32000** When God is on your side there is nothing impossible for him Your right hand O lord is majestic in power your right hand o Lord shatters the enemy **(Exodus;15;6)**Then Jesus said unto his disciples verily I say unto you that a rich man shall hardly enter into the kingdom of heavens and again I say unto you it is easier for a camel to go through the eye of the needle than for a rich man to enter into the kingdom of God ,When his disciples heard it they were exceedingly amazed saying who then can be saved ?but Jesus beheld them and said unto them with men this is impossible but with God all things are possible **(Mathew19;23;26)**let us be bold then and say; the lord is my helper I will not be afraid what can anyone do to me? **(Hebrews; 13; 6)** And is able now and always to save those who come to God through him because he lives forever to plead to God for them **(Hebrews;7;25) He is able to bless you with Favour as a shield (Psalm;5;12)Its only God who can help you to overcome discouragement**-Even my best friends the one I trusted most the one who shared my food have turned against me without god you cannot do nothing depend on God knowing that he will strengthen you in your struggles in some areas say you need him more than the words you say more than the songs you sing depending on him is not a sign of weakness but strength if you depend on him and don't be discouraged you will bear fruits he will help you in family affairs exams business and fight on your behalf and no need for you to do anything **(Exodus14;14)God is able to keep you up from falling**-To him whose able to keep you from falling and to bring you faultless and joyful before his glorious presence to the only God our saviour Through Jesus Christ(**Jude;1;24**)When we have problems or something to ask for help we are reluctant to ask for help in case people think less of us and One author wrote *to fall is bad enough but fall and don't cry for help is worse* some people are full of pride and self-sufficiency they think if I can't get up myself I won't let anyone help me stop being too proud that's what caused you to fall in the first place the bible say those who walk in pride God is able to put them down pride is dangerous it forces you to lie needlessly in a helpless state for days and sometimes years if you ask for immediate help you can get up and move on with life What you think is the right way may lead to death(*Proverb 14;12*) *God is faithful while we were sinners Christ died for us by his blood we are made right with God Jesus Christ gave us another Chance (Romans 5;6) Paul wrote and said there is no doubt in mind ,he who started the great work in you will carry it until it is finished on the day of Jesus Christ ,he is powerful to forgive and forget ,why should you get stuck in the Sin you committed (3years ago) God himself no longer himself remember them ,why should you remember them, he is able to turn a sinner into a saint (Luke 7;36-50-19;5;9)*He forgives all my sins and heals all my diseases**(Psalm 103;3)God is able to give you much more than this** then Amaziah said to the man of God "but what shall we do about the hundred talents which I have given to the troops of Israel ?"And the man of God answered "the lord is able to give you much more than this **"God is able to turn something small into something much Jesus feeds a greater crowd a** boy who had five loaves of barley bread and fish and Jesus feed 500 people **God is able to build you up in Grace** Now I commit you to God and to the word of his grace which can build you up and give you inheritance (Blessings)among all those who are sanctified **(Acts 20;32)God is able to love you when you feel unloved and able to comfort those who are afflicted**-he helps us in all our troubles so that we are able to help others who have all this kinds of troubles using the same help that we ourselves we received from God just as we have share in Jesus Christ sufferings so also through Christ we share Gods great help if we suffer it is your help and salvation then when you help it is your help you are too helped and given strength to endure with patience so our hope is never forsaken God is able just as you share in our sufferings you share in the help we receive God is able to love you **God is able to turn Bad news into Good news**-The king felt sick to a point of death Hezekiah prayed remember the lord I saved you faithfully and royal I have always tried to do what you wanted me to do Hezekiah was healed and given

232

more 15 years and promised to rescue the city many of us want to see sign to prove that God is able but faith is the key to all believe like you believe in Electricity you don't know where it comes from but you see light **(cook and enjoy it)**enjoy faith**(2Kings20;1;6King Hezekiah illness to recovery)God raised people from death** Abraham reasoned that God could even raise the dead and so in a manner of speaking he did receive Isaac back from death**(Hebrews;11;19)** Jesus though was a son of God he cried and made prayer request and tears to God who is able to save him from death **(Hebrews 5;7)God is able to turn disappointment into Divine appointment** Jesus resurrection Mary was disappointed that his lord was taken away **(vs14)** then he turned around and then saw Jesus standing but did not know was Jesus Mary went and told the disciples that was Jesus**(John20;11;18)**Many were doubting and disappointed but God turned the story around into **Divine-appointment (Luke2410;31;Jesus Appears to Magdalene)**What the father can do the Son can do **God and Jesus are able to turn sinners into saints (Luke 7;36;50)**Lazarus was dead but Jesus rose him up to life **(Chapter 11;25)** Jesus said to her "I am the resurrection and the life the one who believe ins in me will live even though they die and whoever lives by believing in me will never die do you believe in this? she replied "I believe you are the messiah the son of God who is to come into the world, **God is able to give us the tongue of disciples and get to know how to use them in due seasons** -The sovereign lord has given me a well instruct tongue to know the word that sustain the weary he wakens me morning by morning wakens my ears to listen like being instructed the lord has opened my ears I have not been rebellious I have not turned away I have offered my back to those who beat me ,my cheeks to those who pulled out my beards I did not hide my face from mocking and spitting because the sovereign Lord helps me I will not be disgraced I have set my flit and I know I will not be put to shame**(Isaiah;50;4;7)**

The tongue of Disciples-

Am healed by Jesus stripes am covered by the blood of Jesus
Am over comer by the blood of Jesus
Am led by the Holy Spirit
Am a new creation
Am a child of God
Am forgiven
Am a partaker of Gods divine nature?
Am strong in Gods power and mightiness
Am establishing Gods word on earth
Am casting all my worries to God
Am blessed from God

Am protected everywhere I go
Am a head not a tail
Am free from all the powers and forces of darkness that destroys my anointing
Am overcoming daily the devil
An heir to Abraham blessings
Am blessing by God and I will continue to praise him with my mouth
Am putting on the mind of Jesus -love kindness faithfulness and good morals
Am walking by faith not sight

" **God can turn failure into success-Failure** –can be defined as conditions of not achieving the desired end or ends /task given and success is achieving your desired goals set,- failure can be more defined as falling short or being insufficient Because you say so I will Master Jesus said to Simon Peter put out into deep water and let down the nets for a catch answered master we have worked hard all night and haven't caught nothing but because you say so I will when they had done so they caught large number of fish that their net begun to break (**Luke5;5**) notice two lesson in this story *God will use your failure to get your attention*-Peter was tired empty handed and disappointed when Jesus spoke to him and he will speak to you through rocky marriages a child you are about to give up or a job seems to be hard for you he does not want you to run away from your problem he wants you to run to him to discover the difference when you invite him into your situation *God can take you back to the place of failure to make you successful* -we assume we are successful at something it was not Gods will but often the truth is that we failed because we relied on our own strength and strategies instead of his When Jesus spoke the fish responded the writer says in the bible they caught such a large number of fish that their nets begun to break so they signalled their partners in the other Boat to come and help them and they came and filled both boats so full that they began to sink God is not limited by your circumstance he is only limited by your unbelief when you obey him you will discover he has too much for you in the store he has too much to the point that it exceed all your expectations how you can overcome stuck(**getting unstuck**) And without faith-It is impossible to please God because anyone who comes to him must believe that he exists and that he rewards those who seek him(**Hebrews;11;6**)have you ever noticed in winter how icy winter brings multiple cars pile ups with drivers in ditches waiting for tow trucks to rescue them we each have a different reaction some surrender to feelings of being powerless others get frustrated and deepen the rut they are in but the wise think twice and wise think rationally of steps they can take in life getting stuck is not always an optional but staying stuck Good news no matter how long you have been stuck the right attitude can get you move on occupy till I came before he left he called his servant and gave them each a gold coin and said see what you can earn with this while am gone (**Luke;19;13**) Occupy means possessions we haven't been called to hold the fort but to go up and posse the land Christ is not coming for a vanquished church but for a victorious church you say you are not qualified but the odds against me don't look good then you need to look at Gods odds according to his mathematics one can defeat a thousand enemies but two can defeat ten thousands if you have faith god will be on your side I will not help them he said then I will see what happened to those stubborn unfaithful people(**Deuteronomy 32;20**)God loves to take something that looks small and you consider not to be important to another level multiply it himself and bring victory out of it (**Judges;6;16**)Gideon and God(**Judges;7;18**)When you are swinging your sword on this side look over your shoulders and you will see God swinging his sword on the other side you are not alone God is fighting for you here some attitude changes you need not to be stuck **Faith** when you have been stuck for a long time forward mission can seem impossible you lack energy and confidence what to do? Getting tractions requires a willingness to act in spite of your feelings God calls this faith and he always respond to it he rewards those who earnestly seek when you act like you believe God will reward your faith and the feeling of faith will follow your action (**Philippians 3;14**)I press on toward the Goal to win the prize for which God has called me heaven ward in Christ Jesus ,flexibility when your faith runs in obstacle your flexibility keeps you in the race ;you need the ability to roll with the punches to bend without breaking don't marry your methods, be willing to make a mind course correction when it is needed flexibility, however is not ambivalence or wish- wateriness flexibility is (**1**)is a commitment to take action a positive mind set alone won't get you un stuck you will have to do something remember big doors swing on little hinges taking a small step of faith will move you a distance and the move you move on a step you get there (**"2) Firmness** resolve not to quit you will encounter problems that leave you no option but to stand still like the Israelites between the red sea and the Egyptian army in the tightest of sport they received this five folds counsel(**1)look for Gods way forward expect him to take action that will help you get you unstuck(2)Be ready to move forward when he opens door.** These are simple but powerful steps you can take when you don't know what to do and what about when you blow it? Acknowledge it re-label it as valuable lessons learned and put it in you-r what not to do next time in your file/life (**3)Forgiveness the guilt that follows failure** can immobilise you but your forgiveness liberates you freeing up your enemy and creativity Forgiveness is two dimension (**a)*first you must receive* God *forgiveness for your*** failure things you have done betrayal angry words dishonesty, broken promises things you haven't done love unexpressed responsibility avoided a child parent or spouse neglected the truth withheld heartfelt confession always brings God forgiveness and open doors not to be stuck God is God of restoration **(Joel 2;25)** I will give you back what you have lost in the years ,when swarm of locust ate your crops it was I who sent this army against you whatever life has taken from you God can restore he may not give you exactly what you want but he will give you what is the best and even when you fall into his corrective hands through disobedience if you repent he will re-instate you to a place of blessing you say but what about the time I have wasted , the opportunities I have squandered and the mess I have made in life ? sometime I wonder if I have fallen so low that even God cannot reach me No there is hope for you ;The bible says behold the lords hand is not shortened that it cannot reach you ,save you no his Ears heavy that cannot hear **(Isaiah59;1)** The Lord says to the people of Israel if you want to turn then turn back to me if you are faithful to me and remove the idols I hate (witchcraft fame pride greed selfishness)it will be right for you to sear by my name then all the nations will ask to bless them and they will praise me the lord says to the people of Judah and Jerusalem plough up you un ploughed field do not sow your seeds among thorns keep your covenant with me your lord and dedicate yourself to me you people of Jerusalem and Judah if you don't my anger will burn like fire because of the evil things you have done it will burn and there will be no one to put it out(**Jeremiah;4;1;4;7;1;27;Jer;8;4;17;Jer;17;1-3)**after wasting all what he had inherited from his father the prodigal son returned home penniless and embarrassed all he wanted was three square meal and a job in the servants quarters but the moment he said Forgive me his father called *for the best robe ,the fattest cow the newest shoes ,and a ring of son* –ship restoring him to his rightful place as a member of the family Even under the crushing weight of the old testament law with the demands that no one could live up to God said if a man steals an Ox and four sheep **(Exodus;22;1)** Now if God would do that for those who lived under the law and on the wrong side of the cross ,how much more will he do for those who he has redeemed ? so you can go to him today with confidence knowing he is the God of restoration restored **(Job)** The Amalekites swept down on king David home town burning it to the ground and taking its families captives in this scene of devastation David and his men lifted up their voices and wept until they had no more power to weep(**1samuel;30;4)**now God will let you grieve your losses because that's healthy but he won't allow you to stay there for so long so God said to David pursue for you shall surely overtake them and without fail recover all ,Did *David got back all whatever he had lost ?,*Yes and much more besides for our God is not only the God of restoration but a God of abundance you say I feel ashamed of the years I have wasted the God who created time can give you more of it (**late-Mandela- Madiba**)I will restore you the years that the swarming locust has eaten, the consuming locust you shall eat plenty and be satisfied and praise the Lord you God who has dealt wondrously with you and my people shall never be put to shame (**Joel;2;25-26**)note the word plenty when God blesses you it will not come an eye dropper or from a rationed supply, no you will be able to sing his love, has not limit his grace has no measure, his power no boundary ,know unto men , for out of his infinite riches in Jesus , ever since Adam and Eve blew it in Eden Gods desire and plan has been to restore to us ,all that we have lost so come to him today and let the restoration be yours(**1samuuel;30;8**)David asked the Lord shall I go after those raiders ? And will I catch them? God said go for them and you will catch them and rescue the captives (**2Corinthians;8;9**) you know the grace of our lord Jesus Christ rich as he was he made himself poor for your sake in order to make you rich by means of his poverty are you saying if only I had not said or done ? You are not so special from others we all have regrets but God wants us to learn from them not to live in them for you know the grace of lord Jesus Christ that though he was rich yet for your sake he become poor that you through his poverty might become rich Jesus Wore the crown of thorns so you could wore the crown of righteous and be in the right standing with God being justified by faith we have peace with God our lord Jesus Christ (**Roman;5;1**)Being justified gives you a right to stand before God and claim his best is your ,Education ,Marriage, Business , struggling or failing Peter the fishermen experienced the same Jesus the restorer said to him launch out into the deep and let down your net catch but Simon Peter answered we have toiled all the night and caught nothing nevertheless he said because of your word I will do this they caught a greater number of fish and their net was breaking so they signalled to their partners in the other boat to come and help them and they come and both boats were filled so they began to sink(**Luke;5;4;7**)Just one word from Jesus Christ can help you to go through the threshold of bankruptcy to adding a second boat so the word today believe for more than you expected because our God is a God of restoration (**Isaiah;35;4**) tell everybody who is discouraged to be strong and don't be afraid God is coming to rescue you God will come with restoration what you give up in order to serve him is nothing compared to what you will get back Peter answered all said to him we have left all and followed you so Jesus said to them assuredly I say to you who have followed me and left your brothers fathers sisters mothers or land for my sake shall receive a hundred fold and inherit eternal life (**Mathew;19;27-29**)that means God can give you back a million times more than what you expect sacrifice in order to serve him are you felling weak and ineffective today the massage is and you have to live on them strength the weak hands and say to those who are fearful –hearted be strong not fear behold your God will come with vengeance with the recompense restoration he will come and restore you and save you**(Isaiah;35;34)**you say but I have lost my joy God can give it to you back in overflowing measure and the ransomed of the lord shall return and come to Zion with singing with everlasting joy on their heads .they shall obtain Joy and gladness and sorrow and sighing will flee away from you say but I have so little to show for my effort ,then stand on these words and the desert shall rejoice and blossom as the rose it shall blossom abundantly rejoice your God is a God of restoration so your best days are ahead of you Jesus said to peter don't be afraid from now on you will catch men so they left everything and followed him Jesus will come to you and help you to succeed and here are several truth you need to know **(1)**when what you are doing is not working he will show you a better way he hill come to your work and help you and when he help you have to help others**(2)** the success he has in his mind for you is greater than anything you can envision for yourself**(3)**Even though it may not make sense at the moment do what he tells you**(4)**your existing system may be not able to handle what he has in mind so be willing to change how you do things when you experience his goodness you will fall at his feet and acknowledge him as your God/lord and when you realise what he has in mind for you will leave everything and follow him **God is able to turn your weakness to a weapon -**Weapon is something you rely on for your protection /defending from harm or if anything of no good try to strike you - **Weakness**–can be defined as failings or defects or lack of strength , firmness vigour or the like in a personal character human weakness are many for example in Praying ,Worshiping Reading Bible Helping Working Preaching God can see something you don't take serious and make it rely on into a as weapon Am content with weakness, insult hardship persecution and difficult for Christ sake for when am weak then am strong**(2corinthians12;10)** Paul was given a gift of hardship at first he didn't think as a gift and begged God to remove it he told him his grace is enough it is all you need my strength comes into his own in your weakness once he heard that he was glad to let it go and happen he quit focusing on the hardship and began to appreciate the gift Now I take my limitations in stride and with good cheers these limitation that cut me down to size abuse ,accidents, oppositions, bad breaks I just let Christ to take over and so the weaker I become the stronger I become Paul learned how to turn his weakness into a weapon by allowing it to drive it closer to God and learn the same too dear friend/Christian you must confront each area of weakness confess it and let Christ take over you might be facing some hard situations wanting to eliminate you turn to prayers prayer answer everything which money does not answer don't listen to critics and complains to the people who have settled for less Your goal should not just be to live longer but to make a different in the world and glorifying God don't lose hope you can begin again through Gods mercies we are not consumed because his compassion fail not they are new every morning great is your faithfulness the lord is my portion therefore I hope in him**(lamentation;3;22-24);Amen**

God is able to heal where there is no hope While Jesus was saying this a Jewish official came to him and knelt down before him and said my daughter has just died so Jesus got up and followed him and his disciples went with him (raised the dead **Mathew 9;18;26**) **A woman who had suffered severe bleeding for12 years** Came up behind Jesus and touched the edge of his cloak ,I will get well Jesus looked around her and saw and said courage my daughter your faith has made you well **Jesus heals the two blind men**- He touched their eyes and said let it happen then just as they believed and their sight was restored Jesus heals **A man who could not speak-** Jesus drove the demons out the man started talking Jesus heals a boy with demons you "unbelieving and perverse generation Jesus replied "how long shall I stay with you ?how long shall I put up with you? Bring the boy here to me "Jesus rebuked the demon and it came out of the Boy and was healed at that moment then the disciples came to him in private and asked "why couldn't we drive it out he replied because you have so little faith truly I tell you if you have faith as small as small as a mustard seed you can say to this mountain ,move from here to there, and it will move nothing will be impossible for you **(Mathew;17;18;20) God has assured us to take away all our worries and sickness**- if you worship me the lord your God I will bless you with food and water and take away all your illness in your land no woman will have miscarriage or be without children I will give you long life **(Exodus 23;25-26);Amen**

God is able; **Fear** is based on what you see and hear ,**Faith** is based on knowing that Gods word is reliable and that he has promised good things to those who believe in him for them ,We should have our hope in the lord **(Hope is the ability to expect)**The hope in him is divine which does not disappoint us for God has poured out his love into our hearts by the means of the holy spirit who's is God's gift to us**(Romans 5;5)**There are these two things then that cannot change and about God so we who have found safety with him are greatly encouraged to hold firmly to the hope placed in us we have hope as anchor for our lives **(Hebrews 6;19)**To have faith is to be sure of the things we hope for to be certain of the things we cannot see**(Hebrews 11;1)**let us give thanks to the God and father of our lord Jesus Christ because of his great mercy he gave us a new life by raising Jesus from the dead **(1peter1;3)**let us hold firmly on the hope we profess because we can trust God to keep his promise **(Heberews10;23)**So many people today are living without hope look at them they smile but their eyes are dead they talk but the music has left their voice but We as true Christians we don't have to live that way divine hope is ours God can be trusted and he keeps his promise is able in everything we should have confidence that he will do what he promised in our lives no one knew the truth of this better than David he had every reason to lose hope after Samuel anointed him to be Israel king he had to wait (*7 years*) while a paranoid ruler occupied the throne he had to flee for his life and hide in a cave surrounded by enemies he saw Israel devastated his friends killed and his family taken captives but he never wavered or threw in the towel faced with circumstances that would wipe many of us out of the psalmist said my hope is in you what then can I hope for Lord ? I put my hope in you(**Psalm;39;7**)His anger lasts only a moment his goodness for a life time tears may flow in the night but joy in the morning(**Psalm;30;5**)In other ward it's getting better and you can't lose with an altitude and hope like that of David became a king because he never lost confidence in the promise of God is able the promises of God him kept focused they kept him on top of the circumstances Christ is not coming back for failures /failed churches but for victorious churches you say you are not qualified - odds are not looking good for you -you need to look at Gods odds according to his mathematics one can defeat a thousand enemies but two can defeat ten thousands God loves to take something that looks small and multiply it by himself and bring victory out of it when you are swinging your sword look over your shoulders and you will see God swinging his sword on the other side your guest and relentless in your pilgrimage turn away from the penny pursuit of possession and position and seek the lord you will not be disappointed **You are not alone God is able** What God has promised you stand on his word and declare it ,if God promised it is able and believe it and receive it in Jesus name God is able in every situation spiritual Weakness, Marriages/ relationship ,Jobs, Finances ,Family affairs, our God is able and our hope should only be in him Abraham believed and hoped even when there was no reason for hoping and become father of many nations we have to believe and hope In God - God is able to provide to you all these if you don't forget his laws and obeying his commands loving him and trusting him as your only God praising him and worshiping him being in union with Christ Jesus Christ observing Sunday ,being righteous (Holy)helping others -**Amen**

QUESTION?

WHY GOD HAS NOT BEEN ABLE TO PROVIDE TO US?

Lack of faith-We don't pray in faith we doubt in what God can do acknowledge God in everything work place, business ,marriage, addictions, he will put you in the right place come to God with faith and you will see miracles in your life happening-
We don't pray (**Isaiah 65; 1-20**)
Our sins -also affect God to open doors for us

Self centeredness ambitions- God bless you to bless others but everything we want it to be (mine) my house, my car, my money
We fail to forgive ourselves and others

We don't testify -yet we know well that we overcome by testimony and the blood of Jesus Christ

We fail sometimes to go to God with confidence and ask him specifically what we want ,how much, why you want it for,**(Mathew;7;7)**We at times bring many things at ago ,Cars, Husbands Money ,Children, it's not bad to ask big but choose what you need first in your life according to the seasons and times ,you are in, ask repeatedly ,be of clear mind,, go to God with all your needs he longs to give you the desires of your heart and pour out his favour, increase, grace, blessings , and promises on you the bible says "You have not because you don't ask **(James;4;2)**Ask the Lord to bless your plans and you will be successful in carrying them out **(Proverb;16;3)**When you step out and ask for all your needs you activate your faith and God to work on your side ,**Amen**

Thanks giving tithes and offering- We want from God but we don't want to give our tithes and offering ,even helping the needy **(Malachi,3;10)**We have not been faithful enough ,the scriptures warn us ,fear the lord and serve him faithfully, with your heart, consider what good things he has done for you, yet if you persist doing Evil both you and your king will perish **(1Samuel12;24;25)Amen**

We are not committed to our God and his commands (ten commandments)-We don't go to church- bible study we only go to church on Christmas and Easter festivals, Make certain that you do not forget the lord your God do not fail to obey any of his laws that am giving you today when you have all you want to eat and have build a good house to live in and when all your cattle sheep your silver and gold and all your other possession have increased make sure you don't become proud and forget the lord your god who rescued you from Egypt where you were slaves**(Deuteronomy8;11-20)**When we neglect God we are neglecting wisdom and his blessing on us we miss his blessing because we only remember him on Sunday and Christmas and Easter God say if you obey me you will eat good things of the land**(Isaiah1;19;20)**God does not want our sacrifices but our obedience life will be better if we acknowledge God in our daily life we won't experience ,depression disappointment, betrayal, loss of our beloved ones- God does not help angels but help the descendants of Abraham Moses urges the Israel to be obedient- Moses said to them obey all the laws that am teaching you and you will live and occupy the land which the Lord of your ancestors is giving you do not add anything to what I command you and do not take anything away obey the commands of the Lord your God that I have given you**(Deuteronomy;4;2),Amen**

Thanks giving tithes and offering- We want from God but we don't want to give our tithes and offering ,even helping the needy **(Malachi3; 10)** We have not been faithful enough the scriptures warn us fear the lord and serve him faithfully with your heart consider what good things he has done for you yet if you persist doing Evil both you and your king will perish **(1Samuel12; 24; 25),Amen**

We are not patient enough to wait on Gods right time- We want to do things on our own yet Gods time is the best and what he promised to you will come to pass we have lost Patience and Hope God is in control no one will take away what he promised you always sing his promises into your life God is always ready to bless you and keep his face shine on you and be gracious the lord turns his face toward you and gives you peace **(Blessings; Numbers 6;24;26);Amen**

QUOTES ON HOPE

The essential of happiness are something to love and something to love where by all these we can achieve them from God I got nothing that I asked for but everything I had hoped for almost despite myself .my unspoken prayers were answered ,The very least thing you can do in your life is to figure out what you hope for and the most you can do is live inside that hope not admire it from a distance but live in it under its roof(**Barbra Kingsolver**) Never let go of hope dream take action and get that transfer to live the life you wish Have faith in your own abilities do not just wish for a thing take action and get it(**Catherine Pulsifer**)We live by admiration   hope and love(**William Wordsworth**)Believe in the incredible power of human kind of doing something that makes a difference of working hard of laughing and hoping Hope arouses as nothing else can arouse a passion for possible(**William Sloan Coffin**)It has never been and it will never be easy work but the road that is built in hope is more pleasant to the traveller than the road build in despair even though they both lead to the same destination Hope is faith holding out it's in the dark (**Georges-Iles**)We promise according to our hope and perform according to our fears Faith walks simply childlike between the darkness of human life and the hopes of what is to come (**Catherine de Hueck Doherty**)Man can live about forty days without food about three days without water about eight minutes without air but only for one second without hope(**Hal-Lindsey**)He who has never hoped can never despair(**George Bernard**)Most important things in the world have been accomplished by people who have kept on trying where seemed to be no hope at all (**Dale Carmegie**) Anticipate good things will happen keep your mind positive and it will amaze you To be without hope is like being without goals what are you working towards (**C Pulsifer**) We judge a man wisdom by his hope (**Ralph Emerson**)If it were not of hopes the heart would break (**ThomasFuller**) He who expects not to achieve will never do so(**C Butler**)The start of something new brings the hope of something greater anything is possible You are never given a wish without also being given the power to make it come true you may have to work for it however (Richard Bach) What oxygen to the lungs such hope is to the meaning of life(**Emil-Brunner**)Optimism is faith that leads to achievement nothing can be done without hope and confidence(**Helen Keller**)Far away there is the sunshine are my highest aspiration I may not reach them but I can look up and see their beauty believe in them and try to follow them (**Louisa May Alcott**)The feeling of hopefulness sometimes comes from someone helping us think back to a time when you had lost hope many times we regained our hope /optimism because someone gave us a helping hand (**Catherine-Pulsifer**)While wishing and hoping makes you a dreamer acting and doing makes you someone who can ,turn dreams into reality (**Nan Russell**) Never give up expect only the best from life and take action to get it(**Catherine-Pulsifer**)In life don't allow to be controlled by*(1)Limited* belief/doubt*(2)Past(3)Other* people opinions *(4)*Relationship *(5)*Money *(6)*Politics Economy (Resources) Environment (7)Fear *(8)*Sin and Shame *(9)*Never let go of hope -Do not forget to hope and be happy (**John Mcleod**)Learn from yesterday live for today hope for tomorrow (**Albert Einstein**)Never talk defeat use words like hope belief faith and victory(**Norman Vincent Peale**) Hope is the last thing ever lost (*Italian saying*) ;**Amen**

WHO ARE YOU TRYING TO PLEASE

PLEASING -means a feeling of satisfaction or enjoyment or Pleasing performance, something that is pleasing gives you pleasure (manners, appearance ,pleasing to the eye of the mind especially through beauty or charm or can be delighting the sense or exciting intellectuals or Emotional admiration - Pleasing through Worship and Praise the scriptures say "Therefore I urge you brethren by the mercies of God to present your bodies a living sacrifice and holy sacrifice acceptable to God which is your Spiritual service of worship (**Romans;12;1**)More than anything Else-however we want please him whether in our homes here or there (**2Corinthians;5;9**)The best way to please God is love him, with all your heart Obey him and his commands ,have faith in him, be kind to others ,have peace with yourself and others, your works should always be residing in him You may ask yourself why should I Please God ?for the reason he created you in his own image ,he has shown himself to be kind and loving to you ,Father full of grace , God wants his Sons and daughters who follow his examples of merciful love and come to him at the end of every day ,All believers and all those who call upon the name of Jesus Christ for salvation their main goal should be to please God -the requirements for all who wants to please God are -that they must seek God by faith ,Walk in the Spirit and not in the flesh, and walk worthy of our calling ,in obedience and being submissive to God's will, all these may seem to be impossible but God wants us to please him and he makes it possible to please him we do these things by the power of His spirit who lives in our heart Those who are in realms of flesh cannot please God-(**Romans 8;8**)the first thing to do is(**1**)**To accept the sacrifice for sin**-that he provided in the death of his son on the cross there is a different in people those who are guided by the Spirit and the sinful nature those who are in their Sins have their minds set on Sinful desires and those who are guided by the Spirit and Christ have completely a new Mindset that is controlled by the Spirit and desire to live in accordance with Christ ,The mind of a sinful man desire is death ,but the mind of the Spirit is Life, and Peace ,Sinful mind is hostile to God ,doesn't submit to Gods laws nor can it do so to please God ,you must accept that you are walking in the Spirit not in the flesh(**2**)**Live by faith** God cannot be pleased by unbelievers or those shrink back from him because they have no confidence in him or they doubt the truth of his promises and declarations or who doubt that his ways are right and perfect both our children and loved one should believe(**3**)**Love-yourself and neighbours** -Pleases God loving Christ is by obeying his commands and Jesus made it Clear that" that if you love me you will obey what I command you(**John 14;15**)Josiah was eight years old when he became king of Judah and he ruled Jerusalem for 31 years his mother was Jedidah the daughter of Adaiah from the town of Bozkath Josiah did what was pleasing to the Lord ,he followed the example of his Ancestor king David strictly obeying all the laws of God **(2Kings 22;1;2)**- **(4) Live in the truth and speak the truth** -for you were formerly in darkness but now you are light in the Lord walk as children of light (for the fruits of the right consists in all goodness and righteousness and truth)trying to learn what is pleasing to God(**Ephesians;5;8;10)**Let my words and thoughts be pleasing to you Lord(*Psalm;19;14)*do your best to win full approval in Gods sight as a worker who is not ashamed of his work one who correctly teaches the massage of truth keep away from profane and foolish discussion which only drive people further away from God **(2Timothy;2;15;16)**May these words of my mouth and this meditation of my heart be pleasing in your sight lord my rock and my redeemer. Are you afraid to speak in case you encounter disapproval? the bible says fearing is dangerous trap and fear is common among people We are meant to live a life which please God not human beings the fruit that please God bears fruit if you buy a fruit tree plant it and take care of it you expect to get good fruits if it does not you will go back and complain where you bought it. Life that pleases God is love of Your God and one another. faith, honest gentleness, Self-control ,Welcome strangers in your home there someone who did and welcomed angles without knowing(**Hebrews13;10)**As for other matters brothers and sisters we instructed you how to live in order to please God now we ask you and urge you in the Lord Jesus Christ to do this more and more for you know that what instructions we gave you by the authority of the Lord Jesus ,Keep yourself free from loving money be satisfied with what you have remember those in prison remember your leaders who spoke Gods massage to you do not let all kinds of stranger teachings lead you from the right way obey your leaders they are watching you without resting **(1Thessolonnian4;1;6)**And when you allow the holy Spirit to take control you will bear good fruits but when you desire human desire your nature will be sinful and evil results idolatry participation, selfishness jealously outburst of anger impure thoughts drunkenness anyone living this kind of life will not inherit the kingdom of God remain in me I will remain in you **(Colossians;1;9;14)**No branch can bear fruits by itself it must remain in the vine neither can you bear fruits unless you remain in me we need to get closer to him and the fruits will come naturally life that pleases God is the life that yarns to know God better keep on growing in knowledge this is to be able to experience more of his blessing Endurance in times of difficult and patient with difficult people means hang in there don't give up to things that may take you away from your God, live grateful do not complain about the Circumstances, Governments, children, food ,traffic Jam ,about Other believers ,Income, Taxes ,Rain we should thank God for everything he has given us it is not how much harder we try to work it ourselves but draining closer to him life that pleases God is the life that glorifies him in our daily life how we treat others our family how we do our Jobs tactics we use to make money the way we handle our mistake The person who is living to please God will begin to see changes in his life and will change in behaviours like**(1)**Those living outside marriage will get married**(2)**Those been abusive in their language turn to kindness**(3)**Those known for using others will begin to serve others**(4)**Those who have been hoarded their resources will begin to invest in the kingdom of God**(5)Those** tearing other peoples name will start building them-For am I now seeking the approval of man or of God ?or am I trying to please man? if I were still trying to please man I would not be a servant of Christ **(Galatians;1;10)**Do not look for glory from human beings like Jesus did not " He said am not looking for human praise but I know what kind of people you are and I know that you have no love for God in your hearts I have come with my father's Authority but you have not received me when however someone comes with his Authority you will receive him you like to receive praise from one another but you don't try to win praise from the one who alone is God how then can you believe me ?do not think however that am that am the one who will accuse you to my father Moses in whom you have put your hope is the very one who will accuse you if you had really believed Moses you would have believed me because he wrote about me but since you don't believe what he wrote how can you believe what I say?**(John5; 41; 46)**And whatever we ask we receive from him because we keep his commandments and do what pleases him**(1John3;22)**Do this not only when they are watching you because you want to gain their approval but with all your heart o what God wants as a slave of Christ **(Ephesians;6;6)**And he who sent me is with me he has not left me alone for I always do the things that are pleasing to him**(John8;29)**But for those who live according to the flesh set their minds on the things of the flesh but those who live according to the spirit set their minds on the things of the Spirit**(Romans;8;5)**but Peter and apostles answered we must obey God rather than men **(Acts 5;29)**When a man ways please the Lord he makes even his enemies to be at peace with him**(Proverb;16;7)**Do not neglect to do good and to share what you have for such sacrifice are pleasing to God**(Hebrews 13;16)**Thus says the lord cursed is the man who trusts in man and makes flesh his strength whose heart turns away from the lord **(Jeremiah ;17;5)**Don't let what you cannot do interfere with what you can do; **Amen**

DIFFERENT KIND OF PLEASERS IN LIFE;

(1)A Pleaser friend- who can't say no resentment may build up but she /he always turns up and takes care of things what she considers as love and loyalty are often exploitation by others who seeks reliance co-dependence and care taking*(b)*A **pleaser child**- is one who at any age still tries to please his parents from report cards to parenting style her decision are coloured or controlled by the options of the parents who raised her and remember what Paul said when I was a child I reasoned like a child when I become a man I put childish clothing away/behind me (*1corinthians 13;11*)-**(c) A Pleaser wiser**- is the one who in his/her desire to be perfect becomes an altered version of the woman her husband fell in love with her-**(d)A Pleaser employee**- consistently works long hours without compensation or appreciation covers others who don't pull their weight and bites her tongue when her/his boss or colleagues take credit for her work (e)**A pleaser Mum** – fears the loss of her children love she is afraid to set boundaries even though they create atmosphere of comfort and respect she equates discipline with division and by depriving her children of rules she ends up missing out on the later life friendship that's the desert of good parents the only thing you should be concerned about is making sure that your words and thoughts pleases God in the end his approval is the only thing that counts (f)**Pleaser husband/ Wife** -those who always try to make their husband and wives happy of what they say sometime are not even of God ,husband and wives just keep quite instead of raising their voices but because they fear of being dumped they end up pleasing them instead of pleasing God -**Learn to say no/ just say no** when you don't learn to say no you just end up disliking yourself as well as people around you (*James 5;12*)Unfaithful people don't you know that to be worlds friend means to be Gods enemy? people who want to be the world's friends make themselves Gods enemies ,don't think that there is no truth in the scriptures that says, The Spirit that God placed in us is filled with fierce desires but the grace that God gives is even stronger than as the scriptures says "God resists the proud but gives grace to the humble ,so then submit to God resist the devil and he will run away from you come near to God and he will come near to you wash your hands you sinners purify your hearts you hypocrites *(James; 4;4;8) You must try to please God alone ,and if he is pleased you are pleased, Some time we just have to accept that not everyone will like us,* above all dear Christians sisters and brothers do not use an oath when you make a promise do not swear by heaven or by earth or by anything else say only yes when you mean yes and no when you mean no and then you will not come under Gods judgement , People you are trying to please in some cases we find it difficult saying it because we are afraid people won't like us in other cases we believe that to be a good Christian we must always say yes to everything ,Jesus said let your **No** be so that you may not sin only when you have a courage to say no will you mature be able to address your own un me t needs and start respecting yourself and others will too so do these things**(1)Think before you respond,** if you need to say I can get back to you ,don't make commitment without consulting God ,your calendar and your family, if you need wisdom ask your generous God and he will give it to you **(James;1;;5)-(2)When your plates are full say so-**responding to so called emergencies caused by somebody else poor planning and sloppy habits won't do either of you any good limit what you say yes to then stick with it don't take on more because you feel pressured guilty or indispensible you will discover that that you are only indispensible until you say no-or die **(3)**Go with your gift God has given each of us a gift which is unique if you have chosen singing in the choir or sitting on the church member committee go where your talent will be best utilised is *this always easy ?* no but unless you learn to do it you will end up investing too much time and energy in what seems urgent and neglect what is important in life don't worry about losing be afraid of losing yourself by trying to please everyone around you ,You are not required to set yourself on fire to keep other people warm ,at your absolute best you still won't be good enough for the wrong person at your worst you will still be worth it to the right person , pleasing everyone is never a responsibility if they like you for who you are good if not it's their problem not yours I can't tell you the key to success but I can tell you the key to failure is trying to please everyone, when you say yes to others make sure you are saying no to yourself **(Paulo Coelho)**Go for someone who is not only proud to have you but will also take every risk just to be with you ,What you allow is what will always continue we have different gifts given to us by God and we find different people expect different things from us and when a lot of people are pulling on you, those expectations can build up like mountains or hills and can bury ,but be honest in your evaluation of yourself measure yourself by the level of faith God has given you ,we all want to please people but we must also realise that they frequently have unrealistic expectation and sometimes selfish ones but because of the fear people we fail to say no to them ,we want to be loved and we are afraid of being rejected all what cause this is because **(1)**We don't know the will of God for our life, Jesus said I carry out the will of the one who sent me ,not my own will **(John,5;30)(2)**We must know Gods will and be committed to it, people will always try to impose their will and agenda on you, we became pleasers because of Pride -If God made you one talented he won't make you two talented assignment ,don't allow pride to take more than you can swallow in order tom have peoples approval , ; (3) we became people pleaser because we trying to be photocopy of others -having then the gift different according to the grace that God is given to us let us use them **(Romans,12;6)** Unless God has graced you to do it , you will fail or collapse under weight of it, realise you are not called to please everyone. **Amen**

SELF -DISCOVERY (WHO YOU SAY I AM)

SELF-DISCOVERY---Means getting to know yourself,**(Awareness of yourself)***What God say about you-,*What you have to find -is yourself first -being true to yourself and everyone around you when you get to know yourself you get acquainted with what you know and what you can do-find out who you are and do it on Purpose ,committing yourself is a way of finding out who you are a man finds his identity by Identifying - if you are left to the world to define you will always fall short, but focus on how God sees you and the truth then you learn more about God and learn more about yourself in relationship with God, you will enjoy Peace and be happy in life and Christ- Find yourself first -like yourself , love yourself first and friendship and love will naturally find you -You have to find yourself first everything will follow you, all the wonders you seek are within you- Knowing others is intelligence-Knowing yourself is true wisdom ,mastering others is strength ,mastering yourself is true Power Don't worry about finding your soul mates find yourself **(Jason, Evert)** When you are being ignored that's a good time to concentrate on finding yourself and creating your own mystery it is a life journey of finding ourselves ,finding our power and living our life not for everyone -When you fight yourself to discover the real you there is only one winner - Finding oneself and ones path is like walking up on a foggy day, be patient and presently the fog will clear and that which has always been there can be seen the path is already there to follow**(Stephen Richards)It doesn't matter what People calls and have named you, What matters in life is what God calls you and named you ,and how he sees you** - It's better to think and somehow ,we learn who we really are and then live with a decision- to find yourself think for yourself - if a man finds himself he has a mansion which he can inhabit with dignity all the days of his life - you have to know yourself so you can at last be yourself**(DH Lawrence)**Be who you are and find yourself so you can be your own person and enjoy life without regrets and then adorn accordingly -Your real self may be hiding somewhere look for it within, when you find yourself you can freely be what you want to be - You never find yourself until you face the truth which is in the word of God ,you can always find the sun within yourself if you will only search - you really have to look inside yourself and find your own inner strength, and say I am proud of what I am and who I am and who am going to be myself and what God say about me- We are adopted as Gods children God has already decided that through Jesus Christ he would make us his Daughters and Sons, this was his pleasure and purpose **(Ephessians1;5)**We belong to God my children and ,I have defeated the false Prophets, because the Spirit who is in you is more powerful than the Spirit in those who belong to the World**(John 1;12;1;John4;4)**But the Spirit produces, Love, Joy ,Patience, Goodness

,Kindness- humanity and Self -control-**Gods temple**-Surely you know that you are Gods temple and that Gods Spirit lives in you, If anyone tries to destroy Gods temple God will destroy him/her(**1Corrinthians3;16;17**)**Am loved by God**-for loved the world so much that he gave his only son so that everyone who believe in him may not die but have eternal life **(John ;3;16)Am justified** -that we have been put right with God through faith we have peace with God through our lord Jesus Christ(**Romans;;5;1**)**I have Christ righteousness**-And just as the mass of people were made sinners as a result of disobedience of one man sin in the same way the mass of people will all be put right with God as a result of the obedience of the one man(**Romans;5;19; 1Corinthians;5;21**)Everyone has sinned and is far away from Gods saving presence ,but by the free gift of God's grace all are put with him through Christ Jesus who set them free, God offered him so that by his blood he should become the means by which peoples sins are forgiven through their faith in him ,God did this in order to demonstrate that he is righteous in this way God, shows that he himself is righteous and that he puts right everyone who believe in Jesus(**Romans3;23;26**)**There is no condemnation now for those who live in union with Christ Jesus**-for the law of the spirit which brings us life in union with Christ, Jesus has set me free from the law of sin and sin(**Romans,8;12**)Sometimes we must lose ourselves to find ourselves by following Jesus Christ -Each man's life represents a road towards himself(**Herman- Hesse**)Lose yourself Wholly and the more you lose the more you will find ,We lose ourselves in things we love we find ourselves there too(**Kristin Martz**) sometimes when you lose your way you find yourself(**Mandy-Hale**)**Tendered and loved by God** -God appeared to them from far away people of Israel(Christians)I have always loved you so I continue to show you my constant love once again and I will rebuild you once again you will take up your tambourines and dance joyfully we are tendered loved by God(**Jeremiah31;3**)**Am chosen by God holy and dearly loved** - You are the people of god he loved you and chose you for his own so then you must clothe yourself with compassion kindness humility gentleness and patience(**Collossians3;12**)**Am holy and I share in Gods heavenly calling** -my sisters and brothers who also been called by God think of Jesus whom God sent to be the high priest of the faith we confess(**Hebrews3;1**) **Am hidden with Christ in God** -for you have died and your life is hidden with Christ in God your real life is Christ and when he appears then you too will appear with him and share his glory **(Collossians3;3)Am saved by grace through faith** -For its by god's grace that you have been saved through faith it is not by the result of your own power /effort but by god's gift so that no one can boast about **(Ephesians2;8;9)Am helped by God** -let us have confidence then and approach Gods throne where there is grace there we will receive mercy and find grace to help us just when we need it(**Hebrews 4;16**) **Have been** given the spirit of power love and self-discipline- For the spirit God has given us does not make us timid instead his spirit fills us with power love and self control(2Timothy1;7)My/your needs are met by God -and with all his abundant wealth through Jesus Christ my God will supply all my /your needs(Phillippians4;19)Am born of God and the evil cannot touch me -We know that none of Gods children keep on sinning for the son of God keeps them safe and the evil one cannot harm them(1John5;18) I have been made complete in Christ -And you have been given full life in union with him he is supreme(Fullness of life in Christ Colossians;2;10) Am firmly rooted and build in Christ-keep your roots deep in him build your lives on him and become stronger in your faith as you were taught and be filled with thanks giving(Collossians2;7)I have just been bought with a price and I belong to God -don't you know that your body is a temple of the Holy spirit who lives in you and who was given to you by God? You do not belong to yourself but God bought you for a price (use your body for Gods glory-1Corinthians; 6; 19; 20) I have a mind of Christ -The bible says who knows the mind of God? Who's is able to give him advice? we however have the mind of Christ (1Corrinthians2;16)I have direct access to God through the Holy spirit - It is through Christ that all of us Jews and Gentiles are able to Come to one spirit into the presence of the fathers you Gentiles you are not foreigners or strangers any longer you are now fellow citizens with Gods people and members of the family of God (Ephessians2;18;19)Am united to the lord one spirit with him-but he who joins himself to the lord becomes spiritually one with him (1corinthians;6;17)Am a member of Christ body-all of you are Christ body and each one of you is a part of it in the church God has put all the places apostles prophets teachers those who perform miracles those with power to heal ,speak in tongues and help others (but, with love;1Corinthians,12;27)Am citizen of heaven-we however are the citizens of heaven and we eagerly wait for our saviour the Lord Jesus Christ to come from heaven (Phillipians3;20) Am a friend of Christ- am the vine and you are the branches those who remain in me and I in them will bear much fruits for you can do nothing without me (John15;5)You are my friend if you do what I command you I do not call you servants any longer because servants do not know their masteries is doing instead I call you friends because I have told you what I have heard from the father(John15;14;15)Am a friend of God -But now by means of his physical death of his son God made me /you his friend in order to bring you holy pure and faultless into his presence (Collossians;1;22)Am reconciled to God -but that is not all we rejoice because of God has done through our lord Jesus Christ who has made us Gods friend, Am chosen by Christ to bear fruits -you did not chose me I choose you and appointed you to go and bear much fruits the kind of fruits that endures and so the father will give you whatever you ask of him in my name this is what I commanded you ;love one another **(John15;16;1) Am a personal witness of Christ-**But when the holy spirit comes upon you will be filled with power and you will be my witness for me in Jerusalem in all Judea and Samaria and to the end of the earth (Jesus taken up to Heaven ;**(Acts1;8)Am Gods co-worker-** in our work together with God then we beg you who have received Gods grace not to let it be wasted hear what he says when the time come for me to show you favour I heard you when the day arrived for me to save you I helped you listen this is the hour to receive Gods favour today is the day to be saved **(2corinthians 6;1)**For we are partners working together with God and you are his field Am Gods workmanship -God has made us what we are and in union with Christ Jesus he created us for a life of good deeds which he has already prepared for us to do**(Ephesians2;10)I can do all things through Christ -**who gives me strength need**(Philippians4;13) Am sure that God who began this good work** in me/you will carry it on until it is finished on the day of Jesus Christ**(Phillipians1;6)Am one of Gods living stone being built up in Christ as a spiritual house-**come to the lord the living stone rejected by people as worthless, but chosen by God as Valuable come as a living stone and let yourselves be used in building the Spiritual temple where you will serve as holy priests to offer spiritual and acceptance sacrifices to God through Jesus Christ for the scriptures says "I chose a valuable stone which am placing as a corner stone in Zion and whoever believe in him will never be disappointed, this stone is one of the greatest value for you that believe ,but for those who don't believe the stone which the builders rejected as worthless turned to be the most important one another Scripture say" this is the stone that will make people stumble the rock the rock that will make them fall they stumble because they don't believe in the word such as Gods will for them **(1Peter4;8)** Don't spend all your time trying to find yourself Spend your time trying to find yourself, spend your time creating yourself into a person that you will be proud of **(Sonya -Parker)**It's not about finding a home that matters so much but finding yourself;-*When you discover yourself-You won't spent your limited time living someone else life* **Am a saint -**from Paul who by Gods will is an apostle of Christ Jesus to Gods people in Ephesus who are faithful in their life in union with Christ Jesus **(Ephesians;1;1)Am the salt of the Earth -**You are like the salt for the whole human race but if salt loses its saltiness there is no way to make it again salty it has become worthless so it is thrown out and people trample on it**(Mathew;5;13)Am the light of the world -**You are like light for the whole world a city build on a hill cannot be hidden no one lights a lamp and puts it under bowl instead he puts it on the lamp stand where it gives light for everyone in the house in the same way your light must shine before people so that they will see the good things you do and praise your father in heaven**(Mathew;5;14)I have been**

rescued from Satan dominion and transferred into the kingdom of Christ-He rescued us from the power of darkness and brought us safe into the kingdom of his dear son by whom we are set free that our sins are forgiven **(Colossians;1;13)I have been given great and precious promises by God** in this way he has given me /us the very great and precious gift he promised so that by means of these gifts you may escape from destructive lust that is in the world and you may come to share the divine nature add faith knowledge endurance -self control and if you have them in abundance they will make you active and effective in your knowledge of our lord Jesus Christ**(2Peter1;4)**We have the power to approach God with boldness ,freedom and confidence in union with Christ and through our faith in him we have the boldness to go into Gods presence with all confidence**(000)**when that comes you will know that am in my fathers and that you are in me just as am in you **(John 14;20)**If you ask anything in my name I will do it**(John;14;12)**I made you **known** to them and I will continue to do so in order that the love you have for me may be in them and so that I also be in them **(John17;26)** Arrogance cause nothing but trouble it's wise to ask for advice **(Proverb13;10)**Pride leads to destruction and arrogance to downfall**(Proverb;16;18)**A journey to discover yourself you need to spend time with your God love your God with all your heart strength and soul**(Mark12;30)**You will know the truth and the truth will set you free**(John8;32)** Always strive to be perfect as the father in heaven **(Mathew;5;48)**The altitude you should have is one that Jesus Christ had**(Phillipians;2;5)**Spend time in ,prayers; reading your bible ,spend time on yourself, write the experience of each day- note or have a journal book- knowing who you are is the best defence against who they think you are - Every man is right in his way ,but God weighs the heart ,When your heart speaks take a note ,find what makes your heart sing and create your own music ,Let your heart guide you, if it whispers so listen carefully Nurture your dreams, discover your passion, embrace your vision ,free your spirit share love with your soul**(Vicki-Vick)**You have been blessed with immeasurable power to make positive changes in your life never let anyone steal your dream stay focused work hard in the impossible -to you let your confidence be in God you will succeed You can change your beliefs so they empower your dreams and desires create a strong belief in yourself and what you want you have to except things of yourself before you can do them problems are not stop guides but they are guidelines don't let the negativity given to you by the world disempowered you instead give yourself that which empowers you**(les Brown)**What lies behind us and before us are tinny matters compared to what lies within us ,we all make mistakes have struggles and even regret things in our past but you are not of your mistake, you are not your struggle ,and you are here with power to shape your day and future ,We cannot pretend to know everything each day -we learn something new your work is to discover your world and then with all your heart give yourself to it, you don't have to look to the left or right just stay focused to your goals *(a)If you lose some friends because you don't let them control your life they were not true friends for you -better let them go (b)if people don't understand you it's okay*(c)**If people start being critical**, *jealous make you look bad don't let them change you, you don't need their approval* -You have the Approval of the most high almighty God, you will succeed in life if you free yourself from what people think about you, what they have said about in the past and what they have named you, if you are to win peoples favour you will be manipulated letting people to squeeze you into their life and plans **(a)**Don't spend too much time trying to win their approval and pleasing them ,wondering what they say about you ,about your family, job, hair style, and dress code, location, tribe ,colour, religion don't make decisions based on people, look on to your God *At (20 years)We wonder what everybody thinks about us (b) At (42-years)We don't care what everybody thinks about us At (60 years) we get to know nobody was thinking about us* The biggest regret in life is*" I wish I had been true to be what God created me to be ,not to just live to meet the expectations of others" Don't allow the world to squeeze you into its mould ,if you want to be what God created you to be ,you need the courage to break the mould, If you get to know yourself without relying on others approval God will pour out his favour ,blessings anointing on you ,* Never be afraid to sit and think find a friend who has been on the same truck for advice to discover yourself Talk and share information with others ,your Experiences, Goals ,Dreams, Visions ,find Teachers, Pastors ,Counsellors ,Mentors, to help you find away to self -discovery isolate yourself from friends who don't build you up enjoy yourself after improving ,God has made you just like Jesus in life there will always be *(1)People trying to squeeze you into their plans (2)People trying to press you wanting you to be who they are either good people or bad-* People they may mean well but remember they didn't create you and breathe into your life they didn't equip you amount you they didn't empower you if you want to be what God created you to be you should have boldness you should not worry about what people think about you and say about you*(a) if you listen to every critics you will never be happy and enjoy life you can't make everyone happy (b) You can't be everyone friend you will never win all the critics in the world* ,Even if you change and do what they ask you they will still find fault in you -you are not yet free until when you stop trying to please everyone, Get to know you are not living to please everyone but your God , many people today live a life where they afraid because they are going to disappoint somebody **(b)** afraid because they may fall out of their good grace **(c)** they may not be accepted in certain level or classes ,you can't try to live what your Parents, Boss, Friends wants you to be -you have to base yourself on what God created you to be -your purpose for life is not the same like for others your calling is not the same like for others you will be pleasured if you want to live like others doing what they are doing God's plan for you is different from theirs you may think people won't like you but everyone has got his own race to run, David fulfilled his purpose for his generation not his father's generation ,your Mother father sisters and brothers they have their purpose and calling ,stop being like them ,go out fulfil your calling ,God doesn't want us to be a photocopy of others, but the Original of what he created us to be ,there is anointing on you which is different from others, if you allow people to squeeze you into their life they will take away your uniqueness and it will affect your Gods anointing ,blessing and favour on you -There areas in life where people expect you to be like your Father or Mother and they may rise criticism about you that you are not like your Father or Mother ,If you chose to live to criticism you will never reach your destiny -Get rid of negative voices ,stay true to what God created you to be, don't compete with somebody don't allow People control you ,don't get upset look forward ,do your best to please God ,and gain Gods approval not man or the world ,Love the praise of God more than mans praise- friends parents wants us to follow their steps or direction but its only God who has the final say we don't want to disappoint them but if you want to make it in life you have to make your choice based on what God and the word of God says about you, better to have the praise of God more than people ,if you follow what God says about your new Opportunities ,Favour. blessing , Love, anointing, friends will overflow into your life, Everyone has an opinion people are always quick to tell you how you can learn your life, dress .drive ,spend your money, raise your children, if you try to please them you will be confused and frustrated and make life difficult, for yourself , Everyone has a choice to make ,if anything doesn't rise you higher and fit into your plans let it go ,some people may try to run your life but if you study them deep they can't even run their life ,good to listen to their advices opinion but rely on God - God does not care about experience no wonder he choose David ,God does not care about age, no wonder he blessed Abraham ,God doesn't care about your Past no wonder he called Paul, God doesn't care about gender no wonder he lifted Esther, God doesn't care about physical appearance no wonder he choose Zacchaeus the shortest , God he doesn't care about fluency in Speech no wonder he choose Moses ,God doesn't care about career no wonder he choose Mary Magdalene a Prostitute-What God say is who you are ; the best way to find yourself is to lose yourself in the service of God and others **(Mohandas Gandhi)**The Lords angles appeared to him (Gideon) there and said "The Lord is with you brave and mighty man **(Judges;6;12)** he couldn't believe it he knew himself as the least in the family and in his Father's house ,he saw himself as the defeated weak and not able but God saw him as strong ,confident and being more than conqueror the question is are we going to believe what God say about us or believe what we feel, think, and the circumstances around us -You may feel *Weak,* today but God calls you *Strong-You may feel Afraid* but God calls you *Confident* -you may feel like a **Victim** but God calls you a **Victor** -You may be in **Debt** but God calls you **Prosperous** -*You may be Sick* but God calls you *Well* -*You may be addicted* but God calls you **Free** -**You may feel Inadequate** but God calls you *Well able*-Today agree with what God say about you believe - you are free forgiven and healed- Am fearfully and wonderful made ,I will praise you for am fearfully and wonderful made ,marvellous are your works and that my soul know well **(Psalm;139;14)**Many of us think there is nothing Amazing about ourselves -We think we are just Ordinary ,Average but Sisters and brothers We have a fingerprint that no one has in life, there will be no other you ;Even Twin Brothers or Sisters differ, they don't have the same personality -Remember you are Original/nobody has your fingerprints, the same eyeballs ,sparkling eyes, the same laugh ,you are original and not by accident he created you God he made you the way he wanted you to be he gave you a special voice, smile, freckles ,hair curl ,and those things makes you different and who you are- you are special to him, and the world would have been incomplete without you ,I Praise you ,because Am fearfully and wonderfully made your works are wonderful I know that well **(Psalm;139;14)**When God he made you he threw away the mould ,when you say" Am Wonderful ,Attractive Healed, Rich, ,Am Vibrant ,Youth Freshness start coming on your way on the Inside your Spirit rise up -Yourself Image begins to improve, and you start seeing yourself Special**,** But all what you have to do first find yourself first ,before you find others, ask God to open your ,hears ,eyes and heart so you can see and hear and love what he says to you, Do yourself favour and read more about self -discovery and you will prosper in your life **(Proverb;19;8)**Whatever you say about your life will follow you .The Lord punishes the people for complaining "The Lord said to Moses and Aaron how much longer are these wicked people going to Complain against me? I have heard enough of these Complaints, now I give them this Answer I swear that as surely as I live I will do just what you have asked ,I the Lord I have Spoken, you will die and your corpse will be scattered across this wildness, because you have complained against me none of you 20Years of age will enter that land **(Numbers14;26;28)**Stop complaining and know who you are in Christ; you are approved by and pleasing to God**(Jeremiah 1;5)**God created you in his own image -you are his apple in his hand , you did not choose yourself he choose you and his pleased with you- you are his most precious creation not every chapter in the bible says God , approves you so long as you don't have any fault or as long as you don't have no mistake, no God approves you unconditionally ,no matter how many weakness you may think you have in life, no matter how many times you fall in your walk with God, you have to get up again and move on and held your head up high ,don't allow the enemy to bring strife into your life by deceiving you into thinking that you are not good enough for the plans of God ,stand strong in your thought knowing that you have been chosen and approved by God ;**Amen**

CONFIDENCE

CONFIDENCE, means -Belief/Rely on, Everyone needs -confidence in God , and -Self confidence and Self discovery ,is not Optional but is Mandatory when you don't have confidence we miss a lot of opportunities in life

CONFIDENCE IN GOD

,You need the confidence of your source **(God -no one can outweigh the source)** We rely on our achievements or affirmation of others but that is placing our confidence in ourselves not Christ , For the Lord will be your confidence and will keep your foot being caught**(Proverb 3;24;26)**,though an Army encamp against me my heart shall not fear ,though war arise against me, yet I will be confident **(Psalm 27;3)** In the fear of the Lord one has strong confidence and his children will have refuge**(Proverb 14;26)** And call on me in days of trouble ,I will deliver you and you shall glorify me **(Psalm 50;15)** Some trust in the chariots and some in horses but we trust in the name of Lord our God **(Psalm 20;7)Amen**
(1)You need confidence of your creator - not what you eat ,education , height , colour, Sovereign Lord I put my hope in you I have trusted in you since I was younger I have relied on you all my life you have protected me since the day I was born **(Psalm,71; 5;6)** Repent and confess your sins ,let his blood make you clean so you can come to him in confidence, Obey him regularly, when we fear God and obey him in everything , he will give us strong confidence **(Proverb,14;26-27)**And this is the confidence we have towards in him that if we ask anything according to his will he hears us , **(1 John 5;14)** But Jesus looked at them and said with man this is impossible but with God all things are possible **(Mathew 19;26; mark 9;23;Jer 32;27)** Let us then with confidence draw near to the throne of grace that we may receive mercy ,and find grace to help in time of need,**(Hebrews,4;16)**You then my Children be strengthened by the grace that is in Christ **(Philippians 2;14)** Blessed is the man who trust in the Lord ,whose trust is the Lord **(Jeremiah 17;7)** Do all things without grumbling or questioning , **Amen**
(2) You need confidence in the potential in you ,
(3) Confidence for Purpose for your creation,
(4) The resource you have,
(5) You need confidence   of your value , knowledge of your Ability **(what you have you are a package of yourself ,if you know your ability people cannot judge you ,you are the best of what God created you to be ,Birds are the best in flying, Fish best in swimming)**

(5) Knowledge of your Uniqueness **(you are original copy of yourself special made by God)**

(6) You need confidence of your **Predestination -knowing your future is Gods past -your future is already known by God -God has the result before the process it's done ,your future already set God don't go low but higher God don't get worst but better wonders he still does -(Jeremiah 29;11) Amen**

You need confidence in the word of God -that what God say will come to pass according to the scriptures ,meditate on his word every day ,meditation will help you to know God and his word is powerful , his word will help you to abide , in Christ and keep your eyes on the above **(Clossians,3;1-2)**Gods word builds confidence remember how God stood with people ,Abraham , raised Joseph from slave to a Prime Minister, ,Moses a stuttering faltering to a mighty leader of the Jewish nation , Joshua to conquer Canaan ,God changed Gideon a coward man to a bold warrior, God Gave Hannah children , Jesus apostles went from trembling fugitives to fearless to preachers once they were filled with the Holy Spirit , Jesus converted Paul from a persecutor of Christians to one of the greatest missionaries of the time **,Amen**

you need confidence to believe that God can do the impossible (Faith) read about the heroes of faith in the bible ,and other Christian books, ,imitate their confidence -and let them be your heroes - remember your former leaders ,who spoke Gods massage to you ,think back how on how they lived and died and imitate their faith -Jesus is the same yesterday , today ,and forever, **(Hebrews 13;7;8)** Visualise what God wants to give you if you have prayed about something and you are sure you want to receive it ,then visualise and believe this is already yours **(read ,Mark 11;24)** Remind yourself of Gods faithfulness ,how he answered prayers of others , ,the testimonies of others will show you the power of God and the power of supernatural divine intervention of God , and give you , confidence , in God and yourself, Welcome trials -trials will build your characters and holiness which in effect will build your faith, God desire to use you because he doesn't see the way we see ourselves especially in our worst days ,it is always good to remember ,that God has a purpose for each of us though you might be feeling useless **,Amen**

You need confidence of the **source of your protection- (God is the** source he knows where the hidden treasures are hidden, Divine Protection, In Economic turndown ,he will protect you, Because everyone will do what is right there will be peace and security for ever ,Gods people will be free from worries and their homes peaceful and secure **(Isaiah,32;17;18)**the reason why he has taken long is because he is preparing you , no one knows your future peoples opinion don't change you ,Do not lose your courage then , because it brings with it a great reward ,you need to be patient in order to do the will of God, and receive what he promised , for the bible says" Just a little while longer and he who is coming will come ,he will not delay , my righteous people however will believe and live ,but if any of them turns back I will not be pleased with him , we are not people who turn back and are lost instead we have faith and are saved **(Hebrews,10;35;39)**,Quietness is a sign of confidence , don't throw away your confidence, **Amen**

God has established your future have confidence , **Amen**

God protects your future have confidence in him **.Amen**

God is committed to your future have confidence in him **,Amen**

God works for your future have confidence in him **,Amen**

Have confidence in God" Job says" all the wealth you have lost will be nothing compared with what God will give you then ,look for the a moment at ancient wisdom consider the truths our ancestors learnt (**Job 8;7;8**) Israel the Lord who created you says" do not be afraid, I will save you, I have called you by name ,you are mine when you pass through ,deep waters, I will be with you ,your trouble will not overwhelm you ,when you pass through fire will not hurt you , for am the God your God the holy God of Israel who saves you ,I will give Egypt to set you free ,I will give up Seba , I will give up the whole nations to save your life because you are precious to me and because I love you and give honour **(Isaiah 43;1;5)**these are all Gods promises and Christians we are assured of him so we should have confidence in him, **Amen**

Trust your hopes not fears ,Don't be afraid of your future have confidence in God and yourself **,(In crisis- Romans,8;31-33)**,Commit to the Lord whatever you do and you will succeed **(Proverb 16;3;4)**You may make your plans but God directs your actions **(Proverb 16;9),Amen**

Today is the end of your worries, because the one who is in you is bigger than the one in the world , **Prayer -** I prayed to the Lord and he answered me he freed me from all my fears the oppressed look at him and are glad ,they will never be disappointed ,the helpless call to him and he answers ,he saves them from all their troubles **(Psalm 34;4;6)** -may he give you what you desire and make all your plans succeed ,then you will shout for Joy over your victory and celebrate your triumph by praising God **(Psalm,20;4;5)**Spend more time in prayers through prayers confidence is build and made more perfect , **Amen**

CONFIDENCE IN YOURSELF-

If you want to be successful you need to develop yourself confidence ,real self confidence comes from ,Self, awareness of your strength and weakness , acceptance of your body ,mind yourself esteem, belief in your skills, experience and ability ,Self confident you don't doubt, you need self confidence in everything you do ,Ministry , God, Work ,Marriage , self confident is the belief that the sun will rise tomorrow morning ,self confidence people influence others more easily , control their emotions and behaviours ,male are more confident than female ,

Self confidence -Makes you attractive- you live the life you dream ,people are attracted to self confidence people,

You became a person of influence- in your society , and people you associate with self confidence giving you more value of your capabilities which means more valuable ,It makes you to put your head up high since you have higher self esteem and proud of who you are **, Amen**

Gets you hired for desired Jobs and Clients,- If you want to steal a business you need express your self-confidence to prospective clients

for Jobs you need to do you need to express self confidence to the Interviewers

,Self confidence - helps you aim for things you only dream about. Amen,

Self confidence helps you to ask for only things you want -if you want to live a life you want you have to be confident , if you are not everyday miracles will pass you by -you won't ask for what you want because you don't have confidence , don't expect people to read your mind self confidence gives you strength and capabilities because you have more of the confidence in you -you feel powerful and stronger , you feel naturally growing stronger and more confident when encountering challenges rather than feeling weaker crippled and defeated by them **.Amen**

Self confidence helps you make right decision - you choose yourself people ,who lack confidence love to please others ,they don't choose for themselves, because they fear they may make a wrong choice**,** when you have self confidence the more energy and motivation to act the more confidence you are that you can achieve things you want to achieve like personal goals dreams ,vision the more motivated and energised you are to take action to achieve them **, Amen**

Self confidence gives you more happiness and enjoyment -,The more you are self confidence the more you are happier with yourself and as a result you enjoy life .**Amen**

Self Confidence gives you freedom from doubt - the more self confident you become - the more free you became of emotional torture , mental torture of doubting of yourself and questioning whether you are really valuable or capable of achieving things you want to achieve, Learn, handle, in this way you naturally replace fear , anxiety with greatness , **Amen**

Self confidence frees us from Social anxiety - the more secure you feel **in** yourself worth regardless of how others sees you the less concerned you are with what others, might think or might not think of you in social situations , you enjoy interaction with others the more happier you are and more confident in yourself , the more you are relaxed comfortable easy you are and this naturally puts you to feel ease with people around you

,others , trust you value you and welcome and co-operate with you   the overall result is better and more enjoyable social interaction ,**Amen**

Self Confidence -makes you productive- Self confidence gives you opportunity to achieve greater success because each of the above benefits contributes to your achievement in a short period which means you achieve your success and enjoy it in life ,you need to be productive and manage time wisely eliminate all the unnecessary activities ,you can't do this without self confidence without confidence you will spend time on things that don't help you to achieve your goals, if you are self confident ,you will be confident in your abilities then you are *Super productive, Amen*

Self confidence contributes to your health life -Because you have less fear ,anxiety - stress free , more peace of mind, and happiness all these gives you the benefit of enjoying the health benefits , including better sleep and health *,Amen*

 In life   never beg someone to be in your life if you Call, Text , Visit and still get ignored walk away, It's called **self respect** ,**Amen**

WHAT CAN BE DONE TO GAIN SELF CONFIDENCE?

Self confidence - be who you are, and say what is on your mind, because those who mind don't matter ,and those who matter don't mind ,create the image that you are beautiful and accomplished in whatever you do ,believe in yourself ,your voice is worth hearing, if you hear voice within you saying you cannot paint then by all means paint and the voice will be silenced „if you belief in yourself your life will take the best ,Visualise yourself as you want to be , to any one that ever told you, you are not good they are not better, we have to learn to be our own best friends because we fall to easily into traps of being our own worst enemies as soon as you trust yourself you will know how to live, with realization of one's potential and self confidence in one's ability one can build a better world, you have to love yourself to get things done in this world , We ask ourselves , who I, am to be rich brilliant, gorgeous ,talented, fabulous blessed ,gifted? actually who are you not to be? A man cannot be comfortable without his approval, see image of yourself that you are proud of , what a mind can conceive and believe can be achieved   create personal boundaries never be bullied into silence never allow yourself to be made a Victim accept no one definition of your life on the basis of your past , present , define yourself learn to say teach others to respect your boundaries , **Amen**

Be confident that things happen for a reason- there things you can change and those you cannot change - realise that if a door closed its because what was behind it wasn't meant for you, you can dream of job but you have to accept life is controlled by God and plans take yourself out of rejection .**Amen**

Action is a high road to self confidence ,and self esteem ,doubt kills dreams than failure ,ever will ,Amen

Be Confidence that change can be of good things -be a change you wish to see in the world change is inevitable in life and happens a lot more than we usually like it, but changes leads us to adopt, we can be scared of a change because its new and unknown but also healthy to mix things up and start new, we need to know that with our already self confidence we can handle the new experience and have confidence in others that they will happen along way, do one thing that scare you, put all excuses a side and remember this ,you are capable, do one thing that scare you every day "if you are insecure guess what ? the rest of the world too- do not estimate the competition and underestimate yourself ,you are better than you think the best way to overcome fear is to face it by doing something that scares you get out of your comfort zone, **Amen**

Be confident to know that It's going to be ok - the confidence to continue living when something horrific occurs ,this can be the hardest thing to gain building confidence after something terrible happen is very difficult but also very necessary ,you need to create confidence to start living again people can influence you to make different choices but its upon you and your life , you gain strength ,courage and confidence by every experience in which you really stop to look fear in face -you are able to say to yourself, I have lived through this horror I can take the next stage that comes along ,you must do things you think you cannot do set yourself to win ,the most beautiful thing you can wear is confidence, laugh at your problems everybody does concentrate on success and forget about failure , negative in our life, many people are discouraged about their abilities, because they set themselves that they goals are too difficult to achieve ,start by setting your small goals that you can win easily once you have laid a foundation on small things you can do big things make sure you keep a list of both small and large achievement ,**Amen,**

Affirm yourself - affirmation are positive and uplifting that we say to ourselves are affective if said loudly in prayers declarations if said loudly God hears our prayers and able to answer , we tend to believe whatever we tell ourselves if you hate your physical appearance , "Practice saying something appreciative about yourself next time when you look into the mirror Am wonderful made ,am gorgeous , beautiful highly blessed and favoured , anointed in Jesus name ,**Amen**

Shift to an equality mentality, -wanting to be someone else is a wastage of a person you are who you are , people with self esteem see others as better or more deserving than themselves instead of carrying this perception see yourself as equal to everyone they are not better than you or deserving than you make a mental shift to an equality mentality and you will see the results in you , **Amen**

Seek help from others-to gain self confidence - honestly is no light testimony of one's integrity to believe in others ,but the way you want others to believe in you having confidence in others has nothing to do with being dependent on them ,but rather knowing they are capable, life cannot be accomplished alone reach out to others ,and follow up with people and they will appreciate your kind words which will in return boost their confidence and yours ,fellowship with others ,don't neglect to meet together with other Christians this is Gods designed way to keep us encouraged **(read ,Hebrews,10;24;25)Help someone else -** helping enables you to forget yourself and to feel grateful for what we have ,it is also feels good when you are able to make a different for someone else , instead of focusing on your own weakness volunteer to ,mentor ,assist to teach another , you will see yourself confidence grow Automatically in the process **Amen**

Care for yourself -Self care is never selfish it is simply a good stewardship of the only gift I have the gift , I was put on earth to offer others , self confidence depends on a combination of good Social ,Physical health, emotional health ,Economic health, - It is hard to feel good about yourself if you hate your physical or constantly have low energy , **Amen**

This is the day the Lord has made let us rejoice and be glad in it **(Psalm 118;24) Amen**

SALVATION

Salvation- Is living by faith in the Son of God, that loved and died for us and Salvation is only to be found in Christ- It is by Gods grace that you have been saved through faith it is not a result of your own effort but God's gift so that no one can boast about it **(Ephesians 2;8;9)** *Salvation is a gift from God ,you don't pay for it, you can only receive it by faith, it's a gift from God* **, the word(God) we read is not interested in our colour but in our souls, then God said and now we will make the human beings they will be like us , and resemble us they will have power over the fish ,birds , and all animals domestic and will large and small (Genesis1;26)** God is not partial , peter began to speak "I now realise that it is true God treats everyone on the same basis those who worship him and do what is right are acceptable to him no matter what race they belong to **(Acts 10;34)** As it is written none is righteous no not one (Romans 3;10) people are not excluded from Gods saving grace on the basis of ethnic ,original, skin, colour, God does not want us to perish - the lord is not slow to do what he promised as some think instead he is patient with you because he does not want anyone to be destroyed but wants all to turn away from their sins **(2Peter,3;9)** Red ,Blue, White ,all are precious in the sight of God , Jesus loves the little children of the world

As time came for slavery to end its is also time men/women of Colour to refuse the language and the images that associates colour darkness(black) with evil and whiteness with good **(Blacks cursed -white blessed)** God wants us all to be saved salvation is for all ,Through salvation our Past has been forgiven, our Present is given a meaning, and the future is secured , saving us is the greatest and most concrete demonstration of God's love, the definitive display of his grace throughout time and eternity, is the work of God to show his glory ,That why he's not going to let it fail, Salvation comes through a cross and a crucified Christ -God proved his love on the cross ,when Christ hung and bleed and died -It was God saying to the world I love you-Salvation is Gods way of making us real people, Salvation is God's grace ,there is absolutely nothing that you can do to save yourself or earn Gods favour ,Saving us is the most greatest and most concrete demonstration of God's Love ,the definite display of his grace(*Which means free gratis for nothing*)throughout time and eternity- Salvation is a gift given ,not a bargain struck,-no one can be saved in virtue of what he can do, Everyone can be saved in virtue of what God can do**(Karl-Barth)**In Christ alone and his payment of the penalty for our sins upon the cross we find reconciliation to God and ultimate meaning and purpose -Jesus died on the cross so that me and you we should have life in its fullness and only through him- the cross solved our problems by first revealing our real problem, our universal pattern of Scape- goating and sacrificing others the cross exposes the scene of our crime**(Richard-Rohr),**Salvation of the world is in mans sufferings (Jesus)**Salvation** is to be found in him alone- In the world there is no one else whom God has given who can save us**(Acts4;14)**Gods word has power , You will also declare a thing and it will be established, for you so light will shine on you**(Job,22;28)** -his word create things ,brings life in eternity ,strength and victory over obstacles, That if you confess with your mouth ,that Jesus is lord and believe in your heart that God raised from the dead you will be saved for it is with your heart that you believe and you are justified and its is by your mouth that you confess and are saved**(Romans;10;9;10)** being born again of not corruptible seed but of incorruptible, by the word of God which liveth and abideth forever **(1Peter,1;23)**The first step in a Persons salvation is knowledge of their sin -Everyone had sinned and is far away from Gods saving presence but by the free gift of God's grace all are put right with him through -Jesus Christ who set them free God offered him so that by his blood he should become the means by which peoples sins are forgiven through their faith in him ,God did this to demonstrate that he is righteous in the past he was patient and overlooked peoples sins in order to demonstrate his righteousness in this way God shows himself is righteous and that he puts right everyone who believe in Jesus Christ**(Romans;3;23;26)**Salvation is not a reward for the righteous ,it is the gift for the guilty**(Steve-Lawson)**Salvation is the root and resurrection is the fruit**(T,D-Jakes)**What must I do to get saved? they answered believe in the lord Jesus Christ and you will be saved **(Acts;16;30;Saving-Faith and real converting grace will always produce some conformity to the image of Jesus)**and your family and we have to put our trust in the finished work of Christ whoever believes and is baptised will be saved whoever does not believe will be condemned believers will be given Powers to perform miracles they will drive out demons in my name they will speak in strange tongues if they pick up snakes or drink any poison they will not be harmed they will place their hands on the sick people who will get well **(Mark;16;16;18)**You were baptised into union with Christ and now you are clothed so to speak with the life of Christ himself **(Galatians;3;27)**What must I do to get saved, Paul did not say Work hard, pray Hard /longer be of more morals or give more and more ,no he said believe in the Lord Jesus and you will be saved, believing is the root of a tree, we call salvation behaving is the fruit that grows on it, I have complete confidence in the gospel, Its is Gods power to save all those who believe first the Jews and also the Gentiles **(Romans;1;16)**For the gospel reveals how God puts people right with himself, it is through faith from the beginning to the end ,the person who is put right with God through faith shall live**(Romans;1;17)**Amen For We do not need to do good works to be saved our good works are just an expression of love and gratitude to the one who saved us the bible says we should be holy and without blame (**Ephesians;1;4**) Even before the world was made God had already chosen us to be his through our union with Christ so that we would be holy without fault before him that may seem to be impossible standard the only that will/can happen is if God takes the righteousness of Christ and credit it to our account and he does God made him who had no sin to be a sin for us so that in him we might become righteous of God(**2Corinthians;5;21**)The moment you place Your trust in Christ God sees you as righteous ,and on that basis he accepts you and you are saved and you should be happy-Therefore he is able to save completely those who come to God through him(Christ)because he always lives and intercedes (Plead) for them (**Hebrews;7;25**)For God loved the world so much that he gave his only son so that everyone who believe in him may not die but have eternal life for God did not send his Son into the world to be his judge but to be his its saviour those who believe in the Son are not judged but those who do not believe have already been judged because they have not believed in Gods son only(**John,3;16;18**)Whoever believes in the Son has eternal life whoever disobey the Son will not have life, but will remain under Gods punishment(**John3;36**)-(**1**)Those who reject me publicity the Son of man will also reject them before the angels of God(**2**)Whoever who say a word against the Son of man can be forgiven but those who say evil things against the holy spirit will not be forgiven(**3**)I assure you those who declare publicity that they belong to me the Son of Man will do the same before the Angles of God there is no one like him (**Mathew;17;5-6**)In Christ is Gods beloved Son in him is well pleased hear him (**Psalm ;27;1**) No one can come to me unless the father who sent me draws him to me, I will raise him to life on the last day(**John3;44**)The lord is our light and salvation who shall we fear, the longer we serve him the greater he becomes ,it is not that he changes but we do (**Mathew;17;7**) Arise and don't be afraid ,he said to his disciples Christians we should arise and have confidence in him and our salvation never is too late welcome Jesus in your life ,Salvation appeals to the ***Rich, Poor, Intellectuals ,the emotional ,Jews and Gentiles*** It affects the past present and the future is the author of our life journey redemption from the past it is concerned about changing people's lives the massage of salvation has been sent to the Gentiles they will listen (**Acts;28;28**) Whatever happens in life we go on living do we? We take no vacation in characters building we cannot walk along the road and stay at the cross road at the same time we need salvation all along our lives(Life) it's not a choice we make from the start of the journey and we stop, It means going on day by day, coming on the side of the truth and justice ,when you receive Christ as your saviour your old nature is destroyed and you receive a new personality (**2Corithians;5;17;18**)Anyone who is joined to Christ is a new being, the old is gone the new has come all this is done by God who through Christ changed us from enemies into his friends, and gave us a

267

task of making others his friends*(soul winning)*When you get saved God look at/ on you and doesn't remember our/your past personality forget the past awful life, look forward for you are a new creature those who look at the past they are lacking understanding concerning the new creation, they have become in Jesus Christ ,when you give yourself to Christ as a sinner you receive **remission**-blotting out sins you receive forgiveness of sins through confession those who conceal their sins don't prosper but those who confess and renounce them find mercy **(Proverb;28;13)**God is just and faithful and just to forgive and cleanse us from all our sins, our God does not remember our sins and iniquities and we are reconciled to him the moment we recognise our sins while we were his enemies Christ reconciled us to God **(2Corinthians;5;19)**at one time you were far away from God and were his enemies because of the evil things you did and thoughts but now by means of the physical death of his son God made you his friend in order to bring you holy pure and faultless into his presence **(Colossians;1;21;22)**To be saved you must believe in the Lord Jesus Christ no one can enter the kingdom of God without being born again, (how can a man be born again? no one can enter into his mother's womb and be born again Jesus replied am telling you the truth no one can enter the kingdom of God without being born of Water and the Spirit a person is born again physically of human parents but born spiritually by the Spirit **(John;3;5;Jesus and Nicodumus question about being saved)Accepting Jesus Christ- you must put your life in his hands God is not concerned with your words as is with your altitudes say "Lord Jesus am sorry that I have been going on my way thank you for paying the price of myself centeredness by dying on the cross please come and take the first place in my life make me a kind of person you want me Amen** Jesus will come and take a place into your life as he promised listen am standing and knocking at your door if you hear my voice and open, I will come in and we eat together with you **(Revelation 3;20)**You have shown me the path that leads to life and your presence will fill me with joy **(Acts;2;28)**hear what God says when time came for me to show you favour I heard you when the day arrived for me to save you I helped you listen this is the hour to receive Gods massage today is the day to be save**(2Corinthians;6;2)**For sin pays its wages ,but Gods free gift is eternal life in union with Jesus Christ our God **(Romans;6;23)**For whoever wants to save their own life ,they will lose it, but whoever looses their life for my sake will save it, Will people gain anything if they win ,the whole world but are themselves lost or defeated of course not, if people are ashamed of me and of my teachings then the Son of man will be ashamed of them ,when he comes in his Glory and in the Glory of the Father and of the Holy angels**(Luke;9;24;27)**Those who do not take up their cross and follow in my steps are not fit to be my disciples ,those who try to gain their own life will lose it ,but those who lose their life for my sake will gain it, **(Mathew;10;38)**Whoever tries to save his life will lose it whoever loses his life for me will save it**(Luke,17;33)**When we accept Jesus Christ we know God forgiveness and friendship and when we put our faith in him he gives us the right to become the children of God we are adopted by God**(John;1;12)**God has already decided that through Jesus Christ he would make us his sons and daughters this was his pleasure and purpose let us praise God for his glorious grace for the free gift he gave us in his dear Son for by the blood we are set free that is our sins are forgiven how great is the grace of God**(Ephesians;1;5-7)**To redeem them that were under the law that we might receive the adaptation of sons **(Galatians;4;5)**When Jesus disciple asked him who can be saved Jesus answered this is impossible for human beings but for god everything is possible Those who follow him can be sure that when the son of man sit in his glorious throne in the new age then you the twelve followers of mine will sit on the throne to rule the twelve tribes of Israel and everyone who has left his house brothers sisters father children field**(Riches)**for my sake will receive a hundred times more and will be given eternal life but many now who are first will be last and many who are last will be first**(Mathew19;16;30)**In the world We are living in today there false believers, those who have not known the truth and they will be expecting to go to heaven and will be denied entrance the best way to avoid being left out is to make sure you have truly put your trust in Christ alone for salvation when you have repented and put your faith in that will lead to a change in your life follow the Lord and educate yourself with his word going to Church does not make you a Christian anymore or does going to the garage make you a car**(J-Peter)** many Christians think going to church they will be granted heaven which is false, many Christians follow false interpretation of bible, by their false preachers instead of them doing a favour for themselves and read the word of God and follow their minds it's good to be feed but you have to take responsibility to see you feed yourself with the word of God -People are still having Sex outside marriage, and doing many Evil things ,they are just Sunday service goers and they don't care about Christ, but when they give their lives to Christ things won't be the same as they believe and trust in God, A good Christians know Jesus is the way and the truth and life no one comes to the father except through me **(John;14;6)**Jesus replies anyone who loves me will obey my teachings, my father will love them ,and we will come to them and make our home with them ,whoever does not love me does not keep my words and the word that you her is not mine but the father who sent me **(John 14;23-24)**We know that we have come to know him if we keep his commands **(1John 2;3)** <u>**WE HAVE A LESSON TO LEARN FROM THE BOOK OF**</u>(MATHEW 25;6)The story of the **Five wise girls** and the **Five foolish girls** at midnight a cry was heard /rang out here is the bridegroom come out to meet him a requirement for being allowed to participate in the a wedding those days was that your Lamp had to be burning but when the bride groom showed up five of these girls were out of oil so they said to the other Five give us some of your oil (**Mathew;25;8**) but hey said what is left will not be enough for you and us(**Mathew;25;9**)while they went to town to buy oil the wedding started and they were looked out the parable teach us four important things(**I)The foolishness of depending on others**- your sister/brother mother father may have been Christians but they won't get you to heaven you must accept Jesus as your personal saviour s you(**2)The futility of Last minute preparation** while they went to buy oil the bridegroom came(**Mathew;25;10**)Remember here Jesus is teaching here about the kind of people who will be living when he returns so here is a question are you putting Salvation off until you are old ? What if you don't live longer(**3)The finality of Judgement**- and the door was shut afterwards the other virgins came also saying Lord -lord open to us but he answered and said assuredly I say to you I do not know you (**Mathew 25;10-12)(4)Morals** -they were virgins yet they were shut out your character and good works won't get you to heaven, by grace are ye saved through faith (**Ephesians;2;8**) are you ready to meet the lord if not put your faith in him today dear friend(**Mathew;25;5**)The bridegroom took a long time in coming and they all become drowsy and feel asleep what else can we learn from these ten virgins (**1)The midnight** crowd while the bridegroom was delayed they all slumbered and slept who slept? The wise and foolish the world as well as the church Paul warns it's high time to wake up out of sleep for now our salvation is near than when we first believed (**Romans13;11;13**)The night is nearly over day is almost here, let us stop doing things that belongs to night /dark ,let us conduct ourselves properly as people who live in the light of day ,stop drunkenness, no immorality or indecency no fighting or jealously ,but take up the weapon of the lord Jesus Christ and stop paying attention to your sinful nature and satisfying its desire, we are in the mortal combat with the enemy who observe no truce /no peace treaties' –the Titanic disregarded five warnings before it hit the iceberg the naval yard at pearl harbour disregarded six warnings before it was attacked Christ is not coming back for the religious but for the redeemed not for the refined but for the regenerated not the respectable but the righteous (**2)**the midnight crisis the urgent massage of this parable is some will have enough to get to them into a wedding others will not so what should we do? Watch therefore and pray always that ye may be accountable worth to escape all these things that shall come to pass and stand before the son of man (**Luke;21;36) (3)** The midnight cry at night a cry was heard behold the bridegroom is coming go out to meet him (**Mathew; 25; 6**) all around us the voice of fear sound where can we go and look for hope, Bankers? Industry, Academics /government? No our hope can only be found in these words looking for the blessed hope and glorious appearing of our great God and saviour Jesus Christ(**Titus2;13**)Do your best to help Zenas the lawyer and Apollo's to get started on their travel and see to it that they have everything they need our People must learn to spend time doing good things in order to provide for real need s they should not live useless lives and that what we should do to get saved not only for ourselves but to win souls too see the good thing in salvation When we believe in the Lord Jesus Christ as your personal saviour you are blessed the blessing are yours, instantly regardless of your knowledge about them new converted believers will not be aware of them ,from the beginning but when they gain Spiritually maturity and growth in the word of God as they grow they become aware of them ,and start experiencing the joy and happiness of knowing Jesus Christ as their saviour, False converts will not enter heaven they will be denied ,the Bible says "not everyone who says to me lord will enter the kingdom of heaven, but the one who does the will of my father who is in heaven on that day many will say to me Lord did we not prophesy in your name and cast out demons in your names, and do mighty works in your name? and then I will declare to them I never knew you depart from me you, workers of lawlessness **(Mathew;7;21;23)**Or do you not know the unrighteous will not inherit the kingdom of God? do not be deceived neither the Sexually ,Immoral nor idolaters nor adulterers nor men who Practice homosexuality, nor thieves nor ,the greed nor the drunkards nor revilers nor swindlers will inherit the kingdom of God **(1Corinthians;6;9;10 ;Revelation;22;15)**There is no Salvation in becoming adapted to a world which is crazy**(Henry Miller)**The Salvation of the world lies in the human heart in the human Power to reflect ,in human meekness and human responsibility**(Vaclav Havel)**Salvation cannot be bought with the currency of obedience ,It is purchased by the blood of the Son of God **(Dieter-F-Uchtdorf)**Work out your own salvation, do not depend on others ,Salvation includes an ongoing transformation in life , salvation is not something God gives you that is going to bless you after you die, it is having the presence of the Lord now **(John G Lake);** If you never made Jesus Christ the Lord of your life, I encourage you to receive this free gift ,let him fill you with his Eternal peace ,Joy so that you can live free , pray father I came to you today giving you all that I am, thank you for the gift of Salvation through your son Jesus I believe he died and rose for me ,I invite you to be the Lord of every my area of my life in Jesus name; **Amen,!**

WHEN YOU ACCEPT JESUS CHRIST AS YOUR PERSONAL SAVIOUR

(1)You must accept Jesus Christ as your personal saviour and agree that one time you had fallen short of Gods glory(2)Trust that God forgives sins and completely does not remember them -Jesus has already paid the price for you/me through salvation our Past has been Forgiven our Present is given a meaning and the Future is secured**(3)**Believe in your heart that Jesus came for you and Loves you no matter what you have done in the Past**(4)**You choose to follow Jesus and use his name in everything you want that is good for the kingdom of God; **Amen**

THE BENEFITS OF BEING SAVED AND FOLLOWING JESUS CHRIST-

When you make Jesus the lord of your life many things change in life immediately and other things are worked out later, you have to work out your salvation by obeying the word of God, and surrendering every area of your life , to Christ do the right things even when its difficult ,resist temptation , and remember its God at work in you to give you the power to work out your salvation he empowers you to overcome all the obstacles he gives you a good attitude fighting on your behalf until you win victory ,but you have to do your best as well ,So then dear friend as you always obeyed me when I was with you it is even more important that you obey me now while am away from you keep on working with fear and trembling to complete your salvation because God is always at work in you to make you willing and able to obey his own purpose , do everything without complaining or arguing so that you may be innocent and pure as Gods perfect children who lived in a world of corrupt and sinful people ,you must shine among them like stars lightning up the sky as you offer the massage of life ,if you do so I shall have a reason to be proud of the day of Christ because it show that all my effort and work have not been wasted **(Philippians 2;12-16)** When you get saved you get to know your true identity your true self in Christ of being who you are and what God say about you -Some people say you are going the wrong way- when yet it is the right way to the truth and true life of you -And never apologize for what you know you are being real in Christ ,be who you are ,and say what you want for those who mind don't matter and those who matter don't mind, have Faith in yourself do not go around looking for a Successful personality and duplicate your personality -If you don't like my words don't listen, if you don't like my appearance don't look, if you don't like my actions turn your head it is as simple as that ,Whenever you go -go with all your heart do your thing and never care if they like it , ride the energy of your own Spirit- if you cannot be a poet be a Poem**(David Carradine)**You were born an original don't die a copy ,-Never be bullied into silence ,never allow yourself to be made a victim ,accept no one definition of your life let God define you accept what you are and this is the first step in becoming better than you are,*(1)***We have access to God's grace** -for by his grace are ye saved through faith and not by of yourselves it is the gift of God for through him we both have access by one spirit unto the father **(Ephesians;2;18)(2)We are adopted by God (Ephesians;1;5) (3)We get an inheritance** -in whom also we have obtained an inheritance being predestinated according to the purpose of him who worketh all things after the counsel of his own will **(Ephesians1;11)(4)We get heavenly citizenship** -and the lord shall deliver me from every evil work and will preserve me unto his heavenly kingdom to whom glory be given forever and ever**(2Timonthy;4;18)We are saved** -elect according to the fore knowledge of god the father through sanctification of the spirit unto obedience and sprinkling of the blood of Jesus Christ grace unto you and peace be multiplied **(1Peter;1;2)(5)You become a servant-** but now being made free from sin and become servants to god ye have your fruit unto holiness and the end everlasting life**(Romans-6;22)(6) We are heirs of God-** joint heirs with Christ and if children then heirs of God and joint heirs with Christ if so be that we suffer with him that we may be also glorified together**(Romans;8;17)**And if ye be Christ then ye Abraham seed and heir according to the promise**(Galatians;3;29)-(7)We become new creatures** -therefore if any man be in Christ, he is a new creature old things are passed away, behold all things are become new**(2Corithians 5;17)**for in Christ Jesus neither in circumcision availeth anything nor uncircumcission but anew creation **(Galatians';6;15)(8)We are reconciled to God** -For if we were enemies we were reconciled to God by the death of his son ,much more being reconciled we shall be saved by his life **(Romans 5;10)(9)We become priests and hath made us kings and priest** unto God and his father to him be glory and dominion forever and ever **(Revelation1;6)(10)We are sanctified** -and such were some of you but ye are washed, but ye are sanctified, but ye are justified in the name of the lord Jesus and by the spirit of our God **(1Corithians;6;11)(11)we are baptised unto the body-of Christ** -in the same way all of us whether Jews or Gentiles whether slaves or free have been baptised into the one body by the same spirit and we have all been given the one spirit to drink**(2Corithians;12;13)We are buried with him** -therefore we are buried with him by baptism into death that like as Christ was raised up from the dead by the glory of the father even so we also should walk in newness life **(Romans 6;4)We have put on Christ-**for as many of you as have been baptised into Christ have put on Christ**(Galatians;3;27)We have eternal life-**and I give unto them eternal life and they shall never perish neither shall any man pluck them out of my hand**(John;10;28)We have peace with God** -Peace I leave with you my peace, I give unto you let your heart be troubled neither let it not be afraid **(John;14;27)We are justified in Gods sight** -now that we have been put right with God through faith we have peace with God through our lord Jesus Christ **We become a friend of God** - I do not call you servants anymore (Longer)because servants do not know what their masters is doing instead

,I call you friends because ,I have told you everything I have heard from the father ,I have made known unto you **(John;15;15)We get in the lamb book of life -**but nothing is impure will enter the city anyone who does shameful things or tells lies only those whose names are written in the lamb book of the living will enter the city **(Revelations;21;27)We receive imputed righteousness even as David-**this is what David meant when he spoke of the happiness of the person whom god accepts as righteous apart from anything that a person does happy are those whose wrongs are forgiven whose sins are pardoned happy is the person whose sin the lord will not keep account of **(Romans;4;8)Our names are written in the book of heavens-**But don't be glad because the evil spirit obey you, rather be glad because your name are written in heaven**(Luke;10;20)We are given a blessed hope of Christ returning -**as we wait for the blessed day we hope for when the glory of our great God and saviour Jesus Christ will appear**(Titus;2;13)We are seated in the heavenly places** In union with Christ Jesus has raised us up with him to rule with him in heavenly world **(Ephesians;2;6) we have fellowship with trinity(1John;1;3)**That which we have seen and declare we unto you, that ye also may have fellowship with us truly our fellowship is with the father and with his son Jesus Christ **(Philippians;2;1)** if there be therefore any consolation in Christ, if any comfort of love, if any fellowship of the spirit, if any bowels and mercies **We have mansions in heaven** (Rooms)there many rooms in my Father's house and am going to prepare a place for you I would not tell you this if it were not so**(John;14;2)**but to enter into those rooms you have to obey the fathers commands **We are born again with a spiritual rebirth -**Jesus answered unto and said unto him verily verily I say unto the except a man be born again he cannot see the kingdom Nicodemus saith unto him how can a man be born again when is old he can enter the second time into his mother's womb and be born again Jesus answered verily verily I say unto thee except a man can be born again of water and of the spirit he cannot enter the kingdom of God that which is born of the flesh and that which is born of the spirit is spirit**(John;3;36)We receive anointing-**but as for you Christ has poured out his spirit on you as long as his spirit remain in you do not need anyone to teach you for the spirit teaches you about everything and what he teaches is true not false obey the spirit teachings then and remain in union with Christ**(1John;2;27)Am anointed by God -** It is God himself who makes us together with you sure of our life in union with Christ it is God himself who has set us apart**(2Corinthians;1;21)The holy spirit will live with us now and forever-**and I will pray the father and he shall give you another comforter that he may abide with you forever even the spirit of truth whom the world cannot receive because it seethe him not neither knoweth him, but ye know him for he dwelleth with you and shall be in you **(John 14;16)We have been sealed by the holy spirit-unto the day of redemption -**and do not make Gods holy spirit sad for the spirit is God mark of ownership on you a guarantee that the day will come when God will set you free**(Ephesians;4;30)Our body becomes the temple of the holy Ghost-**Don't you know your body is the temple of the holy spirit who lives in you and who was given to you by God you do not belong to yourself but God**(1Corinthians;6;19)**your body was bought with a price **We are forever forgiven-**and he said unto her thy sins are forgiven **(Luke;7;48)**I write unto you little children because your sins are forgiven you for his names sake **(1John;2;12)We are redeemed -** they sang a new song you are worthy to take the scroll and to break open its seal for you were killed and but your sacrificial death you bought for God people from every tribe language nation and race**(Revelation 5;9)We dwell in the spirit -**but you do not live as your human nature tells you to instead you live as the spirit tells you **(1Corinthians;3; 16$Romans; 8;9;10)** If in faith God spirit lives in you, whoever does not have the spirit of Christ does not belong to him, but if Christ lives in you the spirit is life for you because you have been put right with God, even though your bodies are going to die, because of the sin of Adam **We have advocates with Christ -**my little children these things write unto you that ye sin not and if any man sin we have an advocate with the father Jesus Christ the righteous **(1John;2;1) We have the possibility to have victory over sin-**sin must not be your master for you do not live under the law but under Gods grace**(Romans; 6;14)We become Christ Ambassadors -**there we are then speaking for Christ as though God himself were making his appeal through us we plead on Christ behalf let God change you from enemies into friends **(2Corinthians 5;20)We are blessed with spiritual blessing -**let us give thanks to the God and father of our lord Jesus Christ for in union with Christ he has blessed us by giving us every spiritual blessing in the heavenly world**(Ephesians;1;3)Our needs are supplied by God -**but my God shall supply all your needs according to his riches in glory by Christ Jesus**(Philippians;4;19)We are given inner strength to accomplish necessary things -**I have the strength to face all the conditions by the power that Christ gives me**(Philippians;4;13)A good work has been done in us -**and so am sure that god who began his good work in you will carry it on until it is finished on the day of Christ**(Philippians;1;6)The lord becomes our helper instead of our judge-**Let us be bold then and say the lord is my helper I will not be afraid what can anyone do to me **We get abundance grace-**You know the grace of our lord Jesus Christ rich as he was he made himself poor for your sake in order to make you rich by means of his poverty**(2Corithians;9;8)We receive eternal love -**for nothing Am certain that nothing can separate us from his love neither death or life neither the angels nor the heavenly rulers or powers neither the present nor the future neither the world above neither the world below there is nothing in all creation that will ever be able to separate us from the love of god which is ours through Christ Jesus our lord and saviour**(Romans,8;38;39)Everything that happens to us is of our own good** -And we all know that all things work together for good to them that love God to them who are called according to his purpose(**Romans; 8;28)God promises his faithfulness to us** -If we are not faithful he remain faithful to us because he cannot be false to himself**(2Timothy,2;13)We are promised to be able to resist temptations** -Every test that you have experienced is the kind that normally comes to people but god keeps his promise and he will not allow you to be tasted beyond your power to remain firm at the time you are put to the test he will give you the strength to endure it and so provide you with a way out**(1Corinthians ;10;13)We are made saints to the church of God** -which is in Corinth to all who are called to be Gods holy people who belong to him in union with Christ Jesus together with all people everywhere who worship our lord Jesus Christ their lord is ours**(1Corinthians1;2)Am a Saint now(Set apart for God)**-receive her in the lords name as Gods people should and give her any help she may need from you for she herself has been a good friend to many people and also to me**(Romans;16;2)Our hearts are un blameable** -in this way he will strength you and you will be perfect in the presence of our lord God and the father when our Lord Jesus Christ comes with all who belong to him **(1Thessolonian;3;13)We have been delivered from the power of darkness** -may be strong with all the strength which comes from his glorious power ,so that you may be able to endure everything with patience and with joy ,give thanks to the father who has made you fit to have your share of what God has reserved for his people in the kingdom of light ,he rescued us from the power of darkness and brought us safe unto the kingdom of his dear son, by whom we are set free that our sins are forgiven**(Colossians,1;12;14)Am called out of darkness** -But you are the chosen race the kings and the priests the holy nation Gods own people chosen to proclaim the wonderful act of God who called you out of darkness into his marvellous light **(1Peter2;9)We receive the power of a sound mind** -For the spirit that God has given us does not make us timid instead his spirit fill us with power love and self -control we no longer have the spirit of fear **(2Timothy;1;7)We are joined in the lord (Saved)**- But he who joins himself to the lord becomes spiritually one with him **(1Corinthians;6;17) Am a personal witness of and the lord Jesus Christ** -but when the holy spirit comes upon you will be filled with the power and you will be witness for me in Jerusalem in all Judea and Samaria and to the ends of the earth **(Acts ;1;8) Am complete in Christ and have need of nothing save him** -And you have been given full life in union with him he is supreme over every spiritual rulers and authority **(Colossian;2;10)For am Gods building** -for we are partners working together for God and you are Gods field **(1Corinthians;3;9)Am a labourer with God himself worker with God** - In our work together with

God then we beg you who have received Gods grace not to let it be wasted **(2Corinthians;6;1) Am dead but my life hid in Jesus Christ** -For you have died and your life is hidden with Christ in God **(Colossians;3;3) Am Peculiar** -he gave himself for us to rescue us from all wickedness and to make us pure people who belong to him alone and are eager to do good**(Titus;2;14) Am Gods workmanship-**God made us what we are and in our union with Christ Jesus he has created us for a life of good deeds which he has already prepared for us to do **(Ephesians 2;10)Am a branch of the true vine and my father is the husbandman(Gardener)**He breaks off every branch in me that does not bear fruits and he prunes every branch that does not bear fruits so that it will be clean and bear more fruits you have now been made clean already by the teachings I have given you Abide in me and I in you as the branch cannot bear fruits of itself except it abide in the vine no more can ye except ye abide in me remain united in me and I will remain united in you a branch cannot bear fruits by itself it can only do so only if it remains in the vine in the same way you cannot bear fruits unless you remain in me am the vine and you are the branches those who remain in me and I remain in them will bear much fruits for you cannot do nothing without me**(John15;1;5)**Be a good Christian who does not let his/her lips and lives preach two different message and your powerful testimony is how you treat others in life ,those who are not true saved Christians Sin on purpose saying I will just repent later even though we are all Sinners we don't Just sin wilfully and deliberately, Whoever say I know him but does not do what he commands is a lair and the truth is not in that person**(John;2;4)**those who live in Christ don't go on Sinning those who go on sinning haven't seen Christ or Known Christ**(1John;3;6)**The person who practice sin belongs to the Evil, one because the devil has been sinning from the beginning ,the reason that the son of God was revealed was to destroy what the Devil has been doing, no one has been born from God practices sin, because Gods seed abides in him indeed he cannot go on sinning because he has been born from God this is how Gods children and the devil Children are distinguished, Gods people honour him with their hearts, not lips and are not far from him, but those who are not of God these people honour God with their lips ,but their hearts are far from God**(Mathew;15;8)**and so these people say they are mine they honour me with their lips ,but their hears far from me, and their worship of me is nothing but manmade rules, learned by rote **(Isaiah;29;13)**If a person thinks that he is righteous but cannot control his tongue he is fooling himself, that persons religion is worthless **(James;1;26)**No person fails to practice righteousness and to love his brother is from God **(1John;3;8;10)** Those who say that they are in light but hate other believers are still in dark**(John;2;9)**They claim to know God but they deny him by what they do, they are detestable disobedience and unfit to do anything good **(Titus;1;16)**Dear friend do not imitate what is, Evil but what is good anyone who does what is evil has not seen God(**3John;1;11**)Why do you call me lord but don't do what I tell you(**Luke;6;46**) knowing yourself makes you to do your things on your own terms ,and get what you came here for **(Oliver-James)**Don't take anything from anyone and never allow them take me alive; I have always loved the idea of not being what people expect me to be yet only my God know who I am ,allow God to fashion you, decide what you are, express and lead you the way to dress and the way to live, don't be into trends and competitions,, Dear Christian do yourself a favour and learn all you can then remember what you learn and you will Prosper (**Proverb;19;8**) In all your area of relationship with God and Christianity ;**Amen**

BELIEVER'S BOOK
SOUL WINNING

SOUL WINNING--Is bringing back those who were lost from God back to God through Salvation, the lost are those who are doing their human desire instead of Obeying Gods law and following Jesus as their Saviour, doing whatever suits them like worshipping other gods, killing, stealing, and robbery committing adultery, gossiping, drunkenness, The lord says wine both old and new is robbing my people of their senses they ask for revelation from a piece of wood! a stick tells them what they want to know they have left me as the woman who becomes a prostitute they have given themselves to other gods(**Hosea;4;11;12**)Its only through Christ we can be saved, In the past we were spiritually dead because of the sin(**Ephesians;2;1;3**)doing our own desires even today people are doing their own desire and need to be saved, but God mercy is abundant and his love is great that while we were spiritually dead in disobedience at that time you followed the world evil way you obeyed the rulers of the spiritual powers in the space the ,spirits who now controls the people who disobeyed God actually all of us we were like them and lived according to their desires doing whatever suited the wishes of our own bodies and minds in our natural conditions we like everyone else were designated to suffer Gods anger he brought us to life with Christ (**Ephesians;2;4;5**)By Gods grace by faith not as the result of your faith (**Ephesians;2;8**)Jesus was a soul winner who brought many back who were lost(**Luke;19;9;10**)Salvation has come to this house to this house today for this man also is a descendant of Abraham the son of man came to seek and save the lost(**Jesus and Zacchaeus**)Through his son God rescued us from the power of Darkness and brought us safe into the kingdom of his dear son(**Collossians;1;13**)God cleanses us but if we live in the light then we have fellowship with one another and the blood of his son purifies us from every sin(**1John;1;7**)To win soul for Christ you have to be a believer and have faith -What is impossible to man is possible to God(**Luke;18;27**)Because every child of God is able to defeat the world and we win the victory over the world by means of our faith who can defeat the world only the person who believes Jesus is the son of God (**IJohn5;4;5**)I have the strength to face all the conditions by the power that Christ gives me(**Philippians;4;13**)Tell the truth Jesus and God are one the father and I are one(**John10;30**)Soul winner shouldn't fear-**No Spirit of fear**- for the spirit that God has given us does not make us timid instead his spirit fills us with power love and self -control, When approaching people God said do not be afraid am with you your god let nothing terrify you I will make you strong and help you I will protect you and save you(**Isaiah ;41;10**)Soul winner should respect each other and trust each other and enjoy each other stay united people when doing the work of God

279

if you can't win it hurts when you win its good if you can't win let someone a head of you win when knocked down get up never let defeat win you it's great to see God using us; **Amen**

WHY IS IT IMPORTANT TO WIN SOULS / GOOD EFFECT

it's a command from God he said(Jesus)to them "go throughout the whole world and preach to the gospel to the whole human race whoever believes and be baptised will be saved whoever does not believe will be condemned(**Mark16;15;16;Luke;5;9;10**)soul winning is a chief business he and all others with him were all amazed at the large number of the fish had caught the same was true Simon (Partners)James and John the son of Zebedee Jesus said to Simon don't be afraid from now you will be catching people soul winning is a chief business to every believers and ministry(**Luke5;9;10**)Jesus was a soul winner and we are expected to follow his steps the son of man came to seek and save the lost(**Luke 19;10**)Those you win for Jesus will thank you in heaven and love you always when people get saved ,**Winning Souls Glorifies Jesus**-righteousness gives life but violence takes it away(**Proverb;11;30**)to win souls it good that we make people aware of the goodness of Christ that he saves and all the benefits of salvation belongs to them (**Luke;16;19;31 ;Mark;42;48**)When we win souls the love of Christ compels us, anyone who is joined to Christ is a new being, the old is gone the new has come so the people we win becomes new creature/creation forgiven their sins and people are being blessed(**2Corinthians 5;17**)**We must win soul because of the judgement before us on the judgement day**- for all us must appear before Christ to be judged by him we will each receive what we deserve according to what we have done good /bad in our bodily life (Faithfully serving God;**2corinthians;5;10**)**We must win souls because of hell**-hell is hot heaven is sweet we know what it means to fear God and so we try to pursue others God knows us completely and I hope that in your heart you know me as well (**2Corithians ;5;11**)**Soul winning is God given ministry**- (mission)all this is done by God who through Christ changed us from enemies into his friends and gave us a task (Mission) of making others his friends also this task is to bring God and you together(**2Corithians ;5;18**)**Winning souls we become ambassadors of Christ**-here we are then speaking for Christ as though God himself were making his appeal through us we plead on Christ behalf let God change you from enemies to friends(**2Corithians;5;20**)**Soul winners will shine as stars forever(Daniel;12;3)**-The wise leaders will shine with all the brightness of the sky and those who have taught many people to do what is right will shine like the stars forever(**The time of the end**)What will you be remember in the world for ? by leading others to Christ as every Christians needs to leave an impact in the world where God sent him and gifted him -Soul winners are the best Christians -Jesus said to them come with me and I will teach you how to catch people **(Jesus calls the four fishermen Simon peter Andrew James and John)** When you win souls Christ will say well done Faithful servant the Master said to his faithful servant well-done you have been faithful in managing small amount so I will put you in large amounts come on and share my happiness**(Parable of the Three servants)**God gives greater opportunity for services rendered in this life and next to those who are faithful in little things, **When you do soul winning you Automatically became a Labour of Christ** -there is great need but few labours as he saw the crowd his heart was filled with pity for them because they were worried and helpless like sheep's without shepherd so he said to his disciples the harvest is large but there a few workers to gather it in pray to the owner of the harvest that he will send out workers to gather in his harvest **(Mathew;9;36;38) We need to win souls so that we avoid a bloody hand** -mortal man he said am making you a watchman for the nations of Israel you will pass on to them the massage I give to you if I announce that an evil person is going to die but you do not warn him to change his ways so that he can save his life he will die still a sinner and I will hold you responsible for his death**(Ezekiel;3;17;18)We should do soul winning because we have limited time to do this work**- as long as day we must keep on doing the work of him who sent me night is coming when no one can work and we cannot win souls**(John;9;4**You don't know what tomorrow holds its time to do it today, **Soul winning will make you prosper**- you will be surprised do your sowing in the morning and the evening too you never know when it will grow well you never know whether it will all grow well or weather one sowing will do better than others**(Ecclesiates;11;6)Soul winning saves any country from sin ,judgement and bad government**- I looked for someone who could build a wall who could stand in the place where the walls have crumbled and defend the land when my anger is about to destroy it but I couldn't find no-one so I will turn my anger loose on them and a like fire I will destroy them for what they have done the sovereign Lord has spoken **(Ezekeil-22;30)If we don't do soul winning we likely to perish without**-a vision of soul winning and disciple winning **Soul winners are wiser know the better things and have better things have less fear**- don't be afraid when Preaching the gospel or labouring to catch souls God has assure you those who want to kill your body they cannot touch your soul fear only God who can kill the body and soul **(Mathew;10;28)Give the gospel and shall be given to you by God** -Give to others and God will give to you indeed in full measure a generous helping poured into your hands all that you can hold the measure you use to others is the one God will use for you **(Luke;6;38-)Amen** look after God interest and God will look into your interest- Soul winning is a foundation of building more churches around the globe (world) Soul winning hurts Satan and make heavens rejoice(**Luke;15;3;7**)**Soul winning it's a privilege**-that angels don't have (**Acts 10;3;8**) **If we don't win souls or do the work of Christ (soul winning)the cult will win them for Satan,** I have no right to boast because I preach the gospel after all am under orders to do so and how terrible it would be for me if I do not preach the gospel if I did my work as a master of free choice then I could expect to be paid but I do it as a matter of duty because God has entrusted me with this task what pay do I get then? It is the privilege of preaching the good news without charging for it without claiming my right in my work for the gospel(**1corinthians;9;16;20**)Am a free man nobody slave but I make myself everybody slave in order to win as many people as possible The servant who know what his master wants of him to do but does not get himself ready to do it will be punished with a heavy whipping(**Luke;12;47**)**Soul winning is part of leisure time and exciting-** Soul winning was done in the past by Christians we have to continue with the journey Soul winning is one of the best way to make friends it increases your love for people brings unity and happiness between the soul winners and souls Soul winning can help you to bring the lost like drunkard prostitute ministers to Christ those who don't know Christ and why he came in the world and died on the cross When we win souls we become grateful to God Developing countries are hungry for the gospel we should open doors to Africa-Asia -china if you don't give attention to those continents and souls other religions will take over instead of Christianity ,**Amen**

THE BAD SIDE/EFFECT OF NOT WINNING SOULS FOR CHRIST

If we do not win soul sits disobeying God-Jesus drew near and said to them I have been given authority in heaven and on earth go then to all nations everywhere and make disciples baptise them in the name of the father and the holy spirit and teach them to obey everything I have commanded you and I will be with you always to the end of the age (**Mathew;28;18;20**)If we don't win souls we are disobeying Jesus the disciples went and preached everywhere and the lord worked with them and proved that the teaching was true by the miracles that were perfumed (**Mark ;16;20**)if you don't win souls miracles will not surface If you don't win souls -You grieve the holy spirit by quitting soul winning do not make the Holy spirit for the spirit is gods mark of ownership on you guarantee that the day will come when the lord will set you free (**Ephesians;4;30**)**You lose the presence of God's in your life-** You become unstable and double minded with one foot in the world and another foot in the church the body of Christ -If you don't win souls you no longer part of great programme /repentance and remission of sins should be preached in the name of Jesus among all nations and so said to them this is what is written the Messiah must suffer and must rise from death three days later and in his name the massage about repentance and forgiveness of sins must be preached to all nations beginning in Jerusalem you are the witness of these things and I myself will send upon you ,what my father has promised but you must wait in the city until the power from above come down upon you(**Luke; 24;46;49**)Those who quit soul winning becomes critical they attack soul winners on the Buses ,Train ,Trams ,Plane ,extra **When you give up soul winning you bring darkness in the community and nations -** People need to know that believers in Christ and the word of God (Bible)and its holiness are still existing if you give up that means there no more prophets in the community and nation **World vision will die Evangelism-**as there no people of vision to preach the word of God and wining souls in the world **The new generation won't know how to win the lost-**So they depart from soul winning history and standards(Younger-ones)

QUESTION?

HOW CAN WE WIN SOULS TO CHRIST/STEPS TO WIN SOULS

Christians and Christ went everywhere in the world preaching and winning souls and Christians we have to win souls today(a)*Feel sympathetic/Empathy for them you put yourself in their shoes* Am the weak in faith I become weak like one of them in order to win them so I become all things to all people that I may save some of them by whatever means possible(**1Corithians;9;22**)There is no difference between the Jews and gentiles between slaves and free people between men and women you are all one in Christ Jesus(**Galatians 3;28**)The voice spoke to him again do not consider anything unclean that God has declared Clean(**Acts10;15**)(b)*Learn the Gospel and scriptures* everyone sinned and was far away from God saving presence but by the free gift of God's grace all are put right with him through Jesus Christ who set them free (**Romans;3;23**)*For the sin pays its wages and its wages is death-* But God free gift is eternal life in union with Christ Jesus our lord (**Romans; 6;23**)But God has shown us how much he loves us it was while we were sinners that Christ died for us(**Romans;5;8**)If you confess that Jesus Christ is lord and believe that God raised him from death you will be saved (**Romans;10;9**)The bible says anyone who calls out to the lord will be saved (**Romans;10;13**)Whoever believes that Jesus Christ is the Messiah is a child of God ,and whoever loves a father loves the his child(c)**Ask God to give you an** *Evangelist burden for others-*ask him to help you see the world as he see it and lay upon your heart a handful of people for whom you can earnestly pray for pray for all those names every day keep a little prayer list and pray for an opportunity of reaching those souls the bible says "Lord lay some soul upon my heart and love that souls through me and may I humbly do my part to win that soul to thee**(d)*Live a Christian life before these people*** "Jesus said you are the light of the world let your light shine before men /women we must have faith obedient love when other hate you love them trust honest we must have a maturity life in the Gospel that others recognise and respect**(e)*Build a good relationship to others*** ,love them remember when Jesus went to the home of Zacchaeus were many sinners had gathered but you as a Christian you must be careful not to be carried away /trapped as well to the same environment God created you for a purpose ,If the opportunity does not come create one some time we wait for the perfect season or time to invite souls to church ,but as a soul winner you can pray and introduce any topic which can deliver you to what you can say to unbelievers and you win them, do your best and impress someone with their need to thirsty for Christ to save them **(f)**Always be ready to Answer questions regarding the Gospel concerning the Jesus Christ and the hope we have in him **(g)Leave the results for God-** We are Gods co-workers responsible for sharing the Gospel but only God can convert the soul having delivered let him do the rest note this Follow me and I will make you fishers of men and Jesus said go there and make disciples (**Mathew 4;19)**Finally our brother and sisters pray for us, that the Lords massage may continue to spread rapidly and be received with honour ,just as it was among you ,pray also that God will rescue us from wicked and Evil people for not everyone believes the massage ,but the Lord is Faithful and he will strengthen you, and keep you safe from the Evil one ,and the Lord gives us confidence in you and we are sure that you are doing and will continue to do what we tell you may the Lord lead you into greater understanding of God's love and endurance that is given by Christ**(2 Thessalonians;3;1;5) ;Amen**

ANOINTING

ANOINTING --Is the Divine empowerment by God ,causing you to do things you cannot do on your own, **Its God who Anoints people -God anoints you /me with Power to overcome, Sickness ,Poverty, and do Miracles,(Given, Supernatural Authority by God)**Listen to these words fellow Israelites Jesus of Nazareth was a man whose divine Authority was clearly proven to you by the Miracles and wonders which God performed through him ,you yourselves know this for it happened here among you **(Acts,2;22)** Gods anointing is God's presence by the Holy Spirit and word stuffed full of power and anointing , if you want to live in fullness of Gods anointing fill your mouth with God's word ,the anointing breaks the yokes -when that time comes .I will free you from the power of Assyria, and their yokes will no longer be a burden to your shoulders **(Isaiah,10;27)**Yokes are, unfair treatment , situations, obstacles ,To be anointed by God means **(To be chosen by God)**,When you have the anointing on you from the Holy one - you will know the truth, God s desire that you plan and live life according to his anointing , not on your own ability and understanding , You cannot be greater without anointing , No man can retain the anointing without putting it to work ,the anointing is given for a purpose in life , It is the anointing that determines your Success and achievements in life, When the anointing is with you the truth is God is with you, the anointing we have received from Jesus is by the Holy Spirit , but you have had the Holy Spirit poured out on you by Christ, and so all of you know the truth **(1,John;2;20)**Am writing to you this about those who are trying to deceive you ,but as for you Christ has poured out his spirit on you, as long as his spirit remain in you, you do not need anyone to teach you ,for the spirit teaches you ,about everything and what he teaches you is true not false **(1 John 2;26;27)** Gods anointing dos not only affect today but affects your tomorrow also , David was anointed to become a King "the scriptures says , " I have made my Servant David a king by anointing him with holy oil, ,my strength will always be with him ,my power will make him strong ,his enemies will never succeed against, him the wicked will not defeat him **(Psalm 89;20;22)**,the Spirit of the Lord will give him wisdom and the knowledge and the skill to rule his people **(Isaiah,11;2)** the anointing enables you to know things you don't know, the Holy Spirit gives you direction because the anointing puts you over ,because you know you belong in the kingdom of wisdom and Gods knowledge , When the anointing is on you things start to change in your life, Miracles always flow in the river of Anointing,- In life don't undermine your anointing ,you will never reach your destiny , People are drawn to your anointing **,In anointing- oil is used as a point of contact ,to smear or rub with oil anointing (Oil is used to anoint, Kings ,**

Priests , Heal the sick people and objects) ,Priest to Baptise a baby with oil , Holy oil means **-(Holy anointing on head)**,David was anointed with the Holy oil on his head ,then take the anointing oil pour it on his head and anoint him **(Exodus 29;7)** Samuel took the Olive oil and anointed David, in front of his brothers, Immediately the Spirit of the Lord took control of David, and was with him from that day on then, Samuel returned to Ramah **(1 Samuel 16;13)** I have made my servant King David by anointing him with Holy oil **(Psalm,89;20)** - Then Samuel took a jar of Olive -Oil and poured it on Saul head kissed him and said" The Lord anoints you as a ruler of his people of Israel , you will rule his people and protect them from all their enemies and this is a proof that you that the Lord has chosen to be the ruler of his people **(1Samuel 10;1-) Anointing of Aaron and his Sons as Priests-** put the Turban on him and tie on it sacred sign of dedication engraved dedication to the Lord ,then take the anointing Oil pour on his head and anoint him , bring his sons and put his shirts on them, put slashes round their waits and tie caps on their heads , that's how you are to ordain Aaron and his sons they and their descendants are to serve me forever **(Exodus,29;6;7;Exodus 40;15)**God anoints those he favour ,and he favours those he anoints, Everyone of us has a Queens and a Kings anointing- Everyone who has the Holy Ghost is anointed ,the helper the Holy Spirit whom the father will send in my name , will teach you everything and make you remember all that I have told you **(John 14;26)**But now you do not live as your human nature tells you ,Instead you live as the Spirit tells you in fact Gods Spirit lives in you ,whoever does not have the Spirit of Christ does not belong to him **(Romans 8;9)**,God is always good follow your dreams ,your own purpose, embrace Gods anointing on your life no body owns me anything ,am not disadvantageous ,am equipped and empowered and anointed by God ,Anointing is activated where there is Faith and without faith the anointing Oil is nothing , faith is the channel through which the anointing flows , Fasting is what prepares you for new anointing, -the anointing you honour is the one you are entitled to benefit from, the anointing you sow into is the anointing you reap from -You love what is right and hate what is wrong that is why God your God has chosen you and has given you the Joy of an honour ,far greater than he gave to your companions, **(Hebrews 1;9),**There is nothing wrong today to be anointed by someone , but we have to make sure that the purpose of anointing is an agreement with the scriptures, God always uses men Servants to impact your life with the anointing of the Holy -Spirit , the Oil its self does not have power but empowered with God and the Holy Spirit makes a change, (*Don't seek the anointing Oil, but seek God*) and produce wine to make them happy ,Olive oil to make them cheerful, and bread to give them strength, **(Psalm,104;15)** don't be contented with oil anointing ,Its essential to have the holy and happy life , that you seek to be anointed with the new oil do

BELIEVER'S BOOK

not be satisfied with the past experience seek to have new revelations of Christ to your soul, seek the renewal application of his precious blood for/to your conscience , Seek the fresh oil ,the scriptures says "believe in the Lord your God and you shall be established ,believe in his prophets and you shall prosper **(2 Chronicles,20;20)** And by a Prophet the lord brought Israel out of Egypt and by Prophets was he preserved **, (Hosea 12;13)**The Sovereign Lord never does anything without revealing his plans to his servants the prophets **(Amos,3;7)**Every day pray for fresh anointing ,you can't win today's battles without new anointing into your, family, church , marriage, business you need God to open doors, blessings favour , protection you can't open by yourself, you are anointed to work into difficult situation , every time you say am anointed   blessed and highly favoured ,fear ,stress disappointment all yokes are broken, never undermine the power of anointing pray in the name of Jesus for the anointing to face battles confronting you in your life pray for anointing that moves yokes without the anointing some battles you can't win them Amen the bible say "Don't harm my chosen servants ,do not touch my prophets **(Psalm,105;15;1 Chronicles 16;22)**Now I know that the Lord gives Victory to his chosen King he answers him from his holy heaven and by his power he gives great victories **(Psalm,20;6) God anointed Jesus -** The Lord says "here is my servant ,whom I have strengthen ,the one I have chosen , with whom am pleased ,I have filled him with my spirit and he will bring justice to every nation , he will not shout or raise his voice or make loud speeches in the streets or put out a flickering lamp he will bring lasting justice to all , he will not lose hope or courage , he will establish justice on earth ,distant lands eagerly wait for his teachings **(Isaiah 42;1-4) Jesus was anointed by the Holy Spirit -** the spirit of the Lord is upon me because he has chosen me to bring the good news to the poor ,he has sent me to proclaim liberty to the captives, and recovery of sight to the blind to set free the oppressed **(Luke 4;18;19 Isaiah 61;1-6)** You know about Jesus of Nazareth , and how God poured out on him the Holy Spirit and power ,he went healing all who were under the power of the Devil for God was with him **(Acts,10;38) Christians today have the anointing to heal the sick -**Jesus sends out the Twelve ,they drove out many demons and rubbed Oil on many sick people and healed them **(mark 6;13;Luke 9;1-6 Mathew 10;5-15) Anointing Objects - (Exodus 10;9;11) Moses** then dedicated the tent and all its equipments by anointing it with sacred oil and it will be Holy ,next dedicated the Altar all its equipment by anointing it will be completely Holy also dedicated the washbasin and its base the same way **(Exodus 10;9;11; 30;25 Leviticus 8;10;36)** How to receive your anointing **?- (1)Daily encounter with God through his Word** -to open your eyes and show you his will , direction , plans and goals in your life , all of us then reflect the glory of the Lord with uncovered faces and that the same glory coming from the

287

Lord who is Spirit transform us into his likeness in an ever greater degree of Glory **(2Corinthians 3;18) (b)Through prayers and faith (c) Through being close to those who are anointed or Favour connection (d) Inviting the Holy Spirit in your life on a daily basis to lead you and teach you ;How to Bless the Anointing Oil?-** Obtain olive oil ,place a small amount of Oil in a Viral- Pray a blessing over the oil ,store the Oil at room temp, Father I pray that you anoint this oil in your heavenly name , I pray that you cleanse it of any defilement (Impurities)On it, make it Holy for the work of your glory, may this be done in the name of the Father, Son, and Holy Spirit **(Oil blessing Prayer),Amen**

BENEFITS OF ANOINTING (1Samuel 10;1-16)

Then Samuel took a jar of Olive Oil and poured it on Saul kissed him and said "The Lord anoints you as a ruler of his people Israel .you will rule his people and protect them from all their enemies and this is a proof to you that the Lord has chosen you to be a ruler of his people ,When you live today you will meet two men near Rachel's tomb at Zelzah in the territory of Benjamin ,they will tell you the donkey you were looking for have been found , so that your father isn't worried any more about them but about you and he keeps asking what shall I do about my Son ? You will go on from there until you come to the sacred tree at Tabor where you will meet three Men on their way to offer a sacrifice to God at Bethel ,one of them will be leading ,three young goats another will be carrying three loaves of bread and the third one will have a leather bag full of wine, they will greet you and offer you two loaves ,which you are to accept ,then you will go the hill of God in Gibeah where there is a philistine camp, at that entrance to the town you will meet a group of Prophets coming down from the altar on the hill playing harps drums, flutes and Lyres, they will be dancing and shouting ,suddenly the Spirit of the Lord will take control of you and you will Join in their religious dancing and shouting and you will became a different person ,you will go ahead of me to Gilgal, where I will meet you and offer burnt sacrifice and fellowship sacrifice ,wait there seven days until I come and tell you what to do" when Saul turned to leave Samuel God gave Saul a new nature, and everything God had told him happened ,when Saul and his servant arrived at Gibeah a group of prophets met him and joined in their ecstatic dancing and shouting ,people who had known him saw him doing this and asked one another what has happened to the Son of Kish? has Saul become a prophet ?"a man who lived there asked "how about these other prophets ,who do you think their father fathers are? "this is how the saying originated, ***"Has even Saul become a prophet?*** when Saul finished his ecstatic dancing and shouting ,he went to the altar on the hill, Saul uncle saw him and the servant he asked them , where have you been ? "looking for the donkeys" Saul answered "when we couldn't find ,we went to see Samuel "and what did he tell you ? Saul uncle asked ,he told us that the animals had been found "Saul answered -but he did not tell his uncle what Samuel said about his becoming a King**(1Samuel 10;1-16)**

BENEFITS OF ANOINTING !

- **Anointing helps you to know things you don't know-** the holy spirit leads you and gives you direction, and Victory - Now I know that the Lord gives victory to his chosen Kings , he answers him from his holy heaven and by his power he gives him great victories **(Psalm 20;6) Amen**
- **Makes you a head, King (Commander in charge)** in life, in Spiritual realms, Politics , Business , work place ,Ministry ,Amen
- **Anointing brings you from nothing (dust) to someone** -become king ,queen , travel places you never travelled before, sit with kings and queens in palaces generation and generation honours you, **Amen**
- **Anointing brings honour - -**people that undermined you in the past, start to recognise you, and your presence because you start to shine a new man/woman in their presence ,Saul was anointed and become a new man , every time you rise from glory to glory , you change daily and graduate from the level they know ,advise your friend to stop studying you, because the anointing on you is more powerful than what they think and call you , **Amen**
- **Anointing helps you to locate the missing blessing** -, Donkeys were missing but Saul found them after the anointing on him ,you will find ,your relocated blessings ,jobs marriage , contract when the anointing is on you .**Amen**
- **Anointing attracts favour and blessings from other sources-** people look for you to help you, three men carrying three Loaves of bread favoured Saul with two loaves , favour suspends, Laws ,education and high qualification ,favour suspends ,colour , religion**, height ,Amen**
- **Anointing Empowers you/me, for a new assignment-** because you are equipped, favoured, and anointed, no one can touch you , you can do what God has called and chosen you to do, - there was no King in Israel before God appointed Saul ,so God created a vacancy for Saul ,God is God of creation , from nothing to something , God is going to create a vacancy for you, at your work place , Political fields , Ministry, if you are single someone of Gods choice is coming , Many people depend on the, Economy , Education . Colour, other gods , God s anointing has power to

change everything wait on his time and depend and put trust in only him , **Amen**

BELIEVE- DECIDE- ACT AND STAY FOCUSED -IN EVERYTHING IN LIFE TO SUCCEED AND FILLFUL YOUR GODS PURPOSE ON EARTH; AMEN -AMEN